Acclaim for David Lipsky's

Absolutely American

**A *Time* magazine, *San Jose Mercury News*,
New York Daily News, *Providence Journal-Bulletin*,
and *Amazon.com* Best Book of the Year**

"Duty, Honor, Casual Sex: Plain American hedonism is powerful at West Point, David Lipsky found, but so are discipline and self-sacrifice.... A superb description of modern military culture, and one of the most gripping accounts of university life I have read. This book must have been extremely hard to organize, and yet it reads with a novelistic flow. How teenagers get turned into leaders is not a simple story, but it is wonderfully told in this book."
—David Brooks, *The New York Times Book Review*

"A labor of love. While Lipsky's friends back home wrestled with nagging, existential questions, he steeped himself in the demanding yet salubrious routines of cadet life, reveling in the youngsters' camaraderie and marveling at their commitment to the academy's core values, 'Duty, Honor, Country.' The result is an immensely rich collection of portraits of young men and women put under very adult pressure by an institution that itself must constantly adapt to the society around it. Lipsky [establishes] a dramatic tension that holds for the next 300-plus pages. A genuinely evocative and wonderfully detailed portrait of an absolutely American institution." —*Newsday*

"A fascinating, funny and tremendously well written account of life on the Long Gray Line. Lipsky approaches the cadets like an anthropologist stalking the elusive Yanomamo tribe, and with good reason: he's in a weird, weird place. Take a good look: this is the face America turns to most of the world, and until now it's one that most of us have never seen. A mesmerizing and powerfully human spectacle." —*Time*

"Five years before 'embedded media' hit the lexicon, *Rolling Stone* writer David Lipsky scored unprecedented access to West Point. Through the Army's late-'90s identity crises to its sharp refocus after 9-11, he watched the class of '02 drill for 47 months to become 'superior beings' worthy of filling the boots of Douglas MacArthur. Lipsky has written the addictive *Absolutely American,* a story that could inspire even nonmilitary buffs to follow the cadets' careers like those of their favorite sports stars." —*Newsweek*

"Masculinity has traditionally been associated with the military. *Absolutely American,* which vividly traces West Point cadets through their four years at the Academy, deals with both sexes and tells a lot about the changing definitions and conditions of masculinity and femininity in the new century."
—Elaine Showalter, *The Washington Post Book World*

"Illuminating. . . . Lipsky has done a distinguished service to a proud school." —*Entertainment Weekly*

"Although confined to one geographic area, *Absolutely American* covers a vast sociological, political and psychological landscape. . . . Neither an institutional hagiography nor a scathing, Seymour Hersh–like exposé, [this] is an assiduously researched, evenhanded examination that focuses on the changing value systems of the institution and the people who experience those changes. Lipsky has written an important, insightful book on the current state of our premier military academy and on the intrepid first West Point class to enter the War on Terrorism." —*Houston Chronicle*

"A sunny portrait of a group of young men and women. . . . [Lipsky] is effective as a chronicler of personality." —*The New Yorker*

"Lipsky is fascinated by the rigors of the academy and how a diverse group of young men and women struggle with its challenges. He achieves the impressive feat of writing from inside cadet culture. Unusually complete and perceptive. . . . Lipsky's understanding of their lives is remarkable." —*Chicago Tribune*

"Wonderfully engaging, a surprisingly nuanced portrait of these cadets."   —*The Atlanta Journal-Constitution*

"Most will be delighted to find a new twist on the subject of military education. This book shows that West Point thrives under resilient leadership and a class of future officers that is human, while still being moral, real and enthusiastic. In short, this book is 'huah.'"
—*San Antonio Express-News*

"A once-skeptical *Rolling Stone* writer spends four years watching teamwork, hard work and self-sacrifice gain meaning for fledgling Army officers, children of a society that glorifies consumerism, individualism and instant gratification."   —*Providence Journal-Bulletin*

"Whether Lipsky is trudging through the woods with tired and hungry cadets or sitting in on barracks-room bull sessions, he marvels at the sense of duty he finds. Wonderfully upbeat. . . . A charming book."
—*St. Louis Post-Dispatch*

"An unprecedentedly in depth examination . . . [at a time] when all the lessons and discipline, which seemed anachronistic in the sunny days of peace, prove suddenly, vividly necessary."   —*Men's Journal*

"A richly anecdotal portrait of West Point during one of the most dramatic transitional phases in its 200-year history."   —*The Onion*

"Superb."   —*Publishers Weekly*

"An exhaustive and very human account of West Point and its cadets."
—*The New York Observer*

"Freshmen could learn a lot by reflecting on a book that suggests that the main problem with traditional American values is that we do such a poor job of living up to them. So could we all."
—*The Charlotte Observer*

"Goes inside the walls of the academy to discover and portray the cadets and the officers who train them, giving civilians an up-close look at the real West Point experience. [Lipsky] captures the language, emotion, history and motivation of the extraordinary people he profiles. Illuminating. . . . Captivating and compelling."

—*The Courier-Journal* (Louisville, KY)

"[Lipsky] followed [the cadets] into mess halls, barracks, classrooms, bars and training exercises. He watched them do push-ups, polish their shoes, get drunk, cry, throw up and grow up. Lipsky chronicles it all. . . . [It] reads like a novel." —*Alabama Mobile Register*

"Highly recommended." —*Library Journal* (starred review)

"The latest, best, and I hope the last of its kind. Shows what West Point does . . . taking apathetic and uncommitted young people and developing them into talented, capable officers, sometimes in spite of themselves. . . . Illuminates the real, human complexities of the military academy." —*Army Magazine*

"Lipsky takes up the problems of maintaining West Point's unique culture—the military squared and cubed—in the face of a general culture that offers a host of temptations. . . . Outstanding." —*Booklist*

"[Told in a] breathless narrative fashion that routinely builds each anecdote to a climactic finale. This formula provides some of the most memorable passages in the book. These vignettes [can] sound like clichés, [but] the message here is that in an age of irony and cynicism, West Point proudly embraces such clichés, and Lipsky's ear for dialogue and his eye for specific detail breathe life into these chapters. Lipsky's book stands out as the most accurate and engrossing look at West Point, warts and all, as it exists today." —*Pointer View*

David Lipsky

Absolutely American

David Lipsky is a contributing editor for *Rolling Stone*. He has written for *The New Yorker*, *The New York Times*, *Harper's Magazine*, and *The Boston Globe*, among other publications. His fiction has appeared in *The New Yorker* and *The Best American Short Stories*, and his novel, *The Art Fair*, won acclaim from *The New York Times Book Review*, *Newsweek*, *People*, and others. His honors include a MacDowell fellowship and a Henry Hoyns fellowship. Lipsky lives in New York City.

BOOKS BY DAVID LIPSKY

Absolutely American
The Art Fair
Three Thousand Dollars

Absolutely
American

Absolutely American

FOUR YEARS AT
West Point

David Lipsky

Vintage Books
A DIVISION OF RANDOM HOUSE, INC.
NEW YORK

Photo insert credits: Cicerelle, DeMoss, Washington Mess, Goodfellas, Rash on bed,
Bergman and Powell, Ferlazzo, and lunch formation: courtesy Mark Seliger/Corbis
Outline. Adamczyk: courtesy of Joseph Adamczyk. Keirsey: courtesy of Hank Keirsey.
Vermeesch promotion, Vermeesch at Beast: courtesy of John Vermeesch. Herzog in
Kosovo: courtesy of Don Herzog. All other photographs by David Lipsky.

For the fighting guppies,
and for Eamon Dolan

OF ALL THE INSTITUTIONS IN THIS COUNTRY, NONE is more absolutely American; none, in the proper sense of the word, more absolutely democratic than this. Here we care nothing for the boy's birthplace, nor his creed, nor his social standing; here we care nothing save for his worth as he is able to show it.

Here you represent, with almost mathematical exactness, all the country geographically. You are drawn from every walk of life by a method of choice made to insure, and which in the great majority of cases does insure, that heed shall be paid to nothing save the boy's aptitude for the profession into which he seeks entrance. Here you come together as representatives of America in a higher and more peculiar sense than can possibly be true of any other institution in the land.

— PRESIDENT THEODORE ROOSEVELT,
at the West Point centennial, 1902

CONTENTS

PREFACE

I CAME TO LOVE, really love, road marching. It's called a suck or a haze at West Point, but I think the cadets aren't being fair to it. There's something wonderful about being in a column of marching people: the gravel popping under soles, the leather flexing in boots, the kind of saddle-top sounds as the ruck (what a backpack gets called in the Army) frames settle. Occasionally someone, out of sheer misery, sighing *Oooh,* or just blowing out air, which in the general silence is like a whale breaching and then slipping back under the surface. You can watch a leaf float down from a tree or stare at the guy's rifle in front of you. The boiling down of life to its basic questions: Can you do this? What kind of person are you, and what can you make yourself finish? Can you hang with the rest of us? Those questions don't get asked much, in the civilian world.

One night I got stuck with a West Point company that was spending the entire evening on patrol in the woods. They had brought ponchos in their rucks and I hadn't. It was about two in the morning when the rain started. A nice earth-smelling drizzle at first. Then it became a pretty hard, thundery storm. I'd never noticed that rain makes different noises on different articles of clothing: a kind of spreading, sinking hiss into a shirt, a loud spattery ploink! on jeans. One of the cadets offered me his poncho, but of course you couldn't accept it. In the dark, I found my way to two trees that had grown so close together that their upper branches formed a canopy. I obviously wasn't going to sleep, so I marched back and forth all night under this umbrella, rain dripping into my ears and down over my lips. Then, in the morning, at five, everyone shook themselves off and we marched again.

I never liked the military at all as a kid. My father told us it was the one profession we couldn't pursue: if my brother or I joined up, he promised to hire strong guys to come break our legs. In his eyes, compared to the military, hired leg-breaking was an act of kindness. So when *Rolling Stone* magazine first assigned me to write about the United States Military Academy, I fought it. And I mean fought hard, as hard as you can fight *Rolling Stone*'s publisher, Jann Wenner, who can be firm and cajoling in a kind of (at least to a writer) irresistible way. When I gave in, and traveled to West Point, I was followed by members of the Academy's Public Affairs Office. They chose the people I could speak with, they sat in on the interviews. I saw my way out; I was thrilled and relieved. I said I could not do the story under those circumstances, and I left. A few days later the colonel who oversees the daily management of West Point — Joe Adamczyk, a thin, steely man the cadets nicknamed Skeletor — called back to say it was fine. There would be no one picking out ideal cadets for me to interview, no one escorting me, no doors closed. I could have the run of the place. "We have nothing of which we should be ashamed," he said.

So that was the first step toward my love of road marching. Very different from my original idea of the Army. And there was no avoiding the story anymore.

It had all seemed so foreign, a kind of dense green forest. Slowly, the trees parted a little, enough for me to step inside, and then I could feel the basic goodness of the place. As I listened to the cadets and understood how they were living, I had a strange, funny thought. Not only was the Army not the awful thing my father had imagined, it was the sort of America he always pictured when he explained (this would happen every four years, during an election cycle) his best hopes for the country. A place where everyone tried their hardest. A place where everybody — or at least most people — looked out for each other. A place where people — intelligent, talented people — said honestly that money wasn't what drove them. A place where people spoke openly about their feelings and about trying to make themselves better.

One reason *Rolling Stone* wanted me on the story was that I'd become a kind of young-person specialist. You specialize at a magazine. On news stories, I mainly covered universities and students. I must have traveled to about thirty-five colleges in the five years before I first went to West Point. From tiny places like Wisconsin's obscure, home-made-feeling Beloit to a thirty-thousand-student factory like the University of Georgia at Athens to places like Harvard and Yale that made me feel like maybe I wasn't changing my socks often enough. I'd also written about young TV actors and the young rich and young media executives, people who had every reason to be consistently delighted. And of all the young people I'd met, the West Point cadets — although they are grand, epic complainers — were the happiest. That was probably step two on the path toward my love of road marching.

Here's three: My friends had reached the phase, in their early thirties, when things slow down and you can relax and look around yourself again for maybe the first time since college. Before that, life is like sticking your head out the window of a fast-moving car: everything is rushing at you, flattening back your skin, your eyes are blinking and you can barely overhear your own thoughts. Most of those thoughts are "Will I find a job?" and "Can I find a partner?" and "What kind of life am I going to have?" By the early thirties, this stuff had quieted down, and my friends were thinking, "OK, I've found a life." And then the second part hit: "Is this the life I want? Does the job I'm doing matter to anyone else?" It was right at this time that the Army and the Academy dawned on me, and I saw what it meant to live as a group, to share experiences, and to have that sense that other people were honestly looking out for you. And I have to say, that looked pretty good to me too.

And so, a road march. Everyone dressed the same. Everyone with a clear assignment: You will depart from this first point and you will arrive at this second point, and it will be clear to you when you have accomplished this. It will be difficult (in the Army, they say challenging). In place of the anxiety that comes from jobs that involve only the brain, the pleasure of a task that would engage the entire body. When cadets faltered, other cadets would softly encourage them. "Come on. You can do this. I know you can do this." The sound of the boots and the smell of the road and the sun on the leaves and this soft, encouraging undertone. When cadets fell, other cadets would move forward, lift them up. I remember, during my first road marches, feeling simply blessed.

*

The magazine originally treated the assignment, when it began in 1998, as a journalistic public service. That summer, the West Point superintendent, a three-star general, had parked with some other military leaders at the sort of big roadside welcome center that features a TCBY and a Great American Pretzel Company (so that even rest stops offer the channel-surfing pleasures of a mall) and where there is usually one restaurant with sit-down service. The superintendent was wearing his green class-B uniform, and so were the hungry officers in his party. The hostess looked him up and down, from polished shoes to epaulets, then she smiled and thanked him for the selfless work he was doing as a member of the Parks Department. The superintendent wondered if maybe the gap between the civilian and military worlds hadn't become too large. A few weeks later, the superintendent and the commandant arrived at the *Rolling Stone* offices in their full uniforms, marching past black-and-white photographs of Eric Clapton and framed guitars. The initial idea was for me to spend a few weeks on post, follow around a bunch of plebes, write something short. I ended up staying most of the year.

When that time was over, I didn't believe the story was fully told. I decided to rent a house in Highland Falls, and stayed until the plebe class graduated four years later — the only time West Point has let a writer in for such an extended tour of hanging out. I saw cadets in combat with themselves, unlearning many of the skills and instincts that had brought them to West Point; I saw some cadets thriving; I saw lots of suffering (academic, physical, homesickness); I saw spot meanness and acts of great generosity. My friends were full of questions: What kinds of people still wanted such a regimented life? Why would cadets willingly put themselves through it? Didn't they realize the way they were living was out-of-date? Those were questions I set out to answer. But I mostly wanted to give people the experience of spending forty-seven months at the United States Military Academy, an experience that only around sixty thousand people have had since the place got up and running two centuries ago. I learned how to read a uniform and how to tie many types of knots. I learned that soldiers are people — that when I flip on the news and there's some officer in a helmet standing before a tank, I'm looking at someone a lot like myself, who's lived through most of the same events I have, eats the same drive-through, can trace the same internal map of favorite movie dialogue and TV scenes, but who has made the decision to put on a uniform and serve in the nation's military.

I've changed the names of several cadets, mostly at their request, including people involved in an honor hearing and three cadets who endured various hardships — a consuming relationship, loss of rank, separation from the Academy. Scott Mellon, Kim Wilkins, Loryn Winter, Nick Calabanos, Mrs. Como, Virginia Whistler and James Edgar are fictitious names — real people under a verbal false nose and eyeglasses. Otherwise, the names and nicknames in this book are the cadets' real ones. I followed the men and women of one company, G-4, from the months they arrived at West Point until the day they graduated; this is their story.

PART ONE

The First Year

Whitey's Dilemma

I F YOU IMAGINE the ideal West Point cadet, you'll come up with someone very much like Don "Whitey" Herzog. Since meeting his first veterans, Whitey has wanted to go military. "Just something special in their eyes," the twenty-one-year-old explains. "They learned brotherhood, service — they learned what real honor is." For ten years, Whitey ran his life like a checklist: West Point, then the Infantry, then the Rangers, the Army's elite.

At West Point, cadets wear gray, but when they dream about their futures, it's all green, the posts and uniforms of the United States Army. Each summer — while their civilian peers are walking the beaches or rubbing their eyes at some internship — the United States Military Academy sends its juniors and seniors to spend five weeks in their futures, leading troops with regular Army units. Because he's the number thirteen–ranked military cadet in the one-thousand-member class of 1999, Whitey got his dream in July of 1998 and trained with the Rangers. They outfitted him with laser-sighted weapons, night-vision goggles, a hundred pounds of gear and tackle, and sent him on practice missions: evacuating pretend hostages, breaking up pretend ambushes. They'd fly to some classified place, do the job, swing back to base with the sun coming up. Riding outside a helicopter, Whitey felt the wind slam his face, watched his boots sway over the Florida night. "Three in the morning, going over supermarkets and bars," he says. "I was thinking, 'Man, I wish my buddies back home could be seein' this.'"

Whitey grew up in the cold pubs-and-hockey town of Buffalo, New York. (His brother-in-law, Mike Peca, is captain of the NHL's Buffalo Sabres.) His parents separated when he was ten — dad a dentist, mom a paralegal. Whitey first heard the words *United States Military Academy* from one of his mother's boyfriends. First day of high school, teachers invited questions for the guidance counselor, and Whitey was the kid with his hand raised. "How do I get into West Point?" he asked.

Like any mountain, the climb to West Point is cut with paths, the ropes and bridges left by other climbers. West Point wants scholars and athletes with good leadership potential. So Whitey ran cross-country, grubbed for A's, campaigned for student office. On the side, he was moonlighting as an ordinary teenager: smoking cigarettes, chasing girls, getting drunk at Allman Brothers concerts. Next morning, he'd go be student body president at the Jesuit high school. "Real Jekyll-and-Hyde stuff," he says.

West Point cadets make a simple deal: a tuition-free education in exchange for five years as Army officers. Every September, the seniors pick their branches of service. If you like to drive tanks, you go Armor; if you enjoy measuring the world's challenges on a scientific calculator, you go Engineers. (If you're a business major, you hook up with the Finance Batallion and get called a Finance Ranger.) But if you have the true calling, you go Infantry. Tell a West Point administrator you're considering the Field Artillery, he might nod. Tell him you're thinking Infantry, he'll clap you on the back and grin. Of course, Infantry skills are also a hard sell should you ever decide to *leave* the military. "Think like a civilian employer," one senior explains. "Say 'Engineers,' that implies you can think a little bit. Spend five years with the Infantry, OK, you know how to sleep in the cold and you know how to kill people. It doesn't set you up for success." For the Army, Infantry means you're serious; for Whitey, it was the second stop on his checklist, the road back to the Rangers.

Whitey Herzog is sandy-haired, tall and skinny. He has soldier's eyes: entering a room, his eyes do a quick reconnaissance skim, picking up the areas of interest, filtering out what's nonessential; then they turn friendly. On his uniform, he wears the bronze star that indicates he's in the top 5 percent of his class militarily, which means that for four years he's performed West Point's duties the way West Point wants them done.

None of that meant squat to the Rangers. First couple of weeks he was there, none of the Rangers would talk to him; the enlisted guys wouldn't even salute. Like many male cadets, Whitcy is a dipper — a tobacco chewer. (His third-year roommate taught a bunch of guys to dip, and in May there were awards. Top honor: Grand Master Dipper. Whitey got Rookie of the Year.) One afternoon, Whitey gave an operations briefing, forty minutes with a mouthful of dip, and something told him not to spit. "I only did one time," Whitey says. "I gutted the rest, which is swallowing it." A sergeant — a burly thirty-year-old, a Ranger — pulled Whitey aside and told him everyone was impressed; they thought he'd be spitting every thirty seconds. "You're one of the *We* now," the sergeant said. His last morning, Whitey ran the Ranger obstacle course, and when he finished the enlisted guys were waiting with an official Ranger poster. They'd covered it with signatures and messages, like a kid's yearbook: "Gain Weight," "Go in the Infantry," and "We'll See You in the Ranger Battalion."

So when he got back to West Point, Whitey gave his measurements for the uniform to the Academy tailor. He'd decided to be an Infantry mud crawler with his roommate, Rob "Harley" Whitten, and his buddy Antonio "Iggy" Ignacio. "That's when the stress just started building," Whitey says. One July night his Ranger platoon leader — a twenty-five-year-old first lieutenant, hard-core — had taken him to a bar in Columbus, Georgia, the low-roofed town outside Ranger headquarters. When they were very drunk, the PL announced, "After the Rangers, I'm *done*." Army life had left him feeling cut off from everything that wasn't Army. "I don't remember the last time I was out on a date — I don't even know how to act in front of a girl anymore," the lieutenant said. "I'm so burnt, I just want to get out." Whitey kept thinking about it. "I was choosing what to do with my life," he says. Infantry meant sticking with the military for a career. With his high rank, he knew he'd qualify for a slot in Aviation. And Aviation — piloting helicopters — is a skill you can sell outside the military. You could even fly helicopters for the FBI.

And then the whole notion of *service* began to work on Whitey like a guilty conscience. He couldn't shake the idea that Aviation was a sell-out move. For weeks, wherever he went, he felt two futures dragging over his head like a pair of clouds: he could be loyal to everything he'd always wanted or to all the things he *might* want. The weekend before branch selection, he got drunk at an Army football game, stumbled into a Porta-Potty — not one of religion's glory spots — and started praying. Basically, he asked God to pick the branch for him. "I was looking up at the sky, I was like, 'Someone, please, someone reach down and tell me what to do. How much do I sacrifice if I choose Infantry, and how much do I do for myself if I choose Aviation?'" Twelve hours left, he ended up drunk in Iggy's room. "Igs, this is it," Whitey said. "I'm doing it. I'm going Infantry."

"You sure?" Iggy asked. "I'm not sure you're sure."

But Whitey was the number thirteen–ranked military cadet, a man who'd never wanted anything except to serve his country in uniform. "This is why I'm here," Whitey said. "I may not like all of it, but I can do it, and I can do it good." Iggy nodded, said he supported him. The next morning, Whitey sat down at his computer, dialed up the branch selection Web site. Clock ticking, ten minutes to go. He kept trying to make himself type the word *Infantry*.

The Aura

West Point, the United States Military Academy, is a formation of chapels, playing fields, cannons and buildings on the banks of the Hudson River, fifty miles north of the first towers of New York City. The Academy has a single mission: take civilians, produce officers. You enter the Academy through a Military Police checkpoint and pass rows of stately granite buildings until you're on a green hill above the river. On a clear spring day, you can look across to the rolling treetops of the Hudson Valley, or upriver where powerboats leave creases on the water, and feel that God himself has issued you a uniform and notebook and sent you to one of the most crisply beautiful places on earth to study the practice of war.

When you look into Academy history, you keep bumping into America's history, as if the same story is being told two different ways. Just before his death in 1799, George Washington wrote Alexander Hamilton, "The establishment of a military academy [has] ever been considered by me to be an object of the highest national importance." Three years later, classes were in session by the banks of the Hudson. In its early decades, West Point trained officers to be engineers — men who squinted at rivers, cleared forests and laid the first bridges and roadways for America. Most officers you see in old-time photographs — wide hats, sweeping mustaches — were graduates: Robert E. Lee, Stonewall Jackson, Ulysses S. Grant. The Civil War was an armed West Point reunion, old friends catching up by firing at each other. Out west, graduates like George Custer chased Indians. In World War I, General "Black Jack" Pershing (class of '86) exported West Point standards of bearing to Europe. (One French general wrote home, "Why, these Americans even *die* in neat rows.") World War II shaped up as a big overseas alumni project, with Generals Eisenhower (class of '15), Patton ('09), Bradley ('15), and MacArthur ('03) as leading class officers. General William Westmoreland (class of '36) commanded all U.S. forces in Vietnam. General Norman Schwarzkopf (class of '56) commanded all U.S. forces in the Persian Gulf. When officers like Schwarzkopf talk about the Academy, they don't say "West Point," they say "this national treasure we call West Point."

But with the Cold War one decade in the past, the Academy's history has ceased to be a useful guide for its future. (The military misses the old Soviet threat the way rich families miss the simple, pressing clarity of being poor.) What the military fears now is called the culture gap. By the final months of the Second World War, one in ten Americans was serving in uniform; that number today is closer to one in three hundred. When the draft ended in 1975, civilian culture and military culture shook hands, exchanged phone numbers, and started to lose track of each other; military theorists worry that most Americans have no firsthand knowledge of how their Army lives or what their Army does.

In its campaign against the culture gap, the Academy has retained a glossy New York public relations firm. It has also participated in a Discovery Channel documentary about service academies and allowed a TV crew — the same team responsible for *Dr. Quinn, Medicine Woman* — to film a pilot called *West Point* at West Point, in hopes it would do for the Academy what the successful series *Pensacola: Wings of Gold* has done for Navy flight school. (I have watched the pilot, which turns cadet life into sixty-minute story lines: hazing, binge drinking and the love that flowers between the ranks.) For the same reason, West Point invited *Rolling Stone* to the Academy; as a reporter I was granted unprecedented access to training, personnel, barracks and cadets. In all, I spent four years on post, to find out what kind of men and women would subject themselves to the intense discipline of West Point, and to discover what it means to attend the Academy during the most trying time in its history.

A West Point entering class is literally a high school all-star team. The median grade point average is 3.5; 14 percent are Eagle Scouts, 20 percent are class presidents, 60 percent are varsity team captains. Candidates are flagged from a long way off, like aircraft approaching on radar. The Department of Admissions boasts of having the most sophisticated database in the country: drop a line to West Point in the sixth grade and you'll receive correspondence from admissions every six months until you hit high school, when the rate doubles. More than 50,000 juniors open Academy files; from there, admissions becomes an endurance contest that produces 12,000 applicants, 6,000 physical fitness exams and 4,000 official nominations (from senators, congressmen, the vice president or the president); at the end, 1,200 cadets are left standing. (Even medical histories are fair game: if you have flat feet, asthma, diabetes or any experience with Ritalin or antidepressant drugs, chances are you're out of the running.) The staff spends a careful forty hours with each file. Cadets receive an education that's famously valued at $250,000, and earn $600 in Army pay a month. Each year brings an unforeseen problem. In 1998, when *Saving Private Ryan* was sparking its resurgence of bystander patriotism at multiplexes around the country, the effect on West Point was very different. "We had a number of people call in and close their files after seeing the movie," says Colonel Michael Jones, director of admissions. "They couldn't make the leap that we don't fight those types of wars anymore."

Plebes spend their first summer at Cadet Basic Training — Beast Barracks — where they get *soldierized*. Five weeks of all the things you've seen in movies: sudden-death haircuts, buckle-shining, wall-jumping, scrambling cadets looking perplexed. Plebes report with underwear and a toothbrush; everything else is Army issue. After surviving Beast (the drop rate is about 10 percent), they enter a world where students don't even have the same names they do everyplace else. Sophomores are yearlings or yuks, juniors are cows, seniors are firsties. They join one of the Academy's thirty-two companies, in which every aspect of their lives is overseen by an adult officer called a TAC. (Each company is assigned a letter, number and name: there are the A-1 Apaches, the E-4 Elvis Lives!) They pledge to follow an honor code: "A cadet will not lie, cheat, or steal, or tolerate those who do." And their *development* — as they say at West Point — begins.

Cadets are developed, tested and ranked in three areas: academic, military and physical. These fuse into the most important development area: character. "Every person," explains Colonel Kerry Pierce, director of Policy, Planning and Analysis, "and every program and every experience must contribute to character." Like many adults at West Point, Pierce speaks with a kind of grave, armed courtesy — the voice of someone who knows he's better adapted for the world's challenges than you are but doesn't want to press the point. West Point is a full-immersion experience, what the administration calls a "twenty-four-hour, seven-day-a-week military environment." Cadets don't get summer vacations. Until firstie year, they are required to be in uniform at all times. (A plebe hitting the bathroom for a small-hours pee must slip on Army-issue sweats before stepping into a barracks hallway.) The process of character-building is designed to be exhausting, and when it's not exhausting, to be irritating. A student at West Point is assigned five hours of homework each night, but a cadet's daily schedule allows for no more than three hours of study time. Then there is what's known as Plebe Knowledge: cadets are required to memorize pages of regulations, attack strategies, terrain, weapons, mottos and traditions. They also master greetings: within days of arrival, a plebe has to know the names of the 125 cadets in his or her company — no mean feat when all 4,000 cadets on post are dressed and barbered the same.

Each of the three West Point programs offers a clear way to win and a clear way to lose. Fail more than two academic courses and you're out of West Point. The military program includes field training like live-fire exercises and jumping out of airplanes. (At West Point, military life is presented as a certain kind of courageous fun: it's fun to ride in helicopters and train on tanks; it's especially fun to "blow stuff up." When I tell a lieutenant colonel at the Department of Military Instruction that I think something is "cool," he gently corrects me. "It's fun," he says.) Fail military tasks and you're out of West Point.

In the physical program, cadets take the Army Physical Fitness Test twice a year. Deputy Director Lieutenant Colonel Brian Morgan — who has the light step and honorably squashed features of a middleweight boxer — explains the process. Fail once, you get another chance in sixty days; fail twice, you get a second retest after thirty days; fail three times, pack your bags. Cadets are also measured for weight and body fat; let yourself go, and you're out of West Point. All male plebes take boxing, where the main idea is not learning how to punch but learning how to *be* punched — discovering you can take a hit and keep going. "It's one of the best things for fear management there is," Morgan says, pacing the boxing room, below posters with brawny slogans like "Champions never take the easy way out — pay the price" and "Fatigue makes cowards of men."

The three separate rankings produce a single class rank. And unlike a college, where the stomach-in-your-mouth feeling of checking grades comes only two or three times a year, cadet rankings change every few days; you're always being evaluated. "We develop them across these programs and across the board," Colonel Pierce says, "because as officers that's what they've got to be: physically, mentally, emotionally and ethically ready to do the job." When you're finished, when you've absorbed the Academy's lessons, you leave West Point with a new culture-gap role: domestic ambassador. "There's a growing difference between the values of the military and society, and there always will be," Pierce says. "That's just the bottom line. So that's the dual responsibility: it's up to the officers to explain the Army to society."

Most people spend their teens and early twenties trying on moral codes, wearing them around the store, seeing which ones fit. Part of the adventure of being an American is discovering what your values are and finding ways to put them into practice. Cadets arrive at West Point and are given a ready-made identity — and told it is perhaps the most valuable identity of all. This takes place at a time when every shift and dilemma that's hit the United States during half a century is crowding into West Point at once; what West Point is shivering through is a decade of aftershock. Gender, identity, community, globalism, multiculturalism, professionalism, pluralism, information technology, TV, political correctness, wellness, progress of various kinds — all in the same delayed reaction. The Academy is absorbing what it needs. The cadets are doing their best to stay on top of it, even as they try to unlearn and relearn the lessons of their adolescence, and remake themselves as the people the Army requires them to be.

The Theory and Practice of Huah

First Captain Rob Shaw is twenty-five years old: tall, modest, blond, square-jawed, the kind of cadet West Point adults — *higher*, as they're called in Academy lingo — can look at and say, "Ah, the admissions process is working like a top." For cadets like Shaw, the Army functions as a kind of secular religion. There's a word you hear a lot at West Point: *huah*. (It's the word Al Pacino rode to an Oscar as the retired Infantry colonel in *Scent of a Woman*.) *Huah* is an all-purpose expression. Want to describe a cadet who's very gung-ho, you call them *huah*. Understand instructions, say *huah*. Agree with what another cadet just said, murmur *huah*. Impressed by someone else's accomplishment, a soft, reflective *huah*. Rob Shaw is huah.

Shaw's military rank is number one, twelve places ahead of Whitey Herzog. As a screen saver on his desktop computer, Shaw keeps a rotating sequence of Successories, the inspirational corporate slogans you see advertised in airline magazines. When I'm in his office, Rob's Successory shows a pretty noble-looking eagle above the words *Duty — a Call Heard by the Brave*. Shaw speaks in clipped, dialogue-sized versions of Successories. Moving with an athlete's physical economy — you almost never see clumsiness at the Academy — he tours me around his office in brigade headquarters, shows me the plaque of all the former West Point first captains, signatures in wood, reaching back deep into the 1800s. "You look up and you see Robert E. Lee, William Westmoreland, Douglas MacArthur — General MacArthur went on to do great things, as you know. Those are some big shoes to fill. To be selected to lead people of this caliber, it's just very humbling."

Shaw's childhood was the classic moving-around story. His father had health problems, and the relocations followed his treatment. After high school in Raleigh, North Carolina — "My grades were horrible; I liked to have too much fun" — Shaw ended up at the University of North Carolina at Greensboro. It was another classic story: everybody was going to college, and even though Rob had always wanted the Army, he got on the same train. First year there, Rob pledged a fraternity, drank, blew off classes. "I partied entirely too hard," he says. He dropped out, got a job folding T-shirts at the Gap. Then he enlisted in the Army. "My mother wasn't too thrilled," he says. "She shed some tears over it. She kept saying, 'Why don't you go back to school? We'll pay for school.'" But Rob loved the Infantry, and after two years his platoon leader recommended him as a prior-service candidate to West Point.

At Fort Bragg, for the first time in his life, Rob felt completely at home. His voice turns evangelical when he talks about it. "The Army just *clicked* for me," he says. "I liked the demands, I liked the schedule, I liked the way I was treated. Some people will tell you you get treated like a child in the Army. But more often I see you're told to do something, and if you fail to do it, you're held to a standard. You're treated as a man." Rob had cut through the tangle of civilian life onto the clear, broad plains of the military. "Just stand in the middle of Fort Bragg in the middle of the day — there's such a sense of *urgency*. Airplanes are flying over. Everybody's camoed up, going out to train. Artillery rounds are being shot on the range; the windows rattle. At my college fraternity, we called each other brothers and did rituals, and I thought, 'Wow, this is pretty cool.' But at Bragg I realized what real brotherhood was like — kind of a fire that melds people together. You're doing tough, challenging, dangerous things, for a good reason. It's just an awesome feeling." Rob doesn't like to imagine the Rob Shaw who would have stuck with the out-of-uniform world. "One of my friends from high school, she works for IBM. She's making money, but she doesn't get any fire from it. She's not personally motivated to work other than to pay rent and these sorts of things."

One weekend at Fort Bragg, Rob's dad came to pick him up. They drove off post, passed the long, heavy rows of aircraft at Pope Air Force Base. "And my dad just turned to me and said, 'You feel like you're a part of something big and good, don't you?' I was like, 'Absolutely.' And that's exactly what I *was* feeling: part of something that is big and powerful and inherently good — and I believe the Army is inherently good. You're not chasing money or anything like that. I think it's a noble profession. That's why they call it the service. I literally would wake up in the morning — and I still feel this way, not as much because I'm not in the field Army — but when you see *U.S. Army*, it's a good feeling. It's a good feeling to be part of that organization."

There are a number of acceptable answers to the question "What brought you to West Point?" The one response you should never give is "mom and dad." The idea is that your parents' ambitions will never be enough fuel for the rigors and sacrifices of four years at the Military Academy. Yet Rob came to West Point because of his dad, in perhaps the one allowable context. Robert Shaw Sr.'s medical problems — which had kept the family on the hop — stem from injuries sustained in Vietnam. Before the war he was a high school All-American with athletic scholarships to Dartmouth and Harvard. When the war began he enlisted. A couple of months into his tour, his platoon was on patrol, and broke for lunch. "My dad just called it 'a bad day,'" Shaw says. All of a sudden they're in an ambush; mortars raining everywhere, slugs, North Vietnamese pouring from the trees. His father's platoon leader lost it — hid in a ditch, wouldn't act, wouldn't touch the radio, wouldn't command.

"My dad got torn up pretty good," Rob says. "They put him on the chopper not thinking he was going to make it, he was that blown up." The medic who rescued him was killed by a shot through the head; the helicopter that airlifted him to a field hospital was so riddled, it never flew again. For years, Rob's father walked with a cane; there's still shrapnel around his spine. Rob never found out what happened to the lieutenant who was his father's platoon leader. "But judging from discussions with my dad," Rob says carefully, "I don't think he's alive anymore, because most of his unit was killed. So I guess for me, I look at my father and say, 'I'm going to be the lieutenant that takes care of that Private Shaw in the future.' I want him and my troops to get home because I did the right thing all the way through."

A week into the second term, I follow Shaw and the senior class to a mandatory presentation on Bosnia in the flag-draped auditorium of Thayer Hall. The firsties enter wearing their dress uniforms, in large groups; one thing you notice after a few hours at West Point is that cadets are almost never alone. They find familiar seats ("Front left, baby, front left — I haven't changed my spot in four years") and toss their gloves into their hats; uncapped, the auditorium becomes a bumpy sea of very short haircuts. The presentation has been arranged because there are only 125 days until graduation (a bit of the Knowledge that plebes are expected to recite on command), and as Shaw says, "The Army is becoming real for us. When you're new the goal is so far off, you don't even think about it." Lieutenants just returned from Bosnia — young officers with only a couple of years on these cadets —

step to the microphone and give quick briefings. Throughout the hour, officers walk the rows, looking for sleeping cadets. They shake them by the shoulder, whisper in their ears and lead them to the back of the auditorium, where they have to watch standing up.

Lieutenant John Byrom, class of '95, grins throughout his presentation. "I was in the southern part of Bosnia — mountains, beautiful area," he says. "I had a great time. An example: You're a lieutenant, suddenly you get a call over your radio: 'We need help, sir. We got eight Serbs with AK-47s pointed at us telling us to drop our weapons. What do you want us to do?' Well, that has some *strategic implications* right there." The firsties shout *huah*. "It's tough. It's fun, too. I'm jealous of you all. You get to go out and be platoon leaders."

Dave Stephens, a stocky twenty-four-year-old lieutenant, takes the lectern. "Everybody awake?" *Huah.* "How many of you guys going Infantry?" *Huah.* "Two years ago, I was going through pretty much the same thing as you guys, which was, 'What do the next couple of years have in store for me?' Well, Bosnia. And I can guarantee you, a lot of you guys will be going to Bosnia too." He tells them about Hill 562. "All kinds of missions — you name it, we did it. We *ran* that hill." He ends not on a note of excitement but on the non-rousing note of safety. Force protection. "I don't know what it's worth to you," he says, "but a lot of stuff over there to me wasn't worth losing a soldier. So you just gotta remember, in any kind of confrontation, your number one thing is to get all these guys back home. Unless you want to explain to their parents, it was worth it to *you*." When the presentations are over, the firstie class snaps up from its seats as a unit, holds at attention. The captain at the lectern says, "Dismissed," and the cadets leave together; another night they've been assured that their work is important, challenging, of selfless value to their country.

Private Rash's Problem

George Rash, a plebe in Company G-4, has been having just a terrible time. Rash, the son of two Army sergeants, grew up in Centerville, Georgia. ("It's not even on the map," he says.) He came to West Point because he'd heard that "the military is a great way to go": guaranteed job, guaranteed housing, guaranteed medical — a no-brainer. George is a hard-luck cadet; even his name is a hard-luck name. When he passes upperclassmen, they'll sneer it out: *Rash! Rash!* At presentations, when the call goes out for volunteers, other plebes will nominate George, just for the pleasure of hearing adults say his unlikely name. He's had problems with what's called military bearing: talks too much, looks around too much (between classrooms and barracks, plebes are not supposed to look around or talk at all), doesn't maintain a good uniform appearance. He hasn't done so well on the physical side, either, because he injured his knee in a fall at Captain D's, a southern fried-fish chain; that's the kind of luck Rash has.

Rash's West Point difficulties started right off with Beast Barracks. Beast features road marching — eight miles, ten miles, fifteen miles — and George's feet did not love the boot. "The shoes were too narrow, and I didn't get to change the socks often enough," he says. George came down with trench foot: clammy skin, blisters on top of blisters. "It was ugly," he says with satisfaction. "The doctors had never seen blisters that bad." I ask if this will always be a marching problem. "I hope not," George answers. "But probably."

Rash had straight A's in high school, 1400 on his SATs; he's obviously a bright kid. He wears glasses, and his skin is covered with the kind of pimples a face sometimes grows out of sheer embarrassment. His expression is a perplexed, willed blankness; he's ready to be liked. Things have turned awful, but if he ignores them — who knows? — maybe they'll go back to being good again. None of this is helped by George's being Jewish in a school full of practicing Christians. Every Sunday morning, the post bustles with scrubbed people headed for church, like a small town. (The Academy even has an official prayer: ". . . Strengthen and increase our admiration for honest dealing and clean thinking . . . Encourage us in our endeavor to live above the common level of life . . .") Some of the more devout kids keep trying to convert George, explaining how Judaism is the wrong religion, that Christ is the only path to salvation. "Basically, a lot of 'em say Jesus is really the best way to go," George shrugs.

But Rash's fundamental problem lies elsewhere. West Point operates on a kind of fanatical male efficiency — the efficiency of timetables, faster computers, a road atlas that leads you to the shortcuts. (You imagine one reason for all the acronyms of military life is that somewhere deep in the Pentagon, manpower analysis has revealed how much troop time is saved through abbreviations on a year-by-year basis.) Upon arrival at West Point, cadets are issued a thick book called *The United States Corps of Cadets Standard Operating Procedures.* The *USCC SOP* contains black-and-white photos of the most efficient way desktops, closets, sinks, shelves, uniforms and dressers can be organized; cadets are graded on how well they match it. Even punishments are efficient. Make an error at West Point and your punishment will be something like raking leaves or painting walls; you are corrected, but the correction has maintenance byproducts for the Academy. Plebes deliver laundry and sweep halls; it teaches them to follow orders, and efficiently keeps uniforms circulating and the grounds looking neat. The idea of military dialogue is to hold the word count to a minimum. (At Beast Barracks, plebes are issued their four boiled-down official responses: "Yes sir," "No sir," "Sir, I do not understand," and "No excuse, sir.") The idea of a uniform is to make dressing automatic.

In this world, George is inefficient; he can't tell what information is more important than other information. "His problems are brain-fart-type things," a yuk tells me. "He's just one of those plebes upperclassmen like to nail." George has been corrected, yelled at, told to write thousand-word essays on the value of respect, locked up at attention for forty-five minutes at a time. Even the taunts against him are wonderfully efficient — just his unbelievable name: *Rash! Rash!*

On a damp, warm day in January, George's problems come to a head. He failed the Army Physical Fitness Test last November; today he gets his second shot. The remedial APFT will be administered by a huah young Infantry captain named Jim DeMoss. DeMoss is the TAC officer for Rash's company, the G-4 Fighting Guppies. A thirty-two-year-old Academy graduate, he served with distinction in Operation Just Cause in Panama and in Desert Storm in the Gulf: medals, citations, stories. As a TAC, DeMoss is a combination role model, counselor and disciplinarian for the 125 cadets in G-4.

If George can't pass, he'll get one more shot. If he fails again, he'll be booted from the Academy. The Army is about meeting standards — clear, nonnegotiable benchmarks of expectation and performance — and that's the beauty of it, as opposed to the civilian world, where invisible standards shiver and evaporate as you approach them. Cadets *must* complete at least forty-two push-ups in two minutes; they *must* complete at least fifty-three sit-ups in two minutes; they *must* be able to run two miles in less than 15:54. DeMoss right now is the stone-faced representative of those standards, but it's clear he wants to see his cadets pass. When I first meet DeMoss, I can hardly bear to be in a room with him; he has short hair, an athletic build, and a kind of piercing stare. After I've known him a while, I understand that the stare is a type of social optimism. He's looking into your eyes and hoping he'll find some portion of the drive and ethic he has in his; after a while, all you can do is look up and meet his expression, come what may. The G-4 physical development sergeant, a kid named Jim Edgar, is here with Captain DeMoss as the timekeeper. The cadets meet in Gillis Field House, down by the Hudson, and loosen up — roll necks, shake out ankles. Three plebes: Rob Anders (muscular, cocky, compact), who failed his November APFT through "a comedy of errors" he'd rather not talk about; Rash; and a tall, midwestern, small-eyed, corn-fed kid named Patrick Schafer. Rash paces the floor mats nervously. Schafer moves with grudging deliberation, like an old dog that doesn't like any of the places it's allowed to sit.

Push-ups come first. Anders lays down sixty-six fluid push-ups. Schafer finishes with a breathless forty-seven. DeMoss crouches beside the cadets as they work, checking the time and calling the count, giving gruff encouragement in his soft Texas accent. ". . . Twenty-three . . . twenty-four — come on, now. Twenty-five . . . twenty-six — good work, keep it goin'." Rash tops out at fifty-six, and when he stands he has a farmer's tan: red neck, red ears, red arms.

"Next is the sit-up," DeMoss says. "Minimum is fifty-three. Feet up to twelve inches apart, shoulder blades do not have to touch the ground." Anders settles into position first, Rash holding his sneakers. "Five . . . six — good pace now," DeMoss tells him. "Fourteen . . . fifteen — pick it up." Anders bounces to his feet after seventy sit-ups; his embarrassment has now diminished by two-thirds. Schafer starts slowly, rocking back and forth; DeMoss has to remind him to lace his fingers behind his head. At twenty-two, he's flagging. "Keep goin'!" DeMoss tells him. "Thirty, thirty-one — let's go — thirty-two, thirty-three — come on now, don't raise your butt — thirty-four — come on, let's go. Thirty-seven, thirty-eight — how much time we got left?" Jim Edgar says, "Thirty seconds." The plebe's motions are becoming agony. "Thirty-nine, forty — let's go, pump them!" "Everything you got!" Anders calls. "Forty-one, forty-two, time." And just like that, Schafer has failed his remedial APFT.

But he still has to hold Rash's sneakers. With a cool, dead look in his eye Schafer kneels on the mat as Rash removes his glasses. After ninety seconds, Rash has forty-nine sit-ups and is grunting with an awful defecatory look. He finishes at sixty-one. "Good work," DeMoss says.

They walk outdoors into light rain, cross a slim parking lot. "OK, men," DeMoss says. "Two-mile run. No matter how you did in there, you're gonna give it all on this event. Schafer, you with me? Huah." The two-mile course covers a thin gray crumble of a road between the Hudson River and the West Point sewage treatment facility, which today is giving off its pungent reminder that all men are corporeal and fallible; many cadets are convinced the course skirts the sewage plant for just this purpose. "Fifteen fifty-four is our time," says DeMoss. "You can run in any uniform you want, and you can shed gear along the way if you don't want to carry it. Any questions? Huah. On your marks, get set, go." And the three cadets go trotting off down the road. After a few minutes, the three dots spread themselves out; a shorter, hard-charging dot pulling ahead, a tall dot in the middle and, in the back, a dot with glasses. Anders comes back at 13:40, barely winded. He picks up his sweatshirt and heads off to barracks. At 14:30 DeMoss jogs a little ways down the road to give some encouragement. Schafer is just in view; Rash is still a speck in the distance. DeMoss runs alongside Schafer. "Come on — you want this — pick it up now." Schafer finishes with a 15:49. With an incredible encouragement barrage from DeMoss, Rash comes in at 16:48, nearly a minute behind the standard. He staggers a few steps past the finish and collapses on the grass.

In thirty days, Rash and Schafer will get one last crack at the APFT; if Schafer can't improve on sit-ups or Rash can't pass his run, they'll be out. Schafer needs to add only eleven sit-ups, but Rash has to shave a full fifty-four seconds off his time. He nods "Yes sir" as DeMoss states this to him, but his face clouds over. Walking to barracks, Rash explains his determination to pass: "If you're kicked out, it better be over something significant that you don't have a hand in."

Plebes tend to stick together, to help each other with duties and school work, with the shoe-shining and room-straightening and moral support you need to survive at the scrappy bottom of the military food chain. But in the coming weeks, the G-4 plebes start avoiding Rash, freezing him out, acting like he's already half gone from the Academy. "Nobody's helping him," plebe Jasmine Rose says. "It's kind of bad in a way. He has to cut off so much running time — the plebes aren't helping him because they don't think he's going to make it.""

The Changes

Ten years ago — before CLDS, the Cadet Leader Development System — leadership training at West Point was simple: once you stopped being a plebe, your assignment was to make new plebes miserable. It was three on one, the upper classes competing for the command experience of getting plebes to quit. (The old attrition rate was around 40 percent; it stands at 20 percent today.)

That's all gone now. As of 1998, the cadets have ranks: plebes are privates, yearlings are corporals, cows are sergeants, firsties are officers. They have the responsibilities that those ranks carry in Army life. This is part of a system of changes at West Point so global that inside Academy walls they're referred to simply as The Changes.

In a society like West Point, information is a closed ecosystem, circulating like weather: it travels upward through chains of command, accumulates, pauses, and then rains down as orders. So when a cadet flunks an academic course — or gets into honor trouble or, like George, fails an APFT — the data work their way from company cadets to their TAC and finally to the Brigade Tactical Department, the eye in the sky, which watches everything. "The cadets think we're just a big spy network staying up twenty-five hours a day," explains Colonel Joseph Adamczyk, the brigade tactical officer. Adamczyk, in his forties, has the stringy, whittled, cheerful look of a man who just parachuted behind enemy lines to attend a surprise party. Cadets call him Skeletor — after the needling villain of the cartoon *He-Man* — because he's the Academy disciplinarian. Walk the post in scuffed shoes, in a wrinkled or otherwise unserviceable uniform, with sideburns below ear tips, and Adamczyk will appear beside you to ask why you aren't meeting the standard. His reasoning is militarily sound: If you can't keep the amateur military hardware of West Point *mission-capable,* how will you make out with a helicopter, or a tank? Adamczyk tells me the following joke: "West Point represents two hundred years of tradition unhampered by progress." He graduated with the class of '72 — when being in the Army meant being in the Army in Vietnam — and understands the need for The Changes. "Society has certainly evolved," he says, "and West Point has evolved."

The smaller changes are atmospheric, as if the Academy has been receiving transmissions from *Oprah*. Cadets now take courses in stress reduction, eating disorders, nutrition and what's called wellness. Plebes learn the Wellness Wheel. "It's a circle with spokes coming out from the center," explains Colonel Maureen LeBoeuf, whose official title as director of physical education is Master of the Sword. "The spokes are emotional, physical, spiritual, intellectual, career, social. If it's not balanced, the wheel won't roll." Tobacco — that Army mainstay — is now frowned upon; alcohol — the serviceman's rowdy old pal — has become the kind of guest who's not really welcome in the house. (A poster called "Risky Business" is required decoration for cadet rooms. The poster begins, "The decision to drink is RISKY BUSINESS.") Even racy photographs have made their way into an annex to the *USCC SOP:* "Cadets need to refrain from displaying or viewing sexually explicit materials that could be offensive to others . . . the decorum expected of a society of ladies and gentlemen dictates . . ." (I follow Colonel Adamczyk on a barracks inspection, during which he lifts a framed snapshot and turns to the cadet. "We've got a picture here of a young lady celebrating what is obviously some sort of a birthday party — one-point-five-liter bottle of wine up to her lips. I'm not too sure she would be too flattered to know that various and sundry folks were lookin' at it.")

Each of the thirty-two West Point companies has a separate chain of command with posts the cadets fill: honor representative, military development officer. The companies also include a respect-for-others officer, to promote racial and sexual awareness, and a community service officer, who encourages cadets to dust their hands off and get involved. "They do wonderful things," says Colonel Barney Forsythe, vice dean for education. Serve in soup kitchens, bang together A-frames with Habitat for Humanity, design Web sites for women's shelters. In the spring, cadets are "huggers" at the Special Olympics — they wait for athletes at the tape with an embrace. Which raises a question: I ask Forsythe if this ever interferes with the Army's traditional role of applying coercive violence. He talks for a moment about "broad spectrums" and "operational requirements." Then he says, "It's really tough. I won't speak for the Army, I'll speak for myself in this regard. I don't know that we've fully sorted all this out yet. How to, on the one hand, prepare people for the violence of combat, yet equip those same people for the midrange peacekeeping operation and the humanitarian maneuver. Helping cadets not only to learn the sort of traditional warrior spirit — physical courage, obedience to orders in the heat of battle — but also to develop a genuine respect for other people and their welfare is a huge challenge." These are elements of what some cadets call the "Nice-Guy Army."

The largest changes involve plebes. "In 1968," Colonel Adamczyk says, "when I came to West Point, society lived on the myth of West Point toughness: the physical harassment, the verbal denigration, the deprivation." Hazing — even after CLDS — had always been unofficially tolerated at West Point. A firstie could grab a plebe for *shower detail:* put him in a poncho, yell, lock him up at attention against a wall, make him recite Knowledge for hours until he passed out. Plebes would sweat so much inside the poncho it looked like someone had showered there. A plebe who kept making Knowledge mistakes might be ordered to a firstie room for *hanging out* or *swimming detail.* Every cadet has a wall locker, a closet with two doors that swing out. For hanging out, a plebe would dangle by his pits between the closet doors. For swimming detail, the plebe would lie across the tops of the doors and make swimming motions for however long — minutes, half hours — the upperclassman felt was deserved. (As a plebe, Rob Shaw was forced to wear a female's uniform and had chicken nuggets dumped on his head.) The administration itself engaged in a kind of haze; whatever privileges you'd managed to win as an eighteen-year-old, you surrendered instantly. (Going to the Military Academy was like being sent away to a military academy.) No music, no telephone, no opportunity to go off post; TV was a glowing, distant memory. As late as 1995, plebe year was so frightening that new cadets would pee in their own sinks rather than risk the walk to the bathroom, where upperclassmen were probably ready and waiting with some kind of haze.

In 1997, Commandant General John Abizaid arrived and began enforcing the no-haze policy. As of 1998, if you hazed a plebe with even violent yelling, you'd be reprimanded; if it happened repeatedly, you'd be expelled. (The *USCC SOP:* "Cadets found to have committed hazing [are] subject to separation and/or court-martial.") The model now is to correct plebes in a firm, polite voice. Plebes no longer have to *ping* — a kind of racewalk — between barracks or wear knee socks pulled all the way up, which made them both eyesores to the landscape and unmistakable as targets. Plebes can listen to music through their computers the first semester they arrive at West Point; plebes are given walking privileges outside the reservation; plebes have phones in their rooms; plebes have TV cards in their computers, which take major channels plus CNN.

Hard-line graduates e-mail the superintendent complaining the place is soft, will turn out soft officers. In the world of abbreviations that is West Point, the old graduates have developed a shorthand expression for what's wrong. They say, "The corps has" — which is short for "The corps has gone to hell." Adamczyk doesn't have much patience for corps-has: "No class — although they will always tell you — has a tougher plebe year than any other class." But there's even some corps-has among cadets. "When I was a plebe, we stuck in our rooms out of fear," Whitey Herzog tells me. "Now the plebes are staying in their rooms, but they're watching TV. They're watching *Friends*."

Meet the Goodfellas

L ate January at West Point is known as Gloom Period. Gray weather, gray walkways, gray uniforms, sky pressing down. Because it's Gloom Period, it's a good time to get the hell off post and do something fun, so Whitey Herzog calls his three best friends and arranges to drive to a bar in nearby Tarrytown, New York; there'll be drinking, there'll be music, there'll be girls. Brian Supko — captain of the corps' baseball team and once drafted by the Toronto Blue Jays — is seeing a girl at Marymount College; she'll bring friends to the bar.

As they say in the joint, no one makes it through alone. Whitey runs with a crew — together they're known as the Goodfellas. "We all pretty much had the same calling to be here," Whitey explains. "Didn't come for grades or sports. And it's funny, whenever we get together, there's never a night where for forty-five minutes we don't start talking about what we'd do in battle. We talk about war, how much it matters to us. Some people think maybe it's not cool to always talk about combat and shit, but I'll tell you what, the Goodfellas, we do. We joke about it —

that sounds kind of sick — but we believe it, and someday that's going to be put to the test."

One night — before they were called the Goodfellas — they rented the video: they saw guys working their way through an organization, soldiering, watching out for each other, learning a code. They said, "Hey, that's us." All firsties wear West Point rings (in the old days, graduates were called *ring thumpers,* because they would knock their rings against desks so other West Pointers would notice), and the Goodfellas had their crew name inscribed on the inside rim. When Whitey wrote the inscription on the order form, the woman looked up. "Oh, so you're one of the Goodfellas?"

It's Yearling Winter Weekend at West Point, and General Norman Schwarzkopf is speaking at the Saturday yearling banquet, so Whitey arranges for the Goodfellas to head out after that. There's also going to be a concert, which Whitey doesn't plan to attend. Friday lunch, an announcement is made in the dining hall: "Attention all cadets: the uniform for the Dave Matthews concert is dress gray with blazer option. Civilian clothes are not allowed in performance at Eisenhower Hall. Please continue eating."

The West Point landscape is structured to remind cadets how important their mission is — so that any place the eye touches down, in some idle moment, there is the potential for character-building. Statues of honored graduates dot the campus (Patton, MacArthur), and the library is hung with pictures of Academy heroes (J.E.B. Stuart, Eisenhower, more Patton), as if to continually advertise the West Point experience to people who have in fact already decided to attend West Point. On the outsides of buildings are plaques commemorating the feats of West Point grads in battle, which cadets stop to read. "'Albert Leopold Miller, 1 July 1898, for bravery and coolness' — wow, shit, check this — 'after being shot through the *head.*'" General Schwarzkopf's visit serves the same purpose — the fact that this man has traveled here, stepped out from the TV news programs to eat, talk and share the airspace with the yearling class.

Before the banquet, the yearling classes of G-4 and H-4 meet for a reception. West Point is a continual dress rehearsal for life in the military, so when cadets gather at an official social, the objective is not so much for them to have a good time as it is to learn how to comport themselves at Army functions. Once a year, the TACs of each company invite their firsties to dinner: cadets learn how to RSVP to an invitation, how to make conversation in a superior's living room, how to write the thank-you note. Jim DeMoss, the G-4 TAC, is here. So is Captain Andrea Thompson, the TAC of Whitey's company, the H-4 Hogs. The cadets are in the full dress uniform, with its many buttons and its big Frankenstein bolts at the neck. Captain DeMoss's wife hands out drinks. A frisky Oklahoman, Mrs. DeMoss tells me that when she and Jim were first married, "we made a rule — Jim couldn't talk in acronyms."

DeMoss and Thompson have quite different leadership philosophies. Jim DeMoss grew up in a military household, graduated from West Point in 1988. To be invited back as a TAC is a great plum and a career advancer. "I mean, I've been fortunate enough that everything, all the stars have lined up for me," he says humbly. Almost everything Jim DeMoss says is humble in this way, and could be printed in a phrase book for Army life, and this is the mark of Army success. Not that you learn to cleverly mimic the official Army philosophy, but that you absorb it so thoroughly that when you speak from the heart, what comes out is the official Army philosophy.

In many ways, Jim DeMoss stands for West Point as it's always been. His office in the Forty-seventh Division is spartan; every decoration has Army significance. Coins from his old regiments, Army insignia, Army photographs, Army slogans. I ask him about the medal — the Bronze Star with Valor — he received for work in Desert Storm, and he shrugs it off: "Definitely I got it because I was in the position of responsibility. It's like everything else — mostly because of my soldiers. I was in the right place at the right time." When he does academic counseling (kids failing courses), he sends cadets off with Army-style motivation: "Now get out there and kick some English butt."

Andrea Thompson, thirty-two, grew up in Sioux Falls, South Dakota, and has the hard, flinty beauty of the plains states. In many ways, her command style is an expression of the new, more culturally fluent West Point. You get the impression that Jim DeMoss spreads himself over G-4 and says, "I am the standard, do the right thing"; Thompson seems to say, "Don't look at me, be yourselves, and surprise me by that being the right thing." She graduated from the University of South Dakota on an ROTC scholarship and planned to spend only a few years in the Army. She's now past the ten-year mark. "The people and the lifestyle appealed to me," she says with the soldier's basic mix of romance and pragmatism. "I love the team concept. And what other job do you know of where you're going to depend on people to your left and your right to save your life?"

Captain Thompson keeps a GI Joe lunch box on her desk; she's got a Slinky on her cabinet and a Gumby doll on her filing chest. Symbolism: "So my cadets know you always have to be flexible." Walk into her office in the afternoon and you'll hear her playing Liz Phair or Hole's *Celebrity Skin* through the crappy boom box she bought at the PX store. "She's cool as shit," Whitey says of his TAC. "She's straight up; there's no gimmick. I think she's a real person. She likes to party and have a good time and that helps, because she understands a lot."

Many male cadets are here with dates. The dates look like astronauts' wives; there seems to be a uniform standard of prettiness for cadet girlfriends. The dresses the girls wear mostly follow the prom-dress model: crossing straps, flounces, corsages. Some expose shoulder tattoos. Cadets aren't allowed to get tattooed while at West Point (nor is anyone allowed to wear a tongue stud, though if you stare in people's mouths while they talk, you'll occasionally see a flash of illicit steel). But their dates are, and when I attend similar banquets for cows and firsties I see more tattoos, more piercings, as their dates continue their voyage into civilian life.

The Goodfellas hook up about an hour later. Whitey rolls by in a big four-door Olds; Brian Supko parks next to him in a snappy BMW. (Firsties are the only cadets allowed to keep cars — POVs, personally owned vehicles — on post, and there are a lot of cars. At the end of junior year, West Point offers each cadet what's called a Cow Loan: $18,000, at an incredibly low interest rate. Half tends to go for a car and the West Point ring, the rest gets invested.) The Goodfellas load into two vehicles, stop at the all-night grocery to grab a few packs of condoms ("It's gonna be a party-fest," Whitey explains; they've signed out for the night and booked rooms at the Best Western), then make the half-hour drive south.

The Goodfellas operate like an interpersonal squad. Supko, a handsome preppy kid from San Diego, father a Marine colonel, is the face guy. "Brian's the player in the crew," Whitey explains. (Supko says, "I don't know how it got started, but like the joke around school is that my major is women.") John Mini, a shallow-chested, deep-voiced cadet from Redding, California — near the Oregon desert, where he and his dad shooed kids doing Satan-worshiping stuff off the lawn — is the brains. He was a chess prodigy at age thirteen, walked into the Junior Nationals on an impulse and walked out undefeated two weeks later with the championship. He's branching Armor. Twenty years from now, the other Goodfellas are sure they'll turn on CNN and see General John Mini giving a briefing; he has that quiet, reasonable presence.

Antonio Ignacio — Iggy — is the Goodfellas' enforcer, a burly, thick-voiced Filipino. His dad was a Philippine marine, brought the family to America in 1983 for the better life. Sixteen years later, his son is graduating from West Point. Iggy is going Infantry and is hard-core on military discipline; one night, he took a cigarette, put it out against his forearm, turned to the Goodfellas and said, "This is for if I ever let you down." He and Whitey call each other *pare,* a Filipino word that more or less means "best buds." He turns a few cigarettes upside down in each pack, so when the Goodfellas draw one, they might get lucky; when he wants to change the subject or doesn't want to answer a question, he says, "'Cause the sky is blue, and God loves the Infantry." Whitey is the Goodfellas' squad leader, the NCO, the guy who stirs the drink.

(Nicknames: since plebes aren't allowed to address each other by first name, cadets usually end up with a name based on family name or their hobbies. Supko is Suppy, Ignacio is Iggy. Whitey's roommate is Rob "Harley" Whitten because he practically grew up on a motorcycle. Don Herzog ended up with "Whitey" after Whitey Herzog, the former manager of the St. Louis Cardinals. John Mini's name functions as a nickname by itself just because it's so much fun to say: *John Mini.*)

After thirty minutes, the Goodfellas pull into the Tarry Inn, an Irish bar Whitey has chosen because of the jukebox. He feeds in five bucks and plots the tunes: Stones, Van Morrison, Allman Brothers, Hendrix, Grateful Dead — the music he's loved since high school. John Mini and Iggy go to the bar and begin the process of liquoring up. Suppy talks to the women, laying down the conversational smoke until everyone can get comfortable. The Goodfellas make their standard toast, an inversion of the West Point honor code: "If you're going to lie, lie to save a friend. If you're going to cheat, cheat for a friend. And if you're going to drink, get drunk with the Goodfellas." They do a shot of Jack to their future military careers: "That we may never fuck up on our soldiers." Then there are drinking games: if a Goodfella is caught holding a beer with his right hand instead of his left, someone will call "Bull moose!" and he has to pound it down; if Iggy, say, feels like pulling a don't-move, he'll shout "Don't move" and Whitey, or whoever, has to stay frozen until Iggy says, "Get the fuck out of there." At first it feels like dumb frat stuff; then you realize the subtext. These kids are practicing to be soldiers: following orders, being aware of what they're doing, perfecting the bonds that will determine their careers. There will be a payoff in their future; for frat kids, it's all about socking away future memories, constructing a past. "The friends I make here, they're my buddies," Iggy says. "They're my family, man. That's all there is to it."

The Goodfellas talk in a kind of cadet slang that serves two purposes: it keeps nonmilitary personnel out, and it locks you in, since who else can you speak to in what's become your native language? The West Point ring is the *GLS*, the golden leg spreader, for the effect it has on women. A cadet who's getting it done has his *shit squared away*, is a *stud;* a cadet who isn't is *ate up*. A cadet who doesn't do anything is a *slug;* a cadet who turns in other cadets to make himself look good is a *toolbag*. Correcting someone is *developing* him. Correcting hard is *ripping shit*. *Getting jacked up* is being taken out of action; *racking* is napping. And, like most cadets, they speak with a modified southern accent — Army model — in which the gerund ending *ing* simply doesn't exist, and words like *isn't* or *didn't* become *idn't* and *dudn't*. Even West Point officers speak this way, to suggest some appropriate and basic male discomfort with language, with the world of thoughts instead of deeds, as if words can be made a little more boss by using a knife edge to flick away excess letters.

What brought the Goodfellas together before they were even the Goodfellas was the hardship of the old plebe system; they were probably the last class to go through hazing, and it's a system they appreciate and miss.

"If you'd come our plebe year, you'd have seen sumpin' different," Whitey says. "Iggy gets really down about it 'cause he cares, he's hardcore. When he was first sergeant" — a company's highest-ranking cow — "he'd rip shit, and he'd correct it." Having their shit ripped made the Goodfellas tight; one of the efficient byproducts of plebe-year stress is what's called *unit cohesion,* the bonds that cadets form. In battle, what often drives soldiers isn't simple courage but a complicated version of crisis loyalty, the desire to not let down their friends. Suppy, Whitey, Iggy and John Mini survived plebe year together. "First couple months, we were scared to leave our rooms," Whitey says. "We had the stories of guys not going to the bathroom, everything. Pretty quickly, we knew how we had to act out in the hallway, what was expected of us. The thing about it is, if you were squared away and you kept tryin', the upperclassmen eventually respected you."

Whitey takes a tug of beer. "This one guy, he ripped me so many times my team leader had to confront him. He hammered me." Branch Night of that year — in November, when seniors learn how they'll serve — the plebes had to write the firsties congratulation cards. Whitey asked to make this guy one: "'Congratulations on going Armor, I respect what you're doing. Cadet Herzog.'

"When they came back from drinking all night — and that night's wild — me and some plebes were cutting through the bathrooms. And that guy's in there pissing, he goes, 'Halt.' We all halt. He goes, 'Everybody leave but Herzog.' They left. OK. We don't do this anymore — it's called blood-branching, a bonding thing. But he gets in the stall, hands over his head. He goes, 'All right, you've been waiting for this all semester. Give me your best shot.' And he puts the Armor pin in his T-shirt, no pin backings. And I just go — boom! — I hit him right there as hard as I could. Then he had me pull the pin *out.* Blood everywhere. But then he took me in his room and gave me a cigar. We smoked cigars together and talked."

In that guy's eyes, Whitey had passed a test. "That's why I love plebe year," Whitey says. "That's why I've stuck it out for four years. I accomplished something. For me it was huge." And knowing you could take it — take the punch — helped with everything *after* plebe year. "I'll tell you, it helped with the Rangers," Whitey says. "I mean, four days before our first mission, briefing rooms, planning, sleeping three hours a night, everything. Then we get up, I'm wearing body armor, which is heavy as shit. Long airplane flight to the objective, get on a helicopter for an hour — which is loud as shit. Fly there, run around, fight. That just wears you out. But I knew from plebe year that I could handle it. I knew I could handle stress, I could handle a little insanity for a little while. So what happens to these plebes when the bullets start flying?

I've got two plebes on my mess hall table. You know, they're pretty good, they're disciplined, they're quiet, they sit there. But I say something — 'How many days till I graduate?' — if I say it even a little stern, they go, 'Oh-oh-oh.'"

Goofballs and Gomers

Kevin Hadley, George Rash's roommate, did not have a difficult time in Beast Barracks. "It was tiring," the slim eighteen-year-old says. But Kevin grew up in rural Westfield, Indiana, putting in the hours at his dad's veterinary practice. "That's hard work. Lot of people board their dogs there. Feed 'em, spray down their poop, walk 'em, pick up their poop, lot of poop — it's all about poop." A few weeks into Beast training, a friend of Hadley's from back home dropped out. "He was kind of a preppy dude, a golf player. Well, I knew he wasn't gonna make it — he was too *sensitive*. I don't jell with sensitive people. When I heard that, I just laughed. I was like, 'This justifies this place, if he can't make it.'"

Companies G-4 and H-4 are located next door to each other, in tall buildings called divisions. (The majority of the companies live on long hallways in MacArthur and Bradley barracks.) Cadets live two to a room like college students; what makes division rooms unique is the floor-to-ceiling pasteboard partition between the beds, which cadets call a spank wall. No matter where George and Kevin sit in their room, there seems to be a spank wall between them; they just don't like each other. "We both know what buttons to push," George says, "and we don't mind pushing 'em."

While George, wearing headphones, watches *The X-Files* on his computer, Kevin explains what brought him to West Point. "I was thinking guns and glory." Today's cadets are the children of the Reagan buildup, the lift-weights-and-kick-Soviet-butt movies like *Rambo*, *Rocky IV*, *Red Dawn* and, especially, *Top Gun*. Kevin's dream was to be a fighter pilot — which meant the Air Force Academy — but his bad eyesight meant the Military Academy. He plans to go Infantry. "I wanna do cool stuff and take advantage of my opportunities here," Kevin says. He looks darkly at George. "What insults me is that you come here expecting a certain standard. It's nothing that nobody else dudn't say. And when other people are goofballs or Gomers, it pisses me off. It insults me when people who can't do fifty push-ups wear the same uniform as I do. Or anybody that makes excuses or honor violations and can't meet the piddly standards that we have around here. If you can't, fine — I'm sure you'll be fantastic at another college. It sounds all huah, but it comes down to you're gonna be leading men someday."

But however bumpy Hadley's roommate situation gets, it still represents an upgrade over last semester. After Beast, Kevin found himself shoehorned into a cramped triple with plebes Josh Rizzo and Reid "Huck" Finn — athletes. Rizzo is a bantam-sized second baseman from Flatbush whom the company has nicknamed "Johnny Brooklyn." Finn is a beefy football player from Baton Rouge. After a while, the athletes became two different accents speaking the same kind of bad: up all hours, swearing, passing around the dip can. "It was a challenge," Kevin says, "'cause I'm a very Christian guy, and they were *always* dippin'. And when you think of dipping, do you picture someone who probably goes to parties and gets drunk, or a guy who wants a relationship with God?" Finn was one of those wild-flying kids who make a mission out of obeying as few rules as possible; he could get into West Point trouble even when he wasn't at West Point. In the airport after Thanksgiving break, a suitcase in each fist, Finn pulled on his hat for the scuttle from baggage claim to taxi stand. A firstie spied his uniform and reminded Finn of the rule prohibiting indoor headgear. Finn looked him over, asked who he was. "I'm a cadet," the firstie replied. Huck deployed his sure hand for West Point courtesy: "Well, listen, cadet — we ain't at fuckin' West Point right now." Finn got written up for the hat, plus a bonus for not shaving and for general belligerence. (In the room, Finn had a simple explanation for Rizzo: "The guy was a douchebag.") Whatever else you might say about Rash, as least Hadley knows he's trying.

Plebe Jasmine Rose — dusky-skinned, pretty, half black and half Panamanian — lives two floors down from Hadley and Rash; like the other G-4 plebes, she's been following Rash's problems. She came because her dad was a career enlisted soldier (one of only about 7 percent of West Pointers whose parents are). She liked the look of the military lifestyle, and her father told her that if she wanted to do it, go as an officer. "He said in the enlisted ranks you take a lot of crap from everybody else," Jasmine says. "Being an officer, it's a lot better — you get better pay, and life's easier." Jasmine and her roommate, Maria Auer, quiz each other every morning on news headlines. Another part of plebe Knowledge is being a walking CNN kiosk. Upperclassmen can ask for news updates at any time. (Plebes used to have to read the *New York Times,* but now they read the Web version. West Point efficiency: [a] cheaper, [b] drills students in technical skills necessary for the coming information battlefield.) On Jasmine's door is a copy of the Washington Mess Hall menu, every meal for a month. It might be disheartening to know what you'll be eating four weeks in advance, but plebes must also be capable of telling upperclassmen what they will be served every day.

For Jasmine, the rough stuff is not plebe life but academics, especially math and chemistry. Strange things keep you going at the Academy. Last fall, two G-4 plebes dropped out within weeks of each other: cadets Sanford and Nett. "They were doing great in classes, didn't seem like they were being bothered too much by upperclassmen." One day Jasmine came back from class and Nett was dressed in civilian clothes. That was that. Another afternoon in English class, Sanford asked Jasmine exactly what kind of paperwork he'd need to get signed for quitting; he said he was just wondering. Couple weeks later, Sanford was walking the barracks in civilian clothes. Thinking about it makes Jasmine release a little giddy laugh. "They drop out, I'm still here, and I'm managing. In a way, it kinda made me feel, 'Hey, I'm doing *good.*'"

While we're talking, Rash's head appears in the door. Jasmine's roommate spots George and shouts quickly, "Bye, Rash!" Rash blinks. "I've gotta go down to the study room," he says. "Can't upstairs in my room. Hadley's too loud." "OK — see ya!" "See you," Rash says with disappointment and walks slowly downstairs. "He comes here all the time," Jasmine says. "Like, we don't really *bother* him that much, so he's always over here. Everybody else makes fun of him."

Girls to Men

Upstairs in Arvin Gym, in a warm room that smells of female sweat and floor mats, Section II of CQC is going through its morning training. Female cadets don't take boxing (though the plan is to integrate most of their physical training with the male cadets' soon). What they take instead is called Close Quarters Combat. Thirty plebe females work in two-woman teams, wearing Army sweats and orange mouth guards. The instructors shout reminders like, "It's not enough to injure your opponent — you have to incapacitate them!"

Dr. Ray Wood, director of combatives, explains that women have to be schooled to respond to problems aggressively. "The violence propensity differs greatly between the genders. Men are more socialized to violence — men will fight over a bar stool." The instructors yell directives like, "You're digging your fingers into the arm to find those nerves. Then — groin slap!" The women practice dislodging an attacker who grabs from behind: take the hands, concentrate on the fingers, bend them till they snap. "Now, I'm continuing to worry the joint," the instructor says, "because what happens when I do that?" "Shock!" the class yells cheerfully. ("Can you imagine how nasty gouging someone's eyes out would be?" one cadet asks another after this tactic is recommended.) There is something moving about the training, watching women do away with the advantage men have over them physically.

H-4 cadet Chrissi Cicerelle is here, an attractive, short-haired nineteen-year-old. Like many West Point females, she's basically a tight muscle package. She's working with cadet Alexia Anderson, a slim black girl who's been her friend since Beast. Anderson kicks, grabs; Cicerelle blocks, rolls. When they practice their maneuvers, it looks less like combat training than like a form of confrontational ballet. Cicerelle elbows Anderson too hard at the back of the head, then gives her a quick fake kiss on the hair. When the class ends, the cadets march out of the gym chanting their CQC motto: *Tear it out! Make it hurt!* "Every section has to come up with an aggressive motto," Dr. Woods tells me. "Politically correct and not obscene, yet in keeping with the general tenor of the corps."

CQC is, in a nutshell, a model of the new West Point, where military life is upbeat, cheerful, a series of neat tests and rewarded sacrifices, and Cicerelle herself could be a poster girl for The Changes. She is known to H-4 as Princess or Ms. Priss. "I just totally don't fit into the whole military-woman thing," she laughs. "I still get teased all the time. Like we'll do gas mask drill, and the sophomores will be like, 'Oh, sorry, don't want to mess up your hair.' I'll wear perfume, they'll be, 'Cicerelle — you're a soldier.' I just say, 'Get real, dude. I'm *still* a girl.'"

Cicerelle loved everything about Beast Barracks. "I marched seventy-five miles, I threw a grenade, I qualified on a rifle. It seems so cool and surreal — to think I did all that is just, wow." The only thing she didn't like was sleeping outdoors. "It was disgusting," she says. "I had to sleep in a dirty uniform — I was like, '*Eww*, this is gross.' I wanted a hot shower, I wanted clean clothes, but *no*." The next time she slept outside, Cicerelle solved the problem by packing Wet Wipes and Chapstick.

Cicerelle grew up peeking at her father's West Point uniform, attending West Point football games. Her family is military on both sides going two generations back. Her grandfather was a colonel; her father, after graduating West Point, branched Armor, hurt his back, then ended up a Finance Ranger for six years. "My dad tried to get back in after he left and wasn't able to," Cicerelle says. "He really regrets it."

She sometimes compares herself to GI Jane. She's incredibly neat and diligent — her drawers and closets matched the photos in the *USCC SOP* long before she came — and she can do sixty push-ups and seventy sit-ups. While we're talking, she stops suddenly and salutes. It's five o'clock. A cannon has been fired, and retreat is playing on the bugle — this happens every day when West Point's flag is taken down. All across North Area, cadets are frozen in place, saluting. Then Cicerelle snaps out of it and picks up the conversation without missing a beat. She says that Academy life "is a trip. It cracks me up. You're slaphappy — the stupidest things become funny because you're under so much stress."

She tried to get into the Academy right after high school in Orlando, didn't make it, burned a year among the sorority girls at the University of Central Florida. Cicerelle pledged Alpha Delta Pi, but she knew she'd never stay. "I figured I'd spend two semesters in regular college, see what I was missing," she says. "It was just a joke." No self-discipline, too much partying, girls getting silly-drunk and guys taking advantage. "My heart wasn't in it — it didn't feel like I was part of something special." At West Point, Cicerelle plans to try out for the cheerleading team — the Rabble Rousers — and takes ballroom dancing classes along with Jasmine and Maria. (Fifty years ago, in the non-coed West Point, male cadets danced with each other; now the class is mostly female.) When I ask how it will feel to command a platoon someday, Cicerelle says, "It'll be awesome. It totally blows my mind." When I ask how it might feel to be under fire in combat, she thinks for a second. "Sometimes I'm in phases where I'm like, 'Shoot or be shot. Hey, I'm a trooper.' And then sometimes I think that would really — it would break my heart. But the whole point behind the Army is to prevent situations like that. The U.S. is like a big brother to everybody; making sure everybody's being treated equally, that there's civil rights."

You don't have to be at West Point very long to realize the secret: Cicerelle and her fellow cadets are happier than students almost anywhere else. It's not just that everyone looks incredibly fit. They seem mentally fit, mentally scrubbed; I've never seen less-depressed kids. It turns out that dressing like everyone else, sharing identical experiences, and being told you're on a mission of importance to the whole country does wonders for the teenage soul.

"There's all these pressures we don't have to worry about," an H-4 cow named Erik Oksenvaag explains to me. "In a sense, life here is easy. People are proud to be at West Point — it's a major accomplishment. And everything is very structured for you. You just show up at this time, in this uniform, real simple. I have friends back home who are just starting to graduate, and they have no *clue* what they want to do — you know, they're gonna take a year off to decide. They say they envy me. I know what's coming up, I have an idea where I'm gonna go and for how long. I have a lot of choices already made for me, and I kinda like that."

West Point is almost entirely without irony. During football season there are "spirit missions" (steal the Navy goat). There are "spirit dinners" with theme dress codes (Cowboy Night, Fifties Night, Geek Night). You hear cadets talk about "honor," "character," "achieving excellence," "selfless service," "principles," "developing yourself," and "leadership" without a flicker of a smirk. The four-year program is called the Cadet Leader Development System — what could be less ironic than that? This makes sense: irony is the comic presentation of doubt, and there's not much doubt at West Point. Doubt would be, "We have a System (are we sure it works?) where we take Cadets and Develop them (are we doing it the right way?) into Leaders (do people really need leaders, or should things be more egalitarian?)."

About the twentieth time I heard the Academy described as a "leadership laboratory," I realized that nobody at West Point was worried about sounding original or being entertaining, which are basically aesthetic notions, and I understood the immense freedom this gave them. When I heard another administrator's speech about values, how being a leader "means having the moral courage to do what's right," I thought how reassuring this must be for cadets, since every other educational institution has basically concluded that "what's right" doesn't exist, beyond the grim brute rule of not teasing anyone else.

Cadets entering West Point step into an irony-free zone, a place where sarcasm has been fought to a standstill. And an irony-free zone turns out to be an immense relief for human beings: a relief not to have to worry about sounding foolish or whether somebody's statement has a subtext; a relief to accept the apparent meaning and move on. "It's just an incredible release," John Mini tells me one night. "To be able to talk about what actually matters to you in life — how you feel about important things — and be supported. You're not worried about projecting the right image. I would never have done that in high school, it wouldn't have seemed appropriate. Why would you bring out that kind of personal stuff? Here we have such a close bond — we're all in the same profession and might have our lives depend on each other. It's a total release."

When a cadet dies at West Point (illness, accident) the corps holds a Taps Vigil. At 2330, four thousand cadets stand at attention on the Plain outside Washington Hall. Taps is played, and a bagpipe gives "Amazing Grace." Then the cadets turn back to barracks, but if you wait long enough, you'll see a small group in the dark, the cadet's friends. They stay on the Plain a while longer and mourn.

Cadets complain all the time at West Point — plebes complain about recognition and upperclassmen; cows complain about not having their own cars, yearlings complain about off-post privileges, firsties (and cows, yearlings and plebes) complain about Colonel Adamczyk — but I came to see West Point as the happiest complaining place on earth.

A Matter of Honor

The terms of success at West Point are belonging and not-belonging. The official word for expulsion is *separation;* you're nosed out, cut off from the pack, shipped far away from the brotherhood. The expression for failing an honor code hearing is *being found* — your secret, that you weren't really good enough for West Point, has been discovered. Michelle Timajo, a Filipina from Spartanburg, South Carolina, is a yearling in Company H-4. She's a yearling-year expert, since she's doing it a second time, this one as punishment. The West Point honor code is simple: "A cadet will not lie, cheat or steal, or tolerate those who do."

Two years ago, Michelle signed out of a last-hour duty assignment, saying she had to get to economics class. Then she went to her room and slipped into an accidental, unscheduled nap. A squadmate confronted Michelle a few days later; Michelle explained she'd meant to study, hit class, then head for cheerleading practice, but had conked out instead. The squadmate reported Michelle to the H-4 honor representative. Michelle made an official statement that she'd been asleep for fifteen minutes; her roommate testified that it was more like half an hour. Her charge was lying on the sign-out sheet: "intent to deceive."

In a typical West Point year, there are 105 honor cases: 60 percent are for intent to deceive, 30 percent for academic cheating, 5 percent each for stealing and toleration. About ten cadets will end up getting separated for honor. "They're going to be responsible for the lives of other human beings," says Captain Charles Stone, director of the honor program. "And there's no time to go out and check up on each other." Michelle entered a four-month honor process, which included an Honor Investigative Team, an adviser, character witnesses, JAG attorneys and a hearing with nine cadets serving as examiners and jury.

Michelle's hearing lasted thirteen hours, from 0730 until 2030; she fidgeted with her rosary the entire time. Michelle was exonerated on the initial charge of lying to skip class. But she was found guilty of having lied in her statement about how long she napped. As punishment, Michelle was *turned back,* ordered to complete sophomore year a second time. Cadets who survive honor are essentially on parole; they can't express unhappiness with the process, because then they will seem unrepentant. But what bugged Michelle was being found innocent of the original offense while being punished for her conduct of the honor process itself. One cadet asks, "How gay is that?"

Daily life at West Point is organized the way people in the Middle Ages believed God oversaw the universe: every encounter is supposed to develop the cadets in some way. Cadets wake up each morning at 0630;

they pour through their doors looking slightly seasick. Plebes — another duty — stand in the hallways at full attention, chanting out the uniform of the day. This is *calling minutes*. *"Attention all cadets . . . There are five minutes . . . until assembly . . . For breakfast formation . . . the uniform is . . . as-for-class . . . under gray jacket . . . wearing black gloves . . ."* (Calling minutes is Cicerelle's favorite duty. "I've got a loud voice — on my day, you can hear me all the way outside.") The West Point day is about Accountability. At 0655 there's breakfast formation in front of Washington Hall: the cadets stand at parade rest for ten minutes, heat or cold, rain or shine, while their first Accountability is taken. (In rain, no one is allowed an umbrella — too sissyish; instead, they put plastic wrap around their caps and wear ponchos. In snow, they stand while flakes fall past their nose.) Once a week there's a haircut inspection. Upperclassmen walk the ranks, look down, look up, say "Good shoes, good hair," move on.

Breakfast and lunch, which are mandatory, are eaten at designated tables. Four thousand cadets stand behind their chairs, a voice announces "Take *seats*," four thousand cadets sit down. Plebes serve the meals: announce food, beverages, portions ("two-and-a-butt servings of rice remain"). If they make mistakes, upperclassmen get on their case. "You can't get it right, can you, Muggs? Tomorrow morning I want to see lightning coming out of your ass." This detail work is meant as preparation for the scattershot responsibilities of officership. (Which doesn't entirely go over with plebes. Jasmine Rose says, "It's like, the idea is right." "But they say, 'You make one mistake, you just killed your platoon,'" says Cicerelle. "You think, 'I forgot to put *tea* on the table and I killed a platoon?'") The classes leave in order of rank, which prevents a bottleneck.

From 0730 to 1600 there are academic classes. The march to class is immensely cheerful, an academic troop deployment — the post feels like a small town under jolly martial law. You see plebes greeting upperclassmen, cadets saluting officers. Cadets on the disabled list — *on profile* — wear sneakers, walk with crutches. The injury level is about what you'd expect from a pro football team at midseason: casts, slings, limps. In history class, there's a weapons cart to show which arms were used in what battles; between classes, professors play period music like "Remember Pearl Harbor" to keep cadets in the mood. People hang coats and book bags outside their classrooms (theft isn't a problem at

West Point; dorm rooms stay unlocked), and inside they stand at attention as the instructor enters and Accountability is taken again. Most professors teach in uniform; I'd never seen a cardigan sweater with epaulets before West Point. Classes are an introduction to why the back of the shaved human head has never been prized for its beauty. Many different styles of short hair — the overhead stripe, the buzz-cut temple, the whorls from the center — and always a brain-paunch hanging over the back of the collar.

During free periods, some cadets jog, a few watch the day room TV (eight uniformed cadets staring at a *Jerry Springer* show: "I'm Taking Back My Man"), but most head back to their rooms to sleep. It takes a while to figure out why shades are always drawn and the rooms have soft lighting. The rooms never quite wake up. Cadets get about five hours' sleep a night and make up the other three in daylight, same as they'll do in the regular Army. Males brag about naps the way they might about meeting some unbelievable woman. (Your blanket is called a *green girl*, since that's who you sleep with most.) Cadets are so ready to sleep that even at honor hearings, with careers on the line, JAG attorneys go on sleep patrol, nudging shoulders, checking eyelids.

As long as they're on post, cadets are being judged. Start cursing with your buddies and an officer might appear with tips on deportment. "I was in the bookstore talking to a guy last week," Harley Whitten says. "The worst I let slip was a *damn* or *hell*. An officer came up to me and said, 'Hey, listen: in the past two minutes of your conversation, I heard you swear twice and make one sexual innuendo. You know, that could be offensive. You should watch what you're saying — you're not alone in barracks.'"

After four, when they're not at drill — parade practice — cadets are required to participate in athletics. All cadets must have what's called a lifetime sport, and if they're not on a varsity squad, they must compete intramurally. "Athletics teaches a lot of lessons," Colonel Pierce says. "Leadership, unit cohesion, sacrifice, the group goal is always more important than the individual." Dinner is not mandatory; cadets order a lot of takeout. The line to meet the pizza van is often fifteen cadets thick, and the restaurants know the West Point meal schedule — when it's cod night, they fire up extra pies. ("Those guys must really hate that beer-batter fish.") At night, plebes and yuks study for a required three hours (Evening Study Period), but juniors can go to the Officers' Club, and seniors have the Firstie Club: beer, jukebox, ping-pong, karaoke night. By 2230 cadets are setting off for their rooms. Cadets are sentimental about any departure; there are hugs, back slaps and complicated handshakes. The corps feels like one huge team exiting the locker room. At 2315 tattoo is played, 2330 is taps, and midnight is official lights out. A CDO, company duty officer, walks the halls making Taps Check, taking the day's final Accountability from room to room. "You get a pretty good feel for the company when you see what people are doing late at night," says John Pandich, the H-4 company commander. "It's funny. The same yearlings and plebes are watching TV, same people are working, same people are always on the phone. And then the big tough football guys are all curled up under the blankets like little kids."

Gray Trou and Hudson Hips

Michele Timajo hangs around a lot in the room her boyfriend Curt Byron shares with Mike Ferlazzo. The room is generally pretty hopping. Ferlazzo is a smoker, part of the H-4 smoking circle; a firstie named Jessica "Coop" Cooper sort of irritates him by using his room as a 12 × 23 ashtray. Ferlazzo is also an apprentice Goodfella, a close friend of Whitey Herzog's. He was one of Herzog's plebes last year, and they bonded over cigarettes. "Whitey was tough on me for a long time," Ferlazzo says. "He was an awesome platoon sergeant, because he was one of the guys who actually cared, who'd actually come around, attend to morale and shit like that. He'd come in, tell us not to get down, we had a lot of good stuff coming up."

Ferlazzo is a blond, thickly built kid from Valley Stream, Long Island. His father was a Brooklyn fireman, then a fire marshal, then an arson investigator, and Mike spent a lot of high school playing hooky, tagging along as his dad's muscle, excavating sites. Mike's brother graduated from West Point in 1995; his father was a Marine in Vietnam. "My dad grew up, rolled with a terrible crew in Brooklyn — I mean, I don't even wanna *know* what they did, they were bastards — then joined the Marines. Just because of the era — everyone went to Vietnam, unless they were a bunch of college pukes." He laughs. "I guess my prejudices are slipping out, huh?" His dad worked the crash crews at

Khe Sanh, the encircled Marine base in Vietnam, putting out aircraft fires on the landing strip. Came home, stayed in the fire business. "So I'm definitely not a military brat," Mike says. "Pretty much why I came is because I wanted this *radical* experience. I was at a point where I was like, You know what? I'm eighteen, I wanna do something that in a couple of years I'm gonna look back on and go, 'Yeah, that was pretty extreme, that was pretty radical, I'm pretty proud I did that.'"

Plebe year was even more radical than he'd anticipated. Ferlazzo's accent is a compound of Brooklyn and Long Island, the national cadence for "Are you fuckin' with me?" "I got totally busted on for it," he says. "Because no matter what I said, it sounded like I was being a wiseass." Ferlazzo would say "Yes sir," and what came out sounded pretty much like "Are you fuckin' with me?" Upperclassmen would say, "Ferlazzo's got an attitude problem." So he had his harassment, but that was pretty much the radical stuff he'd put in for — "the whole big game." He laughs. "You know you're gonna suck down shit." That isn't what bothered him: "For me, the biggest thing to suck down is girls, not finding a female."

Women first arrived at West Point in 1976, but they're still here only in small numbers. Step into the Academy from the civilian world, it's very hard to live in an environment that's 85 percent male. Ferlazzo points to the empty picture frame on his desk; it represents his quest, which is for the woman who can fill it. Most male cadets go off post for women. There's a strange prejudice against dating female cadets. They're referred to as *gray trou,* because of the gray pants that cadets wear. Sleep with one, it's probably because you were wearing *gray goggles.* Tell your friends about it, you've earned your *gray wings.* The women are teased because the carb-intensive diet (four thousand calories a day) fills them out, producing *Hudson hips* — though this didn't look quite true to me.

On-post dating is a tangle: you're not allowed to kiss in the barracks, have sex in the barracks or do anything physical in the barracks. If a male and female are in a room together, the old 1950s college rules apply: the door must be left open, and they can't sit on the same piece of furniture. ("That's how it is with a lot of issues at West Point," Whitey says. "They're barracks *and* they're dorms. But they are barracks, so I don't think there should be sex in 'em." You also can't drink in barracks, can't have a VCR in barracks; many cadets play video

games on their PlayStations, since there's no clear policy for those machines yet.) Caught having sex, you're separated. Or, rather — males
believe — the male cadet will be separated, and the female will be
turned back, because there aren't enough to spare. "White men like me,
we're a dime a dozen, you know," a G-4 cow named Trent Powell explains. Ferlazzo says the real reason males don't try to date female
cadets is simple competition. There are more than eight males to each
female. "If they don't like the way you *sneeze,* they can turn around and
they got ten other guys ready to knock down their door. Any girl that's
halfway decent here gets to think they're a friggin' goddess."

The odds are even longer than they look on paper, because one
whole class — plebe women — is off limits. Plebes can't talk to upperclassmen; they certainly can't date them. "Don't let me even talk about
that, that's dangerous," Ferlazzo says. "Because you *can't.*" And once
plebe women become yearlings, they're not going to be on tap for guys
like Mike anyway; they're targeted by seniors. As the saying goes,
"Firstie brass gets yuk ass." Which is why, for the first couple of years,
a lot of cadets stay faithful to girls back home. "You keep shit carrying
over from high school," Ferlazzo says. "You try to hang on to that as
long as you can." Mike gave it his best shot. His girl went off to Johns
Hopkins: phone calls, buses, things petered out. "It's hard shit," he says.
"She's seven hours away with a school full of guys chasing her. You can't
blame her. I mean, I don't think I'd do it."

But there are consolations; the West Point name carries some erotic
weight. Go off post, you can generally swing a one- or two-night
hookup. There was a girl in Mike's town, homecoming queen, during
high school he never had a chance with her. "She was definitely digging
the Military Academy when I came home for Christmas," he says. "Shit
was cool." Whitey and his roommate, Harley, have logged an anthology
of one-nighters up and down the East Coast: meet a girl at a bar in Atlanta — you're finishing Airborne school three hours away — she sees
the uniform, next thing you know you're squinting your way out of a
hotel room. Visit some married friend in D.C., he's got a sister-in-law,
in the morning you're heading back to post with a hangover and a
story. You talk to a girl at some family cookout in Hilton Head, her parents start asking sly questions about how much money Army officers
make. ("That was wack," Whitey says.)

"There are girls who go after people like us," Supko says, "because graduating from West Point, they know we have a successful future. At least — y'know — for a little while." Whitey and Suppy dated twenty-four-year-old roommates from Connecticut; after a couple of weeks, there were pictures of Whitey and Suppy in every room. Spooky shit. Walk in the living room, two framed pictures; head for the kitchen, hit the bathroom, two framed pictures. "They scared us, man," Whitey says.

Of course, plenty of people see the uniform, the crewcut, they start making assumptions. At the Firstie Club, cadets tell me how they often hold back announcing they're from West Point as long as they can. "It's a rare occasion when I'll actually say it," firstie Bryan "Soup" Campbell says. "Not that I'm not very proud of where I am. But it gives people the wrong impression. A stereotype — conservative, stuck-up." I talk to some members of the Mountaineering Club, who ask carefully, "Do you think we're a bunch of social rejects or introverts compared to normal colleges? Because we don't quite fit in with every other group of people there are."

They go to college parties and the stereotype is waiting for them again: "An intense personality," another climber explains. "Doesn't know how to have fun. Does not know how to treat a woman. They think you're this Marine who's going to be an ass to them." So people won't say "West Point"; they'll say they go to a school in New York State. "You come here because you want to do something different," Trent Powell tells me. "But then when you go out, you want to kind of blend. Just be like a college kid, you know? But no matter what you do, you can spot a cadet a mile away. Like our hair, the way we walk. And when cadets go out, it'll be six guys in a trail. And when they leave, six guys leave." The most negative cadets, if they're pressed, will say they attend the South Hudson Institute of Technology, whose acronym is SHIT.

And of course cadets can have a hard time dealing with people on the outside — getting out of the West Point head, shutting down the West Point response system. First Sergeant Eric Parthemore, the top-ranking junior in G-4, is so huah it's caused problems on vacation. "My brother threw stuff on the bed, pissed me off, and I just started hazing him," he says. "It was instinct." Chrissi Cicerelle went home, her sister gave her a bear hug from behind, and suddenly it was close quarters combat — going for the hands, worrying the finger joints. Her sister was on the floor. "And I was like, 'Oh my God, I am *so* sorry,'" Chrissi says.

Right now, Ferlazzo has to decide whether he'll stay at West Point. The first two years of the Academy are a free pass: drop out, no hard feelings. Leave any time afterward, you're going to owe service to the Army as an enlisted soldier. The first week of junior year, Ferlazzo will be asked to make what's called Cow Commitment: walking into an auditorium, raising his hand, swearing an oath. "Before I came here," Ferlazzo says, "I was totally my own man. My parents respected me. I was in my own car, doing my own thing. Came in here with my bag of underwear, I lost everything. I became an absolute nobody. That's the whole philosophy of West Point — you're literally a bag of underwear. Everything you had before, you're pretty much walking away from it."

A lot of cadets make the Army their religion, but Ferlazzo isn't sure about that. "It's not enough," he says. It's like the middle of *Scarface* when Al Pacino has suddenly climbed to the top of the Miami underworld. "He goes, 'Is this what it's all about? Eating, drinking, fucking, snorting?' It's funny, 'cause in the military every mission has an end state, and when you reach that end state, you know your mission has been accomplished. So where's my end state? At least here, you can fall back on graduating from West Point — I'm gonna be part of something great.'"

The Two Covenants

West Point days are so efficient they even include the night. Each class gets its banquet (one thousand cadets blinking as a Medal of Honor recipient explains, "You have to be in awe of the fact that the parents of this land have taken their most prized possession, their sons and daughters, and turned them over to you"). And each company holds what's called a Dining-in: 125 cadets occupy a private dining hall, propose toasts, eat off Academy china. Tonight, George Rash and Company G-4 ("the Fighting Guppies") are dining in a room that's bright with flags. Lieutenant Colonel Michael Chura of the Department of Military Instruction delivers the address. "It may sound arrogant and egotistical, but it's the damn truth: if you are not a superior being relative to your soldiers, then they are not going to die for you. When I say 'superior being,' I mean you've got to have it on the *wall*. Because I'm telling you, you haven't experienced anything yet. You have not experienced combat, you have not experienced people who are cold, tired, hungry — people who are scared out of their wits. And when that happens, they will look to you: 'Lieutenant, *do* something.' So do not forget, you must be that superior being."

Plebe George Rash isn't feeling very much like a superior being right now; he doesn't even know whether he'll be here next month. A couple of weeks ago, he flunked his second Army Physical Fitness Test. One more failure and he's separated — out of West Point. Most of the G-4 cadets treat him like he's gone already, a temporary cadet, a ghost at the Academy. *Unit cohesion* is the term for the brotherhood West Point life produces — each time George reaches for it, somebody aims a kick.

Rash and his roommate, Kevin Hadley (the two plebes basically hate each other), are sitting with yearlings Adrian Cannady and Arthur Johnson. "Please pass the butter and salt," George says. "Yo, man," Hadley says, "you're gonna rot your arteries." The table snickers: *Rot your arteries!* "Probably," George says morosely.

As with every other aspect of life at West Point, Dining-ins are full of tradition. Cadets are "called out," forced to admit private indiscretions. Then they either drink a special punch (it includes water from the G-4 guppy fishbowl) or accept punishment. When cadets choose the punch, Cannady can't believe it: "That's nasty. That's just ignorance. There's been things floating *dead* in that tank all year." Two firstie roommates opt for punishment; their sentence is to croon "You've Lost That Loving Feeling" to each other. ("That's punishment for *us*," one cadet calls.) After a bar, the whole company joins in, shoes stamping for the beat, and the swirl of unit cohesion is so strong, you can feel yourself linking with everyone in the room, the differences being sanded away; you're getting *bonded*.

"I'm just glad I chose West Point over the Naval Academy," George says.

"Why?" his table mates snort. "Why's that, Rash?"

Once George Rash flunked his second APFT, his problems became the company's problem. Captain Jim DeMoss, G-4's TAC, has taken a hands-off approach, to let this be a *developmental opportunity*. "The cadets are in charge," he says. George needs to hit 15:54 on the two-mile run; his actual time was 16:48, and the odds against him look pretty long. DeMoss is not so sure the cadets are helping Rash. "I'm skeptical," the captain says with a shrug. "I would hope they're really involved. But sometimes I have to brace myself for things not working out as idealistically as I want them to." Ryan Nelson, a sturdy, sleepy-eyed firstie, is company commander of G-4. Nelson grew up on a dairy farm in Ivanhoe, Minnesota — "the Storybook Town," population 751; the streets have English-saga names like Norman and Saxon. Nelson was a farm kid. High school came sandwiched between chores: milking cows, feeding cows, weaning calves. "My mom likes to give me crap," he says. "She says, 'West Point is a vacation for you. I bet you hate coming home because you have to work.'" I ask why so many cadets seem to come from towns like Ivanhoe — Nelson's high school was so tiny he played both sides at football, offense and defense. "In a small town, one thing you see is people who go off to the Army, and they become kind of your role models," he says. "It's the small-town-hero-type thing. And then people kind of see the Army as an opportunity to get *out* of a small town, you know?"

When George Rash failed the APFT, Nelson decided to assign him the best cadet trainers possible. Yuk Steve Lagan is one of the highest ranked cadets militarily in his company — he could help with George's military bearing. And cow (junior) Jake Bergman is the number one cadet in G-4 physically — get him involved and you get his roommate, Trent Powell, two for the price of one. "I gave them Rash as a special project," Nelson says. "To see what they could do."

In January, Rash typed Steve Lagan an e-mail: "If I don't pass in 30 days, I'm out of here, and Captain DeMoss has said that he will recommend separation. Without someone telling me to get ready on a daily basis, I'll probably forget and put it off till it's too late. I definitely am willing to put out the effort on this." Steve Lagan — born and raised in Noble, Oklahoma — is one of West Point's many hard-core Christians. He has Christian cartoon characters on his computer screen-saver (from a show called *Veggie Tales*, where animated carrots and tomatoes offer religious instruction), and he has an *In Touch* magazine on his desk (the back-cover ad asks, "Have you ever met people who believed those stories from the Bible were *really* true?"); when I curse, he winces. His non–West Point e-mail address begins "Mygodreigns." But his determination to help Rash is pure West Point. "If he doesn't pass, it'll be a bad representation of me," Steve says. "I don't want to have to say, 'My plebe got kicked out because I couldn't keep him in shape.'"

Walk into Jake Bergman and Trent Powell's room, you'll probably find them sitting around with their shirts off, reading bodybuilding encyclopedias and taking nutritional supplements. (They don't eat the West Point food — too many calories; they eat fruit and protein bars, drink powdered breakfast mix. They refer to the two Schwarzenegger lifting books as "the two covenants.") Bergman — a smart, massive kid from Diamond Bar, California — tells me there's no slang term like *musclehead* for the serious lifter community at West Point, but that's what he and Powell are: muscleheads. One thing they dislike about military life is how much it cuts into their lifting time. They keep five-pound jars of whey protein stowed under their desks, bottles of Ripped Fuel, a muscle enhancer called Phosphagen HP and Androstene (slugger Mark McGwire's choice) on their shelves. There's a video collection of all of Schwarzenegger's films and a poster of Schwarzenegger from *Commando* on the back of the door. Generally, door posters are supposed to be military in nature, but Schwarzenegger is holding a grenade and wearing face paint, so he squeaks by. Bergman is the planning guy, Lagan the hands-on guy. It's Bergman's job to work up the training schedule for Rash — he receives daily updates — and Lagan's job to put it in practice.

So every morning, Rash reports to Lagan's room before dawn to do uniform drills and go over Knowledge. Three times a week, Lagan brings Rash down to the track. Other days, he sits Rash on the bike machine. "We only have a month," Lagan says, "so we have to crank this into high gear real fast." By the end of week one, Rash has clipped twenty seconds off his run time. Lagan figures that if he can cut another twenty seconds each week, Rash stands a chance of staying at West Point. And under pressure, Rash is hardening: "I won't fail," he says.

One Nickel at a Time

At 0520, the post has a powdery silence, a handful of sweatsuited cadets jogging through puddles. Erik "Ox" Oksenvaag, a half Taiwanese, half Norwegian cow, is leading his plebes to Arvin Gym for some early-morning physical training. Ox is five foot nine, dark-eyed, strong-jawed, hair high-and-tight. For 0520 PT, plebe Chrissi Cicerelle is entirely presentable: French manicure, gold ring, gold watch, diamond studs in her ears. Cicerelle and Ox work through sit-ups, pull-ups, push-ups, leg lifts; there's a lot of intercadet contact. Resistance drill: Ox lays his head between Cicerelle's ankles, grips her socks; Cicerelle stands above him and Ox swings his ankles to her chest level, where Cicerelle pushes them back. They strain and grunt (Ox: *Ungh!* Cicerelle: *Oh!*) together in this faintly sexual way. But success in a coed military environment means ignoring the fact that you are in the coed military environment. ("You know how you get these born-again Christians?" Oksenvaag says. "Here you get born-again virgins.") When Ox kicks Cicerelle in the breasts, he apologizes, and she says, "Yeah, right, you're making me a soldier," and Ox offers to compensate by letting her kick him in the nuts.

Behind them, cows Jake Bergman and Trent Powell are playing a pickup game of basketball. They've managed to work it so they're playing skins: they lurch around the court with their perfectly cut chests looking buff. In his second week of training, I learn, George Rash has shaved another twenty seconds from his run time. Helping Rash is like working an unfamiliar muscle group for Bergman, since Jake has mixed feelings about the Academy. "This place — to be blunt — like, sucks," Jake says. Powell jokes, "It's a $250,000 education shoved up your ass a nickel at a time."

They make a strong case for not being huah. "There's rules for *every-thing*," Jake says. For how wide dorm windows can be opened, for book bags (all black, no visible logo). "Even when it's not in the rule book, it's still a rule. Like there's a policy, we're not allowed to chew gum in class. No one knows why. It's college, but it's like high school." Jake was recruited to play football. West Point flew him in on a visit, toured him around the weight room, took him to a bar; the one military thing he saw was some plebe getting hazed in the post office, and Bergman thought it was pretty funny. "I laughed. I didn't know that was going to be *me*." Jake wanted USC. "But I didn't really have a lot of choice. Thirty-two grand a year, my parents said they wouldn't pay for it, you know?"

Trent Powell grew up outside Houston, part-timing at his dad's truck stop, the Triple-T, named for the three kids: Trent, Toby, Timo-thy. Trent hosed down cattle trailers, scrubbed beer trucks, clinked through the smell of hops. He and his parents had a deal: they'd pay for a private high school if he got a college scholarship. Trent wanted Academy life. "There's the glamour portion as a young kid — you know, being in uniform, having some wild, crazy time." He laughs. "I didn't know what I was getting into." Trent and Jake lift two hours a day; their mornings are spent planning when they can get into the weight room. "You can make fun of it," Jake says, "but the gym is like our social function. It's the thing we have that we can get away from this place. Everyone says we're addicted to it. I'm definitely in the best shape of my life."

The Army Bergman and Powell are being developed for is, as of 1999, an organization in transition. No one seems sure what the mission is — troops have been used to put out forest fires and manage hurricane relief — and this worries them. They don't know whom they'll fight, can't guess where politicians might send them. The Cold War would have been easier. "We don't know who our enemy is," Jake says. "We don't know what we're going to be doing. It's just so *vague*. The scary thing is, we still train with doctrine from like ten years ago. And we're goin' to be fighting through cities — it's no more like warfare with big huge divisions where there's huge tanks." This problem is being raised throughout the Washington defense establishment. A Pentagon administrator asks me, "What do you think we're socializing them for up there? War-fighting. Everything is geared to war-fighting. When they leave, what do they do? Peacekeeping. When was the last time anyone did war-fighting? But they spend four years . . . in their mind, that's what the Army is." The official shows me studies: cadets exhibit negative attitudes toward peacekeeping and global missions.

Jake Bergman isn't interested in Kosovo. "We want to deal with something legitimate. We don't feel like baby-sitting. I mean, we should get trained in, like, negotiation skills and things like that. But we don't get any of that stuff."

Last year, for a class in the Behavioral Sciences and Leadership Department (BSL motto: "Building strong leaders"), Jake did a study. "It was about how to keep people from dropping out of the Army," he says. "What the major problems were, why people aren't staying in." The model is supposed to be a twenty-year Army career, with retirement at half-pay. "West Point attrition is huge," Powell explains. Jake wasn't surprised by the numbers he got. "*You're* probably surprised," he says. "'Cause you probably come here thinking all these guys all want to serve twenty years. But to tell you the truth, we sit and live it every day, so I wasn't surprised. Very few people you meet now want to stay twenty years. Like, you look at the statistics from the class of '95, '96, and that's what the trend is — getting out as fast as they can."

Like many cadets, Bergman and Powell both enrolled at the Academy thinking they'd go career. "You're not sure now?" I ask. "No, no, no," Powell says. "It sounded like fun," Bergman says. "You do career, wow, you're forty-three when you're done. On paper it sounds great. You can start a whole new career. You're forty-three years old. You're young! And the West Point ring opens doors for you." For that same report, Jake did a survey of adult officers. The results fell in line: salary concerns, family stress, deployments. "You don't get paid enough," Trent says. "My dad's friend is CEO of a Fortune 500 company," Bergman says. "He's like, 'There's so much market for West Point graduates.' The pension plan's great, but I mean, God, these companies, they can do better than that now. Seriously, you could probably make three times as much money within five years."

And there's the problem of being twenty-three, twenty-four years old on military bases, away from girls. "Y'know," Powell jokes, "I'm at the peak of my testosterone level right now. I feel like my stock is going down every day I get older." Military deployments will take guys to places like the Balkans or Korea. "That's prime time for meeting your spouse or somebody," he says. "You're in one of those places, who are you gonna meet? And if you do meet a woman, who's to say what she's going to do when you're spending nine months in Kosovo? How is she going to have a career when you're changing posts every three years?" "Not many girls want to be with a guy that, like, at any moment's notice is going to be in Haiti for six months," Bergman says. "How much would that suck if you picked up and left? Girls nowadays, they don't want to have to play with that." This surprises me, after the many official presentations about responsibility and selfless service. "A lot more people here than you'd think, think like us," Powell says.

Chicken Legs

Female cadets arrived at West Point in 1976, one more milestone for the bicentennial year; 119 enrolled, 61 graduated. Retired West Point superintendent General William Westmoreland extended some best wishes for their success: "Maybe you could find one woman in 10,000 who could lead in combat," he said. "But she would be a freak, and we are not running the Military Academy for freaks." Female plebes saluted upperclassmen with the traditional "Good morning, sir," and the upperclassmen would respond, "It was a good morning till you bitches got here." Female rooms were vandalized: a bunch of rowdy guys busting in, throwing the eggs, working the shaving cream canister, masturbating into the underwear. "I don't know how those women did it or why they did it," says Laura Worthing, an H-4 firstie on brigade staff (a big West Point honor). "I wouldn't have been the first female to come to West Point, no way. Coming here scared me, I didn't know how I would be accepted. But I was like, 'OK, there's a lot more women now, the men are getting over it.'"

Laura grew up in Inman, Kansas: straight A's, all-state athlete, valedictorian. She was recruited for the basketball team. "The kind of guys that come to male-dominated schools are a little different," she says. "Maybe they're not into girls as much — they have a different mentality about females, that's for sure." A West Point cadet toured her high school on a public relations trip — handsome, straight-backed. All day long the Inman girls walked the halls saying, "Oh, look at that." "So at first," Laura says, "I figured all the guys would be cute. They're not all cute. It's weird. There's some guys that will hit on any female cadet; then there's guys that will not even talk to girls. Can't stand 'em, ignore 'em, won't interact with 'em." After four years, Laura has learned which male cadets to avoid: "The ones with the high-and-tight haircuts that are all military, you don't want to speak to them."

These cadets, the females agree, have never accepted that West Point is only 85 percent male — they want the other percentage points back. "There are guys who say West Point would be so much more fun if there weren't women," H-4 firstie Angie Robinson explains. "They could curse, run around naked and spit everywhere, and no one would care." ("To be honest," Harley Whitten tells me later, "that's part of the reason I went Infantry. Won't be around women and won't have to think through everything I'm gonna say. Can let a 'fuck,' 'shit' or 'damn' slip out.")

Chrissi Cicerelle's friends smirked when she got her acceptance letter. "Eight guys to every girl," they said, "you're not gonna have a problem getting a date." Cicerelle laughs: "But you know, get real, because girl cadets don't count. People say, 'You got a date this weekend?' They go, 'Yes sir, but she's a female cadet, so she dudn't count.'" "No guys like female cadets," Angie says. "They say we're fat, we're ugly, masculine, nasty. Well, it's strange, because everyone hates female cadets, but a bunch of them are engaged to female cadets, so *someone* likes female cadets."

Of course, if you date on post, pretty soon you start thinking about kissing on post, sex on post, and eventually the night will come when the regulations don't seem so binding and it makes sense to give it a shot. "People have sex all over the place," Angie says. "They just *sneak,* like everything else." In Laura Worthing's old company "there were two cows and two yuks. They were in the same room, actually. And one couple was having sex, and one was havin' oral sex. They had loud music on — you need to be quiet. Well, it was late at night, and the officer in charge heard noises coming from that room. And he just went through the door, snapped on the light, and uh-oh. Two of 'em got kicked out, two of 'em left for six months and then came back."

Angie Robinson is half black, half Hispanic, both parents Air Force reservists. Her fiancé is Army, West Point class of '94 ("so he's in the business"); she met him one summer in Spain, a high school junior ducking questions about her age. Dating him senior year — she lived twenty minutes west of Washington, D.C. — Angie learned what to expect as a West Point female. Her boyfriend and his pals could be pretty funny about it. Angie met one guy's cadet girlfriend. "She kept talking about West Point, she was really excited about this Spirit Dinner, she was like, 'We got all dressed up, it was the 1950s, it was fun.' And I was thinking, 'Is this girl for real? Does she not have *any* sort of cool?' Angie applied without telling her parents, just to see if she'd get in. Her parents found out, they said, "You got into West Point?" Yes. "The *Military* Academy?" Yes. Then they said, "You have to go."

Angie shares a triple with Jessica "Coop" Cooper and Kim Ferguson.

The women sidestep the four-thousand-calorie-a-day mess hall diet; their room has a rice cooker, a fridge stocked with tuna fish, fruit, vegetables, cereal. The post dietitian told Angie the solution was smaller portions. Eat a third of what they serve you — a tablespoon of rice, for example, or a chicken leg. "I said, 'I can't live off a chicken leg,'" Angie remembers.

Post Night

There are two days when Order of Merit — class rank — becomes most important at West Point: in September, when firsties pick their branches of service, and then six months later, when they pick their posts. At 1920 on a foggy, wind-cut Thursday night, the Academy feels deserted: empty walkways, sodium lights, sleeping buildings. A minute later, the mess hall doors kick open and the paths teem with firsties. They pour out doors in BDUs — the camouflage battle dress uniform — slapping each other's butt, pounding each other's shoulders and wishing each other luck. They shout, "This time next year, I could be in Bosnia!" and grin at the unbelievableness of it, eyes taking in the grounds: from here to Bosnia.

The branches assemble at different auditoriums, so the Goodfellas are in separate locations. John Mini is with the Armor guys, learning about Fort Knox, which is tank central. Brian Supko is at Aviation — the plum branch, helicopter skills are marketable. Supko grew up playing sports and bunking at round-the-world military bases with his Marine colonel father. (One day, he opened up the paper in high school and there was his father, pointing his weapon down into an Iraqi hatch, screaming. "And you go, 'Hey, that's my dad,' you know? 'That's the guy I argue with if I don't get my allowance.'") Long before the Toronto Blue Jays made a grab for him, the old surfwear company Gotcha saw the twelve-year-old Brian Supko riding the waves at California's Camp Pendleton and offered him a sponsorship. "My friends were saying, 'Hey, you can stay with us and surf.' And my dad said, 'No way, get in the car, we're going to Korea.'" So it must seem to Suppy like one more high-quality outfit is bidding for his services, issuing the uniform, laying down the rules and codes.

Infantry is meeting in Washington Hall's fifth-floor auditorium; 186 men, 186 BDUs, 186 first choices, 186 people on edge. There are three glory posts (Italy, Hawaii and Germany). There are some other cool posts (Fort Carson, Colorado; Fort Lewis, Washington). Then there are huah posts: Fort Bragg, Fort Drum, Fort Benning, Fort Campbell. Below that are posts people don't want for a variety of reasons: Korea (a hardship tour), Fort Hood (middle of nowhere), Fort Polk, Louisiana (because it's Fort Polk, Louisiana; Polk has only one slot). Harley Whitten is here; he'll be married when his service begins, so he wants a fun place where he and his wife can start their lives. He's hoping to snag one of the five spots in Germany. First Captain Rob Shaw is sitting near the front, his heart and jaw set on Fort Bragg. Bryan "Soup" Campbell from H-4 is in the middle of the room. Soup has wanted to be an officer since elementary school; *Top Gun*, Desert Storm — every couple of years there was something new to make the idea stick. "I'd have come here if I'd had to pay for it," he tells me. He wanted to become a Navy SEAL, but he's red-green colorblind, and red and green are just the colors the Navy likes people to see. He wants Fort Campbell. And Goodfella Iggy Ignacio is here, right in the front row, hoping for Fort Drum; Fort Drum is a light-infantry unit with a high op tempo — they deploy all the time. Iggy wants to get down to it.

And in the back of the room TACs and officers are moving with light, vicarious excitement. Lieutenant Colonel Hank Keirsey (chief of military training) is hunkered in the upper rows. Keirsey is a beloved huah figure on post: bearish, round-voiced, barrel-chested. "Twenty-three years ago," he says, squinting at the cadets, "I did this same thing in the same room." Captain DeMoss shipped for Bragg after West Point. He's showing a postcard of the fort to H-4's company commander, John Pandich, who hopes to make the same choice. The TACs and officers want to see huah choices, cadets as motivated by service as they were. Jim DeMoss rubs his hands together and says, "Gotta be a mud crawler." On the wall is the Infantry slogan, the bravery and sturdiness of all West Point training in two words: "Follow me."

Brigade Tactical Officer Colonel Joseph Adamczyk stands, makes a quick too-much-celebrating-leads-to-tomfoolery speech: "I will remind you, there is nothing worth getting in trouble over between now and graduation — you've got too much to lose. So, please." Then Captain Mark Borowski, the young Infantry branch representative, goes over the rules of selection. On the wall behind him are the names of eighteen Infantry posts. A row of Iron Mikes — paper likenesses of infantrymen — is lined up beside them. Each time a cadet picks a post, one Iron Mike comes down; when there are no more Iron Mikes, that post is closed. "Once the last word comes out of your mouth," Borowski says, "sit down, you've made your choice. Everybody get my message about spelling-bee rules?" The auditorium does a big laughing *huah.* The TACs and officers go into deep nodding when Borowski announces, "I know there's a lot of stress out there. But there's not an officer in this Academy — at least no officer worth anything — that wouldn't trade any job that they have to go be a platoon leader. You're going out there to be with Joe" — GI Joe — "and a lot of you don't realize how precious and what an honor and a privilege it is to be asked to lead American soldiers. So you should not leave here with any head hung low. You have got a lot to look forward to." *Huah! Hoophoop!*

And the first cadet — "Powell, Matthew" — is called. He stands and says, "Italy." The cadets shout, *Awww! Huah!* One of the officers in back mutters, "Startin' early."

And after four cadets, just like that, the post is gone. Borowski announces, "Italy is closed," and the last Iron Mike comes down. *Outstanding! Huah!* The cadets rumble, nod, lick their lips. Then they start going after Hawaii. One kid takes Campbell and gets some relieved chuckling: *Pretty cool! All right!* Each time someone takes Bragg, Jim DeMoss nods deeply, says "Huah." Each time a cadet takes Germany, Harley Whitten mutters, "Come on — stop picking that one." There are three Germanys left, two Germanys. The cadets high-five each other, hug, do a raise-the-roof. The cadets get rowdier with each pick; the room bursts with good fellowship. "Whitten, Robert." Harley stands, takes Germany, and does a big end-zone, stir-the-pot dance while the cadets cheer. "Germany," Borowski announces, the Iron Mike coming down, "is now closed." *Huah!* John Pandich gets Bragg, sits down to a flurry of backslapping, flicks open a cell phone. "I got it, Mom. Bragg. I'll call you later. I will call you back later."

The Iron Mikes start peeling away from Hawaii, Bragg and Carson. Below them wait Fort Hood, Fort Riley, Fort Sill and *Polk,* all their Iron Mikes in a row. The cadets eye Polk, wince. Whitten grabs a cell

phone. "Hey, Michelle?" His fiancée. "We got Germany. Good stuff."
Kris Karafa of G-4 pockets the last Hawaii, Borowski says, "Hawaii is
closed," the room goes berserk. Jim DeMoss says "Huah!" A lot of the
tension scatters; no more cool posts, the anxiety of one sweet place
maybe waiting for you is gone.

Bragg and Alaska start closing up — Shaw grabs a Bragg. Captain
DeMoss comes and sits behind the last row of cadets, slapping shoulders, massaging necks. A cadet named Bryan Moore pulls Bragg and
later says, "DeMoss was so happy I thought he was gonna *tackle* me."
Soup Campbell picks Fort Lewis, comes back to where Harley is sitting,
looking a little stunned. "That's a load off," he says. "I didn't know Fort
Campbell was gonna go that fast. I was fucking *sweating*." Harley tells
him Lewis is a good post. Soup asks where Harley would have gone if
he hadn't pulled Germany. "You know, I have no clue. I was one of
those guys who didn't have a second choice. Not Fort Drum and not
Korea. You just don't want to be that guy who gets Polk." Huge cheers
when Korea closes. (No chance of a hardship tour now.) Cadet Stone,
who takes it, slaps a hundred hands. Although dipping is prohibited
outside barracks, Harley passes Soup his tin of Kodiak; Soup takes a big
pinch. "This is Infantry," Harley says, "we're supposed to be dipping."
Iggy's name is called, he rises. The cadets shout, *Iggy! Woo-hoo! Igs!*
Iggy gets Drum. Bragg closes. Alaska comes down. "The last frontier,"
Captain Borowski says, "is now closed." Then a cadet Gonzales stands
up. He looks around, straightens, says "Fort Polk." And the auditorium
goes insane, cadets stomping their feet, whistling, banging their hands.
Huah! Yeah! Hoop-hoop! Polk! Gonzales! "He'll be laughing at *you*,"
Captain Borowski says, "when he's collecting jump pay and you're
not." "Huah," Jim DeMoss says.

When it ends — the last ten Iron Mikes are Fort Hood; each cadet
who stands, pretends to think it over, says "Hood," gets a laugh —
there's huge applause, backslapping, hugging. The last bit of mystery
about their West Point careers has been resolved: these 186 men know
where they're going to serve the next three years. In a sense, because
they can see their future, West Point has just become the past. You can
feel the cohesion in the room, the cheerful envy and relaxed competi-
tiveness and affection and comradeship, all the emotions men are ge-
netically schooled for. They feel like an army. Lieutenant Colonel
Keirsey paces to the front of the room, stands on a chair. "OK, at ease,"

Keirsey says. *Huah! Huah! Hoop! Hoop!* "There are soldiers out there, kids looking for leadership. They'll go the last mile, they'll run as hard as they can. They're hard, and you'll be just as fired up." The room goes absolutely silent; the cadets blink at Keirsey. "So don't worry about it if you didn't get *exactly* the right post. Because we don't know what division will go to the frontier of freedom here. But I can guarantee you this: this class *will* move out, will go into the ranks of the Army. And somewhere, in some disputed barricade along the frontier, you will meet your destiny. And you will stack this nation's enemies like cordwood."

The biggest cheer of the night. "Stack 'em like cordwood!" one cadet yells. "Something to *drink* on, baby!" they shout.

The huah glamour of post selection — the deep emotion of men meeting their fates together — becomes complicated when you understand a primary concern at West Point. It's called five-and-fly. The bargain that cadets make to train at the Academy is very simple. Come to West Point, and we'll pay for everything. (Since you'll be in uniform, we'll also toss in $7,200 a year in salary.) But you will lead men and women for five years in the Army. And the weight of our history, and the values of honor and selfless service we teach, could persuade you to give us your career. (The Academy's recruitment poster runs, "At West Point, much of the history we teach was made by people we taught.") But since the mid-1980s, an increasing number of graduates have been hitting that five-year mark and leaving the Army — they're five-and-flying. Each time Captain DeMoss hears a cadet pick Bragg or Benning or Drum, he hears something else: a cadet who loves the Army the way the TAC does. A cadet who picks Italy loves travel; a cadet who picks Fort Drum, in the chilly upper reaches of New York State, loves the Infantry. In the class of 1970, only 12.2 percent of West Point graduates left the Army when their five was up; these were cadets who saw the tail end of Vietnam. For the class of 1993, that figure nearly tripled, to 32.4 percent. (In 1993, when the class of '88's five-year term was up, that number was close to 50 percent.)

In his Founders Day speech — an annual address to graduates — Superintendent General Daniel Christman listed retention as the first of West Point's challenges. "It is clear," the general said, "that USMA graduates are retaining in the Army at a much lower rate than in years past.

We are trying to address this issue of 'commitment.'" The superintendent works in a large wood-paneled office on the fifth floor of Taylor Hall, a room with the U.S. colors, an Academy banner, and Christman's three-star flag. High on the walls hang photos of former superintendents going back to the early 1900s. When Christman looks at the pictures, he thinks of his responsibilities. "The real challenge is, don't get it too wrong," he says, smiling. He keeps a *Lion King* Pumbaa doll on one of his polished side tables. "I just like Pumbaa," he says. "You know, when a young kid comes in, it's an icebreaker." Upon assuming command in 1997, one of the first things the general did was revise the Academy's mission statement to emphasize military careers. "That's why I put the third action verb in place: 'to educate, train and *inspire* the corps of cadets for a career as an officer in the United States Army,'" Christman says. "I wanted to make it very, very clear that we are here to produce career Army officers. But we can only do so much."

Like most people of my era, I have little connection with the military. I grew up with the luxury of a volunteer Army; service was something other people did. So I've never felt anything like the military brotherhood that took over Washington Hall 5401 during post selection; it seemed about as admirable a feeling as a country could produce. (Iggy Ignacio keeps a Marine Corps card pinned above his desk: "Civilians can not and will not understand us, because they are not one of us. We're the corps. We love it, live it and shall die for it. If you've never been in it, you shall never understand it.") It seems that for a good number of cadets, the feeling is just a feeling, the surge in the chest after a movie. The feeling is there, it's a thrill, it's gone.

In recent years, when graduates have received the option to leave before five years, they've taken it. Field Artillery is a popular branch because cadets believe officers can sometimes fly after only eighteen months. (Jake Bergman and Trent Powell talk about Field Artillery.) Sophomore Mike Ferlazzo's brother graduated from West Point in 1995. I ask where he's serving, and Mike chuckles. "He's not," Ferlazzo says. "He got lucky. He got out. After three years, he goes, 'I've pretty much accomplished all my goals in the military.' He wanted to go to law school, saw the opportunity, and he took it."

Each year, the Academy's Office of Policy, Planning and Analysis conducts surveys of the incoming class, asking what brought cadets to West Point. The number one answer is "overall reputation." "Wanting to be an officer" is number two. "Self-development" runs close behind at number three.

When post selection ends, the cadets head for their rooms, place calls to the home front. Then it's the clubs, Officers' and Firstie. The Firstie Club is so mobbed, people stand shivering outside, comparing posts. "I can't believe where I'm fucking going," a girl tells Whitey Herzog. "Fort Riley." Inside, the place smells like a tactical strike on a brewery. A cadet pushes his way toward the door: "They're all out of pitchers. I'm going back to my room to beat off, so at least I can get some sex." Cadet Orlando Johnson slaps Whitey's shoulder. "I'm the little black dude up front who yells 'Fall in' every morning," Orlando tells me. "Hey, write this: 'From the time Orlando Johnson calls "Fall in" in the morning, his day is constant military development.' I'm gonna get me a beer."

The Officers' Club is pandemonium. Officers, firsties, cows, noise, beer, whiskey. The cows look carefully at the firsties, watching their futures drink in front of them. Shouts chop back and forth like artillery volleys: "Someone should set a policy: do anything wrong, get posted to Drum!" "Fuck you — I posted tonight, and Drum was my *first* choice!" Whitey and some buddies commandeer two tables near the corner. A female cow named Lynn comes by to wish Whitey well: "You're the best platoon leader I've had since I've been at West Point." Whitey slams back a Heineken and says, "This is why the military is awesome. Because we get to drink beers all night and celebrate where we're going."

The cadets theorize about West Point's drug scene: "There's three drugs we have here," Harley Whitten says. "Sleep is a drug. Porn is a drug. And nicotine." "Masturbation!" "That's a subset of porn." "Beer," cadets shout. "Dip. Motrin." "Motrin," Harley laughs. "They issue that stuff here like candy. Because you really start to hurt." There's a favorite Internet pornography site for cadets, Persian Kitty's Adult Links. With classic military efficiency, it's a broad clearinghouse address that can direct you to whatever specific type of porn you're after. (The superintendent included a Persian Kitty reference in a speech last year, which made the cadets go wild.) "But there are very bad things on the Web," cadet Matt Johnston says, pulling an official face. "And it's a temptation we must avoid because we are future officers. We're respectable people."

After an hour of shots and beers, Whitey slides off his chair, approaches a sergeant with a pro wrestler's build who's been silently drinking at the end of the bar. In a platoon, sergeants run the troops along with the lieutenants. Whitey wants advice, comes back grinning. "I told him I was with the Rangers this summer," Whitey says. "He goes, 'I don't give a fuck.' He goes, 'Just be yourself when you get to your unit. Don't be a ring thumper. Be your fuckin' self.' It was cool." Whitey gulps more beer. "I don't want to talk to this sergeant and have him say, 'Yeah, you went through West Point, you're gonna be my good lieutenant.' I want the sergeant to tell me, 'No, man, fuck it, you gotta be *real,* relate to the people, gotta be open-minded, and if you can do that, then you can lead my soldiers.' They're not my soldiers, they're his. He's a high-ranking sergeant. He's an old sergeant — you know? He's kinda old — I mean, *look* at 'im. That motherfucker, dude, I'd trust him in combat. That's the kind of guy that lieutenants look for, right there. Incredible fucking sergeant."

A kid named Justin Gordon, who's posting Fort Sill, Oklahoma, jokes, "All my dreams were shattered tonight." He's Field Artillery: "Cannons — anything that fires from far away. It means people won't shoot at me if they fight the war." Whitey grabs cadet Rob Bohr. "I will never — c'mere. I will never let you down. Put down that fucking beer. I will never let you down, brother. I will never let you down." Another cadet lurches back from the bathroom. "They were playing that song 'Thank You' in the pisser, and I was looking up, saying, 'Thank you for this beautiful life, man. Thanks.'"

They toast to Military Intelligence, Infantry, Aviation. Harley Whitten proposes a toast to battle. "What do you say? We're gonna start a war, drum up a little business."

"We're gonna defend the United States," Bohr says.

Whitey lifts his glass. "Here's to hearing the lamentations of the women and children of our enemies, dude."

"We protect the oppressed!"

"We'll go into Bosnia and we'll clean things up!"

"We're gonna clean up the whole damned world!"

"And we're gonna make it perfect. And it's gonna be like *The Wizard of Oz.* Ha-ha-ha!"

"I'll wear my clogs!"

"Dude, you need more beer."

"Airborne!"

"I do need more beer."

Whitey's Burden

When he sat down at his computer last August, Whitey Herzog picked Aviation instead of Infantry. He knew what he was doing — deciding against the military for a career. "I was like, 'This is the rest of my life,'" Whitey remembers. There were ten minutes left. "And I just couldn't press Infantry. The answer was always there, it was just a matter of facing it." He laughs. "When it's ten minutes before the deadline, you face it." Whitey will spend the next six years as a helicopter pilot; he'll train with Brian Supko at Fort Rucker, Alabama. When those years are up, the plan is goodbye to the Army.

When he speaks about his decision, Whitey sometimes dips into the unease he must have felt in August, when he prayed for God to give him some signal in the Porta-Potty. "You know, there's only a few things that are important to me in life, and one of them's service to the military. I'm dead serious about *that* one hundred percent of the time." Whitey had been so sure about Infantry, he'd been measured for the uniform. "I was going to go Infantry and go with the Rangers. Always wanted to do that, had my heart set on it. I never failed any major goal in my life. And I had to accept that: Can I go with Aviation and still serve as much as I want to?"

A few days before post selection, the Infantry uniform arrived anyway. Whitey opened the box, looked at the gear for a long time. Blue is the Infantry color — blue-striped cap, blue suspenders. After a week, it began to seem like unclaimed luggage at the airport, a suit made for somebody who was never showing up. He sent the uniform back. "I'm never going to know if I made the right decision," he says. "Yeah, the contract says 'Hey, I'm good to go,' but that's no way to live life. You know — *selfless service*. That's why I hurt." He smiles. "No regrets."

Whitey grew up hoping to be an officer; he wanted to do something for the country. "Nowadays most people don't think of the military for that. But that's what I thought I'd be good at. I love the freedoms of our country. I love the fact that my friends can go do whatever they want, even little shit — I wanted to preserve that." Whitey has always loved music (at West Point, first thing he'll do back from class is turn on the

CD, raise his hands and say, "Ladies and gentlemen, James Marshall Hendrix"). He even chooses women on a musical scale. "The Dead's too far one way, Tupac's too far the other. The kind of girl you'd find at an Allman Brothers concert, with a nice pair of jeans on." His high school friends — beer drinkers, Deadheads — are mostly kids who didn't even go to college: one works in a restaurant, another's a bike messenger. Whitey was afraid he'd lose them over West Point. "That was my big worry — you know, the Army isn't for them." After Beast training, families are allowed a weekend visit; Whitey walked out of the barracks hungry for a friendly face. Two of his high school buddies stepped from behind a tree — long hair, beards, tie-dye. The other families were craning their necks, people with cameras and kids. What were guys like this doing at West Point? "But I didn't give a crap about that," Whitey says. "They supported me, they were proud of me. They thought it was cool."

A cadet uniform is like an old-fashioned steamer trunk: look at the stamps, they tell you where it's been. Over his left pocket, Whitey wears the wreath that means he's kept a 3.0 academically, physically and militarily. (This puts Whitey in the top 15 percent of his class.) He wears Airborne wings, the National Defense Service ribbon, a military-skills badge and the Army Achievement Medal, for Special Operations training missions with the Third Ranger Battalion. Cow summer, West Point sent Whitey to Mexico with three other cadets for some cultural ambassadorship. They toured Mexican army units, colonels got them drunk, generals fed them on yachts. "When we visited their military academy, the entire corps put on a show for us. And I ain't shit, man — I'm some kid from Buffalo who loved to have his beers every day after high school with his buddies. And here we were, their whole school did a parade for us. The cadet that escorted me had tears in his eyes. He's like, 'This is my honor.' I said, 'I admire the discipline, it's my honor too.' He's like, 'No, it's *my* honor,' and he took off his academy symbol, gave it to me. I gave him mine." Whitey knows everything about the Army — units, divisions, weapons — the way some kids know sports teams. Mention a battle, he knows how it was won; mention a movie, he'll tell you how the Army makes sure Hollywood always gets one uniform detail wrong, so no foreign power with a costume director can wreak havoc. He knows it because it's what he's always wanted.

A week after post selection, the Goodfellas — minus Supko, who has an away game with the baseball team — hit a local bar to celebrate. They have about 110 days till graduation. The Goodfella Whitey is closest to is probably not Suppy, who'll live with him at Aviation next year, or John Mini, who's smart in a lot of the same ways Whitey is smart. It's Iggy. For both men, the military is the thing they care about, a rescue from disorder.

Iggy's father grew up poor in the Philippines, lost both parents, swept buses for a quarter, had one pencil in school; he wrote very lightly to make the lead last. His dad joined the Philippine Marines and learned the fellowship stuff; his father's Marine Corps comrades are the men Iggy calls "uncle," a Filipino sign of respect. "I saw the brotherhood that my father had," Iggy says. His voice is raspy, sharp. "The civilian world is so different, you know? Maybe it's ignorance that I say that, 'cause what can I say about the civilian world? But the military, the thing I saw most was, you couldn't find as good friends, or you wouldn't become good friends so fast. You go through all the same shit, and it's not just you." Iggy's mother came from a tiny Filipino town, did poorly in school; it was years before anyone realized she needed glasses. In 1983, Iggy's dad brought the family to California — no future for children in the Philippines. Iggy had to repeat the first grade because he didn't speak English. In elementary school his mother would help him study. "That made me real proud," he says. "Then after a while I started getting into accelerated courses and she couldn't help me anymore. But even when she didn't understand, she'd still sit with me, try to do it."

The Ignacio family lived in Long Beach, California. "Not a good area. It wasn't like ghetto style, *Boyz N the Hood*. But, like, it could get bad." Some nights, sitting in their house, they'd hear tires screech, gunshots, tires screeching away. Iggy was in a special program at Long Beach Polytechnic High, but those weren't the kids he hung with. Iggy would be out with the crew, dancing at house parties. "That's why I loved my high school. You had guys with the brains in a school that was ghetto style, we were all mixed. What I'm saying is, you can put me with the gangsters and I'll get along. And you can put me with the fuckin' brainiacs, I'll get along, too." The Ignacio family was tight with a Filipino family whose children ran the gangs. "And they would always look at me and my brothers like, 'Why can't you jump in with us?' I'll tell you straight, it was my parents that saved us."

There was also junior ROTC. Half the kids in Iggy's program were gang. Another mix: disciplined kids, discipline-problem kids. "We lost some, converted some." Senior year, Iggy commanded the city's entire corps. When he got West Point, it was what his father had hoped for when he left the Philippines. "In this country, you can start with nothing and come out fine," Iggy says. "That's why it's so important that I'm here. It's not just for me — well, I *am* here for me, but there's other things involved. I want to take care of my family." Iggy branched Infantry because he loves the Army; he selected Fort Drum — usually the first unit to see conflict — because he wanted to deploy fast, get out and soldier. "See, that's what made the crew tight," Iggy says. "We all believe in the same ideas."

At the bar, the Goodfellas do some beer talk about service. John Mini gets drunk, tells his friends the tanks will always be there for them. Iggy says his greatest fear is that he might somehow let them down — "that it'll be just words," he says. Whitey says, "If there's a moment that I don't want to fail, it's that moment. Whether it's for lives, oil, economy — that's our job. Alls I ask is that one chance."

The breakdown among West Point firsties is between the hard-core and the relaxed. It's as though there are two different trains rolling through West Point; for a while, they're the same train, and the cadets ride along comfortably, eyeing each other, figuring out who's who. Then, with firstie year, they hit a juncture and split off. There's a tension. "Touchy issue," Whitey says. "A lot of guys here, they're great guys, but they don't seem to ever talk about combat and all that; they're so relaxed, I can't figure out why they're here. Just to graduate, get the West Point ring and get out."

Sometimes Iggy hears kids talking about leaving early, shipping to graduate school, taking computer science so they can head-start their job search. "I don't agree with that," Iggy says. "You want to be a lawyer? Go to Harvard. You want to be a math guy? Go to MIT. You want to be a combat officer, you come here. We're here to lead. And that's *changing*. It's changing because society's changing. And you hang around guys who talk negative enough, you'll catch up on it. It's like we're outnumbered, you know what I mean?"

The $120,000 Rumor

It's a cold February day — the sort of afternoon when the river winds are like opening a freezer — and I'm walking with a cadet who chose the Academy over Princeton and Yale, full rides. This choice in itself is a victory for the Academy. I ask how the cadet decided; I expect to hear about the value of service, the honor of leading America's sons and daughters. "It's free," he says. An athletic scholarship brought the cadet to West Point. "I had a bad knee injury coming out of high school. And if something happened where I wasn't able to play ball again, then I'd probably be in trouble about being able to stay there. They'd take away my scholarship — they can do that. Not to mention, the military paid for the surgery. So that was key. Don't think *that* wasn't going through the back of my mind, either. I'm trying to be smart."

This is what cadets say all over post: "It's free." "My dad heard it was free here — that was the end of the story." "They provide you with just about everything — clothing, food, education. It's free money. I'm like, 'I'm all over that.'" "Free education. And there's tons of opportunities coming out of this place."

Lieutenant Colonel Joseph LeBoeuf — who resembles a harder-nosed Anthony Perkins — is course director of PL 300, one of two required courses in military leadership. As a man who teaches the art of motivating soldiers to a common purpose, LeBoeuf (class of '74) has kept an eye on the retention problem. You can see that the subject gives him pain. "This is by no means Academy policy," he says to me carefully after class one day. "It's just my perspective." He starts talking about the class of 1986. Fewer than 30 percent of its officers are on active duty. "Their notion of service today is different than ours was," he says. "Cadets aren't committed. I think we have a culture that's focused on *I*: 'What's in this for me?' Then we're trying to convince cadets that the service ethic is as important and relevant as being a lawyer or a doctor. You know, a lot of 'em will talk about their afterlife. We didn't talk about that when I was a cadet."

Every year, LeBoeuf asks cadets to write a short essay discussing their intentions for the future. "And most of 'em say, 'I'm gonna get out and be a lawyer,' 'I'm gonna be a doctor,' 'I'm gonna be a racecar driver.' You know, they don't talk about professional service for twenty years in the Army; they don't speak in those terms." Somewhere along the way, no matter how much they've heard about service and character at West Point, what Colonel LeBoeuf diagrams as *noise* enters the system. Cadets hear the first whispers of the noise in Beast Barracks: article of faith, when you leave the Army, stop by the Association of Graduates, they'll hook you up with a $120,000-a-year job on Wall Street. And then there are headhunting firms that specialize in finding jobs for West Point grads. "The noise is saying, 'You come out, we'll double your salary, we'll give you this, we'll give you that.' The financial stuff."

For cadets who five-and-fly, the West Point mission statement has a built-in fail-safe, an honorable fallback position. It's not just a career as an officer in the military. It's also "a lifetime of selfless service to the nation." If the training doesn't take, and graduates leave the Army for whatever reason, there'll still be some national benefit, some return on investment. Graduates will carry the military's character lessons into the civilian world, spreading them around. The way this boils down in cadets' minds is as principled self-fulfillment. The answer non-career-minded firsties give as to how long they'll stick with the military is always the same: "As long as I'm having fun." Once it's not fun, it's a suit and tie.

"There's two sides to that coin," Harley Whitten tells me. "Because when you go out into society, yes, you're gonna be an active citizen is what they're figuring, and hopefully a good one. I'm definitely gonna stay in for those five years. But I don't feel I owe anything past that — it's gonna be more, 'How does this affect *me?*' But you're also here for your own profit. I'd be lying if I didn't say, 'Yeah, I'm usin' the Army for my own benefit.' I'm havin' a *blast* here, y'know? And I'm gonna use my West Point education as much as I can. And hopefully make tons of money in the civilian world — but in an ethical way."

The problem is, West Point bills itself as a sharp choice for career-minded kids. If the Academy faces a problem with cadets once they leave, admissions faces the same problem before they even arrive. Over the past twenty years, West Point has reinvented itself as a "tier-one college," the kind of school that promises not just a future but a *lifestyle.* Come to West Point and your degree will put you on a footing with graduates of the Ivy League and the other green planets in that clubby solar system: Stanford, say, or MIT. At the new West Point there's no more hazing, there are academic majors. The application brochure — it doesn't downplay the Army environment — opens to half-page quotes reminding prospective students that West Point is not just a military academy, it's a university: "When I was selecting a college, I wanted one that was very strong academically. I chose West Point"; "I'm impressed by the education I'm getting here. My friends are amazed at the classes I take."

An officer who asked not to be identified explains: "Who would we bring in otherwise? Midwestern boys that have low grades but good patriotism? For the reasons that you don't want people to come here, they're coming here. And that's for the prestige of the institution, not for the Army career."

The point man for the Academy's first question — how do we attract the best candidates? — is Colonel Michael Jones, director of admissions. Jones has no illusions about how difficult his job is; the students he wants tend to have plenty of options. "In all the stuff we lay out," he says, "what we really emphasize is, 'We're trying to make you the best lieutenant you can be.' Now, in getting you there — and this is where we really hook the parents, so to speak — we lay out the great education. We compare ourselves to the Ivies when we talk about how we stack up with Rhodes scholarships. We compare ourselves to the best engineering graduate schools in the country when we talk about the Hertz fellowship. You lay that out. It puts us right there with the Ivies, MIT, other tier-one schools."

How does the Academy attract high school students? "When you lay out what the program and the education can do for them in the future," Jones says, "it really sells itself." What can the education do for them? "They know it's a very strong program that prepares them for life, not just for the Army. If they don't stay in, the education and their leadership experience positions them very well to do what they want to do." How hard is Colonel Jones's job? "Exceptionally difficult. If I didn't do my searches, we wouldn't fill a class." What do candidates ask about? "A typical question is, 'Well, I think I want to be a lawyer.' And up until a month ago, I'd have to tell 'em, 'Well, we have a "field of study" — you can sort of minor in it.' But as of this year, we'll have a major in law."

At a time when the military is reassessing its global role — in the past decade, there have been twenty-seven Army deployments; in the four and a half decades before that, there were only ten — it is surprising to learn that the Department of Military Instruction does not offer a major. In fact, in a school of four thousand students, only thirty even minor in the actual study of the art and science of warmaking. The department offers courses on Low-Intensity Conflict, Battlefield Operating Systems and Strategy; the most popular class is Public Speaking.

"Well, you know," Lieutenant Colonel Michael Chura of DMI explains, "those other classes could also be popular. But if somebody's pursuing, say, a physics major, they may not have the time to take some of these courses. One would think, though, that they would add an *edge*."

By their fourth year, many cadets view the Army as an obligation and not a mission. In their minds, they made a very clear bargain with West Point the day they signed the acceptance letter. *That* was their service commitment: they were agreeing to four years at the Academy and five years in uniform. The military side is a long summer job. (One West Coast cadet tells me, "It really hasn't been that hard. I could be at UCSD, and I'd be going to classes but I'd be working on the side, trying to pay for school. The way I see it, I'd be working long hours wherever I'm at — I might as well do it here.") For some, the training at West Point becomes a sort of Outward Bound experience, an adventure camp. There are weird refinements. Cadets are trained for joint troop movements in a war room computer simulation called the JANUS lab: combat netting hangs from the ceiling, lights flash, mortars whistle and machine guns fire on a soundtrack. During Beast Barracks, you have to spend time in a bunker full of tear gas; when you come out, your eyes are running like crazy and you've got a string of snot dangling from your nose. A photographer snaps a picture of each cadet and gives it to them afterward, something for the scrapbook.

Chris Eastburg, a looming Californian — he branched Engineers, and has the build, walk and features of an actor playing an officer in a movie — wanted the challenge. "I go home now, I sit around campfires and BS with friends, and everybody wants to know what I've done. I've been around the world. I jumped out of planes, jumped out of helicopters, got to play with explosives, got to spin doughnuts in a seventy-two-ton tank. You know, not everybody gets to do stuff like that. You go home, people are like, 'That's cool.' If what I'm doing is an adventure, if I'm having a good time, I'll stick with it. And if it's not fun anymore, I'll get out."

I take a walk with Captain DeMoss one evening. The post makes different sounds at night: train whistles, the sneaker tap of cadets jogging, the laughter of upperclassmen walking to the clubs. Somewhere a cadet calling, *Fall in*. Captain DeMoss talks about his tenth-year West Point class reunion: the strange experience of wearing his uniform and meeting people who had stopped being in uniform. "My class is down pretty close to twenty-five percent still active," he says. People telling Captain DeMoss, "I can't believe you stayed." Captain DeMoss saying, "I can't believe you *didn't* stay."

DeMoss isn't sure why so many cadets don't want to stick with the military. "It's disconcerting," he says. "But I'm not in the position to judge other people. This is the hard part of bein' someone who's made a commitment in my life to do this. It's hard to see people and *not* hope that they're as inspired and as excited about the Army as I am. Of course, I'd love for everybody to stay in the Army for a career. You know, I'm the mud crawler. Like, I think there oughta be a *twenty-year* commitment when you graduate." DeMoss's eyes sweep the post: lamps, flagpoles, granite. "I mean, this place gives you *so much*, and it asks for so little."

Through the Woods

Throughout March, Whitey Herzog is training for the FTX (Field Training Exercise), a corps-wide war game held at Camp Buckner. It's going to be an in-the-forest operation — crossing streams, taking hills. Whitey is Company H-4's military-development officer, the detail man for the operation. One night, he heads to a briefing in Washington Hall. (Another cadet keeps checking his watch: "*Felicity* comes on at nine, so we gotta be out of here.") Over the next three weeks, he will spend a couple of daily hours nailing down a chain of command, taking recon walks, rehearsing key maneuvers, arranging weapons, transport and strategies.

One afternoon, he's crossing North Area with his rifle when a new officer stops him, a captain just appointed to the faculty of DMI. The captain shouts, "Hey, you — c'mere!" Whitey trots over. "That weapon feels good, doesn't it?" "Yes sir," Whitey says, "it feels good — but an M-4 carbine feels better." The carbine is a rifle cadets don't train with; a Special Forces weapon. "I started walkin' away," Whitey remembers. "And the captain goes, 'Carbine! C'mere, you!' So I ran up to him, stood at attention. He's like, 'What do you know about the carbine?' I said, 'Sir, I used it this summer. With my unit.' 'What unit?' 'Sir, Ranger Battalion, Third Battalion.' He was like, 'Oh, my God!' Started swearing up and down — 'Jesus fucking Christ.' He named like half the officers I worked with. I say, 'Yeah, I know 'em all, sir.' So he's like, 'And you're goin' Infantry, right?'" Whitey didn't pause, and wouldn't lie. "'No sir.' You could see his face go. He just went off, hazed me, gave me a hard time for about five minutes. But I knew he was just testing me to see if I'd back down from my choice. And I didn't.

"And finally he says, 'All right, that's good. We need good aviators too.'"

An early-spring afternoon. The FTX starts at 1400; crisp light, leaves crunching under boots. John Pandich, Ox Oksenvaag and Whitey lead a file of thirty cadets. The cadets have twigs in their helmets, faces painted with green stripes, ears smudged to deflect the light. They step over logs, lie stomach-down in pine needles. Guns fire every few minutes far away (blanks), a distant popping sound. Herzog is silent and focused. He gives Army hand signals you know from movies: everybody down; eyeball a target; two scouts on the horizon. The platoon climbs along a stream. After sixty minutes they reach the objective, a gutted house on a hill. Three visible enemy soldiers are guarding. Oksenvaag sets up a support-by-fire position behind a log; when he lowers his head, you can't see him. Whitey changes the grip on his rifle. The attack begins, and most of the platoon takes a beating; booby traps, hidden enemy rising out of gopher holes. Someone throws a smoke grenade. When the smoke begins to lift, it's Whitey who's made it through fire and cleared rooms on the objective.

Afterward, the platoon heads for a clearing. They lean on rocks, sip from canteens. It's 1600, shadows getting low. Whitey puts down his rifle. "I gotta tell you, man," he says. "I've decided it's not what I'm gonna do with my life. But there's a fire in me when the guns open up."

Saving Private Rash

A few days before George Rash takes his last remedial Army Physical Fitness Test, Steve Lagan brings him to the track, runs him through the two miles. Rash has to beat 15:54. Lagan gives him a pace — "Great time, keep going" — then accelerates it: "A few seconds behind, catch up to me." When they're done, George Rash has passed a practice PT test for the first time. He comes in at 15:34; twenty seconds' grace. Word goes up to Bergman and Powell; they tell Rash to keep off the track until the actual test. Rest the legs. Rash says he feels outstanding — "A little nervous, but not nearly as if I hadn't passed." Lagan receives permission to run the course with him on test day. The day before, he puts George on the bike for twenty minutes. That night, more directives from Bergman and Powell. "Push-ups and sit-ups, just do the minimum," Bergman says. "You've gotta save your energy for the big one."

On APFT day, George has a slight cold. Everyone comes to Arvin Gym to cheer him on: Company Commander Ryan Nelson, plebe Jasmine Rose, her roommate Maria Auer, George's roommate Kevin Hadley, Rob Anders, Jake Bergman, Trent Powell, Steve Lagan. Aside from Lagan, they won't be running, but they're in track uniforms for support. The only ones not there are George Rash and Patrick Schafer, the G-4 cadets actually taking the test. (A mix of cadets from other companies — stringbeans, fatties, cadets in casts — are also taking the exam.) Captain Matthew Michaelson of the Department of Physical Education — small, dark-haired, wiry — is administering today's remedial. He looks at his watch, looks at the overhead clock, looks at the waiting cadets. "We'll give them two more minutes," Captain Michaelson says. Two minutes go by. The captain shakes his head, leads the test takers to the mats.

Schafer and Rash arrive just as the captain is beginning the push-up exam. The two cadets grin nervously; Nelson comes over and tells Rash to tuck in his T-shirt. "I've got some standards I'm going to tell you about," Captain Michaelson announces. "If you're a man, minimum score to report pass on this event is forty-two. If you're a woman, minimum score to report pass is nineteen." He hands out booklets with the standard, waits for the cadets to read them like an instructor at Motor Vehicles. "You have two minutes to do as many push-ups as you can. Count loud, so I can hear." *Huah.*

When it's Rash's turn, Steve Lagan kneels beside him to call the count. The G-4 cadets watch carefully ten feet away. George pauses at twelve for a moment, then keeps going. ("Good push-up," Michaelson says. "Parallel to the ground, hips as one unit.") "Good job, Rash!" Jasmine shouts. "Another twenty-four to go," Bergman calls. "Forty-one," Lagan says. "Forty-two — you got it — forty-four, forty-five, stop." Rash nods, stops. G-4 cheers.

Schafer is the last cadet on push-ups. "Body as one continuous unit," Captain Michaelson instructs. "No." Schafer gets red-faced, hits a wall at thirty. "One minute left," the captain says. "Parallel to the ground. No. You're not getting it." Schafer breaks through forty-two. "You're there," G-4 calls. Captain Michaelson gives the cadets three minutes to rest before sit-ups.

"Minimum score to pass is two minutes, fifty-three sit-ups," he says. "Rule Two Twenty-six: in accordance with the new standards, men and women must do the same number of sit-ups to pass the event."

Sit-ups begin. Michaelson walks above the cadets. "No! Hands behind your head." A cadet named Davis, Company E-3, fails the event. His friends groan, say they hope he won't be separated.

Rash looks around for Lagan, gets into position. Maria shouts, "Come on, Rash!" At eighteen sit-ups, George pauses, tosses aside his glasses. He rests at forty-two, neck and temples purple. "Good job, huah, good job, huah," Lagan counts. Rash hits fifty-four, fifty-five, and stops. "Rash!" G-4 calls.

"All right, who's next in the chute?" Captain Michaelson asks. "Last call for sit-ups."

"Schafer! Cadet Schafer!" Jasmine yells. This is the event Schafer failed one month ago with a forty-two. He lies back on the mat without expression, takes a breath and begins. At forty-five seconds, he has twenty sit-ups. "Come on, Schafer! Push it!" "One minute," Captain Michaelson calls, standing over the cadet. "All right, Schafer — you can pass it, keep goin'!" Schafer hits thirty-six, thirty-seven. "Forty-five seconds," Michaelson says.

"Good job! There you go!"

Schafer is having a hard time moving. "Come on, come on!"

Schafer reaches forty-five, forty-six. "You can do it! Pull up! Do it!" G-4 is going crazy, pleading, straining, bending in sympathy. Schafer makes it to fifty sit-ups. He needs three more. He has thirty seconds. And he locks up.

"Go go go!"

"Fall back! Get up! Get up!"

"Fifteen seconds," Michaelson calls.

"Three to go!"

"Get up!"

"Ten seconds."

"Two to burn!"

"Let's go!"

"Come on."

"Five . . . four . . . three . . . two . . . one, that's time." Schafer fails with fifty-one sit-ups. He sits on the mat red-faced, silent. After a moment, he walks to the end of the gym, stands apart from the other cadets, looking cadaverous, with a silent, caved-in, devastated expression, his eyes like tiny soldiers peeping over the turrets of a fort. He knows he's just been separated from West Point.

"OK, listen up," Captain Michaelson says. "Cadets, come around me, please. Everyone has ten minutes to move out for the two-mile run."

It's cloudy, Lagan runs alongside, Rash wears a balaclava, the G-4 cadets cheer him on at the halfway mark and then at the finish line. "Lookin' good, Rash!" "Yeah, baby!" George passes easily with a 14:44, a full minute to spare. Lagan is hardly winded; for a second they stand together at the line. Lagan grabs his shoulder. "Listen up," Lagan says. "You've passed it now. You never fail another one in your entire career. Got it? Only improve from here, all right?" Then G-4 converges. Powell pounds Rash on the back, Nelson shakes his shoulders. In the center, George nods, blinks, smiles; for the first time, they are taking him into the brotherhood. Bergman screams into his face, "You know what? You *never* quit. You *never* quit. You don't ever give them the chance to end your career. You never let them make that decision for you. Never."

"If I didn't feel so sick, I'd feel good," Rash pants out, hands on knees.

"All right, guys who just took the test," the captain says, waving his hands. "C'mere. One last thing: for you guys that just passed? Congratulations: you are now at ground *ze-ro*." He laughs. "All right? I'm not tryin' to bring you down. You did a good job. It shows a lot of improvement. But the point is, you have now reached baseline minimum. There's no officer in the world — in this Army, anyway — that's ever gonna accept baseline-minimum standards, and there's no troop that's gonna accept it. I do congratulate you. You did a nice job meeting . . . the standard. But that's it. Let's move on from here."

Rash walks off. Six months later, Trent Powell will tell me of his shock and satisfaction watching a crisp George Rash correcting plebes on North Area.

A few days after the APFT, Schafer meets Captain DeMoss in his office. DeMoss informs the cadet he will be recommending separation — no hard feelings. "I wanna give you another PT test if you are separated," DeMoss says. "If that's the case. Because I want you to prove to yourself that you can pass the test." DeMoss makes Schafer promise. The TAC tells him he cannot give up — his situation is not final; the Academy is tricky, and for all DeMoss knows, it might decide to give Schafer one absolute last chance anyway. A week later, Schafer voluntarily resigns from the Academy before the final decision has its chance to come down. He changes into civilian clothes, packs his room. There won't be any adults in his orbit to tell him that he is on a mission, that he is a superior being, that he has an awesome responsibility or that he is doing the most valuable thing a young person can do for his country. He's flying back to Michigan to see about enrolling in a technical school. The morning of his departure, DeMoss stops by, reminds him of his promise. He walks Schafer to his office and makes him take the test again. Schafer passes.

Keirsey's Cigar

Three bodies travel the West Point sky — compass points to steer by, lights full of clues and portents. General Christman, the supe, is a bright, encouraging star. Snap a salute to him on

Thayer Walk and even on the gloomiest day you feel your luck, and your purpose: you've joined a sophisticated, modern Army. Colonel Adamczyk, Skeletor, is a dark comet. He crashes behind you and suddenly you've got a whole new adventure: you're hustling back to barracks to trim fingernails, fix uniform, polish boots and brass. And the last is Lieutenant Colonel Keirsey, the sturdy green planet of the soldier's life. Keirsey has the gift of inspiration, which is the gravitational tug of your best future.

Keirsey, forty-four, works in DMI as the director of military training, the huah of huahs. Keirsey has a chest as broad around as a tortoise shell, a gravel voice; even his fingers are muscly. Meeting Keirsey at West Point is like driving out to Arizona and discovering that the Grand Canyon is brick red and very deep. Cross post, and cadet talk amounts to one long Keirsey conversation. His name has become an adjective: that's so *Keirsey*. Cadets say it, grin, add a head shake and a disbelieving chuckle. "That man . . . he's the real deal . . . he's the hardest . . . he's cool as shit! . . . He's Patton . . . I've never met anyone . . . You have to talk . . . Have you talked yet . . . Did you meet . . . ?" "That guy is the best thing that ever happened to this place," Calvin Huddo, a yuk in H-4, says simply, then adds the most fieldstripped West Point compliment. "I'd follow him onto a battlefield."

His expressions work their way into cadet dialogue like scouts: soldiers aren't physically fit; they're *steely-eyed and flat-bellied*. You don't jog fast; you *run like a scalded ape*. And you don't defeat America's enemies; you *stack them like cordwood*. Keirsey's gestures leave an imprint in the memory, like light on photographic paper. "He gave us the route for this run, it's called Mind-Fuck Hill, it doesn't *end*. We finally work our way up, we're all dying, it's a rock pile with a view, what the hell did we do this for? And there's Keirsey, sitting up there on top of his Harley. He gives this speech about hunting deer, how they never stop, how humans need to become more like the deer. So that whole year, that's what we'd say before every game: Be the deer." Everybody has a Keirsey story, which follows the strict, formal pattern of an Army fairy tale: a cadet starts flagging, Keirsey shows up, the cadet achieves more than he ever intended.

"We were gonna patrol one night. Two in the morning, we looked up and there's Keirsey marching out of the damn woods with his face all camooed up." "We all went to his house one time and he found a way to fire us up about clearing deadfall off of his *lawn*. Honest to God — I was genuinely excited about doing yardwork."

And Keirsey could recover the words you needed. Iggy Ignacio spent cow year as a first sergeant: rolling the halls, tightening screws and hammering down the standard. Word came down about a big meeting. Juniors only, to chew over the direction of the Academy, likes and dislikes. Instead, higher was laying out changes for next year. It snapped something in Iggy: the meeting was about making things easier. "It was about being weak on the plebes and shit," Iggy remembers. "That wasn't the way we came up, and when I got back to my room I felt disgusted. I felt like I'd had this idea, that West Point was going to be the hardest fucking thing in my life. And it was hard, yeah — but it wasn't what I expected."

So Iggy got methodical. He took the gray West Point pin out of his cap and removed the insignia from his collar. He put strips of dark hundred-mile-an-hour tape over the West Point patch — the helmet and sword — on his shoulder. He left *U.S. Army* showing because the Army didn't have anything to do with it; Iggy saw West Point and the Army as separate entities. "And I kept my name showing because I was proud of my name." That afternoon there was a boot-and-shoe layout — polishing and edge-dressing. A firstie spotted Iggy opening his door in this muzzled, amnesiac uniform and turned him in. So Friday morning, Iggy had to report to the TAC, Major Rice. They stared at each other across the desk for a long moment. Major Rice was Armor, quiet and thin-lipped. "Iggy," Major Rice said, "I should break you."

Instead, Rice told Iggy to report to his office again Monday morning. He said, "I am going to send you to see someone." So there went Iggy's weekend: frets, guesses, rolling over to try to find the worry-free side of the pillow. Maybe he'd have to sit down with Adamczyk or the supe. Maybe he'd have to explain his motivations to a military psychiatrist at CPD, which stands for the Center for Personal Development, but which — because cadets believe that having a psychiatric anything on your record leaves a cloud over your career — everyone calls the Center for Personal Destruction. When Iggy reports Monday morning to Major Rice's office, the TAC stands and asks, "Ignacio, do you know who Lieutenant Colonel Keirsey is?"

Iggy crossed the post, emotions bubbling. "Inside I was like, 'What?

This isn't any fucking punishment.'" And Iggy stands in Keirsey's office, surrounded by the souvenirs of a successful Army career: slogans, coins, old company guidons, Iraqi trophies, objects that comprise a tangible military résumé. Looking at the lieutenant colonel, Iggy knows why he denatured his uniform. Iggy tells him he feels sick, he doesn't believe he's *earning* this. And Keirsey tells him about the warrior spirit, that he has to believe in higher, they're squared away. Iggy says, "We're making weaker soldiers." Keirsey says, "Guys like us, they keep us around, 'cause when the real shit happens they know they're gonna need us. That's when they pull us out. And then they put us down again. You should never feel sorry for yourself. If you ever have any issues or problems, you come to me." And then Iggy starts crying.

A couple months later, at the Infantry bash, Keirsey put his cigar down for a few seconds. Iggy pocketed it, sealed it in a Ziploc bag and saved it for two years, till he'd graduated and posted and the cigar was just some dried tobacco-colored chips in the back of a drawer.

Butter Bars

One night in the middle of March — windows cracked, spring feathering the breezes — Whitey Herzog got an idea. He counted out eighty Post-its with his roommate Harley Whitten and pasted them up in the shape of a calendar on the back of their door. Every night at taps they'd peel off a day. At first, this creation was pretty dismal to look at — each yellow square represented weather, duties, hurdles. But suddenly Whitey was unpeeling the last Post-it, and Harley was saying "Now the angels sing," and it was Grad Week.

During Grad Week old grads ramble the barracks, searching out their cadet selves, creaky hands reaching for everything — sinks, closets, bunks. Parents remember the cadets as children, seeds they planted four years before in the wholesome ground of the Academy. And firsties — rushing party to party, goodbye to goodbye — size up each other's features, hunting for the future officer inside the cadet. The Firstie Club is full of hollering and beer accidents, a rush-hour party on a subway car, everybody smashed in and chugging toward the same stop. "I can't believe . . . !" "Time to go to *work,* baby!" "Yeeeeah." Every conversation gets abbreviated, goodbyes interrupt goodbyes.

"You want to take everybody aside," Whitey says, "tell 'em how much you care about 'em, how much you're proud of 'em for finishing, how much you look up to 'em as peers. But there's not enough *time*." Every couple minutes you see guys shoving away chairs, grabbing each other's arms and just nodding. Survivor grins: they're graduating West Point.

Grad Week has liberated Whitey from second thoughts. "Every motivation you thought you lost," he says, "you didn't." The feelings come back to Whitey like lost mail, with his love for the Army inside and intact. "Here I am, this is what I'm for. Good feeling — it's gonna be tough, but it's gonna be worth it. Scary feeling too." He pounds back beers with Iggy and Supko, the Goodfellas firing one another up the next stage. "Graduate from a civilian college," Supko says, "you're gonna go out and do well in the world. For us, it's like, 'Guess what? You just passed a four-year test. And you've got another five-year test right ahead of you.'" "And you fail this one," Iggy nods, "people could die."

Whitey counts down the last hours before commencement with the good, packed-ruck feeling of every duty met, sitting and laughing with Harley Whitten because there's nothing left to say. Mike Ferlazzo pops by, in the gray squirt of hours between 0200 and 0400, to burn their last cigarettes together. ("That was nice," Whitey says, "just talking and chilling. I did that for a firstie buddy when I was a yuk.") Two hours later, the operation Whitey has been waiting for since he first heard the words *West Point*. A thousand uniforms bob uphill through the morning shadows to graduation. The weather is running a preview of what the sun will be able to accomplish by August, the cadets get sweaty and lightheaded, everybody grousing and chuckling with lack of sleep. Whitey and some buddies sneak into the ice hockey rink and cool off. Then they sit down and watch the supe shake every hand in the class. The hats sail into the air. Then the cadets have a last West Point order to follow: back in his room, Whitey removes the cadet uniform for the final time — the Academy becomes a pile of gray jacket, white belt, white pants — and changes to Army green. In a shady spot under some trees, Major Andrea Thompson raises her right hand and swears in Whitey Herzog as a second lieutenant with the United States Army.

Whitey's parents are here — on a temporary armistice — to pin the rank on his shoulders, the two fresh brass lieutenant's slashes that the

Army calls *butter bars*. Graduation is a family reunion: aunts, uncles, cousins — faces from the Thanksgiving table — turning out to see what Whitey has become. For Whitey that also means friends. Mark Matty was the buddy Whitey was most afraid of losing by going military. Mark was about as unmilitary as you could get; the kind of easy, popular kid who actually looks good smiling in photos, cheeks wide, hair in his eyes. In high school, girls he hardly knew would work up their nerve to call him on the phone. Everybody understood how much Whitey wanted the Army — as freshmen in the cafeteria, Mark bumped trays with Whitey and started singing "I Want to Be an Airborne Ranger."

It was the kind of best-friendship that opens up a side door in your life. Whitey was busy doing high school carpentry (tests, homework), building a ladder out of grades. Mark never gave college a second thought. "We'd go hang out all day in Delaware Park," Whitey remembers. "It was great, it was something I never experienced before. These people were just there because they wanted to have a good life, and they didn't give a damn about your college or your future." Mark taught Whitey music: when they were sophomores, Mark cued up a CD in Whitey's basement. "I want you to hear a song," he said solemnly. "This is Jimi Hendrix." Now Mark is here, applauding the bar-pinning, offering Whitey his first salute.

Graduation over, the post clears out fast, cadets headed off for a last detail of family life. Mark helps Whitey stuff his big Oldsmobile with boxes and clothing. The car quits an hour north of West Point. Mark and Whitey wait out the repairs at a trucker bar, watching hockey on the trucker bar TV. During commercials, Mark slaps the counter and announces, "Hey, this is a new lieutenant, a butter bar — I think that *deserves* a free beer."

Whitey's Buffalo base of operations is an Irish pub called Checkers: Irish flag, Killian's, dartboard, framed newspaper headlines embarrassing to the British. His first night in town, Whitey heads over; first time in a while, he's not thinking about meeting girls, he's thinking about time with friends, one long breather before flight school. And there's Loryn Winter. The impressions pile up fast: ankles, throat, dark hair, perfume, eyes, fingers poking Diet Coke slush with a straw. Loryn is twenty-four, a local girl without the local-girl accent. Just as Whitey's love for the military carried him out of Buffalo, Loryn is the sort of girl whose good looks amount to travel plans. Her face is too polished, her clothes too snappy to be stranded so far north of the nation's party. The timing couldn't be worse: Whitey will report to Fort Rucker, Alabama, in seven weeks. He calls Mark when he gets home, hands jittery on the phone. "I think I just fell in love," he says.

PART TWO

The Second Year

Best Summer of Their Lives

WEST POINT CADETS call their post the fishbowl. Everybody stares at everybody. Four thousand cadets in the corps, TACs keeping an eye on the cadets, higher scrutinizing TACs, Congress overseeing higher and, every so often, the American public rapping the glass, checking up on whether the fish are getting along. But right there at the center, cadets stare at cadets, because it's the post's most entertaining diversion. And since everyone ends up treading in the same bootprints anyway, it's educational. Chrissi Cicerelle, from Whitey's old company, H-4, stood at attention on the Plain and watched the firstie class shrink in the distance. "It felt kinda eerie," Chrissi says. "You're so used to having them around. Then the rest of us marched back to barracks, and that's when it hit us: Whoa — they're really gone."

Next morning, the plebes collect luggage, grab bus seats — West Point relies on converted school buses, and it's a leveling treat at Academy functions to watch graduates who've gone off and become captains of industry boost their diamond-clad wives up a student-sized staircase — rumble the seven miles to Camp Buckner and sign out for leave. The three-week vacation will be their longest since they showed up for Beast. Back home, cadets approach the most mundane fixtures like carnival rides. A bed turns into a Sleep-a-Whirl. The refrigerator becomes the Masticator. (*It's waiting for you — twenty cubic feet of calories.*) A hike down the sidewalk unwinds as outlandishly as Civilians of the Caribbean: a senior citizen, a skate punk, two black-eyed Goths, a gay couple, a fat kid or just some bushy-haired yokel — so much arrayed human variety, your own home street feels Animatronic.

And wherever cadets go, West Point tracks behind them like a gunpowder trail. Slip into the wrong environment — a bong at a party, underage six-packs from the 7-Eleven, even just four kids shaving costs by splitting a motel single — it throws a spark, ignites an honor investigation at the end of the summer. Chrissi Cicerelle flies home to Orlando. Sitting above the clouds, Chrissi realizes she's got everything she wants. She's found a boyfriend — Mark Thompson, a G-4 plebe who was Reid "Huck" Finn's Beast roommate. From the outside, they make an odd pair. Cadets still rag Cicerelle about whether a trigger guard will splinter her manicure. Mark Thompson is super-huah: lanky and tall, Infantry ideal; when he's not talking, his mouth seals into a slashed wince, as if he's so filled with ambition it hurts. (Chrissi has always planned to marry in the trade. "I have a lot more respect for cadet guys. We're choosing the same lifestyle.")

And this being West Point, the relationship is fast-tracking, off to a dragster start. "He says all the things a girl wants to hear," Chrissi explains. "Like, very few guys are not afraid to talk about marriage and commitment and the future. And *he* has no problem with it. So that's real attractive to me. He said 'I love you' after three weeks. I'm like, 'Well, he has to mean it, who talks like this?'"

George Rash spends leave packing up his parents for their relocation from Georgia to Yuma, Arizona. He's glad to strike Centerville off his map. "Weather sucks, a lot of bugs, I'm allergic to half the *plants* in the state." Three weeks later, the class is back on post, the cadets clamp on the green and gray, and Camp Buckner gets its step-off.

West Point training operates on the Army developmental model: Crawl, Walk, Run. (When it comes to character-building, the formula sprouts mystical wings: Be, Know, Do.) Every summer trains something new. Beast is the crawl phase, a six-week cram course in soldiering. By the time they reach Buckner — Cadet Field Training — cadets are walking, picking up advanced soldier skills. Cow and firstie summers spell the run phase. Cows stick around West Point to administer training at Beast and Buckner, firsties take their skills out on the road, testing them with real Army units.

At West Point, there are shadow versions of everything, and for the cadets each year has its particular crawl-walk-run flavor. Plebe year is enthusiasm; you're thrilled to be invited, you're hoping they'll let you stay. Yuk year is the bitterness year; nothing's changed — yearlings don't secure many additional privileges — except you've got another class on the bottom. (A typical yuk conversation starter: "Do I sound like just another bitter yuk to you?") Cow year is the crossroads: you're solidifying your cadet personality, choosing your cadet path, either huah or cynical. And firstie year is graduation: cadet time getting short, West Point sliding toward the rear-view mirror, you're hoping they'll let you leave.

Buckner is the first taste of bitterness. Its Old Corps nicknames have the Southeast Asia ring of debacle: Buck-nam, the 'Ner. Eight weeks of midnight patrols, 0500 wake-ups, dirt, heat and bugs. (Cadets swab their BDUs with DEET, an insecticide so powerful that one dependable Buckner pastime is watching bugs crawl up your sleeve and die.) Cadets bunk in long metal shacks — bays — that look like tin igloos. They train constantly — weapon systems, runs, riding a pulley one hundred feet in the air over Lake Popolopen on the Slide for Life. The official joke phrase for Buckner is "the best summer of our lives." You're in the brush, trying to get your damn rifle clean, some guy asks how it's going, you pop off, "Best summer of my life."

George Rash is now a yuk, spending the summer mastering camouflage, hand signals, the quiet arts. But there's no camouflaging George. His BDU proclaims his giveaway name, the word no one ever reads and thinks, "Boldness — recklessness — audacity." (George's younger brother had his name legally changed to his mother's maiden one, Salinger. Not because *Rash* brings to mind skin irritations. Because his parents, amazingly, gave him the full name Richard Rash. George can't understand the decision. "He just doesn't like *Rash*," George says, shaking his head, "despite the fact that it's an old name with a lot of *history*.") George has been dreading Buckner for months. It's a rematch with his two chief West Point opponents: foot march and the run. After a couple of foot-march miles, the terrain between his feet and his shins lights up like a fire zone, muscle cramps slugging it out with blisters, until finally George sits down. Next time out, cramps across the stomach, continents of sweat mapping his BDU, and George is a heat casualty. Other cadets sneer by, *Rash! Rash!* By July, George reaches the conclusion the post has been waiting for: these are not his skills, not his people. He puts in his request for the paperwork, makes the telephone call to his parents, tells them he's had enough; he's resigning from West Point.

But next morning, he's back in formation, ready for more, head tilted back, glasses catching the clouds. The rumor races around the fishbowl. Rash wanted to drop but his mom and dad told him, "Don't come home." The real story is more complex: two retired parents, fixed incomes, they told him there was nothing budgeted for a civilian college. George hung up and walked back to his company.

Buckner's traditional lore highlights primal fears and thrills. Colonel Adamczyk can talk about dark nights and rustic settings, upperclassmen dropping arty simulators (a flash and a boom to mimic the fall and commotion of artillery) outside the bays at three in the morning. Keirsey will recall the Recondo week survival training where you killed a rabbit or chicken and cooked it into a stew; cadets chattered all year about which cadet would get selected to bite off the chicken's head. (In 1980, some general's kid was offered the honor, and that more or less ended the survival element of the Recondo program.)

These days Buckner lore is hormone-driven. To a lot of cadets, Buckner is the promised land, a discreet territory where every nighttime tree or boulder provides shelter for the hobby that's prohibited in the barracks. (Cadets never give up finding ways around the rule, even during the academic year. "Cadet sex is like a gas," cadet Ryan Southerland explains. "And you know how gas will expand to fill any space? Well, any space that is possible, cadets will try and have sex in it.") There's an Academy all-Caucasian rap group — the scariest four words in music — called White Bread; they record an MP3 duet called "Buckner Love." The male cadet deploys his sweetest line — "Aw, come on, you know I respect you as a soldier" — the female lays down some Donna Summer groans. Another cadet makes a stew out of memories and hankerings, field-tests the results on some squad buddies, submits this contribution to *Penthouse Forum*. It runs under the title "Babe in the Woods" — and the West Point development experience makes its way into a million plain brown envelopes.

I am currently going through a second course of training at a military academy I will leave nameless. I was on a practice course for a land-navigation test, something that I am not very proficient in. I had become hopelessly lost when a member of my class came out of the woods. There aren't that many decent-looking females at my school, and it is very difficult for any of them to make fatigues look good, but she was hot as hell . . . She stripped off her uniform, and she was gorgeous, with an athletic build that had been well-hidden. Before I knew it, she had pushed me back on the dirt floor . . . We didn't have much time. The hour of our exercise was almost up. Once we didn't show up, the Humvee would come to look for us . . . As soon as we stepped outside the shack, we were greeted by cheers and applause. The rest of our navigation companions had been standing just outside all the time. They kept our secret — but never let us hear the end of it. — K. H., New York

(When the issue appears, higher mounts a brief, unsuccessful hunt for the letter's author, and K. H.'s father offers a recommendation. "Please don't do that again," he says. "That's not a real, uh, respectable periodical.")

Female Buckner lore mostly amounts to warnings: Buckner is sex education run on the immersion principle — a believe-it-or-not experience. Whatever sex distinctions have limped through plebe year get plowed under by Buckner. "Once you're there with them for seven weeks, guys no longer see you as a girl," explains cadet Christine Ray, a hardy, practical-minded Christian from Texas. "I don't think anybody's ever ready for it," says Christine's roommate, Erica Watson, a Chicago yuk who speaks with the confident clip of the serious student. "Before, you don't realize what guys are like for real. They go beyond treating you like a sister and you become like another guy in the squad. Men always put on — what's the word? — airs when they're interested in you dating-wise or they're around you as your friend. All those polite fronts go right out the window. They just get gross."

The field environment — life pressed down to the essentials, sun, dirt, rifle — gives some male cadets the vapors. All talk becomes sex talk. A girl pulls out a paperback, sits under a tree, the guys come bobbing over like bees, itching to dispute something literary: "Do the characters give blowjobs?" "Is that a romance novel, or are there guys getting off in it?" Male cadets can't wrap their minds around it: if women are as physically tough as we are, maybe they're just as sexually tough too. Late afternoon, girls racked out on bunks at the bays' female end. A male cadet strips down, drops his boxers, marches over to demonstrate his especially courageous and intimate piercing. "Everybody started screaming," Erica explains. "I wasn't going to look — I really didn't know the guy all that well. That actually didn't make me want to know him much better."

The summer climaxes with a transportation event: one thousand yuks complete the slow jog to West Point in formation. Chrissi is already slipping into the grouchy yuk persona. "I asked my dad, 'Am I ever gonna *like* to see West Point again?' 'Cause I loved it so much before I came — I didn't have the right to love it as much as I did. But I was excited to see the gates that time — no more Buckner, thank *God*." The yuks are now *team leaders;* each one receives the name of a plebe they're supposed to instruct. At West Point, everything is dual purpose, like equipment on the space shuttle. Yuks will get this appetizer-sized taste of leadership, plebes have a chance to download bottom-floor management skills while they're still fresh on the yuks' tongues. (For the rest of the semester, Chrissi is stuck with Buckner — because that's her plebe's name, Private Buckner. "Of all things," she sighs.)

The G-4 Fighting Guppies have acquired a new TAC, Captain John Vermeesch. In the last days of Jim DeMoss, TACing reached a kind of martial Zen: DeMoss wanted to see if you could live to standard on your own. Vermeesch runs things differently; he doesn't mind dirtying his hands up and *pushing* a little. The company braces itself. G-4 cadets receive copies of his Leadership Philosophy in their e-mail, "the things that make Captain Vermeesch tick." They read like Successories on steroids: "You're here to make mistakes. Long as you make them at a hundred miles an hour, go as hard as you can and don't make them twice, you're good to go." "My basic philosophy is that development occurs around a crisis." The new TAC's most mistake-making, crisis-prone cadets are probably going to be Kevin Hadley's two old roommates: George Rash and the one cadet with an even more unlikely name, Huck Finn.

Best Summer of Their Lives II

Because the Goodfellas aren't going to be together anymore — they're lighting out for different posts, Suppy and Whitey to study flight in Alabama, John Mini to master tanks at Knox,

Iggy to face the Infantry music at Fort Benning — they book a ten-day West Coast farewell tour. They open with a couple of dates at the Ignacios'. It's no secret that Iggy's family isn't rolling in money: their house is the squat, fortified type you see in South Central message movies: bars across the windows, grate for a screen door. (Their back yard stops at the retaining wall of the San Diego Freeway; sleeping on couches, the Goodfellas can pinpoint the exact start of rush hour by the moment when every glass object in the place begins to tinkle.) But it's a sweet, relaxing time. Mr. Ignacio shows off the trophy shelf built right above his bed. "I call this my family's *wealth*," Mr. Ignacio says; plaques commemorating his sons' achievements, tiny buffed-up angels hoisting baseball bats and rifles. Mrs. Ignacio serves Filipino rations, sticky and delicious — candied pork, vinegar chicken, bananas in rice. Then the Goodfellas play some San Diego appearances at the Supko household. Leave gives them the bracing sensation of flying under radar. Dining at some harborfront eatery amid seagulls and yachts, they smile from the undercover kick: the civilians could never guess they're watching four young butter bars at the starting gate of their Army careers.

The military operates a sideline: it's also the nation's best underground economy. Once you're in, you can shop at private stores (PXs with unbeatable discounts), visit special hospitals, and, if you're willing to hang around the airfield, fly a private airline, in the passenger cabin of a C-141. The Goodfellas hop a flight to Hawaii. It's only when they're over water, when they finally leave the lower 48, that Whitey feels the cords snap and shakes the stomach-clenching idea that he's missing formation at West Point.

Graduation wouldn't be graduation without a flameout story. This year, Chad Jones, president of the class of '99, a spotlight cadet, took the hit. Cadets have a special separation etiquette. You only say two things — the way vets mention a dead GI and his last battle — the cadet's name plus the infraction that nailed him. "She got into some trouble" means alcohol and a car, a packed night. "Bad trouble" indicates drugs. "Well, he did a stupid thing" spells sex or honor. Chad Jones did a stupid thing. In April, grading his term paper, one of Jones's professors spotted some hand-me-down footnotes. The honor process went up and running fast. It was the last weeks of school, and nobody believed they'd kick out the class president.

Floating in the Pacific (salt on their lips, clouds driving overhead), the Goodfellas look for the moral — their *class president,* separated on honor — but maybe there isn't one. Nobody is sure how West Point values will handle on real-world roads — how do you remember the honor code when there's no Adamczyk around and you're trying to make rent? — and here's an example of a breakdown at the Academy gates. In the airport, the Goodfellas face another uncertainty, one that's dogged them since June. How do men say goodbye to each other? They shift grips on their bags uncomfortably, thinking it over. Finally, they go with the hardy standard. Right hands meet for the shake, left hands tighten into a sideways fist, to thump the other guy on the back. Affectionate but tough, love plus a little backbone of expectations. Iggy's voice, husky in Whitey's ear: "You know, brother — I'll see you when I see you."

Back in Buffalo, love clotheslines Whitey. He's held back with girls for four years, now he wants to share everything he's got and everything he's going to have, what other word is there for that than love? He finds he's got no use for the old cadet relationship deferment — "'I agree, it would be outstanding to fall in love, but unfortunately I have to report for taps.' Not anymore. Just being with Loryn is such a wonderful feeling — I mean, the minute I'm away from her, my next thought is when I'll see her again."

Loryn did some New York runway work for Calvin Klein, and it amazes Whitey to see a girl this professionally attractive imitate voices from after-school cartoons. She calls him Donald, formal and elegant, as if, being a grad, he now outranks having a *y* at the end of his name (unlike Whitey, Iggy, Suppy, or even John Mini). They chart their similarities: music, former relationships, how their parents even divorced when they were nearly the same age. He takes her to every restaurant he can think of, his favorites, anybody's. His West Point stories impress her, and his family connections pay off. They can saw through steaks, kill two salads, split dessert and a bottle of wine, pay a fifteen-dollar check, because the owners know Donald's brother-in-law is hockey star Mike Peca.

Marriage ideas bubble above Donald's head like thoughts in a comic strip. He's on one of those good-luck streaks where everything seems to brighten together: he's an Academy grad, he's in love, and now the Buffalo Sabres are even in the Stanley Cup playoffs. He takes Loryn to

HSBC Arena instead of his buddy Mark. "That was wrong." Donald grins. "I fucked up. I almost don't feel bad because I was fuckin' in love and that blinds you. I'm convinced I'll be able to look at Mark when I marry her and say, 'See, it was OK I took her.' I mean, Mark Matty is one of the greatest Buffalo Sabres fans I've ever known." Three weeks before flight school, he can't hold back anymore; over menus at Applebee's, he tells Loryn how in love he is. Loryn closes her menu and says if he weren't headed for Alabama, she wouldn't have a doubt in her mind. And a thought ghosts through Whitey's mind, the kind you stamp out like a fire: here's a woman who would be worth getting out of the Army for.

Seeing the Elephant

DMI, the Department of Military Instruction, offers courses in public speaking, but to cadets the best training is watching Keirsey. The summer is over, everyone's back on post — Buckner stories, plebe stories and leave stories ping-pong over the mess hall tables — and Keirsey returns to his job of firing up the corps. Everything about him is soldierly — arms, legs, shoulders, eyes, even his atoms seem more tightly packed than the civilian kind. When he speaks, cadets hear yelps and gunfire, drum music quickening, he's a man who carries his own soundtrack.

Infantry's insignia is two crossed rifles. Since everybody knows how risky the duty is, the cadet nickname is "idiot sticks." Keirsey has passed his whole life under the sticks. He was raised at the Infantry's home, Fort Benning. In the 1860s, his great-grandfather migrated to the Indian territories, married a half-Chickasaw woman named Mattie Collins, settled down to a small spread along the Texas border. Because the trains paused at his ranch to collect water and postal bags, the town entered maps as Keirsey, Oklahoma. His grandfather ranched and worked law enforcement. In Keirsey's office, there's a picture of Jim Dan Keirsey on horseback, wearing his sheriff's star, squinting down a dusty main street. In 1929 he trailed a bank robber into a house; there was a quick exchange of shots, and deputies rushed in to find both men dead.

Six years later, Keirsey's father turned sixteen, packed his bags, misled a recruiter about his age and enlisted with the Thunderbirds, the Oklahoma Forty-fifth Infantry. In the run-up to World War II, Jim Dan Keirsey got promoted to lieutenant. He led landings at Sicily and Salerno; mini-Normandys — overcast skies, GIs shouting in the water, Italians sniping down from cliffs. By the time his battalion splashed across the Rhine, Jim had risen to second-in-command. He was acting battalion commander while his men cleared out Nuremberg Stadium, where Hitler had staged his largest, most ornate rallies, as if the whole world could be conquered though sheer force of choreography. Stepping outside, removing his helmet in the dusty German air, he must have felt as if he'd chased the worst criminal in history back into his house, and now he was walking out alive. He taught Infantry tactics at Benning during Korea; in the sixties he shipped for Vietnam. He received three Silver Stars for valor, and told his son, "They were handing them out with the rations."

So in the way other families stick with plumbing or police work, Hank Keirsey followed his dad into the family business. From his father he learned the essentials of command, a list of never and always. Never lead from the rear. Always be bold. A leader is responsible for everything his subordinate does and does not do. Hank applied to West Point because it seemed the surest path to a life like Jim Dan's in the military. The last *silenced* cadet was a member of Hank's plebe company. In the Old Corps, there was no honor code wiggle room; get found, you left. Occasionally, a cadet discovered some loophole to curl up in and stayed on anyway. That's where silencing came in. Standing at his first formation, Keirsey understood just how rocky West Point could get, the firsties pointing out a glum, thin-necked kid who had cheated on an exam: "Plebes, we've got Pelogi here. Don't distribute his mail, never deliver his laundry. Don't sit next to him or talk to him, don't even *look* at him. Pretend as if he doesn't exist. He is an asshole, he is a *lyin'* sumbitch, he is a *scumbag*." During firstie year, Hank made the sixteen-hour car trip from Georgia to Highland Falls with his blond girlfriend, Kathy Hanson, whose own dad had retired a colonel after Vietnam. Hank branched Infantry and headed back to Benning for Ranger school. He trained and patrolled to exhaustion and right on past it, until he couldn't tell whether he was marching or dreaming, past the big sweeping pines that rose like skyscrapers from a city where people were allowed to sleep. He married Kathy at his first post, Fort

Bragg. Bragg is home to the Eighty-second Airborne, the one Army division so huah it gets mental capital letters: The Division.

Then the routine of Army life, climbing the ranks, waiting to deploy — that double sensation you have on an airport people mover, rolling along without getting anywhere. The Keirseys had two boys, J.D. — another Jim Dan — and Kent. In 1989, Hank's unit rehearsed the parachute drop into Panama; then, at the last minute, there was a duty changeover. "That was a heartbreak to me," Keirsey says, gruffly laughing. "Somebody else jumped in on my mission." When Civil War soldiers finished their first action, they wrote letters home about "seeing the elephant." The elephant was the big smashing animal you never got a look at in town. In 1990, Keirsey got his look at the elephant. His unit — 325th Infantry, Fort Bragg — deployed to Desert Shield, for the war people in the Army call "Saudi."

You always imagine deserts in terms of heat. But it was February; temperatures slipped into the forties by moonrise. The *shamal* blew constantly — a fine wind that whipped the tops off dunes, sticking them to everything else. You'd run a finger inside your ear and come out with a grainy hunk of Saudi. Keirsey felt the dazzle in the stomach of setting foot on ground where no one he knew had ever stood. Because Saudi was the first conflict after most of the world started shopping at the same stores, there were surreal touches of home. "What was the Iraqi assault vehicle of choice?" Keirsey asks cadets. "Chevy Suburban." When the trucks pulled in, you had to squelch the thought that you were being attacked by an after-school soccer team. Or you'd get assigned to guard some gleaming new Saudi air defense base, and drop your bedroll beside the summer-vacation smell of an Olympic-sized pool. Or you'd clear a deserted Iraqi bunker: no enemy, only rows of beautiful consumer goods — TVs, a motorcycle — it was like visiting the prize warehouse of a game show. Then you'd hear a whine, draw your pistol, and two healthy Labrador puppies would tumble from behind a curtain. At West Point, Keirsey would stress these details — Chevrolet, dogs, Harley, pool — to reassure cadets that the elephant was not so different from town as they thought, the elephant looked like home.

A moment comes when any hard job gives like a jammed door. It's that flash Keirsey likes to paint for cadets. His came on G-Day — Ground Day — eve, the night before the big Infantry assault. CNN was padding out the news cycle with horror stories about the Iraqi defense. Expert commentators pulled out maps, worked the pointers; the Iraqi plans, they said, were designed to chew up Infantry. First, coalition troops would encounter Iraqi trench lines, lightly defended, with built-in valves carrying gasoline. Step inside, Iraqis would flood the trench, set the petrol on fire. Survive that, you'd have to cross two hundred yards of densely seeded minefield. Whoever was left would face Iraqis firing from triangular forts, under constant artillery bombardment, maybe or maybe not employing a nerve agent.

Keirsey had his men prep what they could. They porcupined their trucks: tearing out seats, ripping off canvas, piling sandbags two layers deep on the floor to absorb shrapnel from the mines. ("That would muffle the blast a bit," Keirsey explains, "so the shrapnel runs a little slower through your leg.") Then the soldiers would aim their rifles over the truck slats in every direction, like spines on a porcupine. Keirsey's regiment got attached to a French armored division, which was good news — the tanks would divert some of the heat from his troops. Keirsey marched up Dead Camel Road (two roads led in and out of camp, both with circumstantial nicknames, and a dead camel had been decomposing on this one for a while; the other route, named for a barking dog, was called Barking Dog Lane) to coordinate with the French. The French colonel outlined his battle plan. The American troops would race across the desert for forty-five kilometers behind the French. "Then," the French colonel explained, "we will encounter the Iraqi resistance. When we find them, we will back our tanks up and move *around* them. And you will go into trenches and root out the Iraqis." Hank wasn't sure he'd understood properly. "Well," he said slowly, "you guys have the tanks. Don't you think you ought to stick around, maybe give us some fire support?" The colonel shook his head. "Oh, no *no*. They will shoot rockets at us. This could cause damage to our tanks. No, we will move away while you clear out the Iraqis."

Keirsey crossed the sand to a scene from World War One: his soldiers dug into foxholes, anxious faces squinting in the wind, ponchos shielding their automatic weapons. As Keirsey tells cadets this story, his voice drops, it gathers the weight of a conversion experience. Except it's what he's always believed — it was more like the revelation of a father's advice proved entirely true. "We're in just the shittiest of conditions," Keirsey says. "Everybody's got their goggles on, bandanas across the nose to keep out the sand. I walk back to where one of my sergeants is dug deep in the red moonscape. Smith, twenty-year-old kid — this is not a Rambo kid, this is your average thoughtful human. 'Hey, Sergeant Smith.' He takes the goggles off. In desperate situations, you want to see people eyeball to eyeball. You look at him and you say, 'Here's what we're gonna do when we wake up tomorrow. We're gonna pile in the truck. And the French tanks are going to take us to where the resistance is. And then, when they find it, they're gonna move away from it. And we're gonna move forward without any support and clear out every last Iraqi. That's our mission — how do you feel about it?'"

Keirsey pauses like a motorist, easing his foot off the gas, so cadets can feel all of it: sand, excitement, the sense of being on the verge of the assault. The cadets stare up. "This is the defining moment of officer-ship," he tells them. "It's what I love so much about the American soldier. Because you expect to hear, 'Bullshit, sir — this is all fouled up.' Smith looks at me. You can see the crust around his eyes where the goggles sat. He thinks it over. 'Huah, sir,' he says. 'I'm going to need to get some more grenades.'" The cadets applaud, roar *Hooop!*

"It's moments like that," Keirsey tells them, cadets straight in their seats, "that make the hair stand up on the back of your neck. What a thing that is, to go forward with that kind of loyalty and courage. Because if you make the call and say, 'I want you to get down in that trench, I want you to move out under that artillery fire,' Sergeant Smith is going to do it. Not only that: he'll bust down the back of the truck, and he'll be bringing more grenades. Makes you want to be worthy of him, because you don't ever want to spend that loyalty unwisely. That's what makes this profession noble, the look in the eyes of troops that'll do anything for you. This is what we do."

G-Day was all images, what Marines in Vietnam called the eye-fuck-ing of war. Keirsey crossed the desert in a Humvee at the head of what amounted to a technology parade; this is what Americans can do. Tanks and armored personnel carriers taking the dunes like boats rid-ing swells, howitzers letting loose, even the sky confettied with heli-copters. "You're finally out of the foxhole after thirty days," Keirsey says, "so it's exhilarating. As you're driving north, you're watching the MLRS battalions — multiple launch rocket systems, carting along six-packs of giant missiles, they're shooting all the time. You feel like singing." Down in their bunkers, the Iraqi defense plan turned out to be to surrender as soon as possible. Head down, arms in the air, Infantry called it the Iraqi salute. Hank spun around a dune and saw a sea of boots, backs, heads — Iraqis lying face-down in the sand. He had to thread the Humvee between them, shouting encouraging words out the door. "Looking *good!* Get some. Don't worry about it!" Hank's chemical officer belched, leaned out his own door and started throwing up, from tension and relief. "Good God, man," Hank said, "the first enemy we encounter and you're blowing your lunch around. How are we going to impress them?" The chemical officer wiped his lips, apologized and vomited again. American troops bumped by in their porcupined trucks, cheering.

All Roads Have Wires

Donald begins packing with one week left to go in Buffalo. He's become a good enough read of people at West Point to see that Loryn is sinking into emotional fatigue. "It was getting intense, scary," he says. "She was confused on the inside — she was hurtin'."

2330 used to mean taps; now it's the start of another workday, punching in for a long stretch of hours on the telephone. What worries Loryn is Donald not being around; Donald knows they can get past that, he explains how the Army schedule isn't as harsh as it appears — while, at the back of his mind, he's struggling to forget everything that lieutenant once told him at Ranger, about how he hardly even saw women anymore. He gives Loryn the soldier promises. "I was desperate by this point," Donald says. "I started telling her all the good stuff. 'Do you know how much time I get off, all the holidays, do you know how often I can come back to Buffalo? This is worth it to me.'" At another restaurant, they sit down in the waiting area, and never get off the bench. "Loryn," he says, "I know how you feel, I know I've got to go into the Army, but that doesn't have to be forever. How do you feel about it? There's no reason not to try this."

They spend the last night back at Checkers. Like a good officer, Donald has performed reconnaissance and prepped the area. There's a bouquet of roses waiting for Loryn, along with a letter explaining that he loves her and how much he wants to continue. If she doesn't feel the same things, OK, they can end as friends. "I said that's the whole point of life. There's one bottom line, either you're in something one hundred percent, or you're out." Loryn answers in the form of a kiss; she drinks, cries, tells him how he should become a writer but she's ready to date a soldier. Donald drives off to Alabama the next morning.

The plan is to link up with Suppy in Virginia and convoy from there. The landscape washes past him — smokestacks, forests, signs for drive-thru and towns — and it's all wallpaper, background for Loryn. Every so often he stops to wipe the bug apocalypse off his windshield. He knows he's crossed South when religious broadcasters crowd the sports talk off the radio. Donald can see this is going to be one of those relationships that eat into a military salary. First hotel he stops at, they're on the phone together — two beds strung by a wire — until four in the morning.

In Virginia, Suppy waves to Donald from a parking lot. They split a Ryder truck and set out on the last leg. They pass presidential birthplaces, old Indian trails, battlefields. Chickamauga in Tennessee, site of one of the last big Confederate victories in the war. In Alabama the gas pumps are the old slope-shouldered, nondigital type, and girls in flowered dresses sit on cement steps talking on the cell phone. Church signboards: *The Lord Gives Strength. One Man Practicing Sportsmanship Is Better Than 50 Men Preaching It.* Then they're past towns where men wear chunky belt buckles with open shirts, cars start looking new again, drivers wear aviator sunglasses and have high-and-tights, and they're back in the military world, another Army colony. Officers stride the sidewalks with the pilot's look of having a business relationship with gravity. In Enterprise, home of Fort Rucker, the houses have signs saying *Welcome West Point Class of '99.*

Right before flight school, there's the kind of military foul-up that spins Herzog's mind back into doubt. Donald had played too much music, sat too close to the amps at too many Allman Brothers concerts with Mark Matty. His hearing isn't strong enough to fly helicopters, where catching instructions or a rotor spinning funny can make a life-or-death difference. "I thought it was God's way of telling me I should have gone into the Infantry," Donald says. But a week later, Donald is cleared. He receives his first pilot instruction. Helicopters sometimes crack up on high-tension lines, blades tangled by the telephone wires that always follow a road. It becomes a flight school slogan, something for the West Point grads to tell each other in the hallway. "Remember — all roads have wires."

Loryn is supposed to make her first visit in the middle of September. A few days before, she tells Donald about a party at her beach house. The party was attended by her friend Rich. "I wasn't worried, because there wasn't anything in her voice to make me worry," Whitey says. Then she calls again. Rich just told Loryn he has plans, and they involve Loryn and the act of kicking it to the next level. "What'd you say?" Whitey asks, mouth going dry. "I don't want to be more than friends," Loryn replies. The edge Rich has over Whitey is one he can't compete with, the key civilian advantage of proximity. A day later, Loryn calls again. Rich just came by the house to say he's in love with her.

Beat Navy

During three seasons, nature stays in uniform at West Point. In winter, trees are white over gray, snow in the branches. Spring and summer, when cadets crowd the walkways in their own white-over-gray uniforms, trees move to green over gray. But fall is casual-dress Friday, no discipline, trees reporting in whatever colors they see fit. That's one sign that it's football season.

West Point plays the beefy Division I game. This means they don't waste time on four-eyed squads like Yale or Columbia. Since 1998 the Academy has been a member of Conference USA, which ensures that nearly every fall Saturday West Point gets clobbered by some big-thighed, ground-thumper team like Tulane or East Carolina. But it also guarantees TV exposure, which helps attract more sports-loving candidates. And none of these games, deep down, mean squat to anyone. What matters a little is beating Air Force. (Air Force, at nearly fifty years old, is the upstart new kid at the service academy table, on the lookout to spark rivalries.) And what matters the most, deep down, is beating Navy.

The two academies have mixed it up since 1890, an annual military super bowl. In their first meeting, Navy scored by faking a punt, which Army protested as being ungentlemanly. Emotions have remained high ever since. The two most common words around post are *Beat Navy*.

Bleachers and tunnels say it, milk cartons and candy bar wrappers say it; rooftops say it, for the benefit of cadets in the clouds. (In a zoologically perfect world, birds would call it from the trees.) Every December, right before they head out for the Navy game, the Black Knights — West Point's team — pad the Washington Hall steps, jittery as horses, and Keirsey delivers the big speech. He stands alone in the center of the stairs, asks four thousand cadets to picture fellow troops following the game at obscure postings around the world. For a finish, he leads the corps in a cheer adapted from the film *Conan*. "What is the good?" *To crush Navy!* they yell. "What else?" *To see them driven before you!* "And?" *To hear the lamentations of their small barnyard animals!*

Huck Finn, from G-4, is up there with his teammates, yelling himself hoarse. First thing Huck or anybody else will tell you: he's a redneck. (His real name, Reid, didn't last long, once everybody heard the accent and that he was from Baton Rouge, Louisiana.) Second thing he'll tell you: he came to West Point to play football — *fuhball* is how he pronounces it. Third thing he'll tell you: that's the wrong damn reason to come to West Point, and he plans to rectify his mistake. Huck has made a deal with himself: he only needs to stay until Cow Commitment. Then, if he's still hating it, he'll pull up stakes. "No matter how much I hate it, I'll consider it quitting if I leave before that," he says. Too many rules, he's in full-time trouble — for sleeping through class, not shaving, poor attitude — "they throw the book at me."

Here's another thing he wants you to know: his West Point problems are not his parents' fault. "My daddy taught me right from wrong." Then he thinks it over. "My mom contributed a lot to that shit too." Huck's father is a salesman with John Deere, in the casual southern style. He'll clap you on the back, start asking where you're from, how the fishing is thereabouts, the contours of the land, what kind of equipment you use on your spread, suddenly he's driving away and you've bought a new John Deere backhoe. Huck shares some of his dad's salesman charisma. Plus, he has a big man's natural authority, which in the physical landscape of the Academy counts as a Harvard diploma. His presence works on fellow cadets like an umbrella in the rain — when he enters the room, they edge a little closer.

Team spirit brought Huck to West Point. Through the end of his sophomore high school year, he played baseball and basketball; then he quit to concentrate on football and the weight room. (The call goes out early to cadets: Lift!) He was a starting defensive end and tackle, on the sort of no-nonsense team that appears in the *USA Today* top ten. "And the dream I always had," he says, "was to get a scholarship to play big-time college fuhball." But although Finn is a smart kid, it's not the type of smart that surfaces on an SAT. Colleges pulled out one by one. Senior year, just before Christmas, he got the bad news from Rice University, and Huck faced a future without fuhball. Twenty minutes later, West Point's coach was on the phone. "And he even didn't bullshit around," Huck says. "He just flat-out said, 'We want you to play here.'" Three weeks later, the coach walked up his lawn to close the sale in person. Huck didn't know much about the Academy. "All I knew, my life was gonna change drastically," he says, "and that it was gonna suck." One guy in his school — a kid he didn't like, Bryan Hart — had been living for West Point, and Huck talked it over with him. "You wear a uniform all the time," Hart said, "and after you graduate there's a five-year commitment" — which didn't lay any of Huck's fears to rest. What clinched it was National Signing Day, the February afternoon when all recruited athletes sign official NCAA letters of intent. Huck couldn't bear to stand by and watch while his teammates went with Clemson and LSU. He showed up at Beast, long-haired and rowdy, lobbing around all the wrong questions. "Yo — what's that little rank thing mean, where they wear the diamond thingie?" Mark Thompson was his Beast roommate. "It means you will address him as 'First Sergeant,'" Mark said.

Huck's best friend at the Academy is Josh Rizzo, an Irish-Italian party legend from Brooklyn, who treats West Point with the casualness of a man who knows he's only a few subway stops from home. Rizzo came up in Flatbush, Police and Fire Department country, where kids dawdle all day long in front of the station house dreaming about the uniform. (Rizzo sees the world through the hard algebra of the squad-car window. People divide into GFDs — good fucking dudes — and dirtbags.) They've done the cross-cultural experience swap. Riz led Huck on midnight Brooklyn party crawls; subway, club, forty-ounce, girls mooning over Huck's accent. Huck invited Rizzo down for a Baton Rouge Christmas, where Rizzo saw his first cows. ("Holy shit, Huck, what the hell is *that,* is that a *bison* or something?") Huck's friends, family, neighbors — they heard Rizzo's strange accent and they rednecked it up. They fixed a pot of squirrel stew. "This is real nice eating," Rizzo said, spitting black kernels into his napkin, "except for all these little squirrel elbows and kneecaps." "Shotgun pellets!" Huck laughed. "Don't you know folks hunt 'em?" They had the same West Point attitude. "I was definitely what would be labeled a fall-out plebe," Huck says. "Someone who doesn't walk down the hall all scared-looking. I wanted everyone to know I didn't give a shit."

Cadets worry that George Rash is somehow too small to ever fill out the uniform. The worry about Huck is that he's too large to squeeze in. Big jawbone, size-fifteen shoes, big meaty-palmed emotions. In class, when he's crouched over his notebook, he looks like an elephant writing with his trunk.

But he's just the right size for football. The Army-Navy game makes West Point worth it for Huck. Everything he's supposed to feel during the rest of the year — heritage, tradition — he gets as one condensed forty-eight-hour surge. The game is staged in Philadelphia, neutral territory, halfway between the academies, in the big decaying home of the NFL Eagles. After the sendoff speech, team buses depart at half past seven. The bus VCR runs fighting-mad movies: *The Matrix, Saving Private Ryan.* In the afternoon, hotel check-in: players drop bags, grab helmets and head back to Veterans Stadium, to chuck the ball around. "You wanna get used to the grass and stuff," Huck explains. "Philadelphia is old school; fall on that, you start bleeding."

At their banquet all the Black Knights go quiet, watching an NFL film called *Field of Honor: 100 Years of Army Football* — antique leather helmets, Heisman trophies, players who passed through the end zone straight into politics. It sucks the breath out: what they do tomorrow could show up on history's reel. The menu isn't designed for elegance, it's just feed, carbo-loading, food to spell you through each quarter. Meat, oil-seared vegetables, pasta. Then the graduating firsties stand, to make what are called their last hurrahs; they want the team to know how much these four years have meant. Around the table there are tears and gulps; most firsties get at least a little humid. Much of what they say is platitudes — "Be sure you make the most of it," "Time flies" — but in the face of life's big events, what does anyone find in their pocket but clichés? The team keeps farmers' hours: the Knights are back in rooms at ten, lights out by eleven. But Huck stays up till two-thirty watching TV — miracle ads, bass-fishing shows — volume turned low. He insists he's not nervous: "Before the first game I was gonna play in, I almost shit on myself. But I don't even get butterflies now."

Five hours before the noon kickoff, the team eats a quiet, calibrated breakfast. Mac-and-cheese, eggs, no sausage or bacon, nothing greasy to turn you sluggish. The buses pull out for Veterans at ten behind a fifteen-car police escort. ("That's pretty cool," Huck says.) On the roadside, fans shake signs: *Go Army. Sink Navy. To Hell with Army, Go Navy.* Silence fills the bus, players tuned in to private soundtracks by headphone. In the locker room they admire the sweet NFL accommodations and suit up, helping each other tuck pads into jerseys. No joking, no talking, lips two tense lines across. A couple of hours before the game, bladders start distilling their natural response to tension, lines stacking up behind the urinals.

At eleven, the team glides on the field for an easy stretch. Huck takes in the ring of artificial light, the bowl-shaped sky, the low rumble of early birds finding seats. Sound cracks sharper, objects drop their shadows. "I love this stuff," Huck says. "I can't believe I'm down on the grass, the place is gonna be full, people paying good money to watch us play, the feeling is just awesome, a thousand times better than sex if you ask me." Navy takes its side of field too; but you don't look at them, because you don't want them staring at you. Huck does practice snaps. Huck is the Knights' long snapper, the special-team guy who shovels back the ball on kicks. Navy sends a coach over to track him with a stopwatch. "So they can see how good a chance they'll have to block the punt," Huck says. "Dudn't bother me at all. I look him in the eye. Bring it on, man: time me all day, because I got all the confidence in the world." Huck's standard snap takes .67 second; NFL centers do it just .02 second slower.

Back in the locker room, Coach breaks the silence. "Everybody take a knee." The chunky noise of joints, cleats, pads pressing the carpet. Football players aren't engineered for bending. Coach quotes stacks of e-mails, from grads and officers: "You never forget Army-Navy." "I can still relive every play from fifty years ago." "Don't lose this game." Most of the Knights have slung so deep into the pregame burrow they couldn't recount Coach's speech for money. "You keep thinking about what the hell you've got to do," Huck says. "You're about to go to war." Kneeling there, the team knows every other quarter has just been warm-up, the overture, West Point football is a one-game season.

The Knights snap to their feet, buckle on helmets, crowd into the tunnel. They breathe in the dusty, cinderblock smell, the scratch of cleats on floor, the tiny extra-lush square of field. The corps of cadets is lining the end of the tunnel. Roommates, squadmates, classmates, all these people dying for you to crush Navy. The guys ahead of you begin trotting through, hands flash out to thump helmets, voices roar. "Adrenaline starts flowing more," Huck says. "Heart starts beating faster. You're waiting, thinking, 'Almost here, almost here.' You can hear everything super-loud, it echoes in the helmet. Then Coach says 'Go!' and it's like *Fuck yeah*. You start running towards that cordon of cadets and it's the best feeling, just *extreme joy*. You haven't felt anything like it since last year at Navy, you only get to feel it four times in your life. When you run through that cordon — they slap your ass to death — and see the field, you feel like you could jump all the way over the stadium."

Once Huck makes it through the cordon, he walks to the punter on the sidelines. "I never felt that good," he says, "in my entire life." The coin is tossed, the game begins. Army loses, 19 to 9.

The Knights stand at attention for alma mater. Huck feels wet in his eyes — for West Point — and lets it fly, cameras darting in for the close-up. The clip gets recycled on ESPN, his pals from Louisiana calling and giving him shit. "Sure, you made fuckin' *SportsCenter*," they say. "You were crying like a wuss, though." Huck shakes his head. "They don't understand about Army-Navy," he says. "This ain't a fuhball game."

The Theory and Practice of Professionalism

Back at G-4, Captain Vermeesch has a warning for Huck. If he can't shape up — stop missing class, start shaving and correct the attitude — he'll lose the privilege of playing Army football. At the new West Point, Huck's troubles now fall under the category of unprofessional behavior.

In peacetime, fads sweep West Point higher — field explorations of the culture gap, authors mapping out paths back to the rest of the country. For a while, a 1997 study of Marine basic training called *Mak-*

ing the Corps offered trustworthy blueprints. Elitism was the culprit. New recruits developed values, which was good, except they ended up convinced that values outside the military were bad, which was itself bad.

Then higher started buying up *Who Moved My Cheese?*, a business bestseller in which readers improve their flexibility through the metaphor of unfamiliar dairy products. "The quicker you let go of old cheese," the book argues, "the sooner you find new cheese." The Army chief of staff, General Erik Shinseki, saw a valuable lesson (the Army had entered a period of cheese diminishment — smaller budgets, fewer recruits, less support); he purchased copies in bulk and organized conferences, where generals were instructed to catch out several varieties of old Army cheese.

But since the late nineties, the most popular culture gap solution has derived from a 1957 study called *The Soldier and the State*. (It still polls number two on Amazon's West Point bestseller list, one slot shy of *The Green Letters* — a collection of Christian meditations — but wiping the floor with *Gates of Fire, Platoon Leader,* and *Tender Warrior: God's Intention for a Man.*) Samuel Huntington, a Harvard sociologist, did what great engineers do: he turned the structural problem on its head. The important thing was not getting civilians to understand the officers' job — that was gravy — it was making sure civilians respected them. His design for the bridge across the culture gap was one efficient word: *professionalism.* You could string the thing up and start moving traffic across it with a single conversation.

Officers in West Point's Office of Policy, Planning and Analysis (OPA) — the developers behind the Cadet Leader Development System — were tracking a problem. Grads were five-and-flying, leaving the Army behind to follow other careers; civilians were talking perks and salaries, parents wanted to see their kids situated in professions, with the kind of degree that's a rain hat in a storm, a résumé in one word and a portable business address. (You'd find the same thing on TV; some nights, the networks seemed to be staging doctors' and lawyers' conventions with romantic subplots.) Huntington solved the problem in his first sentence. "The modern military officer is a professional man," he wrote. "This is perhaps the most fundamental thesis of this book." He attacked the status issue head-on, by assuming its prerogatives. "In our society, the businessman may command more income, the politician may command more power, but the professional man commands more respect. Yet the public certainly does not accord [to] officers the same deference it gives to civilian professionals . . . Professionalism, however, is characteristic of the modern officer in the same way in which it is characteristic of the physician or lawyer."

It was the answer West Point higher needed. Colonel Scott Snook, a Harvard-trained MBA with the broad-shouldered accent of eastern cities, is the author of the latest version of CLDS. "We refocused around professionalism," he explains. "It was a whole different way of thinking."

The word passed hand to hand around West Point like a new high-caliber weapon. For cadets, tidying your room for inspection didn't just save your ass from getting chewed by the TAC; it was *professional*. Cursing not only made you sound like a Martin Scorsese character; it was *unprofessional*. The all-volunteer Army became the professional Army; in 1999, when West Point launched a new department for boosting honor and values, its name was the Center for the Professional Military Ethic; Academy officers pulled all-nighters, wrote papers on The Future of Army Professionalism. (Cadets both caught on and didn't. "God, all day long," Huck Finn sighs, "West Point fuckin' preaches professionalism, professionalism, professionalism.")

Professionalism met the efficiency test. Civilians — parents, boyfriends, girlfriends — got a glossy new way to think about military service ("It's the same as being a doctor or a lawyer"). Cadets had their five-and-fly questions answered with a question: "Why leave the Army to join a profession when it turns out you already belong to one?" (In OPA circles, this is referred to as *professional self-concept*; once you get cadets thinking of themselves as professionals, they're less likely to leave; doctors and lawyers, for example, never stop being doctors and lawyers.) It became the go-to concept in speeches, a kind of vitamin that energized a sentence and nourished cadets' self-esteem. Colonel Adamczyk was praised as "the model of professionalism"; "Duty, Honor, Country" — West Point's motto — became "the professional values of 'Duty, Honor, Country.'" When the Academy celebrated a birthday, the Air Force supe offered these congratulations: "West Point has become synonymous with professionalism." If you sat down to a briefing, professionalism and Huntington were waiting. "I'd like to talk about this notion of 'officership,'" Colonel Pierce would say, fiddling with his Academy ring. "Because it's something that might not be understood by a lot of Americans. It's a profession. There's a guy named Samuel Huntington — works at Harvard, very famous — he wrote the definitive book. He says the military fits the bill."

But professionalism isn't what draws cadets like Rob Shaw or Iggy Ignacio to the Academy. For them, *huah* means loving your work so much you'll do anything for it; *professionalism* means loving your career so much you won't do anything to jeopardize it. If you looked at it under a cool, professional light, why would anybody join the Army? Low pay, relocations every three years, and the chance to risk your life for your country? (Over at DMI, Keirsey puts the question more gruffly: "Why the hell would you want to see yourself the same as a doctor or a lawyer?" He clears his throat. "These kids are special, steely-eyed — it requires more than the nine-to-five dedication.")

In the best cases, cadets choose West Point because of hopes and dreams, the chance to feel strung to something larger than themselves — their shot at a range of emotions beyond personal consideration. The moments cadets treasure in Army movies are the *un*professional ones. The platoon sticking around the smashed French town in *Saving Private Ryan* and dying for a guy they've just met. The two stony-faced Delta Force sergeants (at West Point they're known as D-boys) jumping out of the helicopter in *Black Hawk Down,* knowing they are headed to death. People will risk their lives, or stake careers, for many values, but professionalism is a hard concept to sacrifice for. Many cadets are confused by it. "This whole professionalism thing," frowns Ryan Southerland, a yearling from Oklahoma. "Higher is so scared of being unprofessional, they won't do anything positive, anything to light fires in you. It's just this ideal of professionalism that nobody can really define, it ends up as a crutch for being politically correct." TACs brood over the concept in the same workday hours that they model it for cadets. "I never thought they should call it a profession," one departing TAC explains to me, looking out at the Academy's green fields. "It's more of . . . a calling."

A Number of Adopted Sons

For the first time in four years, Hank Keirsey doesn't give his speech before Army-Navy. He's not in the Washington Hall crowd either, and when cadets glance around Veterans Stadium — checking for the big stride in any cluster of officers — there's no sign of Keirsey there. They don't understand it; the game is chockfull of the stuff — courage, endeavor, uniforms — they know the lieutenant colonel lives for. They wonder if he's turned his back on the corps.

No officer is ever entirely safe; his last tour before West Point, Keirsey bit the bullet and brought his family to Camp Swampy, Camp Armpit — Fort Polk, Louisiana. He helped put together a new school there called the Leader Training Program: exercises for commanders, a course in leading large-scale operations like Saudi. Keirsey wanted the colonels and their staffs to develop the same sure touch for reading a battlefield that surfers use to predict waves. (Officers who visited Fort Polk in the 1990s can still remember his briefings: "It was last hour of a twenty-one-day rotation," a major tells me, "when everyone is usually too tired or burned out to listen, when I first met Keirsey. I never saw such a performance. He taught us more in one hour — and motivated us to train until we got the lessons right — than we learned through our entire rotation." Then the major lists the long-night Army skills. "He is simply a master of team-building and motivation. I've worked with very few leaders who even come close.") When his three years were up, Keirsey asked to go back to West Point.

He was surprised by The Changes. People even *spoke* differently — whole dictionary pages had been silenced. "They'd toned down most of the tough language," Keirsey remembers. "Made it completely acceptable to everybody, so in the end it didn't appeal to anyone, it didn't *inspire*." And there was a new Bedrock Value around. Through most of its history, West Point has had what it calls one Bedrock Value, Honor. (Drop into a slippery situation, where conditions are unclear and you can't find any footing, honorable behavior would always give your boots solid ground.) In 1995, the Academy made space, and the two Bedrock Values became Honor and Consideration of Others. Cadets were supplied an official definition, which sounded like talk-show boilerplate set to cadence: "Actions that indicate a sensitivity to and regard for the feelings and needs of others [*Sir!*] and an awareness of the impact of one's own behavior on them [*Ma'am!*]." The program's founder used the example of posthumous Medal of Honor recipients to illustrate the concept: by jumping on grenades, and thereby saving squad members' lives, these fallen soldiers had demonstrated "an extreme instance of Consideration of Others." (In 1998, the value was streamlined into one high-and-tight word, Respect.)

With the Soviets throwing in the towel, and Desert Storm five years past, the perception was that American power had run its enemies even out of the future. Keirsey had enough sheriff in his heritage to know that when a town is sleeping soundest, rustlers are probably making shadows around campfires, plotting to steal horses and raise hell. He watched cadets in the field. What struck him was that Maneuver Light — the baseline soldier actions of defense and attack — was weak, sloppy, the training uninspired and unrealistic. Instructors would say, "Move ahead two hundred meters, you will encounter snipers, the snipers will engage you" — which didn't train a cadet for anything, since snipers weren't likely to be as red-carpet polite or predictable in combat.

He beefed up Beast combat exercises and added a Polk-style simulation to Buckner. (Keirsey instructed the opposing force to scatter clues. Matches, cigarette butts, bootprints — if cadets hung around that spot, they'd found a good place for an ambush.) He staged terrain drills designed to leave cadets scratching their heads. That way, at the clubs, instead of beer talk, they'd pull out pencils and a napkin and sketch the landscape: How could we have hit the objective better? He commandeered props from the weapons curator and brought them to class for show-and-tell. This is the submachine gun carried by So-and-So on Okinawa. Here, hand it around. There's a helmet worn in Stalingrad; put that on.

The West Point day can pound it out of you. In the squinty afternoons of Gloom Period — when daylight feels demoted — you can forget why you ever joined. That's when Keirsey did his walkabouts. He looked for an internal light switch, the phrase that would fire up a cadet; when he could, he pinned it on an impressive feature. "Look at the arms on you, man," he'd say. "They're *huge* — what've you been doing?" Sometimes, all he'd get to work with was how the cadet met his gaze. Then Keirsey would rumble over. "That's a good-looking *stare*. Looks like you could take out a bunker." He became a subject line on e-mail.

I would like to remain anonymous, because I am not looking for recognition from LTC Keirsey, only that he understand the impact he has had on myself and nearly all the cadets. LTC Keirsey is by far the finest officer that I have ever seen, heard or worked with. He is more respected and more loved by us than any other officer on campus. He seems to be the only officer remaining on this post that realizes that this is a military academy. The reason I am writing is that I realize that not all echelons of the military academy agree. I know some find him a bit too Huah. I would like him to know that if I become half the officer . . .

Then speaking invitations came from cadets. A crowded schedule; the lieutenant colonel delivered what he called his Keirsey bullshit to honor classes, Sandhurst rallies, bashes, tours, Dining-ins, sendoffs. He had just enough too-much, just enough is-he-serious? When he talked about Korea, a notorious hardship posting, he called it "the frontier of freedom," and suddenly it wasn't some bum border check, it was the reason you had decided on the Army.

Cadets would take seats for a company's military development lecture. There'd be Keirsey, talking about entrances and exits, the two sides of West Point, Academy gates and Academy cemetery. "You step inside here and take your shot," he'd say. "All the graduates of this institution are going to leave here as second lieutenants. So don't worry if you hear somebody say, 'Nobody's serving past five years.' What you owe this institution — and the legacy of two hundred years that people have moved out and served in America's conflicts — is complete commitment and intensity for whatever time you *do* serve. And if at the end of five years you decide to leave, you will march and you will hang up your uniform. And you'll walk by the tombstones that line the cemetery here. You'll be surprised by how many people you see from the class of 1966. Class of '66, died in 1967, in service of his country. You walk around in there, you start ruminating: there was not a whole lot of life these guys got to *live*.

"This institution was called on to send its graduates into a firefight, when everyone else is scared. The LT jumps up, and moves to the sound of the gunfire. Now, your goal is *not* to be in that cemetery. But we've got to honor those people, and that particular tendency to lead from the front. So if you feel weak one day, from the mind-numbing cycle of classes and homework, go back to the main mission. It's described on the MacArthur statue right outside this building. 'Your mission is to win our wars. All other public purposes will find others for their accomplishment. Yours is the profession of arms, the will to win, the sure knowledge that in war there is no substitute for victory, and the obsession of your public service must be duty, honor, country.' Any questions?"

In the spring of 1999, when Commandant John Abizaid left the Academy for Germany, to take command of the First Infantry Division, he had a parting gift for Keirsey. A warning: other officers were keeping book on him. "You know, you have people who watch you all the time. They're always circling, whenever you get up to talk. Keep driving on, but be careful."

Every fall, firsties make their selection from a sixteen-branch menu. Six are combat arms: Infantry, Armor, Aviation, two Artilleries — Field and Air Defense — and Engineers. The other branches are what's called Combat Service Support. (For example, Quartermaster: "Sustainer of the Army"; Transportation: "Nothing Happens until Something Moves"; Chemical: "Do You Smell Gas?" — actually, Chemical has no motto, though the insignia is two crossed beakers.) Through the early 1980s, all male cadets were required to branch combat arms — if the government was bankrolling the training, the idea was to maximize the country's investment.

In 1983 that changed, and combat arms has become a sore subject. Mention Infantry, it's considered unprofessional not to quickly add something supportive about Quartermaster. (By the mid-nineties, a West Point officer in a spotlight department like leadership could lose his job by talking too much about combat arms.) The irony is that when Samuel Huntington gave the Army the professional nod in *The Soldier and the State,* it was because of combat arms.

For Huntington, medicine and law can be called professions because of a combination of uniqueness and mission. They are composed of "experts with specialized knowledge and skills," he writes, "performing a service which is essential to the functioning of society."

Huntington asked the corresponding question: "What is the special-ized expertise [and] skill of the military officer? This central skill is per-haps best summed up in the phrase 'the management of violence.' The function of a military force is successful armed combat" — that is, combat arms. The word Huntington used for the noncombat branches is "auxiliary"; they were not members of the military "in its capacity as a professional body." The second irony is that if he were at West Point, Huntington himself would be criticized as unprofessional. The Acad-emy had plucked the word, and peeled away the definition.

Keirsey doesn't state matters that bluntly, but he takes a cadet's re-jection of combat arms as a defeat. "Because everything here, all the cultural icons around the reservation are stacked to get you motivated to go out on the line. Not that we don't need those other branches, we do. But picking it dead last out of sixteen branches always made me scratch my head. You've basically gone contrary to everything we tried to motivate to do. We've somehow" — he laughs — "failed." (Cadets put it more colorfully: "Four years here and you wanna go Finance? That's kind of like pissing in West Point's Cheerios.")

In October, after branch selection, one of Keirsey's subordinates, an Aviation captain named Dan Dent, cooks up a parody of the sort of PowerPoint slide you might use for a briefing. Dent found out which company had the lowest number of combat arms firsties, titled his slide, "Class of 2000 Homo Factor Report." He shows it around, officers chuckle. Keirsey takes a look, says, "Woo, Dan, that's a rough one, man. Make sure that dudn't get out." "It was kind of my humor," Keirsey says, "but twisted with a little extra added distaste. It was bizarre-o."

A couple weeks later, Keirsey gets a call from a frantic cadet. It's Jenny Hull, the deputy brigade commander — one cadet rank down from first captain. "Sir," she says, "there's a slide circulating off Captain Dent's computer. You need to make sure that computer gets shut off now. It's really bad." Dent had gone to deliver a branch briefing to cadets who had picked Aviation. To save time — to access his notes from the lecture hall — he had connected his own computer drive to the Academy computer system. The instant he did this, every one of his files became available to any inquisitive user in the Academy. One fish-bowl hobby is reconnaissance, checking the view from every section of the glass. A cadet wandered over DMI's site, skipped onto Dent's drive.

The cadet opened the slide — funny shit — e-mailed it to a few friends. They also had friends. By taps, the slide had arrived in every mailbox on campus. At next morning's formation, the TACs are walking extra-stiff; by lunch, orders come down from higher to delete the unauthorized e-mail; after dinner, rumors are flying about a court-martial. Dan Dent is in the chute.

At COB (close of business), Keirsey grabs a six-pack, pulls into Dent's driveway. The captain looks disheveled. "Usually," Keirsey recalls, "this was a rock-hard human. He was beside himself." Dent was pacing, mentally tallying what the slide would cost him. "He said, 'What am I gonna do? I've got a wife, I got another baby on the way, third baby. They're going to throw me out of the Army, aren't they?'"

Keirsey opens two beers and gives the captain reassurance. "Dan," he says, "we are going to come through this, one way or the other. Keep your cool, this is just a *shitty situation.*" And then he promises, "They're not gonna be able to kick you out of the Army."

But for higher there are clear stakes. Cadets must see that this is not the face of the new Army. After an official investigation, the recommendation comes down: a general letter of reprimand in Dan Dent's file — his military adventures are over. If this were the business world — or the realms of politics, medicine or law — you'd see arrival in reverse: boxes crowding a desktop, pictures coming off the walls, supervisors treating Dent like a biohazard. Keirsey ponders the Army lessons his dad taught him. Lead by example; an officer is responsible for everything a subordinate does and does not do. He reports to Colonel Smith's office (his boss, head of DMI), faces him across the desk and asks for the responsibility. "Sir," he says, "I am the one who deserves the letter of reprimand."

In early December, he writes to the commandant, "I feel strongly that Dan Dent is a gifted, superb and aggressive officer who needs to be able to go on and serve this Army. I strongly request that if one of our letters must be placed in the official file, that it be mine."

Keirsey doesn't base his decision solely on military ideals of selfless service. "I thought I'd survive the hit, and Dan couldn't." It's a generous gamble. "Even if I didn't, it's the right thing to do. Dent had all these kids, he's a great officer to have around soldiers. Obviously, there was no other choice but to take the blast. So you wanna talk about courage, that wudn't total courage. There was an awful good possibility I'd survive it. And if not — well, I've made my run."

Then Keirsey is in the chute, and the whole thick book is opened. Too much combat talk, too much fitness talk, too much too-much. Conducting an Army investigation is like compiling an anti-yearbook: all the stuff you've forgotten you ever did or said, your personality is committed to paper and pored over. Keirsey does the rushed self-promotion of crisis. He gets character letters from lieutenant colonels, majors, captains. ("LTC Keirsey is a uniquely gifted leader who can inspire men to act nobly merely with his presence and a simple word." "Believe me when I tell you, there are 4000 cadets who strive to grow up and be a warrior like LTC Keirsey" — under the circumstances, maybe not the most helpful accolade. "His is the face cadets associate with the great war heroes they learn about in class; he brings to life the great rhetoric written by Generals MacArthur, Patton and Eisenhower. The cadets *need* that image, and very few officers can fulfill it without appearing phony. This is what Keirsey does best.")

On direct orders, he sits out Army-Navy — "that broke my heart," Keirsey says. Instead, his sons are at the game. They're both cadets now, J.D. a cow, Kent a plebe. In the sheaf of documents that comprise his defense, Keirsey includes a photograph of one of Kent's high school buddies, Ben Smith. Smith was the kind of kid — cigarettes, shoulder-length hair, puka-shell necklace — no officer is ever pleased to discover eating potato chips in his living room. Hank enrolled Smith in the Keirsey PT program (weights, rope-climbing, run), did the military talk, got him to cut his hair. Now Ben Smith is at West Point too. Kathy Keirsey, Hank's wife, asks to speak with the commandant, and Hank brings her by his side. A colonel accuses Keirsey of hiding behind a woman's skirts. Keirsey replies simply, "My wife and I have been a team in the Army for twenty-two years. If she wanted to do it, I thought she deserved to see the people who are trying to terminate my service."

On December 23, Keirsey is relieved of command of Military Training — dismissed from the United States Army. The commandant writes, in his Order of Relief, "LTC Keirsey . . . has created and fostered an environment in Military Training that is antithetical to Army values, professional standards, and the development of cadets into officers of character." DMI's Colonel Smith completes the terminal Officer Evaluation Report. "LTC Keirsey is the most charismatic individual I have ever worked with. I have never met an officer who surpasses his level of technical skills and tactical knowledge." But when it's over, it's over. "Unfortunately, he failed to exhibit three of the Army Values, Honor, Respect, and Loyalty. He has no potential for promotion." Uniform, brass, rank, evaporated. Keirsey is converted to a mental glimmer, a memory at West Point. It's as if he's been separated on honor. Keirsey has met the kind of end that drives supporters under cover. Officers speak about him in hushed tones, on promises of anonymity. "I deeply regret that he's no longer among our ranks. It was a loss for West Point — but it was a much bigger loss for the Army. I would have gladly served under him in combat, and I know I am not alone."

For me, what Hank Keirsey did for Dan Dent is one of the clearest examples I have of West Point values. When I tell civilian friends Keirsey's story, I have to go over it twice, because they keep asking, "Wait, didn't the *other* guy make the slide?" A leader takes care of his soldiers. He puts their concerns ahead of his own. But the cadets never get to learn this lesson from Keirsey. All they see is Keirsey here one minute, gone the next. He considers fighting the decision; but both his children are at the Academy, the fall has been too ugly already, it was hard enough for Hank and Kathy to talk them out of resigning.

Keirsey sends the supe one last letter. There's no bitterness. "Sir," he writes, "I know once a decision is made a good soldier salutes, moves out and draws fire. I am ready to do this." But he includes a request, in the P.S. under his signature. "Kathy mentioned that she would very much like to get the original photograph of Ben Smith back from my appeal packet. It belongs on the refrigerator, with a number of adopted sons."

Half a year later, Dan Dent — now a captain at Fort Lewis, Washington — writes a letter to Keirsey's children.

Jim and Kent Keirsey
Quarters 17A
Wilson Road
West Point, NY 10996

Men,

Nearly 6 months have passed since dark Monday. The pain that I carry from my actions still lies very heavy in my chest. In fact, I can no longer hold in the truth about the measures taken against me and against your father. Herein are the deepest, most honest, most undaunted words I can muster.

No single mortal man has shaped my life as a leader more than your father. From the first time I met him on a rugged steep trail, he instilled in me the traits of courage, toughness, and selflessness that are my touchstones today. My service to your father not only made me a better officer in the United States Army, it has made me a better father. He is simply the hardest, strongest, most unwavering officer I have ever met.

You have probably heard many rumors about what happened within the Department of Military Instruction after I failed to destroy a distasteful joke between buddies. Within 24 hours, I was told I could face courts martial. Some of my friends distanced themselves from the blast radius. However, your father, my boss, simply said from the very beginning, "Stand in the face of your enemies." At a time when any other leader would have devised some clever scheme to deflect blame, LTC Keirsey dug in next to his soldier and said "Don't mess with one of mine." "Steady, Dan," was how he greeted me every day.

The operation culminated one cold day in December, when I was prepared to receive a career-ending letter of reprimand. Just before the round fell on me, LTC Keirsey placed his chest in the cross-hairs. As a sacrifice for one of his men, he offered twenty years of performance, placed loyalty to his men before his own livelihood. Once again, he led by example, selfless service and moral courage. These are values other men only talk about.

The rest of my service to our great Army will stand in tribute to the pain I have caused your father. I have struggled for a long time over my duty to write this letter to you, but I am finally convinced that I am honor bound to tell you the story as it really occurred. Here is the truth.

Good luck and God bless in your future service to our nation. Keep up the fire.

Daniel H. Dent
Captain, United States Army

Black Holes and the Hover Button

On the phone from Buffalo, Loryn can't make up her mind about visiting Alabama. When the other guy says he loves her, Whitey even sends a card, the same thoughts and reassurances Iggy offered him a year ago when he was deciding about Infantry: "You know I love you. Whatever makes you happy, I'll support." Before she gets the card, Whitey picks up the phone and there's Loryn again. "I had a dream," she says. OK, what was in the dream?

"It was about Rich . . . Well, I love him."

Silence.

"You're fucking *kidding* me."

Silence.

"Please just give me a chance, please just let's talk about it in person when you come down here."

"I'm not coming down."

"I was in la-la land," Whitey explains. Counting off push-ups at 0500 PT, Whitey can't keep track of how many he's done — the numbers in his head are dates, visits, phone calls. In aero-med class (a kind of first-aid brief for the sky: cigarettes reduce night vision by four thousand feet, Visine turns to condensed jelly in the eyes at high altitudes, "and that will screw you"), he's thinking about what made the relationship crash. Loryn is his last thought before he goes to bed, his first thought in the morning; then she steps into the dreams in the middle, and Whitey can't even sleep. "I tried everything," he says. "I tried being nice to her. Then I said, 'I don't ever wanna talk to you again, Loryn.' And so she didn't call after that. Then, like an idiot, I dial her on the phone, I'm like, 'I can't believe you didn't even call me, Loryn,' and she goes, 'But you said . . .'" Some of it's the before and after of West Point. By the time you make it in, you've had four years of people saying you're the most exciting commodity in high school, the prime candidate for export. If you make it out, you've had four years of, essentially, officers blowing smoke up your butt, assuring you you're a prime hope for the nation. (Vermeesch circumspectly calls this "blowing smoke up the fourth point of contact.") But once Whitey is off in the Army, Loryn has selected the civilian — just what cadets learn to fear at West Point.

"It devastated me," Whitey says. "She had a choice, and she picked the other guy. Then I got evil." He laughs in apology. "I ripped her, hazed her like a fucking plebe. She was like, 'I'm sorry, so sorry.' I don't know if she knows it or believes it, but I loved her. I wanted to spend a life with her." He sighs. "It crushed me because I couldn't have her. I couldn't be the one to help her when things got bad. I couldn't be the one to make her smile."

Whitey, Supko and a third Pointer named Bart Wilkison — a Nebraskan who runs on the Academy mix: handsome, bright, buff — rent a place together. The housing dream of every firstie, life as a beer ad: sports banners on the walls, Coors in the fridge (right beside the Gatorade — Academy people drink it as though they have an endorsement deal), Nintendo on the TV, pool table in the living room, Smokey Joe grill right next to the swimming pool out back. They have cable installed, and there's a Rip Van Winkle effect; they can't believe there's a whole channel — the E! Channel — devoted to Hollywood, models, Howard Stern and women in bikinis. When Whitey can't sleep, he wanders down the hall, sits in Bart's room, in Suppy's room, and they slowly talk him around.

They're having girl problems of their own. Suppy has brought his square-jawed looks and team captain's confidence to flight school, where they do some damage. He dates a female lieutenant a few houses over, things take a turn, they break up and he dates another female butter bar, the first one gets mad, the second one gets anxious. Scenes at parties, on patios and balconies, the phone ringing constantly. "Don't even answer it," Bart sighs, and then they listen while a female voice on the answering machine attempts a delicate aerial maneuver, criticizing and complimenting Suppy at the same time.

Bart takes out some local women. Cute and funny, with that southern, white-gloved, learner's permit politeness. The relationship hitch couldn't be more surprising to Bart. He grew up in small-town Nebraska, farms and churches. Before he arrived at West Point, he'd never seen a black person except on television, and he got comfortable with the easy racial mix at the Academy. It's not the same outside the gates. A successful date with a sorority girl — nice movie, nice dinner — she folds her hands on the table and smiles. "Hey," she proposes, "do you want to head over to a great bar in niggertown?" So, of course, Bart's got to break it off. Another night, he's driving another nice woman home, he's run a diagnostic conversation over dinner, dropped names of black athletes, entertainers, spiritual leaders, politicians, it's all good. She nods, points through the window at some beater of a car. "Wow, just take a *look* at that old nigger-mobile." Bart finally lands a girl, Kelly, and every sign looks promising. She's attractive, well-spoken, an early-education major. They're together for three weeks, he doesn't even hear a whisper of it; they pass beat-up cars, great bars, she doesn't say a word. Bart relaxes. Kelly shares an apartment with her sister — cable TV, Monet prints, flowers on the mantel, everything neat and modern. Bart and Kelly wake up together, head into the kitchen for coffee, Kelly shakes the milk carton with a frown. "Look at this," she says, "my sister finished off the milk and left the empty container inside. How nigger is *that?*"

Whitey's personal mission is to flush Loryn out of his mind. He takes out some local women — he meets them while grazing at the supermarket, browsing the new-release shelf at Blockbuster — but they aren't college girls. They're adults, feeling their circumstances harden; they want a boyfriend, but they also want a romantic crowbar, something to get them out. Whitey makes an assessment: OK, move into a higher age bracket, early thirties, women who're already comfortable with the shape of their lives. It makes him miss cadet girls; it turns out he had more in common with them than he thought. There was a wider range of personalities and ideas. "The irony of it is, the common belief is that the opposite is true. How you relate to people, it's almost more evolved in the Army. The best thing to do is say what you think and feel, then accept the consequences. You meet these girls in Atlanta, they don't know how to act like themselves in front of you. Everybody's concerned with getting the same things right, they click into a format, and it's not even a fun format."

He ushers at a cousin's wedding up north, meets a smart, thirtyish career woman from Philadelphia — "that's an incredibly sexy age," he says — they head for the hotel bar, then a late-night bar. She keeps telling Whitey how much his officer's poise impresses her. He leans in for the kiss — everything goes well, nice lips, he sits back. Suddenly she gets this weird look and talks for five minutes about black holes. They're ancient collapsing stars, the end result of some very compli-cated math and physics. "What are you doing?" Whitey asks. "I'm sorry," she says. "When I panic, I talk about the black hole." The next morning, it hasn't worked; the thoughts don't even wait for him to get back to Rucker, all he's thinking about on the plane is Loryn. He hardly even notices he's in the air. At flight school he's grown used to that.

Flight school is a pleasure. For one thing, there's the diversion of fresh lingo. Within a few weeks, Suppy, Brian and Whitey have discovered all new ways to confuse civilians as they speak. When you fly, you ride with a *stick buddy*, the other Aviation student learning in the same helicopter. An *IP* is the instructor pilot who trains you and your stick buddy. (IPs are usually retired military with nicotine cravings: "Smoke addicts," Suppy explains, "because we scare 'em so bad.") The first time the IP hands you the stick — the *cyclic* — is your *nickel ride;* you're supposed to find a nickel with your birth year on it so when you land, you can hand it over. And *BCS*, Basic Combat Skills, is gun runs and weapon-targeting, the last phase.

There's the complicated fun of clearing space in your brain, filling it with a new body of knowledge. Aviation students learn the actual speed of a knot (1.1 mph), they learn to always check both sides of the aircraft for traffic. ("Clear right?" "Right," your stick buddy says. "Clear left?" "Left.") They learn Aviation branch lore, how Army helicopters are named after Native American tribes, the Blackhawk, the Apache, the Chinook, the Iroquois (the Iroquois is better known by its Vietnam-era name, the Huey). They appreciate the virtues of the plebe Knowledge system: they're old hands at memorizing data.

Flying a helicopter is like being a one-man band. There's something for each hand and foot. Your right hand works the collective, a stick that controls power; your left is on the cyclic; your feet are on the pedals, one takes you up, the other down. If you make a mistake and the music stops, down you go. When you master everything at once, you can hover. Then the IP says, "You've found your hover button." ("It's so sweet," Whitey says. "You automatically relax, fuck yeah, you wanna *keep* hovering." When the graduates learn hovering, they ask their stick buddies to smuggle cameras on board, to snap pictures with their helmet on, visor down, looking hard.) Then you're ready for your first *supervised solo.* Just you and the IP. Whitey watches the ground sink under him; instead of riding on the side of a helicopter, he's piloting it. When he lands, the IP gives him his solo wings, to sew onto his hat, before he meets the class for his solo party.

The only drawback is possible death. Whitey sits down in a twenty-student classroom — an aviation class is like the earthbound type, desks and a whiteboard — and the lecturer tells everyone to look around, somebody in the class will be dead in five years. The IPs teach you how to survive a power failure by taking you up a few thousand feet and then killing the engine. They announce, "Simulated engine failure." (If you angle the rotors correctly on the way down, you'll catch enough updraft to get them spinning again.) The instructors run crash videos on a screen; you watch pilots die, learn to understand and avoid their mistakes. Wires, bridges, trees, collisions. It's part of what you have to know — you let your concentration lapse, you're done — and it's also part of the dicey pleasure, you have to risk death to master gravity. By December, Whitey has found his hover button.

Christmas in Buffalo: fireplaces, hockey, overworked snowplows. Whitey made the mistake of taking Loryn to all his favorite spots. Now her memory is like graffiti in the corners of every place he's liable to visit. (At least she's moved with the other guy to Los Angeles, so there won't be an embarrassing, accidental meeting.) Whitey decides to spend New Year's Eve — the turn of the millennium — quietly. He smokes on the cold back steps of his dad's house, because his father hates seeing him with cigarettes. At ten he crosses through the house, says good night; he'll face the new century alongside Mark Matty.

They pile into the car, flick on the heater, crunch over wet slush into north Buffalo. Whitey says he wouldn't mind just relaxing at Checkers, but Mark prefers a New Year's crowded with faces, music, women. He teases Whitey, "Hey, your whole *job* is about making decisions." So Whitey decides to make Mark happy — Mark has always looked out for him, and it is New Year's — and they drive to find their friends. They shiver into a bar called 67 West, but everybody's already left for a party. The bartender tells them the address, they cross the street to their car. Mark only clears one direction, Whitey sees fast, wet headlights. He looks up, sees Mark's head bent far over the windshield, and then Mark is flying.

By the time Whitey gets to Mark, blood is smearing from places you wouldn't think of: ears, eyes, mouth, nose, dark on the pavement. The car is twenty feet away, windshield caved in, steam rising over the head-lights. "Mark," Whitey shouts, "if you can hear me, *don't move.*" Whitey hears himself issuing crisp orders — everyone step back, someone call

911 — and then he's bending down for Mark's pulse. In emergencies, you learn how many people on any given street are off-duty paramedics. Two guys materialize at his side. An ambulance glides in, Whitey sees it in pieces: flashers, legs, scrubs, stretcher. One of Mark's shoes got knocked off, it's on the sidewalk, and Whitey runs and grabs it before jumping into the ambulance. There's an awful moment on the cramped ride: Mark comes to and starts fighting away the paramedic's hands. "I'm scared of dying," he says. "I'm *scared*." Whitey leans over him, takes his hand. "I'm here with you," he says. "I'm here. You've got to let them work on you. You're not alone." Mark's oxygen mask gets pooled and raspy with blood. He's never conscious again.

The police want to make the call to the Matty family from the hospital, but Whitey insists that he be the one; the Mattys will need a voice they recognize. Mark's mother asks how serious it is, and Whitey answers, "It's bad. You need to come right now." When she arrives, the first thing she sees is the shoe under Whitey's arm, and that's when her face crumples. Mark squeezes his mother's hand a few times during his five days in the hospital. A priest from their grammar school — one of the big, kindly faces that lean over a kid's world, encouraging you to grow up well — arranges the funeral service. Mark's friends roll in the front pews, laughing and crying, trying to guess how Mark would have wanted them to handle this one. (Mark had a prankish streak, and to honor it one of his buddies swipes a road sign and nails it to Mark's front door, a one-way arrow pointed to the sky.) Whitey heads outside into the gray wind with the other guys to burn a cigarette. He's been wrestling for months now with the risks Aviation entails; it never occurred to him that his civilian best friend might die before he did. Whitey slaps his pockets, asks, "Who's got a lighter?" A voice behind him answers, "I do." It's his father.

Jake Bergman's Last Job

Each of West Point's thirty-two companies is an employment agency, with a hundred percent placement rate. There are chain-of-command jobs for every cadet. Companies acknowledge the old rule of the sea: you have to work every post — scale the rigging, swab decks — before you're permitted to climb the ranks. By the time you become a captain, you understand the function of every member of your crew.

Plebes do the company's cabin-boy work: haul laundry and tote packages, slice cakes in the mess hall. They're learning to follow, their chain-of-command title is Member of Squad. Yuks are their team leaders — they police the plebes. A West Point company is split into four platoons, same as in the Army. (Sociologists speak of the magic number 150 as being any organization's ideal size: large enough to complete tasks, small enough so you never lose track of names or faces. West Point companies average 130.) Cows become platoon sergeants, implementing orders from the firsties, squaring away yuks and plebes for duties like inspection. And firsties are platoon leaders, PLs, the top of their staff tree, keeping eyes on who's doing good things, who's ate up, who's taking an APFT, who needs a tutor for Dirt (environmental engineering class) or Baby Juice (fundamentals of electronics). Once you graduate, you've lived four lives; you know how it feels to be a private, a corporal, a sergeant, an officer.

By firstie year, cadets can also try out for glory positions on regimental or brigade staff (you live in separate barracks, and because there are additional stripes for the uniform, you get the nickname *striper*). The companies also provide other jobs for firsties: respect officer (keeping track of consideration for others), activities officer (arranging white-water rafting trips and barbecues), regulations and discipline officer (West Point dialect: *regs nazi*). But the job most firsties want is company commander: reading reports from your platoon leaders, sending back orders, leading by example, setting the standard. Best of all is having the job second term. Your parents get to see you marching your company at graduation as the loudspeaker voice announces, "Leading G-4 is Company Commander Ryan Nelson, of Ivanhoe, Minnesota." Just like that, you've shed glory on state, town and family name.

Jake Bergman and Trent Powell — G-4's weight room lifers, the *physical studs* responsible for saving George Rash — have their own glowing vision for second term of firstie year: as little interference from West Point as possible. Jake wants to spend his last months golfing, lifting, mixing protein shakes, hanging out with his buddies before the Academy clock ticks out.

So both cadets apply for regimental staff. They're after the same cushy position: not activities officer, *assistant* activities officer — no parades, no hassles, no after-lunch military classes. "You live in an upper-floor barracks," Jake explains dreamily, "so who's going to wanna climb all those stairs just to bug you? And funny as it may sound," he continues, "I'm higher ranked as a cadet than Trent is. But what happens? He gets on staff and I don't. He's right where I want to be, assistant activities officer." So Jake asks Captain Vermeesch if he can grab the XO position — executive officer, the slot Mr. Spock fills on *Star Trek*. This makes Jake Bergman second-in-command of Company G-4. "I wanted it just because XO tends to be a lot less work than being a platoon leader," he says, "so it looks like a good situation." The company commander is Jim Edgar, a tall, freckled firstie (Edgar was the physical development sergeant last January, working the stopwatch at George's first remedial APFT) who's an exception to the West Point rule — hangdog but popular, with a slow voice, as if he can see his words in the air and doesn't want to bunch them up. Being XO means that you room with the commander, fine by Jake. Edgar is a friend of his. This gives Jake a front-row seat when Company G-4 chews itself up. And it also means he's one of the first cadets to hear, in February, when George Rash flubs another APFT.

"He's a great kid," Jake explains, "but he's the kinda person — well, he's just one of those kids, trouble always finds him." Jake still has leftover fondness for George, a residue of last year's APFT. "We really set him up for success, he did so fantastic at the end." Jake shakes his big head. "All that effort, just hoping he'd take the next step."

Together, Edgar and Bergman function as a kind of sink trap, catching the steady flow of corrections and attaboys through Company G-4. West Point companies are self-policing. Recidivist cadets work their way up the chain like ballplayers perfecting their swing. Smaller infractions will earn you a hearing before a company board — your TAC, your company commander, your XO. Once you bat your way out of the infield with a subsequent offense, you appear before a battalion board (more TACs). Slugging the long ball carries you to a regimental board, until, when you finally hit one out of the park — complete failure in academics, DWI, gross insubordination — you make your way to the show: brigade board. Cadets who live through all four boards say they've done the cycle. Huck Finn is pretty sure he's the kind of cadet who'll end up doing the cycle.

Edgar and Bergman are the ones writing up *quill* — punishments, since in the old days quills were what you used to write them — when Huck slaps the snooze button and sleeps through class, and they're among the first to hear when Huck and Josh Rizzo are officially split as roommates. (The cadets are bad influences on each other, a mirror placed in front of a mirror, reflecting one long corridor of not giving a crap about West Point.) And Jake is there to witness the negotiations between Jim Edgar and Captain Vermeesch over Edgar's tricky girl-friend situation.

Ginny Whistler is a G-4 cow. As company commander, Jim should not be romantically involved with a cadet in his chain of command. If the company commander gives in to temptation and shuts the door while in barracks with his girl, or shares the same piece of furniture — the delicate West Point euphemism for being together in bed — how can he order his cadets to not do likewise? Vermeesch knows that love can make cadets do strange things: under the press of rules, even the most casual West Point relationship can feel as excitingly dire as *Romeo and Juliet*. There's the constant, heady provocation: Show me how much this means to you.

As a TAC, Vermeesch is like a couples therapist with veto power. "From my perspective," he explains, "it would be hypocritical to allow Edgar to start in this relationship and then say, 'Well, now you can't have it.' I don't like to deal in complicated issues; I think everything should be much more straightforward." So he strikes what seems like a reasonable deal with Edgar. So long as Edgar promises to avoid even the appearance of impropriety, he can serve his dual roles as company commander and Ginny Whistler's boyfriend. The two shake hands, commander to commander.

So when his friend continues sneaking off to Ginny Whistler's bar-racks, Jake can't believe it. "Stop it," Jake tells Edgar, waving his Popeye forearms. "Just stop it, wake up, something's not clicking in your *skull*." A rumor spreads through G-4: Ginny is secretly hoping Jim Edgar will get turned back. That way, they can spend another West Point year side by side. "The way he and his girlfriend talk about it," Jake says, "it's as if they're *victims* of something, like people are out to get them. But this isn't a normal college, and if you can't accept that, you leave. We all know the rules — you could put Cindy Crawford in the room across the hall from me, I'm gonna graduate from this institution. I'm tempted to just glue his butt to the chair so he won't be able to get to her room."

As the company tries to overlook afternoons of closed doors and probable furniture-sharing, Colonel Adamczyk's baseline premise about *living to standard* starts making new sense. Once you're an officer out in the real Army, how can you expect soldiers to shine shoes, maintain uniforms, if you can't follow the discipline yourself? It's a form of inadvertent leader development: Jake Bergman is a cadet who hates gum-chewing regulations and dust checks (during inspection, the commander will don white gloves, then run a hand inside a drawer or along the frame of a mirror to show cadets his gray fingertip). Here's something he hates worse. "You know me, I don't even like seeing the TAC walking in the company area." Now Jake finds himself hoping to see the rules come down hard. "I said to Jim, 'You are the worst kind of leader, because you're a hypocrite.'" Jim Edgar, preparing to walk over to Ginny's barracks, just uncomfortably laughs.

Super-V

George Rash had good solid reasons for failing another APFT. He lays them out, multiple choice: "Problems with the ankle. Also, my arches were flaring up *real* bad. And I'd just gotten a pair of orthopedics for my sneakers — they broke my feet in, instead of the other way around." Push-ups and sit-ups went fine (George has a soldier's broad upper body), the run not so hot. Rash jogged awhile, walked, ran some, jogged, limped across the finish with a 16:30. (Vermeesch couldn't believe it: "You just don't ever wanna see someone walk at the end — you're walkin', you better be dead or *bleeding*.") But whatever the path, it leads to the same destination: George has to march to the TAC's office and sit down with Captain Vermeesch.

For John Vermeesch, being a TAC is the finish to a before-and-after story. He graduated the Academy in 1990; a little more than half a year later he was stomach-down in Saudi, leading a rifle platoon against the army of Saddam Hussein. Vermeesch wants to see his cadets ready. "I remember feeling as a cadet like it wasn't *real*— that what we do here isn't completely real," he says. "The big reason I wanted to come back was this obligation to tell cadets, 'Hey, it *is* real. What you learn here is exactly how it's going to be when you get out.' What I wrote in my application essay was that I am very committed to making cadets understand the importance of the mission — of winning America's wars, of taking care of America's sons and daughters — and how soon they might be called on to go execute that mission."

Vermeesch's voice croaks and swells when he says something important; it's as if the most significant words grow physically larger in his throat. Vermeesch is an intensely physical man. A little under six feet tall, with something a bit piggish and pugnacious about his features. If he likes what you're saying, he's nodding, marching along with you; the less he likes it, the stiffer he gets — you're marching alone. When he casts around for a metaphor to explain how West Point builds values, he tells cadets, "You stress those muscles incrementally a little more each day — to sum up, it's like lifting." On the subject of George Rash, he gives a pained shrug that carries more weight than his words. When he wants to let you know where he's from, he juts up his hand. "Michigan is shaped like a mitten. Roscommon, Michigan — first knuckle, second finger." The most vital information rolls off his frame; the body is a keyboard for John Vermeesch.

His first weeks in Saudi — getting prepped for G-Day — Vermeesch spent his free time pushing into his soldiers' tents, collaring guys after chow, downloading their stories. "Because the last thing I wanted," the captain says, "was to not know them as people. I knew decisions I'd make in the very near future could impact on whether they lived or died. And the thing driving me was writing the letter home to mom and dad that said, 'Your son didn't make it.' I envisioned myself sitting there trying to write this letter, and not really knowing the kid personally, and coming up with some *bullshit*. It drove me crazy, how nongenuine that would be." Vermeesch isn't sure that's a drive George Rash can understand. "Honestly, I don't know what's going on sometimes in that guy's head."

For the first term — the natural result of George's D at Buckner — Vermeesch put George in what's called the Special Leader Development Program: once-a-month office meetings, the field Army confronting the cadet world, Rash staring at Vermeesch, Vermeesch staring at Rash. "I thought we really made some progress," Vermeesch says; George earned a B in military development. Then, after Christmas break, George flunked his run ("So obviously, first semester didn't work out so well"), and like a pitcher on the mound, Vermeesch has to make an adjustment. Being a TAC requires creative solutions on the fly. "I just don't perceive any common ground with George Rash," Vermeesch admits. So he sends George around for monthly meetings with Captain Lance Richardson, a buddy from his Saudi company who's now teaching chemistry at West Point. They're both brainy guys, and like Rash, Richardson played tuba in high school. "He was kind of the geeky guy growing up," Vermeesch says. "He came into the Army to become a man, and it did that for him. He rose through the ranks, Special Forces, Ranger guy, an exceptionally successful officer." Rash and Richardson, Vermeesch feels, have that common ground, a space where they can hail each other, geek to former geek.

The other problem child in Vermeesch's Special Leader Development Program is Huck Finn. Vermeesch has a better handle on Huck — they're physical in the same ways. He sees in Huck the thing nobody else has, a fine officer. "I was his TAC at Buckner," the captain recalls, "and I thought, 'This guy is gonna be the best cadet I've ever seen.' He's got more raw potential than ninety-five percent of the people here, just a super-stud leader. He can influence people naturally, but to what end is he gonna influence 'em?" Huck could end up a before-and-after story too. But he's like a twisty math problem where Vermeesch can't find the proper integer to plug into the formula.

One mid-February Saturday — snow dusting the building sides like stuff left too long in the freezer — there's a TA-50 inspection. TA-50 is your temporary Army gear: canteen, ammo pack, gas mask, flashlight, a deep-pocket-sized shovel called an entrenching tool. Cadets are required to scrub their tackle down, arrange it on a towel in an attractive, combative table setting. Huck just spills his ruck upside down over his rack. The equipment has gone untouched since Buckner; actual leaves pour out, along with a terrarium's worth of dirt. Then Huck wanders down the hall. He hears a voice shouting, "What the hell is *this?*" and he laughs — whoa, somebody is getting *ripped*. He strolls back to his room, and there's Captain Vermeesch, lifting his crusty shovel with two fingers. Vermeesch moves in for the correction, eyeball to eyeball. "Cadet Finn" — then the TAC's face stops dead. "Did you *shave* today?" One more screwup, Vermeesch promises him, and Finn will have batted his way up to a battalion board.

Vermeesch arranges a marathon special counseling day: eighty minutes with George, eighty with Huck. He opens up their peer evaluations — thumbs-up, thumbs-down, here's what your cadet critics had to say. George listens and nods as the captain lists his shortcomings: physical skills, communication skills. Vermeesch tells George that if he fails his next APFT retest, he'll be *highly* recommended for separation from West Point. (The constant shock for officers is that George simply listens, offering no explanation, showing no emotion. But George does have a response: "Ouch," he tells me.)

Huck doesn't even want to read his evaluations. "Well," Vermeesch says, "you've gotta see it." Huck stumbles out of the office shaken, wanting to drop some big redneck tears. "Wow," he says. "People had some not-nice things to say about me. I am an absolute asshole. In fact, these kids think I am the *biggest* flaming asshole around here." Crushing reviews; one star, half a star. "Huck Finn does not care about West Point, Huck Finn only cares about himself." What cut most were the cadets who wrote, "I can see cadet Finn starting a fight with one of his classmates, and I can see cadet Finn punching his classmate right in the face." Huck sighs. "And bro, that's not me. I swear, if the TAC ever has to show me one of those forms again, it's gonna say something different."

Then, in March, another problem arises that puts Finn and Rash in the shade. It starts with Maria Auer, Jasmine Rose's roommate. Maria comes from upper Wisconsin, the icy dairyland where Canadian pronunciation (*aboot* for *about*) flattens the local accent. Maria has been sneaking out of her room in the evening — a regs violation — to study, she says. The rumor is that Maria is actually sneaking into her boyfriend's room. Vermeesch pulls the two cadets aside for the brass-tacks question: Are you guys messing around in barracks? They swear no — even Maria's boyfriend's roommate vouches no — and a week later, they're discovered on the same piece of furniture, under the covers, watching *Seinfeld*. G-4 braces itself for a strange spectacle. How can Jim Edgar hand around punishments when everybody in company knows he and his girlfriend have been breaking the identical rule? "You can't stand in front of people and give out quill," Jake Bergman says, "while you're doing the same dumb shit. It's just the ultimate hypocrisy."

Jake is surprised and bitter. "There's a lot of nice people here, but Jim is truly one of the nicest people I've ever met, so how can he do it? I told him, 'How can you look at yourself in the mirror and do that?

You're a snake.' And I'm not the type of person to go talk to a TAC *ever.*" But when Vermeesch makes his way to Jake's room, the XO has already prepared his answer. "Sir," Jake says, "I'm not going to give you details about it, Jim can give you details. You're asking me to confirm rumors, I'm telling you the rumors are for the most part true, and the situation's been out of control since February."

Vermeesch motions for the company to fall in around him after morning formation. He says he's had it with male-female relationships in company, with people breaking regulations. Maria stares at her boyfriend, other couples exchange worried looks. "Because Captain Vermeesch had heard different rumors about other cadets," Maria says. "He's like, 'I will burn you to the ground.' I'm looking over at my boyfriend like, 'That's *us*. We're going to get burned.'" The rule-breaking ceases, and that's how Vermeesch acquires his nickname: Super-Vermeesch, Super-V.

Spring break is a jump into ten days of civilian life; a high dive, a swim, a splash through the non-uniformed world. The cadets limp back the following Sunday showing different degrees of tan above their collars. (Jake hits Cancun — bikinis, alcohol, whooping — and doesn't fully recover his voice for a week.) Vermeesch has already met with Jim Edgar. Fifteen minutes before 1900 formation, the company commander pulls Jake Bergman aside and warns him something's coming. Then Jim Edgar stands in front of his company, and the G-4 cadets get to witness something historic, an act they've never seen or heard about before: a West Point company commander resigning his command.

When Edgar steps down, his XO automatically becomes company commander. The cadet charged with enforcing the regulations is now Jake Bergman — a cadet who hates regulations. Jake accepts the promotion with grace. "Pretty ironic, huh?" he says. "Asking to be XO really bit me in the butt." He laughs. His first thought isn't about the honor or leadership experience; it's just going to mean more work. "These last couple months are *not* going to be very fun. I kinda feel like I'm in charge of a sinking ship, I've just gotta keep it floating till graduation."

Becoming a Man

Huck Finn is trying to do better. But it isn't like football, where you've always got the other guy's helmet crashing in as a reminder of what you're supposed to do. There's nowhere to grab — how do you block out your own random impulses?

A week after counseling with Vermeesch, Huck passes up a mandatory lecture in Thayer Auditorium. "And they sent around an e-mail, the subject line was 'Attendance' — it said, 'If you weren't there, let me know.' So I coulda gotten away with it — I mean, no one woulda ever known. But I was like, 'Well, shit, I missed it.' So I e-mailed back, and I knew what was coming for me. I was like, 'Damn, might as well just call up the fuhball coach now and tell 'im I won't be there.'"

And just as Super-V promised, Huck arrives at his first battalion board — with Major Andrea Thompson, who's now the battalion commander — and receives maximum punishment, a sentence straight out of Greek myth. Finn is a physical cadet who loves being around people; he's ordered to pass the rest of the semester indoors and alone. Sixty days of room restriction, the kind of home confinement low-ball criminals get handed when jails overflow. He has authorization to leave for class, meals, ninety daily minutes of exercise in the yard, and that's it. And there's no more football, which is what Huck came to West Point for. Huck stays in his barracks for seven weeks.

By day fifty, his chair pulled to the window, smelling spring and the crust of cadet barbecues, he decides he'll sign whatever is necessary to reopen that door. He's ready to file his LOR, his letter of resignation from West Point.

Spring is the busy season for drops. Headshake, embarrassed smile, the phone call home. For yuks, it's a last chance to use the door before penalties apply. Cow Commitment falls the first day of the next year, and from then on, the first two years will be treated as a deposit. Agatha Glowacki — the one cadet George Rash has a crush on — leaves West Point for the sweaters and ivy of Harvard. Captain Vermeesch admires her decision. "She's a wonderful young lady, just not *selfless*, and she knew about herself enough to realize that she could never place other people's interests in front of hers to the extent this profession demands." Chrissi Cicerelle has had a rotten year, and it's all been Mark. Every day they're having their standard argument — does West Point have to be the way West Point is? — and cadets see them moping around post. They have the scowling weather look (private clouds under clear skies) of a couple in trouble. Chrissi is about ready to resign — but then her roommate does it for her. And seeing the costs convinces Chrissi to stay. "It's a lot to walk away from — not only all the time you've put in, all this is gonna do for you in the future."

Spring is also high season for separations. Adrian Cannady, the yuk who was shocked that anyone would willingly drink the grog at last year's Dining-in ("that's just *ignorance*") is about to become a firstie. "Almost done it," he says. "One leg of the race to go, man — the last quarter mile. Almost there, man, *almost there*. It's *emotional*. It's like — you just want to get on your knees sometimes, because you just been through so much stuff." Instead, Cannady gets the word, separation for academics. He heads back to Texas to await decisions from the Army, his last quarter mile just hanging in the air.

George Rash doesn't want to end up in the same boat. Vermeesch has given him the warning: another APFT failure and he's out of West Point. No one trains him this time. He's a yuk, he is expected to motivate himself. "It's all on me now," George says. Back at Beast, when his toes grew blisters on blisters, George smiled: it meant calluses were forming. George is developing a West Point callus. "I took a lot of last year personally," he says. "I've mellowed out a lot." And the other cadets have mellowed toward him: they no longer sneer *Rash!* Meeting George now generates a more diverse set of responses. "Some of 'em take it pretty well," George explains, "and consider having met me a good thing. For a variety of reasons. Some because they've learned *from* me — others because they've learned to be *not* like me." Video games have been George's balm, his emotional convalescence. He plays the on-line role player EverQuest. "Also referred to as EverCrack," he says, "because it's extremely, extremely addictive." Selecting a video game character is like walking a dog, displaying your personality on a leash. It's your subconscious declaring your survival strategies and your sense of self. "I play a monk," George explains. "Monks have no magic at all. Our defenses suck, we can't take hits the way a warrior can. But we *heal* damage unparalleled by just about any other characters. When I'm fighting battles, I have to keep flicking on reverse view to make sure I'm not getting ganged up on and attacked from behind. And my character has got a new skill, it's called 'feign death.' Basically, it means the monsters think I'm dead and leave me alone."

Sergeant Mike Tierney thinks George's cadet career is dead in real life. Tierney is G-4's TAC-NCO: each company gets a noncommissioned officer, to perform the same up-to-the-elbows tasks — training, inspecting, motivating soldiers from ground level — that NCOs do in the field Army. Tierney is red-haired and fair-skinned. He has a broad smile, and the shipwreck humor of NCOs everywhere: We are pleased to have accurately predicted that things would eventually turn to crap. On a mild April Saturday, he administers the remedial APFT to the Fighting Guppies. He's pretty sure this spells the end of George's line. "George missed the last time by forty-five seconds," Tierney says, "and that's an eternity in the run game."

No G-4 cadets turn out at Gillis Field House to cheer George on; it's just cadets who are also on the firing line. Anthony Bowers and Ahmond Hill are track stars. They move at the easy glide of cadet athletes — people for whom any movement is a minor sport; they're here because the last APFT conflicted with a track meet. Steve Cho is a thickly built Asian kid with small red acne colonies on his cheeks, giving him a fed-up look. Amy Saul is a chunky plebe. (She's George's plebe, his Member of Squad; taking a remedial APFT beside your plebe is the kind of blunder other cadets notice.) Marcus Genova is from Colorado, a wiry, watchful kid with more hair on his legs than the track cadets — shaved for speed — have on their heads. Marcus has weak stomach muscles; because he's always on the verge of being separated for sit-ups, Tierney has enrolled him in G-4's PT-for-Life program. Every time a G-4 cadet takes the APFT, Marcus has to turn out too. He frowns like a man waking up to find he's back in a repeating dream.

I ask George how he feels being back here, with another two-mile run between him and graduation. "Slight cough," he says, clearing his throat. "Otherwise not too bad." Push-ups come first. Amy kneels, flexes, knocks out forty-five. "That's pretty damn good for the women's standard," George tells her; he's working his way toward APFT statistical mastery. "And it's passing for the *men's*." George's turn comes, he scrunches way past the necessary forty-two. "That was an all-time best for me, Sergeant Tierney," he says.

"Good," the sergeant says. "You just do the run, you'll be all set."

Tierney is wearing a new leather jacket. He leans back against his motorcycle, folds his arms.

"I now know I can do seventy-five push-ups," George muses. "All I have to do is drop a minute on my run."

"Can't do it walking," Tierney replies.

Then sit-ups, on the chilly lawn in front of Gillis. Bowers and Hill take turns, pressing down on each other's Nikes; they don't deign to touch the more imperfect cadets. They encourage each other in clipped gym patois: "Run it baby, burn it baby, come on come on come on, burn it and run it baby." Genova chugs through twenty sit-ups, thirty — actually cuts a concussive fart at thirty-five — and reports another glum pass to Tierney. "Fifty-six." The cadets trade places. Their knees are blotched red, and field dandruff — leaves, grass — sticks to their shins. Before his turn, George lays aside his glasses with a vaguely Supermannish gesture of resolution and grit. He flies past the minimum, then reaches for his glasses, repackages himself as Clark Kent and reports his seventy-three. Sergeant Tierney and the cadets watch the Army lacrosse team warming up one field over, sticks fanning the air. "Thinking of giving up basketball for lacrosse, Amy?" Tierney asks. George chooses to field the question. "Looks like fun," he says. "But my eye-hand coordination is not that hot."

In anticipation of the run, the cadets shed sweatshirts and gloves. They stand at the start, beep their digital watches into timer mode, bend back their legs. George's face goes blank. Sergeant Tierney makes a quick speech: "Those of you going out to the field this summer, stay in shape, or your tour could get ugly real fast. Otherwise, when you do PT, we *enlisted* soldiers will say, 'I heard that cadet Rash was ate up like a soup sandwich.' You don't need that, you don't want it. Everybody get the message? OK. Ready, set, go."

The cadets pad softly down the road. George has fifteen minutes and fifty-four seconds to stay at West Point. Tierney climbs aboard his bike and swaps predictions with G-4's physical development officer.

"My time for George is sixteen-fifty. Unless he's been working really hard at it." The heads are bobbing away: the track is a basic straight line, like an errand to the store; you run to the end, turn around, gun your way home.

"He's got a pretty easy pace going there right now," the PD officer agrees. "That looks like an eight-minute-mile pace. He's behind Amy —

she only needs eighteen-something, he needs to go under sixteen. He should be ahead of her."

White lines finger through the sunburn on Tierney's neck. "The only question is, who's gonna finish first, Bowers or Hill? See, they're running together." By the ten-minute mark, you can see the athletes' shoulders bouncing up and down. By eleven minutes you see their steady, unruffled features, and at eleven and a half you can hear their speech: "Come on burn it move it you want it." "You guys gonna hold hands?" Tierney yells, leaning over his handlebars. "Come on! We're hoping for a real race here!" They finish in tandem, 12:19. The two athletes simply start walking — no panting — like automobiles smoothly shifting from a high gear to a lower one.

Tierney flattens his hand against his forehead, searching for George. "Oh, he ain't gonna make it. Amy is going to beat him. George Rash is getting ready to walk out the gate." Two minutes later, the rest of the cadets finish together at a panting gallop. At 14:20 George's tiny head comes into view at the end of the gray road. He's a quarter mile away and it doesn't look promising. There are ninety seconds left; in spite of himself, Tierney yells.

"Let's *go*, George!"

"He could still do it if he pushes it," the PD officer says.

Tierney shakes his head. "He needs eighty seconds for the quarter mile — that's a big push, especially now."

Then, also in spite of themselves, the cadets trot down the course, space themselves out evenly along the last quarter mile; it's the group ethic drawing them, and a group wants to see every member succeed. As if he can't bear a competition he's not part of, Bowers drops his sweatshirt and skims back down the road. Then he turns around and starts to pace George. At 15:00, George's features become distinct — head lowered, cheeks working, with the exploded-grape look of a person expending every last bit of effort. The cadets shout, "Move it, Rash! Come on! *Kick* it!" At 15:30 you can see the thumbnails on his fists, the heaving neck. At 15:40 you can see his half-closed eyes. Tierney begins to yell out the time. "Fifteen forty-five. Fifteen forty-six. Fifteen forty-seven." Now you can hear George's breath, fast and ragged. The cadets shout, "Knees up! You're *right there!*" George closes his eyes and stretches his body forward. Tierney lifts his watch, "Fifty-one, fifty-two, *fifty-three,* fifty-four . . ." as George thunders past.

George stops dead, bends over, grabs the hem of his shorts for support. George Rash has once again found a way to stay at West Point. Tierney is staring at the numbers. "Fifteen fifty-three, you had a second to spare, George." And then the sergeant moves on to the standard Academy gesture of raising the bar. "Good job. Take another minute off that, you're doin' good."

Steve Cho pats George on the back, George holds up one finger. "I thought. I was gonna. Die at end. I was thinking: I failed, I failed. But I'm never gonna. Just quit on myself."

(Tierney tells me later, "Bowers saved the day. Rash wasn't going to make it otherwise." Bowers converts his action into simple gym terms. "It wasn't that big of a deal. You kind of get, um, caught up in your own private misery sometimes. Hearing somebody's voice snaps you out of it. I just told him, 'Hurry the hell up.'")

The pile of sweatshirts sorts itself back to original owners, Bowers breezes past George, and George raises his head with a squint. "Thank you, Bowers." Bowers says, "No problem."

Does passing feel good? "Actually, I just feel congested," George says. "I've had this cold for a couple of weeks. I'm just glad my shin splints didn't flare up." He pulls on the heavy gray cotton sweatshirt: *USMA* — United States Military Academy. "I really need to get back, get cleaned up, and start studying my Hebrew. I have my bar mitzvah coming up in three weeks."

To the cadets' surprise, Jake Bergman proves an excellent company commander: firm, fair, decisive. Since he's not in trouble himself, he can hand out punishments without fear or favor. (Not that his opinion of the job changes: "It's very time-consuming, and the people who run this place don't have any common sense.") He protects his plebes when the Academy tries to take away a weekend pass, he raises everybody's morale by living to standard. For the first time all year, it feels as if G-4 has its shirt tucked back in. "I try to give my guys every opportunity I can," he says. His leadership style has the armed decency and resolve of Schwarzenegger dialogue. "You always give people a warning. And if they do it again, then you *slam* them." But when he speaks about his success, he finds the modest voice of his old TAC, Jim DeMoss. "In theory, any cadet ought to be able to step in and do the job," Jake says. "It's just that I have such a great staff." When the parents arrive for graduation, he will march G-4 in the parades, and the announcer will say, "Leading Company G-4, Company Commander Jake Bergman, of Diamond Bar, California," and Jake will find himself stiffening and grimacing with pride. To everyone's surprise, his lifting buddy, Trent Powell, has found religion, and is shipping for Infantry training at Benning.

And Huck Finn gets his brush with religion too. You could call it Stockholm syndrome, but by day fifty-two of his confinement, he's reconciled to staying at West Point. "I went to my platoon leader on the fiftieth night," Huck says. "I'd sat in that room long enough, I'm at the low point of my life. I told him, 'Hey man, screw this, call up Captain V right now. I want to start out-processing tomorrow morning.' He's like, 'Tell you what, why don't you sleep on this? You come back here tomorrow night, tell me the same thing, I'll call him up right then.' So next night I went back up to his room, but he must of known I was coming; he wasn't in there. So I was just in such a pissed-off mood I just went to bed. And I woke up the next day and I'd kinda forgotten about it. Really weird like that."

The more Huck broods over it — in the last creeping days before his parole — the more Captain Vermeesch doing exactly what Captain Vermeesch said he would do makes Huck want to remain in gray. Because West Point is that sort of cause-and-effect place, where the action follows the promise as neatly as the rising steps of a staircase. "I love the man," Huck says simply, "for doing what he said. I needed it. If he hadn't of brought the wood and unleashed fury on me, I would of been like, 'Wow, this guy's not as hard as I thought, this place isn't as hard I thought, it's just like every other place.' See, I kinda always have viewed West Point as the best place. And if I leave the best place, then I'm settling for second best, and that's just something I can't ever do."

By the Army's definition, he may not have reached manhood yet, but according to the Torah, George Rash becomes a man near the end of his yuk year. The West Point Jewish chapel — concrete and glass, with the main window stretching up like an arrow toward God — sits on a hill overlooking the trees, barracks and fields of the Plain. Inside, the corridor's watercolors are painted in the Delacroix style, with subject matter relatable to the cadet: *The Priests Leading the People into Battle; Joshua Thanks GOD for His Victories; Huge Hail Stones Rain Destruc-*

tion on the Armies of the Amorite Kings. Rabbi Lieutenant Colonel Richard White, the Jewish chaplain, explains that they're worth "beaucoup bucks." He spreads his arms wide: "Look how visible we are! West Point has had Jewish representation from class *one* — 1802 graduated two officers. One was a Jewish boy from Baltimore, Simon Levy. We've been a part of this team since the very beginning." His branch insignia is the double-arched tablets of the Ten Commandments.

Inside the sanctuary, a chunky Star of David that looks like a piece of munitions hangs suspended twenty feet above the sea of dress-white skullcaps, cadets sitting rigid and solemn in their dress uniforms. The local Jewish community has turned out with yarmulkes that are unusually informative. Some read "Jewish War Veteran." Others say, "WW II — Hudson Valley" or "Executive Committee," some carry combat decorations and service pins. With typical West Point efficiency, two cadets are being bar mitzvahed on the same morning. Standing by the ark, Jason Blaustein has a swim team captain's chlorinated poise; George wears a proud grin, and chants a surprisingly beautiful Hebrew. You look around for George's family, and then there's the clatter of a collapsing video tripod, a female voice whispering "Shoot," and you know exactly where they are.

The two bar mitzvah cadets uncap the tinkling cones from the Torah scrolls. They read their portions, and at that moment enter Jewish manhood. Rabbi White watches, a small finicky-looking man with eyes in which friskiness is being channeled and squeezed back in. By coincidence, the day's Torah reading is from Leviticus, the *Parshat Kedoshim,* the holiness code that God gifts to Moses, a kind of oral version of the Ten Commandments. Do not steal, do not bear false witness, do not lie. When it's over, the cadets deliver speeches. Blaustein grips the lectern. The Bible, it turns out, is also directly relatable to cadet life. "While reciting my portion," Jason begins, "I thought of walking into my TAC's office, listening to a long list of things I had to get done. So I sympathized with Moses, listening to God on Mount Sinai; it was very similar to the experiences that I had this semester as a first sergeant. Enforcing standards upon people is very difficult; that's a lesson for all leaders." He clears his throat. "One verse that stood out to me as a West Pointer is 'You shall not steal, neither deal falsely, neither lie one to another.' A correlation can be drawn from this statement to the cadet honor code: A cadet shall not lie, cheat, steal, or tolerate those who do." He nods. "It is heartening to know that God approves."

Then George stands, with the slight gulp of a man who's just heard somebody else deliver his speech. But he spins the material his own way. "I'd like to thank you all for coming," he says, fingering up his glasses. "This couldn't have happened without many people: my family, Jason's family, the rabbi, a lot of good people, and a lot of other people. I probably wouldn't even *be* here if it wasn't for the support of the faculty and all my friends that helped me through these last two years." George is standing at the summit of another West Point year, a place most canny gamblers would have wagered he couldn't reach.

"As *I* was reading the Torah portion, what I actually thought of was the UCMJ — the Uniform Code of Military Justice — and the cadet honor code. This seems to fall somewhere in between." He clears his throat. "It just sets down some very general basic rules on how to live your life and how to be a good person. And basically tells you to follow the golden rule: Do unto others as you'd have them do unto you. Treat people fairly and justly, and keep from being needlessly cruel to others. As for what bar mitzvah means? Generally it symbolizes the coming into adulthood — I guess I always was a late bloomer." George waits for titters from cadets and the Rash section to subside, then closes with: "As a youth, I never really had any need for a religion, till I came here."

Then the big meal. George's aunt says "knock wood" and actually raps his head. Cadet Steve Ruggerio, George's invited G-4 guest, is dining at the Rashes' table, unsure of what he's doing there. ("George asked me to come," he says. "I was surprised, because I really don't know him very well at all. And then he told me he considered me one of his best friends here. And I was like, 'OK.' That made me feel almost a little bad. Because this kid obviously thinks a lot of me, and I barely even know him.") Cadets ask George what he's doing this summer and he replies, "Squad leader, Beast Barracks. I've scared a lot of people with that thought."

PART THREE

The Third Year

R-Day

APPLYING TO WEST POINT is a clerical road march. Fifty thousand high school juniors step off together, filling out the official request-for-information forms. From there it's a test of stamina, a battle of attrition.

Twelve thousand candidates complete the application. Six thousand make it to the physical aptitude examination stage, a fitness pop quiz — push-ups, pull-ups, standing long jump, three-hundred-yard dash. Service academies are the only institutions in the country that will measure how far you can toss a basketball from a kneeling position. (A little under seventy feet is the minimum.) Four thousand candidates are nominated by their senators or congressmen. The congressional nomination is a round-robin event, ten candidates competing for each slot, elected officials taking a turn as admissions officers, sifting through transcripts, recommendations, and clean-cut photographs. (Especially ambitious parents will snag jobs at a congressman's in-town headquarters, hoping to gain their kids an inside track.) If your parents are career military, you can jump the line and apply directly to the president. If one of them happens to be disabled, deceased, POW or MIA — or a recipient of the Medal of Honor — your file skips all the way to the superintendent's desk at West Point. Then the folks at admissions get down to the elimination round, stacking valedictorians against team captains, yearbook editors against debaters. Two thousand hardy candidates are pronounced qualified for admission, but only about twelve hundred get offered actual West Point places. They receive a plaque in the mail. In many small towns, friends and neighbors stop in for viewings.

To the home front, a West Point cadet is a successful immigrant, golden and fortunate, someone who can meet their siblings at the docks. Chrissi Cicerelle's sister, Marie, bunked with Chrissi two Februarys ago for a candidate visit. Chrissi took Marie to class, toured her around the snow crust on the Plain, stood her in the back rows of formation. (On second-semester Fridays, you'll find candidates backing every company, doing their best to look martial and severe in sneakers and jeans.) Marie's last night, Erik "Ox" Oksenvaag swung by Chrissi's room to train her for the company's Field Training Exercise. Tactical basics: low crawl, react-to-contact, react-to-ambush. "*Ambush* will usually be a device like a claymore mine," he said. "Now, that mine is gonna eliminate a big chunk of the squad in the kill zone immediately. You'll probably be on point — so you're gonna be one of the first cadets to get killed."

"*Ew*," Chrissi said. Marie giggled and Chrissi frowned. "Shut *up*, Marie."

"It's OK," Marie told Ox. "I know my sister's prissy. I'm prissy too."

"So you're coming next, huh?" Oksenvaag asked, standing and wiping his hands. "Class of 2004?"

"Roger that," Chrissi replied. "She's got her nomination. She's just waiting on admissions." A year later, Marie received her thumbs-up and the plaque. Now she's one of the new plebes crowding into Highland Falls, watching the clock wind down on civilian life. Parents, childhood, radio music, fast food, free speech, all becoming items for the scrapbook. Palms go sweaty from the press of goodbyes. It's the second-to-last morning of June, Reception Day.

R-Day is the last leg of the admissions march, the first step in the long haul to butter bars. Over the next twelve hours, new cadets will get divided, weighed, processed, sworn in. They'll be tested by upperclassmen wearing red sashes and trained. At sundown, twelve hundred former civilians will march smartly across the Plain as uniformed soldiers. (West Point overpacks in the face of the four-year journey; only about a thousand will graduate.) Logistics are so tricky that the Academy performs a complete dress rehearsal two days before R-Day. Local civilians play the part of new cadets; every year, a bunch stagger away in tears.

Huck Finn's job is to instruct arrivals on reporting to their first sergeant, the diamond-thingie-wearing cadet from his own R-Day. (Eternal-recurrence fans will appreciate that the first sergeant is Huck's own R-Day roommate and Chrissi's boyfriend, Mark Thompson.) Huck is trying to keep a lid on himself. "We had those civilians comin' through on R-Day practice," he explains, "and I don't know how it happened — I just started getting up in their faces, louder and louder — but two little girls started crying on me. So maybe I need to tone it down some. But everyone agrees this is how it needs to be, it has to be hard, everybody gets broken in on R-Day."

Families start collecting at the foot of Michie Stadium in the snappy 0630 weather, breezes giving the leaves a ruffle. Mothers wear *West Point Mom* baseball caps, dads check battery levels on their video cameras. Because this is West Point, there are some wild cards. One father sports a *Joint Counter-Intelligence Training Academy Instructor* windbreaker and is getting into something heavy over his cell phone. Another trim dad, whose polo shirt reads *National Security Agency,* looks patriotically abstracted, as if he's receiving satellite data through his sunglasses. New cadets wear denim cutoffs, camo trousers, hometown sports jerseys, platform shoes with butterflies in the heel. Some hold sweethearts' hands, exchanging tight goodbye squeezes; others maintain a precise, embarrassed teenaged distance from their folks. Officers fan through the crowd on atmosphere-lightening duty. "Come on," a major chuckles, "no second thoughts now! Keep it moving. Hey," he points, "don't let *that* one get away." A captain explains, "We do it because the families are nervous." But the parents mostly look intrigued, like participatory tourists: they've come to see their kids fuse with a national monument.

The families click through turnstiles, take bleacher seats in groups of forty as officers rise with hospitable speeches. "Today," the officers begin, "is both a culmination and a beginning, the beginning of new and unparalleled opportunities." Dads hoist video cameras to their eyes, the one-armed salute people pay to the future: this meets the memory criteria, this is souvenir-worthy. "As you go through this day," officers say, their advice heartening and worrying the new cadets, "remember to *listen closely.* If the person in front of you says 'Step up to the line,' then do not step *on* the line and do not step *over* the line. And remember that you are not alone. Every member of the professional cadet cadre, every member of the long gray line, and every one of your classmates has experienced this day. Throughout the morning, there'll be things that happen — some to your classmates, some to you — that at this time will not seem very funny to you or them. But years from now, I can promise, when you reflect on this day, yes, many of you will smile." Already the Army is extending its reach, planting its flag on upcoming recollections.

Then a female cadet introduces herself, a representative from their crisp and poised future. "Following my briefing," she announces pleasantly, "all friends and family will be asked to move downstairs and depart the area. You will be going on alone from here." Parents can't resist glancing at children, faces an open question: Are we prepared for this? The kids click their necks, crack knuckles, as if at the starting line. "All right," the cadet says. "At this time I will now ask parents to prepare their final goodbyes. You will be moving out in ninety seconds." Moms gather children in close, eyes become puddles, dads shift uncomfortably, as if what's being rated is their ability not to make a scene. ("All right . . . knock yourself out now.") As the kids begin their determined jog down the cement steps, the parents look stunned, proud, and *lightened;* they flex hands at their sides like long-distance travelers after putting down the bag they've been carrying for eighteen years.

The kids collect downstairs at the concrete lip of the field until all forty are together. A cow, part of the upperclass cadre overseeing R-Day, issues their first command. "Shift bags to the left hands, candidates." Then they step onto the AstroTurf, and leave the spectator part of life behind. The cadre member marches them across the fifty-yard line; the last thing they hear from their parents is applause. As they enter the dim tunnel at the stadium's other side, they're greeted by the glowing reassurance of a Coke machine. They've traveled — by crossing a few hundred feet — from a world in which they were infinitely treasured to one in which they have next to no value at all. Unless they finish Beast, they won't get to be called plebes. Until they sign today's forms, they won't even be *new cadets.* They're *candidates.*

Cows wait by a table with sharp orders. "Bags up on the table. Don't look around, candidate. Hurry up, you've got places to be." "Take that *hat* off! Fill out one tag for each piece of luggage — do it now — last name, first name, middle initial. Are you *smiling* at me, candidate?"

One kid is so nervous he has to fill his tags out twice, pen mapping jittery lines like an EKG. An eager father pushes into the room, face deep in his viewfinder. "Whoa-whoa-whoa," the cadre says, "sir . . . ?" "Let's *go,* candidates! I'm glad you think something is funny — you have yourself a *real* nice day." "Stand up *straight,* candidates. Now take your bags, follow the cadet guide. We're moving out by bus to Thayer Hall." Buses pull up, brakes hiss, doors fold open.

Once the candidates are aboard, the cadre break into chuckling and bragging. R-Day is training for them, a chance to lead. "Did you see the guy I asked for his hat? I thought he was gonna swallow it." "I had a *smiler.*" "That one kid had a guitar! Guy had a fuckin' *guitar* on R-Day. I don't know what the hell he thinks he's gonna use it for."

The buses (*Candidate Shuttle*) rattle in silence as dozens of internal videotapes clip through the same basic scenes: home, lawn, high school, TV, grandparents, here. The doors clatter open, a cadre member's head appears at the stairs. "All right candidates, you have twenty seconds to get off this bus. Let's move." As the candidates spill out onto the Thayer Hall sidewalk — a mammoth gray structure containing a maze of classrooms — the cadre lines them up. "Head and eyes will remain straight forward at all times." West Point now has dominion over what you're permitted to see.

At R-Day you surrender your old self in stages. You've already left behind family and control over your environment. In the fluorescent Thayer hallways, you hand over your belongings, then file to the treasurer's office to give up your cash; any sum greater than forty dollars gets banked. Cadre members stalk the lines of candidates, wearing the summer white-over-gray uniform: white gloves, white belt, shining brass, bodies giving a martial squeak and buckle as they walk. "No talking," cadre announce. "Do not move, do not smile. Hands will remain cupped at all times. You need to look at anything, look at my wall." Unless you had an unlucky home life, this is the first time anybody has spoken to you this way. The candidates are just blank eyes now, mouths so tight the lips appear to be hiding. The cadre march them down the halls, volunteers distributing clothes from tables. Then the males and females are channeled into separate classrooms — windows, whiteboards, industrial clocks marking time — for changing.

Now the Army demands your clothing. In their dressing room, male candidates tug on black gym shorts and white T-shirts with a speed that suggests graded events. "You *must* put on a jockstrap," a TAC-NCO commands. "Let's go — move with a purpose." There are lowered eyelids, specks of modesty. You can spot ex–big-time athletes by their ability to skin themselves out of their drawers as if it's just another pregame. One shy kid tries to yank his athletic supporter over his shorts. "No — nothin' on *underneath* the jockstrap."

Then the Academy takes custody of your actual skin. "If you have," the sergeant booms, "any tattoo, brand or body piercing, regardless of whether it is visible while wearing a uniform, you must declare it at this time to the registration desk at my rear." A rising firstie — Josh Reeves, shaved head dusted with a five o'clock shadow — operates the digital camera and Dell laptop computer. "What does that say?" Reeves asks, pencil pointed at a candidate's shoulder.

"'John 15:13.'"

"OK, what does the verse mean to you?"

"For me? It's about friendship and dying, sir. Dying for something greater than yourself."

The next candidate steps up. "Leazer, sir."

"All right — Leazer, David R. Hold up your arms, I gotta see it. Any meaning to those symbols?"

"Reverence, Honor, Patience."

"Is that Japanese characters?"

"Chinese, sir."

"OK, next, step up. What does that word mean?"

"That's my dad's nickname for me when I was a little kid, sir."

"His nickname for you? *Paws?* OK. Next, get up here, candidate Pascarelli. Left shoulder blade — what does that mean?"

"That's a Metallica logo, sir."

"What does it mean?"

"They're a music group, sir."

"Thanks a lot. Even though I may not look it, I know what *Metallica* is. What does it mean to you?"

"Metallica, sir."

"OK, next."

During a lull, Reeves explains the rationale behind skin inspections. "I don't know if you're aware of what happened at Eighty-second Airborne a few years ago. White supremacist stuff. That's what we're looking for. Take the Confederate flag — all right, that's a tough one. It's southern pride, so it's not necessarily indicating anything. We're looking for more direct: 'Supreme White People' — that'd be bad. German eagle with a slogan under it. 'AB' means the Aryan Brotherhood — that'd be a dead giveaway. Also we're checkin' for gang symbols. They always go on the knuckles. Anything that shows below the hands or above the neck in a class-B uniform is a no-go. Only thing I've seen today that's a semblance of bad said 'Men of Ruin.' Not sure what it meant. Next. What is that? Gotta show me."

"It's a bar code, sir."

"It's a *bar code?* For what?"

"Don't know sir. It's just a bar code."

"What about the numbers? It's your birthday? OK, that's the coolest one yet. Sergeant, why don't you try running the Scantron over this tattoo?"

"I see people's *drawers* being left behind in here!" the sergeant shouts. "Pick — up — your trash. Do *not* leave your underwear behind in my room!"

Then the candidates are marched to the next station, a wide classroom cleared of desks; doctors and nurses wait in white medical coats as the Army takes charge of your body. "Good morning," the doctor says. "This is the medical station. First thing you're gonna do, if you wear glasses or contacts, is walk right across the hall to optometry; they have your new glasses there. Second stop you need to make is the pharmacy. We need to see all prescription and over-the-counter medications you may have brought. Then you're gonna proceed down the hall and take your oath."

The Army-issue spectacles are bulky Clark Kents. The official military acronym is big-shouldered and ragging at once: TEDs, tactical eye devices. Candidates hit the pharmacy and turn over their meds. For a lot of women, this means pulling out saucer-shaped birth-control holders — no room for privacy or embarrassment. For the medics, the pills suggest these candidates may need further checking.

"You keep these and finish these during basic training," the nurses say. The girls blink. "When you get down to your last two, you come see me for more. When did you get your last ob-gyn exam? Don't let yourself run out of this stuff. When was the last time you had your blood tested?" Candidates surrender fistfuls of painkillers, muscle builders, accident menders, placebos, bad-luck tonics and more — the medicine cabinet spells parents wouldn't send you off without. Neosporin, Sting-Ease, Bengay. There's a heavy emphasis on remedies for the foot, Beast Barracks' most sorely tested body part: Aftin, Actin, Tinactin, Gold Bond Medicated Powder, Johnson's Foot Soap ("soaks away misery"). Spectrum multivitamins, Mega Man Dietary Supplement, One-a-Day Plus Iron, Flintstones Chewables. "Somebody's got Flintstones?" a major calls out, rattling the bottle. "This is great. Keep taking those Flintstones, they're delicious."

And now you're ready to become a new cadet. Candidates line the hallway before the classroom where they will take their oath. Identical T-shirts and shorts (the air fills with the inky, just-off-the-shelf smell of new clothing), and whole klatches of kids wearing matching TEDs like a commando chess squad. They wait at the vague version of attention you pick up from the movies, take deep breaths before entering the room. For most candidates, this will be the first promise they've ever made to their country.

Captain Lisa Davis, a cheerful red-headed JAG attorney, hands out ballpoint pens from a box as forty candidates occupy desks and pore over the cadet oath. One tall kid, whose folks I'd bet are lawyers, marks small checks beside each clause on the page. This is the one moment of R-Day when candidates won't be rushed. ("It's their contract," Davis later explains, "and they're so young. We give 'em all the time they need.") Then Davis clears her throat and stands. "OK," she says, "I want to make sure everyone understands what they're getting themselves into by signing off on this." Her voice is solemn without being scary, like a driver's ed instructor pointing out ice on the road. "What the oath means, um, is that you agree to protect the Constitution, and you agree to be loyal to the United States and its sovereignty. That you will serve and defend your country, and you agree to follow your officers. Anybody have any idea what the UCMJ is? The military has its own special set of laws called the Uniform Code of Military Justice; they apply to you in or out of uniform, on or off duty, anywhere in the world. You fly to Florida for spring break, something goes wrong down there, they can court-martial you up here." The candidates' eyes widen, Adam's apples bob. "OK. Any questions on your cadet oath?"

The legalistic-minded kid raises his hand. "Ma'am, isn't the term of service like *five* years? Because here it says . . ."

"OK, good question. Five years of active-duty obligation, plus three years reserves, so the oath says eight years."

The hand comes up again. "Ma'am, as far as the eight years goes, is time served here —"

A black candidate goes for the laugh: "Man, we just got here — what's your rush?"

Davis taps the desk. "OK. By signing this contract you are stating that you are unmarried, do not have custody of a child, and that you have read, understand and will abide by the Statement of Policies. Anybody have any questions on what I just said? OK." She stands up straight. "Next thing we're gonna do is swear you all into the Army. Raise your right hands."

This is the first Army song the candidates sing together. The male voices drop low and serious, females lift solemn and high. They speak of stirring things — true allegiance and fealty, the Constitution. It's the most they've said since leaving the bleachers. "OK, congratulations, you're all in. Good luck. Make sure to leave both signed copies of your contract at the back of the room." An immense scratching noise as forty new cadets sign their names. The cadre has returned. "New cadets, on your feet. Proceed to the door front to rear, move out!"

Now the Army absorbs your vital statistics — data you had no hand in creating that nonetheless add up to you. Eye color, hair color, Social Security number, home telephone and address.

"Gary? Your father's name is Robert?"

"Yes, ma'am."

"And your mother's name is . . . ?"

"Karen."

"And you reside at Twenty-two Elm Street, in Sullimac, New York?"

"That's my father — my mother and I are at a different address."

The hometowns they recite are mostly *near* better-known places. "It's just south of Tacoma . . . About twenty miles from Tulsa . . . You drive half an hour past Bakersfield." Underdog towns with scenic names, the shy towns from the back of the class. "Zephyr Hills, Florida," "Forest City, North Carolina," "Grand Island, Nebraska," "Four Corners, New Mexico," "Friendsville, Maryland," "Little Falls, New Jersey," "Marshfield, Massachusetts," "Roswell, New Mexico." ("It *is* a very strange place, ma'am.")

New cadets now wear two cardboard tags, on strings pinned below the waistband of their shorts. One is identification; the second has a row of boxes, to be checked off after the completion of each R-Day task — uniform-fitting, barbershop, lunch. When cadre members need to see how far you've traveled down the line, they simply lift your tag. "Did I instruct you to move, new cadet? Face my wall. All right, at this time I'll ask if anybody needs to go use the latrine." Nobody says a word in the men's room. Washing up, they steal dire glances at themselves, not certain what face they'll find in the mirror.

Then the Army takes your hair. The cadet barbershop is a lazy wind from home, the day's most hospitable sight. Top 40 tunes from the radio, flowers in water, steel thermoses with the afternoon's slug of coffee, smiling civilian women in blue smocks. Every few minutes the guy working the push broom sweeps away what looks like a whole discarded wig. (The barbers place bets on the R-Day yield. Last year's take was 422 ounces.) The chatty barber, what everybody hates, now seems an oasis of civility. "How you feeling?" the barbers ask. "I hope nobody's hassled you too bad yet." "Was it OK saying goodbye to your mom and dad?" "You've got scratches all over your neck — were you in a catfight or something?" Scars, nicks and dents bloom beneath the razors. "See, I bet you didn't even know you had this." Barbers pat the heads. "This head has never seen the light of day before, so it's going to be very sensitive, you're probably gonna want to find some sunscreen." "We feel bad doin' this," they confide. "You come in here with your own identity, and you walk out all uniform."

Now you're shorn of everything. You look, act, dress like everyone beside you, for maybe the first time in your life. In five hours, West Point has reduced you to just the meat your parents made, topped by its frenetic, calculating brain. The cadre marches the new cadets out to Central Area — an open square, gray buildings staring down. An awful sound rises from the margins. It's the Cadets in the Red Sash. New cadets stiffen at the noise.

The cadre introduces them to the basics of the Army body language: how to stand, how to listen, how to respond with the grammar of obedience. "New cadets, I will now teach you the proper position of attention. It's easy if you remember one simple principle — push up at the top of your head." "New cadets, this is the proper salute. Notice I keep my arm parallel to the ground, hand like a knife edge. Notice, I am not showing you my palm — no one wants to see the palm of your *hand*, new cadets." "Your title is New Cadet Doe, and you will always refer to yourself as New Cadet Doe. If you are addressed or corrected, you will respond in a crisp, direct, unequivocal manner. I will now teach you how to report to the Cadet in the Red Sash."

The new cadets have dreaded it all day. You can't move on till you report successfully, no matter how many attempts you must make. Local citizens actually turn out to watch the red sash cadets snarling, clicking and growling. One yells, "You are not *running the show* anymore, new cadet!" The new cadets in formation triple blink, trying not to look.

"You will come up to Cadet in the Red Sash's line," the cadre instructs. "Stand at the position of attention, render the proper salute. Say 'Sir, New Cadet Doe reports to the Cadet in the Red Sash for the first time as ordered.' You will listen to what the Cadet in the Red Sash has to say — you will *do* what he has to say. Then you will render the proper hand salute, say 'No retreat, sir,' and move out. At this time do you have any questions, new cadets?"

"Yes sir. Can you please repeat that phrase again?"

"You should have been listening the first time, new cadet. New cadets, pick up your barracks bags. You will now stand behind the first line of tape." They wait in lines eight deep, to report to the Cadet in the Red Sash. Four stand in a row, sashes knotted at the waist, voices coming quick and harsh like spitting-mad auctioneers. Your stomach goes heavy, and then the shoulders in front of you clear away and the red sash fills your eyes.

"Step up to the line not over the line or behind the line. New cadet, step up to my line!"

"Sir, New Cadet Whaley —"

"New cadet, look where you're standing. I told you step up to my line, understand? Try it again."

"Sir, New Cadet Whaley —"

"You are *still* not up to my line. Now drop your bag, new cadet. New cadet I'm telling you to *drop your bag*. Now, are you going to salute me? Are you going to report to me? Get to the back of my line, think about what you've gotta do." Whaley hurries away.

"New cadet, step up to the line!"

"Sir, New Cadet Doe reporting to the Cadet in the Red Sash as ordered."

"Are you saying your last name is *Doe*?"

"No sir, my name is —"

"Drop your salute. Get to the back of the line. New cadet, step to the line!"

"Sir, New Cadet Klinker reporting to the Cadet in the Red Sash for the first time as ordered, sir."

"Drop your salute. You will only say 'sir' at the beginning of the sentence. This is not the Marine Corps, this is the Army, we do not make sir sandwiches. Start over!"

"Sir, New Cadet Klinker reports to the . . . Red Sash . . ."

"Are you gonna make a correction, new cadet?"

"Sir, New Cadet Klinker reports in to the Red Sash for the first time as ordered, sir!" Another sir sandwich; there's an exchange of frowns.

"New cadet, step up to the line!"

Cadets in the Red Sash know exactly where the kids' soft spots are — they're reaching back to their own R-Days, recycling the words they feared most. "You're in my world now — do you understand? You are not at home with mommy. You don't like this, you can go back with mommy right now. Quit lickin' your lips! Pay attention to detail, that'll save somebody's life one day!"

"I'll go over it *one more time*. 'Sir, New Cadet Doe reports to the Cadet in the Red Sash for the first time as ordered.' Do you understand? Get that show of emotion off your face, new cadet. Nobody cares if you're frustrated. Do it right."

"Sir, New Cadet Morrow reports for the first time as ordered!"

"New cadet, I just *told* you *two* times. You have three seconds to pick up your bag and move out to the back of my line. New cadet, step up to the line!"

"Sir, New Cadet Macleod reporting to the Cadet in the . . . in the Red Sash . . . for the first time . . . as ordered . . . May I make a correction?"

"'May I make a correction' — you gonna put a 'sir' on that?"

"Sir, may I make a correction?"

"Yes!"

"Cadet Macleod — New Cadet —"

"Drop your salute."

"May I make a correction, sir?" Silence. "Sir, may I make a correction?"

"One more thing: the proper format is 'New Cadet Macleod *reports*,' not *reporting*. Y'understand?"

"Sir" — his tongue tangles up — "Neeew Cadet Macleod reporting —"

"Wait. Are you a *neeew* cadet or are you a new cadet?"

"*New* cadet. Sir, Cadet Macleod reporting —"

"Drop your salute. So you're already a *cadet* now? Guess what — you're on R-Day, that's *day one*. You've got six more weeks before you're a cadet. Do you understand?"

"Yes."

"Gonna put a 'sir' on that? Get it right!"

"Sir, New Cadet — New Cadet — reporting —" It's the last thing to go: he has forgotten his own name.

"New cadet, step up to the line!"

"Sir, New Cadet Jefferey reports — to the cadet first sergeant as ordered. Excuse me —"

"Drop your salute! Is 'Excuse me' one of your four responses? What are your four responses, new cadet?"

"Yes sir, no sir, no excuse sir, sir I do not understand."

"I don't wanna see you rolling your eyes — I don't *care* if you're shaken up. Maintain your military discipline at all times. Do you understand?"

"Sir, New Cadet Jefferey Jay reports in to the Cadet in the Red Sash for the first time as ordered."

"Did you just say your first name? Are we *friends* now, new cadet?"

"My first name is not Jefferey, sir. My last name is Jefferey."

"Is *that* one of your four responses?"

"No excuse, sir."

"You will speak when spoken to, new cadet. Drop your salute. Do it *right*."

"Sir, New Cadet Jefferey reports in to the Cadet in the Red Sash as order —"

"Reports *to*. Do it over, you've got *one* more chance."

A deep breath — and suddenly it's just you, conducting your first Academy conversation. "Sir, New Cadet Jefferey reports to the Cadet in the Red Sash for the first time as ordered."

"Drop your salute. New cadet, you are now a member of Charlie Company, Cadet Basic Training regiment, the *best* company in CBT. As a member of Charlie Company, the highest standards will be expected of you at all times. What's that? Is that a show of emotion on your face, new cadet? Are you *smiling*?"

Jefferey salutes. "No retreat, sir."

"No surrender."

The new cadets report to barracks, change into their first West Point uniform, spend the afternoon absorbing drill language at a Berlitz pace: parade rest, present arms, about face, left face, dress right dress. At 1800, when twelve hundred new cadets march across the Plain for the oath ceremony, there's no way to tell they woke up this morning as civilians.

Going Commando

For the new cadets, Beast is a chance to discover whether they've got the stuff for the Army; for the upperclassmen, Beast is a shot at seeing if they can lead. Cows like Huck Finn get the nod as Beast squad leaders (ten new cadets to a squad) and platoon leaders (four squads to a platoon). First they teach the Army housekeeping: polish brass, prepare shoes (Huck hosts shoe-shining parties: warm the official low-quarter shoes with a lighter, this opens up the pores, lets the Kiwi sink in), hospital-corner beds. Then they charge ahead to advanced entries from the Army vocabulary: hold a rifle, march on post, march on the road, maintain your honor.

Then cadre lift their eyes to the ephemeral; they want to have new cadets loving the place fast. Stroll the post on a warm July night and you'll hear platoon leaders on the Plain lecturing skinny, nervous new cadets, waving their hands toward Gothic towers, glowing windows, the stars. "You might not like it right now. But it'll click on you. It *clicks*. What some civilians say is antiquated, we call that tradition right here. I could live at this place forever." The new cadets swallow eagerly. Their PL's voice is the only human sound among crickets, breezes, a jet plane. The PL sighs. "That's about all I got for y'all. I just wanted to bring you all out when it was dark, but not so dark that you couldn't see. And just have you look."

For Huck Finn, Beast is practical as could be, it's his make-or-break time. He told Super-V — and got Vermeesch's stamp for the plan — that based on how things panned out with squad-leading, he would decide to leave or stay. Vermeesch is like a man in a hospital waiting room, full of hope and anxiety. "When I first met him, I thought, 'Of all the cadets in the company, this guy is full of so much tremendous raw potential. If he makes it to being a lieutenant, his soldiers are going to just love him.'" Vermeesch shrugs. "I've been trying to convince him to stick around."

The new cadets have more immediate concerns. "We're hungry all the time," they say, "have you got any food on you?" "I just don't understand," they grouse, walking out of the practice gas chamber site, "why you would purposely subject yourself to breathing in a potentially hazardous gas, just to prove to yourself that it's not *that* bad." You hear many complaints on the base question of underwear. "They only issue tightie-whities, not boxers. A lot of people are going commando — no underwear." "There's no *way* I'm wearing it," another guy says. "This is a wet climate. You could get like jungle rot. I got it on the three-mile road march." I pop by a complaint session with Huck's squad. What emerges is Beast poetry.

> *It's better than we expected.*
> *What are you talking about? This is horrible.*
> *I miss TV.*
> *Everyone misses TV.*
> *We all miss back home.*
> People *have* lost *their* minds.
> *Nobody's sleeping.*
> *I can't remember why I came here.*
> *I came for the challenge.*
> *Society doesn't have a moral-ethical background anymore. People are so self-centered and materialistic.*
> *I don't know, that's like preachy. I mean, we're not at war with the country.*
> *I'm here because I need discipline. Because if I was at a regular college, I would never go to class, I'd just party.*
> *Finn is doing great.*
> *He's a jerk.*
> *No, he's awesome.*
> *He's the best squad leader.*

Huck is up at dawn and planning after midnight while the squad dreams. He shaves every morning, with a touch-up in the afternoon — he's even shaved his head. For motivation — it becomes his squad's mascot — he's lugging a fifty-pound tank round everywhere he goes. His own motivation comes from someplace inside, someplace deep: "I just love those little fuckers," he says. "It makes me wanna work for 'em." The new cadets blink at Huck with those big, know-nothing eyes — how could he show them any way to act but the right one? First week, he pulls everyone out of bed, gathers them into one room ("2330 during basic training, if I got caught, boy, that woulda been my *ass*") and makes them a simple proposition. "All right," he says, "everybody take a seat — or stand — I don't care what the fuck you do." The squad is doing good things; no doubt about it, they're a damn fine squad. "But lemme put it to you this way: Why the hell don't we just decide right now to be the best fuckin' squad around?"

Toward the end of Huck's three-week turn as squad leader, the company moves out for emergency medical training. The site is in the woods above the cadet chapel. Huck's squad tromps past motivational signs planted by the trailside, stir-the-heart words in blocky Army font: *Candor. Values. Duty. Devotion. Courage. Strive. Drive On. Heart. Unity. Country.* They form up in a dusty clearing, Finn leads them in the pre-exercise throat-clearing, the verbal incentive check and scream-off.

"How you feeling, Second Squad?"

The yell leaps back, cadets feeling their way with a surprising muscle, the boot-shaking power of the massed human voice: *Motivated-motivated, downright motivated! You-check-us-out! You-check-us-out! You-check-us-out! Hooooop!*

It's impossible to see any R-Day left in them. "How motivated?"

Fired up! Fired up! Hoooh-hahh! I wanna KILL somebody!

They charge down what are called lanes, over an obstacle course staffed by the Army Medical Corps. Adult NCOs portray gruesome battlefield casualties, wilting and moaning around convincingly gory pretend injuries. "My arm! Oh my stars and whiskers, I'm hit in my arm!" (One of the sergeants carries around a big wooden Hollywood makeup kit: masks and prosthetics. *Gunshot Wound, Chest. Atomic Burn, Face. Compound Facture of the Femur. Leg Amputation. Protruding Intestines, Stomach. Face in Shock.*) The cadets scurry into the field with first aid. ("Spread out! One grenade could take out every last one of y'all!") One sergeant lies groaning under a tree. "Ow, ow, ow. My leg. My *right* leh-yug." The new cadets kneel, bring out splints and tape. "No, my *other* right leg." "No apologizing on the battlefield, new cadet," the casualty says. "Say 'sorry' on the battlefield, it was too late, huah?"

At the finish, Huck's squad receives the maximum score for the first-aid training.

It's the summer of drops at Beast Barracks. No one knows why for sure; it's a mystery to higher, a shame to the cadre, a distress for the TACs. By the halfway point, more new cadets have tossed in the West Point towel than during nearly the entire course of last year's Beast. (The resignees depart on shuttle vans with some self-hating glares and smiles. One explains to me, "I was like — I *kinda* wanted to come here. But I let a lot of other stuff cloud my thinking: everybody was so amazed — *West Point* — all the friends asked to come and see the little plaque. But heh-heh, it's a lot easier to say it than to do it. The hardest stuff was where they'd be like: 'Are you guys *excited?* Are you ready to come be Army professionals?' And then you gotta pretend to be excited." The explanation most TACs eventually lead with on the resignation form is "Life Goals Not Compatible with Military.")

At the official halfway mark — what's called Change of Detail — Huck's company takes the flag for best in Beast, and Huck walks off with Best Squad Leader. He comes away with a Finn-style Successory. "I guess what I learned as a *leader* is, if you try your hardest, those little fuckers are gonna do their best too." He's entering the fall with some square-jawed resolve. "I'm gonna stay outta trouble from now on," he says. "I don't want to let Captain Vermeesch down." But he's driven by more than devotion to military ideals. "I wanna keep my position for football."

A few weeks later, Huck crosses the Plain, marching some new cadet football players to the stadium; by coincidence, he passes his old squad. "And I was missin' 'em real bad right then, you know? I wanted to be back around 'em all again. And one of the kids sees me, he gives me the company greeting: 'Go Wolfpack, Sergeant Finn!' And the whole squad just erupted, everybody screaming. I almost started crying right there. That's probably a better feeling than I ever got playin' a football game."

The Braves

Beast is split into two details, which gives a new roster of upperclassmen their swing at command: George Rash is now on deck. The new cadets have been warmed up for him. They're already speaking West Point dialect. They *pass off* Knowledge, they *sham out* of duties. ("I wasn't shamming — I was at sick call.") They've *dropped* for push-ups. They've discovered that the secret acronym for TEDs is BCGs — birth control glasses (because you have no chance, cadets believe, of getting laid while wearing them). And they've learned why *ass* is the most popular slang term at West Point. The ass is the unprotected flank, the one important body terrain you can't even see — if you get shot at, you can always duck your head, you can jerk your arms and legs, but what can you do about your ass? At West Point, the ass is on the chopping block; it's either getting *ripped* or it's getting *sunshine piped up it.* There's *chewed* ass and, if you have quick enough footwork, *covered* ass. Your ass gets *hazed,* if you're taken out for some really exhausting PT it's *smoked,* if you move too slow you get *a boot put to it,* on a bad day you're *assed up* or have *gotten the ass.* All this in addition to the civilian usages, which still apply. Vermeesch reminds his Beast chain of command to send their new cadets to parade rest during room inspections, "because — I mean, think about it — nobody likes to stand at attention for some asshole who's going through their stuff. So my advice to you would be, do not be that asshole."

John Vermeesch in the field is a changed man. He's an infantryman, a field guy; West Point offices are not his natural habitat. He's like something domesticated sprung from captivity, one lean crackle of energy. He prowls the ranks of a drizzly road march, head snaking and bobbing, sniffing out sore spots and the wobble of surrender. A new cadet starts to crumple under her thirty-pound ruck. Vermeesch paces in front, gives her a tow on his ruck straps. After a mandatory ten-minute break, he plants his ruck on the gravel by his toes, leans forward, then saddles up in the Infantry style: the pack goes trapezing up and over his shoulders until it bangs down hard against his back.

It's been a wet summer, the smell of mud as pungent as in a greenhouse. (The new cadets have picked up the traditional Army salute to poor weather: "If it ain't raining, we ain't training.") After a march, while the cadets flick muck off their boots, and some Bible studiers kick back for a discussion of the Scripture — "you open up Ezekiel, start reading about the dragons, that stuff is *deep*" — Vermeesch talks about the essence of officership. In the field he's more direct, as if his argument is up and patrolling by his side.

And as much as the Academy talks values, Vermeesch knows that officership is half physical: what the body says is just as important as any words. The brain can overpromise, say "I'll be there at 0530, count on it," and then not show up; the body is either there or it isn't. "Just like this road march," Vermeesch says, "you can either choose to quit or you can choose to drive on. In this profession, the end state is taking care of your soldiers. Being able to overcome whatever pain or discomfort you're feeling — and they have to know you'll do it — in order to not let 'em down." Vermeesch isn't sure that's a drive George Rash could understand. "And I question whether he has the capacity to ever learn that, which is a hard thing to say."

It's 1930 and breezeless, evening bats make sorties among the treetops. Through a tangle of foliage and past a valley, you can make out the soft roof lights and car parks of Woodbury Commons outlet mall. A cadre member has leaned her canteen with a cake of soap on the fender of a Humvee; new cadets use them to wash up for chow. Vermeesch takes in the two competing views, rough-and-ready military versus the consumer glow. If George doesn't succeed this summer, Vermeesch would like to see him walk down into that valley. "He has to get this figured out in the next month," Vermeesch says. Cow Commitment is four weeks away. "I think being a squad leader will be exceptionally good for him. He's gonna be forced to face all his weaknesses, lead from the front. And my hope is, either George steps up and is able do it. Or if he can't, I hope that he recognizes it for *himself*. And takes appropriate measures." Vermeesch's voice croaks, the hard concepts jamming his throat: soldiers, leadership, quitting.

George knows the stakes. "If I fail this summer," he explains, "I could get kicked out of the Academy. Or, if not kicked out, definitely go through a *looot* of remediation. But I'd have to screw up pretty badly."

Rash is lacing his boots for Change of Detail. Beast II is the toe cruncher, the boot splitter, a grudge match between head and foot. Beast I features the three-mile, five-mile, six-mile road marches, the shallow end of the pool. In Beast II the marches turn serious: six-mile, eight-mile, twelve-mile, fifteen-mile. "Those last two are gonna be ugly," George predicts. When he was a new cadet, road marches were charted in foot injuries; this year he's taking preventive measures. "It's hard to find the really good socks," he says. "Good socks help. What the medics actually suggest is, not only powder the feet, which I do, but also wear knee-high pantyhose. *Then* the thick wool socks over those, then boots."

George can't believe he's back at Beast; he's excited, spirits high.

"Two years ago, I was in *their* position. And now here I am in charge of 'em. Go figure. Half of me is saying just, My God. And the other half is saying, *Thank* God, two years are done, only two more to go." What's he discovered? Rash shakes his head. "That a human can learn to put up with practically anything. Anything, given enough time, becomes tolerable." He brightens. "And I had a *looot* of friends, they carried me through." When George says a happy thing like this, you try not to think of Steve Ruggerio.

George has decided to adopt an easygoing leadership style. Three quick rules: "Do what you're supposed to do. Do it when you're supposed to. And . . . don't piss people off too bad. Past that I don't really care." It's a mutual non-aggression pact between leader and led. He's not going to put on the huah act. (This is part of George's odd integrity: he won't pretend to be something he's not; in the whole time I know him, I never hear him utter the word *huah*.) "If you fuck up, I'll have to be a hardass — and I don't wanna be a hardass, so don't fuck up."

And then the night arrives, Change of Detail; new cadets lined against the walls, the new cadre throwing a yelling festival in the corridors. "What are you gonna *do* when you're firing a live round?" someone shouts — not to the new cadet getting corrected, but to the girl by his side. "You gotta think for you *and* for the guy next to you!" George is leading Fourth Squad, Third Platoon, Company B — Bravo Company. (To keep things clear over the radio, the military adopted the phonetic alphabet: A is Alpha, B is Bravo, C is Charlie, so on through Zulu.) Bravo Company's nickname is the Braves. "Before we went away for leave," explains Captain Chris Engen, Bravo Company's summer TAC, "we had arranged to be the Bulls — the Raging Bulls. But Colonel Adamczyk, the BTO, wanted to ensure that the name sent the right message and didn't exclude people. And when you think about it: Bulls . . . not inclusive, there's a male connotation." Engen chuckles ruefully. "When the cadets found out, they said, 'Well, what about Braves? Braves is a male kinda thing too.' And finally you've gotta say, 'Look, just follow the order.'"

Upperclassmen stare down freshly shorn new cadets during the first day of their West Point careers. For most cadets, this is the worst day they'll experience at the Academy.

Cadet Chrissi Cicerelle, in BDUs, or battle dress uniform, developing her "violence propensity."

Major Jim DeMoss of Company G-4 inspects
a lunch formation. Cadet Eliel Pimentel stands
at attention at right.

Washington Mess Hall, where four thousand cadets eat at once. The mural
depicts General George Washington's military exploits.

The Goodfellas, in the class-B uniforms they'll wear in the Army. Left to right: cadets Don "Whitey" Herzog, Brian "Suppy" Supko, John Mini, and Antonio "Iggy" Ignacio.

Cadet George Rash during his yuk, or sophomore, year. A name tape is affixed to his bed frame, polished shoes are arranged underneath.

Cadets Jake Bergman, standing, and Trent Powell in their home away from home, the Arvin Gym weight room.

Colonel Joseph W. Adamczyk, nicknamed "Skeletor" by cadets, in an official portrait. As the brigade tactical officer, he's in charge of assuring that the Academy's exacting standards of dress and behavior are enforced.

Lieutenant Colonel Hank Keirsey (then a major) in Iraq, Operation Desert Storm, 1991. Charged with instilling in cadets the skills and attitudes they'll need as warriors, he is the embodiment of "huah."

Cow, or junior, Mike Ferlazzo salutes in his as-for-class uniform.

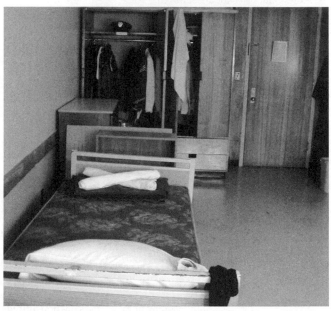

An exceptionally tidy West Point room.

Every morning at 0655, rain or shine (or darkness), the entire corps of cadets gathers on North Area for breakfast formation.

Marching into Washington Hall after lunch formation on North Area, cadets wear their foul-weather gear.

Major John Vermeesch at his promotion ceremony. His father and his wife, Lynsey, pin his new rank insignia on his shoulders.

Vermeesch, in his element, at Beast, the intensive six-week training new cadets endure before they begin their plebe year.

George Rash (front row, left) listens to instructions in Gillis Field House before his final two-mile run.

The Corporation: Eliel Pimentel (holding phone), Matthew Kilgore (checked shirt), Rob Anders (facing camera), Kenneth Wainwright (holding camera).

Eliel Pimentel works the grill at a G-4 barbecue. Rob Anders
watches him.

Cadets Ryan Southerland and Betty Simbert,
meeting away from their computers, in Ike Hall
for Branch Night, 2001.

Ryan Southerland, above the crowd, at the Army-Navy game.

The hours. Cadets march for five or more hours at a time, back and forth across Central Area, as punishment for various infractions.

Captain Rafael Paredes greets cadets at hours formation on Central Area. Cadet Jasmine Rose stands at right, Rob Anders on her left.

Cadet Huck Finn—"doing what I do best"—walking hours on the Area.

Huck Finn (center) rallies G-4's team before the last event of Sandhurst, a grueling contest of soldier skills, from marksmanship to rappelling down a cliff.

Lieutenant Whitey Herzog in Kosovo, with schoolchildren.

Lieutenants Iggy Ignacio and Whitey Herzog, burning a few cigarettes in Watertown, New York. Both sport fresh high-and-tight haircuts.

George Rash tries on the class-B uniform he will wear if he becomes a lieutenant. Captain Paredes, in BDUs, is checking the fit, while Kenneth Wainwright waits his turn in the uniform soldiers wear at black-tie functions.

Thayer Walk, twilight.

Ryan Southerland collects money for the Goat, the lowest-ranking cadet, who receives a dollar from each of his one thousand classmates on graduation day.

Beast II Squad Leader

For the first ten days, George is a terrific squad leader. Beast II, when you're not road marching, is skills training: seven days after Change of Detail, the 132 members of Bravo Company camp in two-person tents near the Basic Rifle Marksmanship range. It's a rainy, cool night. (The cadets have now mastered a second weather joke: "It's not rain, it's liquid sunshine.") You toss a blanket over the wet grass, the porous canvas tent admits a sheen of moisture (like the beads on a beer can) so it's not like sleeping under a drizzle, it's like sleeping in the clouds. Rest comes like airplane sleep, an act of logy will. At 0430 the camp wakes up, and I have an encounter that shows me how it feels to be a new cadet at Beast. I'm using a Maglite to find my other boot when Cadet First Sergeant Ryan Southerland raps the outside of my tent: "No *white light*, new cadet." I feel: embarrassed, confused, eager, put upon, tired, excited. A shock and a comfort: there are rules for everything.

Outside, in the morning gray, the tents look like a herd of animal skins, wrinkly and mysterious. Betty Simbert, a small, energetic black junior from Miami, is trying to shout her squad into action. "Let's *go* First Squad! Bring those tents down!" (Betty, who's a cheerleader, makes most orders sound like advanced pep; she's the best cadence caller in Bravo Company, it ticks her off when Southerland swipes her chants.) Matthew "Mac" MacSweeney — a cow from Westchester, New York, with the boozy good humor of a friar — spent the night rubbing his eyes in the rain: fireguard duty. While the new cadets clink out their tent poles and fold the canvas, he complains to Simbert with the mix of discomfort and boast that comprises an Army gripe. "I sat outside and froze my ass off. I'm still wearing wet BDUs. Four in the morning, in just half an hour, we stopped forty new cadets going to the latrine. No rifle and no Kevlar." The rule is, any time you venture outside, you must be ready for an assault; Kevlar is the Army nickname for your helmet, which is made of Kevlar and can stop a bullet. "No battle buddies either. A battle buddy is there because he or she is supposed to hold your rifle — they're not allowed to take 'em inside the latrine. Four years ago, some kid dropped his rifle down the latrine. And, uh, he ended up having to climb in after it."

Betty makes a face: "*So* harsh."

The cadet commander of Bravo is a muscly, thick-faced kid confusingly named Chuck Sargent — so his title this summer is Cadet Captain Sargent, like a form-letter misprint. He pulled fireguard detail with Mac — a safety duty that's usually a new-cadet job — so the kids could be better rested for marksmanship qualification this morning; he's stumbling around, annoyed and sleepless like a frustrated mom. "You do that for these guys, and they can't follow the simplest rules. One kid's latrine excuse was he had to go *really* bad."

When you wake up in the field, you clean your room so effectively it's not there anymore. Within ten minutes, the tents disappear into rucks, and there's a line of new cadets in front of the latrine shack. The latrines contain one of the Army's most intimidating field traditions: toilet seats side by side, like benches on mass transit. The new cadets conquer this design flaw by going in at a modest one at a time. (The urinal is just a long canted sink with a drain at one end and no faucet — you're the faucet.)

First Sergeant Ryan Southerland is Bravo's enforcer, the cadet with the Keirsey assignment of keeping you fired up; under an overhang, he motivates the new cadets by reading Vietnam-era Medal of Honor citations he dug up on the Web.

"This lieutenant," he declaims stonily, "did some great work in rain much harder than this. 'Realizing his platoon could not hold very long, and seeing *four* enemy soldiers moving into his position, First Lieutenant Joseph Marm moved quickly under heavy fire and annihilated all four. *Then,* seeing that his platoon was receiving intense fire from a field machine gun, he deliberately exposed himself to draw its fire, thus locating its position . . .'" It builds to the standard Army close, words slotting into place, combat's panic and quick breaths compressed into a formula of achievement. "'First Lieutenant Marm's *gallantry* on the battlefield, and his extraordinary *bravery* at the risk of his life, are in the highest tradition of the U.S. Army, and reflect great credit upon himself and the armed forces of his country.'"

Southerland fixes his moody eyes on the mass of new cadets. "Rain doesn't matter. Fatigue doesn't matter. Exhaustion doesn't matter. Do the mission." *Huah.*

The company breakfasts under another overhang, new cadets joking and yawning in small clusters. Army order of precedence dictates that the highest rank dines last; only after your troops are fed can you think about chow. Cadet Captain Sargent follows Southerland through the line, Captain Engen piles up his tray in the rear. The meal is chunky, greasy-smelling stuff that packs the belly like a ruck. Egg patties, sausage patties, hash browns, biscuits, orange slices of American cheese (it's no surprise the great heyday of fast food came after World War II GIs shipped home; pre-cooked foods under keep-warm lights is Army dogma).

Chris Engen is a tanker. His blond head is as smooth as a tank round. His smile trains on you slowly, as though it's revolving on treads. Engen has been watching George Rash improve. "He's going pretty good," Engen grins. "He's confident, I'm seeing that confidence increase, now that he's been doin' it a few days."

By next night, Rash's leadership is growing even stronger. He taught Squad Tactical Training, leading his unit through a combat simulation. He ran it like the playbook — split them into two teams, sent one flanking through the woods, pushed the other one forward in small bounds to draw fire. In the end, Rash's squad took out four soldiers and gained the objective, the graders paying his work the highest Army compliment, "Outstanding." George walked downhill looking thrilled. "That was gut-wrenching," George says, "and it was exhilarating." Engen smiles after him. "His cadets are very motivated. He's doin' a good job."

This evening, Bravo Company is spending the night camped in the foggy, muddy grasses of Lake Frederick. Dinner's over — lines for latrines are at post-movie levels — and the air is full of the kind of spicy ocean smells that can make you forget what season it is. Ryan Southerland leads me over the squelchy mud to George's squad. Southerland hails from Norman, Oklahoma, with a solid plains build. He's muscular and heavy-browed, parents divorced, mom a teacher, dad a farmer who wanted to paint. "So my middle name is O'Keeffe," Southerland says. "After the painter, Georgia O'Keeffe. I use her paintings as computer wallpaper, always have. *From the Plains, The Lawrence Tree, From the Faraway Nearby.*" It's probably the last thing Georgia O'Keeffe even expected, to have a measured career assessment delivered from a set of BDUs. "Her early collection, all the cityscapes and everything — the more industrial, mechanical sort of canvases — they get a little lost in the shuffle. But they're beautiful."

Southerland has the kind of bone-deep huah that makes most rules seem like surface stuff, a tie you put on for company. "Are you familiar with Army values cards?" he asks. "They call it a leadership card, a credit card everybody's supposed to carry around with values on it, and then you get another one to wear with your dog tags around your neck." Southerland won't touch it. "That's not how I operate. I don't carry my values on my neck. It's how you act, not what you carry in your pocket."

George is walking the narrow avenue between tents. "I'll be glad to be back in garrison," he says. "Hot showers." A new cadet in another squad misplaced a rifle today — a hasty search, an angry TAC lecture, this is the kind of mistake terrorists just *lurk* for — so George is performing a squad weapons check. The new cadets treat him simply as a leader. "Make it run, Sergeant," they say, after he issues orders. He spots one kid deploying toothpaste in his tent. "You're supposed to brush your teeth over there — *that's* the hygiene area. OK, pull your rifles out and show 'em to me." Muddy hands, barrels pushing through tent flaps. "OK, thank you," George says politely, the rhythm of the civilian world in his command style. After everyone has shown their rifles, George is done, but he doesn't leave. Captain Vermeesch would smile if he saw this: George is putting soldiers first. "Hey, Fourth Squad," he says. "Make sure you put on dry clothes, 'cuz it's gonna get cold tonight. If you have to, wear your field jacket. Also, change your pants. And I'll help with bungee cords." In foul weather, you string your poncho over the exterior of your tent. George shows me how it's done on his tent. "I put that up there two days ago — not two days ago. I put it up yesterday. Only about a dozen other tents in this whole bivouac," he says proudly, "managed to keep them on."

George is one of the most truthful people at West Point; it has nothing to do with honesty, which is conscious truthfulness. George can't help it, some finicky instinct sends him chasing down the longest, narrowest, least rewarding corridors of veracity — his answers are so complete that his listeners can walk away with no idea what information he considered most important. "This is full circle," Rash says. "Two years ago, I was out at Frederick doing the exact same things as them — or if not the *exact* same, pretty damn close to it." In Fourth Squad, he's got some George Rashes of his own. "Three problem children," he says, shaking his head. "One can't stop grinning. Another is just shy of beating his roommate up — the roommate doesn't help, by being basically a slug. And the other one, Calabanos, just doesn't have the proper attitude." This detail is as near to being an exemplary cadet as he's ever been. He even speaks in Successories, but his have a Rashian overlay: "It's a lotta responsibility. Leadership — sometimes it's exhilarating, uh, refreshing. And it's not quite a giddy, heady feeling. But it feels good." He pauses, thinks some more, locates a truth. "Other times it's extremely frustrating, if not just downright annoying."

The Only Time You Can Think About Quitting

In the morning, Bravo Company polishes off the hand grenade course. They buckle up in flak vests, lob fragmentation devices over a concrete wall; their targets are bowling pin–shaped plaster figures called Ivans — snarling Soviet Cold War troops who've taken some beating and chipping over the years. The windows in the bunker shake, bits of metal splinter down into puddles. Bravo charges through the sniper course, tossing pretend grenades into machine-gun nests. (One cadet throws the equivalent of a wild pitch and frowns: "Oh, fudge.") Then the cadre give the saddle-up command; Bravo has an eight-mile road march back to post.

The cadets separate into two files; they flex and clank down the margins of the road. Their features grow strained and fixed, with a dried-sweat stare, facing the quiet, basic human question: Can you make yourself go a few more steps? PT squads of upperclassmen jog cheerfully down the center, singing in cadence: "You got mud on your face, a big disgrace, never gonna make it out of this place." Then they're gone, and it's silent but for a tree squeaking in the wind, boots crushing gravel, canteens rattling against rucks. There's the clacking, dropped-tennis-racket sound of a slipped rifle. Upperclassmen murmur low commands: "Keep your intervals." The cadets pass chapels, then chain-link fences, road signs, the mowed lawns and brick walls of officer housing. For the first half of a march, there are the high spirits of any group on the move, where everybody not in the column seems to be missing the point.

When rain comes to the forest, it filters down through terraces; leaves first, then thick branches, then the drumbeat of water hitting 150 BDUs and Kevlars. The first groans rise from the quiet. Faces drop the effort of expression. By the midway point, the first stumbles. The cadre creeps in, hustling down the middle lane, issuing commands. "Anthony, Manders — help Moore!" Squad leaders step alongside, match their stride to yours. It's not just that you shouldn't quit; nobody will let you. Legs, boots, determination and will belong to the unit. "We're close. You can do it. Don't let down your company. Don't let down your squad. Don't quit."

The cadre begins the repetitions of motion hypnosis. "Come on, Averakis, we've moving onto a flat piece of land. You can do it, Averakis; we're more than halfway there." The cadet murmurs seep in, an undertone. "You've got to want it. I know you want it. Let's go, let's go. There you go. We've got a little short downhill. You're doin' great. Stay with me. Here comes the downhill." And if this wears off, a bad-cop squad leader leans in, face full of camo. (At West Point it's called *happy paint*.) "You will *not* stop. Mental toughness. Mental discipline. Quit — that word is not in your vocabulary! Fall out — those words are not in your vocabulary!" Then the kind voices soothe in again. "Let's go. Stay with me. If you need me to carry you, I will."

New cadets prepare to fall out. "I don't think I want to go on," a hurting cadet will announce. "You don't *think* you want to, Averakis? Well, you're going to." The other new cadets break silence around you. "Come on, Stephanie." "You've got this." "We're all behind you." If the words won't lift you, there's actual, physical hefting. "Grab onto my ruck. You started this — whether you like it or not, you're going to finish it. The only time you can think about quitting is when you're done."

The new cadets understand. The decision to quit isn't yours alone — it can't be — because an Army isn't just you.

"You're not gonna stop, Av. I don't care how you feel."

"Grab my ruck."

"Uuuh! Anx! Mmph! Oh my *God!*"

"Grab my ruck."

"Quit thinking it's hard. Fight it."

"Love it! It's easy!"

"Last hill. You can do this."

"Now let go of the strap. You are going to finish it on your own."

After the morning rains, the afternoon has turned bewilderingly hot, air lending clothes the damply warmed effect of a restroom hand dryer. As the cadets cross grass, their steps are muffled, items delicately shifting; when they march back onto blacktop, the clanking is like a train. Calls come down the line. To not bunch up; to drink water; to help your buddy up the hill. The column winds into the forest, new cadets reaching for tree trunks, the mud as thick as frosting. A plane glides overhead and necks tilt back. "Take *me*," a new cadet named Sullivan jokes. George reaches out and shuts the open canteen on somebody's ruck. At the bottom of the hill, you can see actual steam rising off cadet necks. "We've got just over a mile to get to the top," George tells his squad, then thinks it over. "Maybe a mile-point-six."

MacSweeney breaks out his bagpipes — he studied the instrument with the Catholic brothers at prep school — and offers the company motivational wheezing. Bravo weaves up the last hill before the halfway break. George begins encouraging his people, the same mix of coax and prod G 4 gave him two years ago. "Pick up your feet. You're doing all the work if you're dragging. Gravity will help you out. You'll already be a third of the way up the hill once you hit that corner." His cadets are wilting into the dangerous T shape. "You can do this," George says, breathing hard. "Keep on goin'! Let's go, Calabanos. I know you all can finish this. Sims, Rosenfeld, catch up. You don't wanna be a fall-out like those Rough Riders" — the cadets who've already fallen out — "in the back." The road begins to flatten out. "Two hundred meters," George calls. "This is the top of the hill. Everyone's gonna finish this!"

George doesn't have any fall-outs. He looks over his squad, who've gone for the long refreshments table, grabbing apples and Capri Sun juice boxes. Sergeant Constance Ashford, a tart-tongued middle-aged woman who's one of Bravo's two NCOs, glances up at MacSweeney and his bagpipes. "That would definitely let the enemy know *exactly* where you were at." The new cadets whimper and joke. "My feet are killing me." "Mine have no feeling. I feel like I died and came back to earth. Except for my feet."

Then Bravo mounts up for the second half of the march, curves down the same hill they just climbed. Suddenly George slams into a road sign. Time snaps backward; George Rash is in plebe year again. He rolls on the ground, his new cadets halt and gawk. "Keep moving," Sergeant Rafael DeLeon tells them. (He's Bravo's second TAC-NCO.) He sizes up George. "Dehydration. Put his ruck straight — use it as a back brace, sit 'im up. Where you got your cramping at?"

"Ooof," George says. "Thighs and calf. I was sweating too much, lost all my salts — or my electrolytes." George's face doesn't show disappointment, or any personal thing. He's disappeared in a squinting generic: injured cadet. The cadre swing by — dark appraisals, shaking heads. "He's done it," they mutter, "too many times." The medic coasts in, greets George with some Army humor: "What's up, highspeed?" Flies alight on every arm, every shoulder, but today they've sworn off George. "They won't land on me," he says morosely. "I stink too bad."

Bull Hill

The new cadets have only ten more days of Beast, so Bravo passes afternoons on post, knocking out required honor classes. They're standing at the riverbank, waiting anxiously to cross into plebehood. They take an APFT, all eleven hundred of them, in shifts so as not to crack Gillis Field House. West Point specializes in freak chances: George Rash is overseeing the two-mile run. He gives the morning weather an APFT gourmet's appraisal. "Good day for a PT test. Cool, but not *cold*. Slight breeze to keep you drier." In two days, Bravo will be marching twelve miles back to Frederick; a week later, they'll attempt a march route that covers the fifteen miles back. George isn't worried, he's philosophical. "I can do it," he says, "if my feet don't give out on me."

Bravo steps off at 0630, and by 0730 the weather is so sweltering — the sun pressing down like an iron — that one new cadet has brought out a plant mister and is spraying down marchers as they pass. The new cadets sing a cadence: "Little hill, no sweat. Big hill, better yet." Bravo starts its long, winding crawl up Round Pond Hill; same hill, same pace, same groans as last week. But George doesn't make it as far. His body makes three separate thumps going down: shins, butt, ruck. The sweaty medic pounds down the road. "You better be almost *dead*, cadet

Rash. I was at the top of that hill." The medic won't even open his first-aid kit. "You do not need an IV, and I'm not going to give you one." An FLA — a field line ambulance, a Humvee bearing the red plus-sign logo — pulls in and picks up George. He stares ahead, utterly defeated, like some hard truth has come to him. "I can't perform the task as a squad leader," he says, "so what good am I?" The back of the FLA, with its swaying medical gear, bangs and tinkles like a restaurant kitchen. George sighs, feeling what this means for his future.

In the Keller Army Hospital waiting room, Katie Couric is throwing to Al Roker's forecast on TV; the march is half over, and the *Today* show is still running. Magazines wait on tables, George sits in a comfortable chair. It's like being restored to the civilian time stream, a sane, ordered world. When nurses send you out, they don't say "Mental toughness" or "Never quit"; they smile and urge, "Have a *safe* day." George follows a nurse, she draws the consulting room curtain. She asks, "What happened?" and George answers, "I was definitely not made for the Infantry."

Meanwhile, Bravo is making its ascent up Bull Hill. This steep, endless incline is the Cadet in the Red Sash of the marching world. The cadets approach over a dry stream bed, rocks giving their footing a hard time as a little more civilian gets marched out of them. Halfway up the hill, new cadets begin to wheeze with each step like broken accordions. "Get control of your breathing," Captain Engen says. "Keep it going now." Gold Bond powder flies through the air, spilling off necks and out of boots. "Let's go, Bravo!" Engen urges. The cadets are bent double; you've never really heard foot-dragging until you've heard 150 pairs of feet actually drag. This is what George is missing in the hospital. Then the landscape turns sweet, flattening all at once. Engen dashes ahead — pumping down on his knees with his palms — and turns around with his arms opened wide. "OK, Bravo, this is the top." He beams. "I first made it here in the summer of 1987." *Hoooop!* "Come on and join me on the top of this hill!"

Hammered, Slammed, Toast— You're Done

Whitey Herzog's parents had a colorful divorce, so he's already familiar with the process, how memory can shrink even the biggest experiences. That's what's happening with Loryn: the recollections are working down to a manageable size. But though he waits all spring, Mark Matty's death never loses its original dimensions. He begins to understand it's the sort of event that can shift your direction through life.

Mark's funeral lasted for hours; it wound up at some girl's shaggy Victorian house, the boys taking pulls on their flasks, getting angry, getting drunk, then angry-drunk. They found a Halloween jack-o'-lantern on some lazy neighbor's porch, dragged it into the street, stood on the steps winging it with beer bottles. They hauled somebody's Christmas tree out onto the sidewalk and tore it apart. They were mounting an assault against the calendar — how could people celebrate holidays when their friend was dead? When the cops showed up, Whitey helped everybody get the street clean, working the broom, bagging the garbage.

Back at flight school, Whitey wrote Mrs. Matty a letter: he said he couldn't stop replaying the night. He was watching it through his military eyes: like an officer with his troops, he'd lost one. He wrote that he was sorry he'd been there. Mrs. Matty wrote back, "You're not only in the military — you're my friend. And so you'll get no response from me when you say that. No authority in the world could have prevented what happened to my son. I'm just so happy you're the person who was there with him." A few weekends later, he flew north to Buffalo to spend the day with Mrs. Matty. She asked if he'd mind walking outside to the back garden and keeping her company while she read the newspaper. Whitey stood there chucking tennis balls to the dog. ("The dog doesn't know what happened," Whitey says. "The *dog's* sad.") After a while Whitey turned around to find that Mrs. Matty had folded the paper. "Her face was glowing, just because I reminded her of Mark with his dog. It was wonderful to do that for her, she enjoyed it so much."

Whitey knows from watching crash videos that family tragedies can endanger pilots as surely as wires strung across a road. "One guy was having marital problems — severe problems — and he shouldn't of been flying. The camera was mounted in the aircraft behind him, and you can see him go right into the ground. If people are having trouble and they're not one hundred percent focused, they die." Now Whitey can't concentrate. He zips into his flight suit, grabs his helmet, reports to the flying line, and his mind remains in Buffalo. One day he takes the aircraft up, flies like hell, back on the ground his instructor pilot lights a cigarette and asks what's the problem. Whitey tells him. The IP smiles. "Jesus Christ," he whistles. "Damn LTs — always trying to do everything themselves. Man, if you're hurting, you don't feel like you can fly, you *tell* me."

West Pointers follow the can-do movie gospel imparted by Cinderella sports tales, romantic comedies and revenge thrillers. There's no problem that cannot be overcome through a combination of determination and positive attitude. This makes them a tough market for psychologists. When his commander advises Whitey to seek grief counseling, fear is his response: he doesn't want it on his record. And fretting about career repercussions isn't conducive to opening up. "I went," he says, "but it wasn't helpful. It was just an evaluation, what I needed was fuckin' *talking*. The psychologist was a captain, very cool. He told me, 'You're fine, you're grieving, you're a very healthy person mentally, so just grieve. Don't even worry about this going down on your file or me telling your commander. There's no need.' I said, 'Thanks, sir, I appreciate that.' The one uncool thing he did, he tried to make me cry. I'm a semi-intelligent guy — I knew what he was doing. 'What was Mark like? How does this feel?' And he just looked at me. He was waiting for me to get emotional, it's not gonna happen. I was just whistling: 'All right, sir, let's go, next question.'"

Just as doctors have pet names for emergency room regulars, and firefighters for the many ways flame can take a building, soldiers are on a nickname basis with injury and dying. You're *lit up, jacked up, tore the hell up;* you can get *broken, hammered, slammed;* worse comes to worst, you're *waxed, whacked, toast* — you're *done.* But this makes it sound like rotten sports luck, having to do some time in the penalty box. What Whitey knows is, people never get out of the box.

After the funeral, he saw a picture of Mark on someone's piano, and he understood he was never going to see him again. For months he tries to put this into words for friends at Rucker — it's the lesson Mark Matty always hoped to teach him when he was still alive. "I've learned that life is short," he says, "and life is precious."

Back at the Academy, Whitey could have hashed this out with the Goodfellas. But they're hard to get a hold of; they've got their own Officer Basic Courses to complete. John Mini is finishing strong at Knox, near the top of his class, packing up to ship for Germany. Suppy is cruising toward the end of flight school. He'll graduate in the top third (the Army has three ratings for officers: above center of mass, center of mass, and below center of mass), and soon he'll pick his career aircraft. He's leaning toward the Blackhawk, which will give him a shot at the Aviation equivalent of Special Forces, Task Force 160. He's mastering Basic Combat Skills — firing live rounds, lurking behind the treeline, then swinging around to hit targets sliding by on a railroad track. For him, it's almost as fun as surfing. He flies nights, 1900 to 0200, racks during the day, so he can't be around when Whitey would talk.

Iggy is knocking out the Infantry course, whose hurry-up-and-wait quality makes Buck-nam seem like a well-oiled machine. (Whitey bumps into his old first captain in Atlanta, and even Rob Shaw admits he's hurting on motivation.) Infantry climaxes with Ranger school, another elimination round, so Iggy is preparing for the sixty days of no food, no sleep, endless training and patrolling. What you learn is how much punishment you can take; in war movies, when a costume department wants to make an actor look hard, they'll stitch the yellow and gold Ranger patch on his left shoulder. (The patch is called a tab.) It's so crucial in the Infantry community that some failures will risk court-martial and wear black-market Ranger tabs on their uniforms.

If Whitey had made different decisions, he'd be on the ground getting ready with Iggy right now. Instead, every morning he wakes up, tries to get himself stoked for flight. "Walking to my helicopter," he says, "I'm like, 'I don't wanna be *doing* this.' I wouldn't mind dying if I'm out with soldiers and we get ambushed. That's different, I'd be OK with it — I've done my part, if we get hit, we get hit. If I was in my helicopter at two thousand feet, a bolt fell off and I was headed towards the earth, my attitude right now would be: I'm *pissed*. There's lots of stuff I wanted to find out about, I'm fuckin' pissed off that I'm gonna die because a machine has broken down."

His number one priority has always been serving his country, so he studies, passes test rides, inches toward the end of training. One afternoon in May he's on the phone with Mrs. Matty, and she cuts him off with the key words: "You're not happy doing what you're doing, are you?" Whitey doesn't know what to say; it's the question nobody's asked. The words slash out. "No. Not at all. Not one bit." Mrs. Matty thinks about it. "If you're not happy, then you have to do something else." Whitey hangs up feeling better than he has in months. He tells Brian, tells Bart, tells Iggy, rehearsing the decision in his mouth. West Point is there with the terms, helping him make sense of the whole year. "This year," he says, "has developed me." Then he goes to his commander and puts in his request for branch reassignment. He doesn't want to be in Aviation anymore. He wants something on the ground, something controllable: he wants Finance.

You've Been Visited by the BTO

Hank Keirsey has departed into the clouds of the Army afterlife, and that leaves just two points in the West Point sky. Supe sightings are rare — his job, like any college president's, includes a good amount of off-campus fund-raising. So Colonel Joe Adamczyk, Skeletor, the brigade tactical officer, is now the most inspirational figure on post. Keirsey stood for military exploits, the adventures still to be found threading their way under modern life like a system of cables and pipes. Adamczyk embodies regulations, living to standard. Cadets scurry out of his eye-line, grin when he nails somebody else. But he's their daily reminder that more and different things are expected of them than from anybody else.

If you were to watch the BTO progress across North Area from above — from, say, an upstairs barracks window or the Washington Hall roof, where smokers gather — it would bring to mind a state trooper cruising the highway, cadets braking and swerving aside. Some cadets actually jump indoors. "I've never seen him cross the Area and *not* make a correction on somebody," Mike Ferlazzo says. ("He's one lean and slender individual," Huck Finn says. "You can spot him from a long way off, and you stay as far away as possible.") Adamczyk sends cadets ricocheting back to barracks with too long sideburns, because they've forgotten to wear a belt with their civvies or tuck in their shirt, because the overall effect "makes you look like you pump gas at a service station. Is *that* how you represent this Academy?"

As the BTO, Adamczyk is the TAC for the TACs, the boss of bosses. Captains who left their cadet status behind a decade ago metamorphose into flustered plebes at his side. (Hearing he's canceled a meeting, TACs will whistle "Forget your troubles, come on, get happy.") When he goes on a regimental inspection, he'll start ticking off infractions in the entranceway. "Somebody taped a memo to your regimental sign, they left the tape residue behind. Someone left a coffee cup on your heating unit, you've got some stains. And look up there." A ghostly spider web is riding the air currents near the ceiling. "Think that just happened this morning? Busy spider." There are learning points in this. For the TACs ("Keep an eye on your standard maintenance; it's gotta get done and it ought to be done to standard"), for cadets ("You're gonna be responsible for critical pieces of equipment when you leave here — tanks, helicopters, weapons — and a soldier only does what a leader checks. When leaders adhere to, set, and enforce the standard, life is good"). And there's a severe Martha Stewart homily to bestow on everyone: "People make an immediate assessment of a unit based upon its entranceway. If it doesn't present a neat, clean appearance, they're gonna say, 'Here's a unit that doesn't have much pride.' Entranceways are one of an organization's most important aspects."

On the whiteboard outside his office, Adamczyk writes a new biblical verse every couple weeks. One week he'll post Proverbs 15:10, "Stern discipline awaits him who leaves the path; he who hates correction will die," or 15:32, "He who ignores discipline despises himself, but whoever heeds correction gains understanding." When you come back, it'll be Proverbs 12:1: "Whoever loves discipline loves knowledge, but he who hates correction is stupid." But there's a warmth to Adamczyk. Under Washington Hall, he posts a weekly Xerox called "Rumors of the BTO," with a snapshot of Adamczyk holding his finger to his lips. The rumors are: "Please give blood this week. Support mankind . . . Ever wonder why DWI is illegal?" — picture of a gory, mashed-up car — "Be careful during this weather, don't take 'risks' you don't need to take. Think *SAFETY!* . . . Do something nice for someone. Go Army!"

During summer training he is everywhere. In August, when Rob Shaw returns to West Point to marry General John Abizaid's daughter in the snug Catholic chapel, the BTO is kneeling on the altar beside them, to the left of the Catholic chaplain. (The priest's white hair is the longest in the church; in West Point's stubbled environment, men of God look countercultural and racy.) Then he's outside, grinning on the patio, as Rob and Sherrie Shaw walk through the traditional saber arch. Cadets in dress gray line up three on each side; at "Attention!" they raise and cross their swords. When the couple reaches the end, the last cadet lowers his blade like a tollgate, forcing the Shaws to kiss; then he uses it to swat Sherrie on the behind: "Welcome to the Army, Mrs. Shaw." Another August morning, he's piling into his Humvee, first inspecting it like a cadet's uniform. Then he's rolling off to visit cadets in the field.

Being in the BTO's company is an exercise in rigor, a demonstration that there is a right way to do everything. It's also a demonstration of one sad, entropic principle: left to their own devices, people will generally go wrong. At the Basic Rifle Marksmanship range — cracked smell of gunpowder, new cadets sitting back to back cleaning M-16s, sprinkling Gold Bond on their toes — he spots a pile of green blankets left unprotected by a tree. Then he steps over a gray-and-yellow puddle of latrine runoff. A cadet tells him it's water, and Adamczyk says, "Water? It's seepage." "Sorry, sir," the cadet says. "You're right. It's urine."

Adamczyk came to West Point in 1968, from Harrison, New Jersey, whose down-heeled visuals HBO has made famous with *The Sopranos*. (When Adamczyk feels homesick, he can look over the actors' shoulders for familiar street corners and storefronts.) "I had Sisters of Charity elementary school for nine years. I went to mass every day in grammar school, Benedictine monks and priests in high school — *and* an Irish-Catholic mother. West Point was *easy*." In the disorder of the times, a teenaged Adamczyk watched the glow of the Newark riots, fires across the river. When he reported to school in downtown Newark next morning, St. Benedict's was one of the few buildings still standing. "And the only reason why it wasn't destroyed was it had a Benedictine abbey attached, and the monks just absolutely refused to leave. They stood their ground even as the riots were going on, folks *respected* that, they didn't mess with them." This taught Adamczyk a valuable lesson about toughness and holding your position.

Officers who endured the Army of the sixties and seventies have the same narrow-eyed disposition as civilians who survived the Depression. At the Vietnam-era Academy, before cadets left post to march in Veterans Day parades, they were schooled in ignoring taunts and defending the flag in case the crowds attacked. At Adamczyk's first Infantry unit, he walked into the home front's big muddy: low morale, alcoholism, a drug addict whose nickname was Slow Death MacGregor. "Every payday, old Slow Death would get his paycheck, head downtown, buy a new set of clothes. And before the weekend was over, he'd be back in the barracks, no idea what had happened, no clothes, and flat *broke*." Adamczyk had graduated too late for Southeast Asia. "You feel a little cheated," he says. "You train, prepare — not because you savor war, but if there's a conflict going on, you automatically feel you should be there."

In 1975, Adamczyk was reassigned from Fort Bragg to the Old Guard, outside Washington, D.C. Because the Old Guard is a ceremonial division that often appears on television — inaugurals and funerals — they are platonic visions of soldiers. At first, Adamczyk hated the spit-and-polish routine. He'd just come from The Division, the Old Guard was like a unit constructed by a BTO. Everyone was over six feet; Adamczyk is five foot ten. At his first function, a captain asked, "Hey, I want to know how tall that lieutenant is." And Adamczyk balled his mental fists and responded as Huck Finn might: "Sir, tall enough to beat the shit out of anybody in this room." After a few years — parading and planning Arlington funerals for the Vietnam dead — Adamczyk refined his answer: "Someone said, 'Jeez, I thought you had to be six feet in the Old Guard,' I'd say 'If you're six feet and you're in the Old Guard, it's because you're six feet. If you're my size and you're in the Old Guard, it's because you're *good*.'"

Adamczyk's Old Guard experience left him as perfect a garrison officer as Keirsey was a field officer. The Army eventually sent him to Germany, to Hawaii, before winging him back to West Point — a pretty luxe ride for a boy from Harrison. What he wants cadets to know is that he walked a tight path in the Army, and found it to have surprising views. When Keirsey met cadets, he searched for verve. Adamczyk builds his impressions on demeanor, posture, handshake, appropriateness of dress, on the same principle that says a healthy animal will keep its fur clean. But both men look first in the eyes: Will a cadet directly meet your gaze? For Keirsey, this meant you had the right spirit inside, and so had nothing to be ashamed of. For the BTO, it means you have everything correct on the outside, and so have nothing to be ashamed of. Adamczyk's twins are both at West Point: Matthew will spend next year as the brigade XO; Leslie is in H-4, the same company as Keirsey's oldest, J.D. Next year, she'll room with Chrissi Cicerelle.

At 1600, Adamczyk parks his Humvee in the Keller Hospital lot. "I try to come at least once a week," he says. "It's a responsibility of leadership, checking on your soldiers. And there's the training aspect: somewhere down the line these kids are going to have soldiers in the hospital. Hopefully they'll say, 'Oh yeah, I remember when I was in the hospital Colonel Adamczyk came by to see me, maybe I ought to go visit my soldiers.'" The wide, creaky elevator doors open on white hallways and prints by Monet and Matisse, and then Adamczyk goes room to room. Cadets are laid up with heat exhaustion and soccer accidents. ("You're gonna look more macho with that scar," the BTO says. "Yes sir," the new cadet replies, "mean and tough.") The cadets are surprised to see the BTO and shy to engage him in conversation. In one room, Adamczyk sits with a new cadet checked in with a muscle pull. "I saw you yesterday," he says. "You were on the road march, hollering 'Let me keep going, let me finish.'"

The new cadet, a black kid from Tennessee, wrinkles his face warily. "I apologize about that, sir."

"No apology necessary. You're from Memphis? So when Army plays Memphis, who you gonna cheer for?"

"I'm going to cheer for Army, sir. I plan on being a West Point graduate, this is my home now, sir."

"Good for you, huah."

In the next room, Adamczyk finds a worried mother occupying her daughter's bedside chair. "I didn't call her, sir," the cadet says quickly.

"I hear 'blood disorder,'" the mother says, "and I *freak*."

"You a little bit calmer now, Mom?" The BTO smiles, using her civilian rank.

"She's leaving tomorrow morning, so I know she's OK. As long as she's not dying, I'm OK."

Adamczyk turns to the cadet in the next bed. "Is she spoiling you too? I know the mothers never come up here and just spoil their own kids." In the rooms where cadets are absent, for treatment or tests, Adamczyk fishes a card out of his BDU pocket, leaves it on the pillow: *You've been visited*, it says, *by the BTO*.

Cooperate and Graduate

If Joe Adamczyk had returned to the hospital the next day, he would have found Nick Calabanos, the most Rash-like cadet in George Rash's squad, being treated for trench foot — the condition that sidelined George as a new cadet. And if he stuck around for a few hours longer, he could have watched George Rash himself being lugged in, nearly unconscious.

West Point likes to immerse cadets in their imperfections. Huck Finn is bad about rules: so when summer assignments came around, he was teaching new cadets to make beds, polish boots and follow regulations, learning he could do the same. George got Beast II — the marching portion of Cadet Basic Training.

Early in the summer, John Vermeesch gave George his high-stakes warning. "I told him that as of now I wouldn't want to serve with him as a lieutenant," Vermeesch says. "So this summer is very important. I hope he can step up and lead from the front. And if he learns he can't, before Cow Commitment, I hope that he recognizes it for himself. At that point he has to say, 'I can't be an Army officer.'"

Cadets have a fixed motto: "Cooperate and graduate." The idea is that cadethood is too much for any solo operator. But when corps opinion turns against a cadet — if peers think you're bound to wash out, or that you'll be an embarrassment if you do survive — there are any number of ways to stick a boot in your path. After he falls out of the twelve-mile march, cadet opinion solidifies against George Rash. They know Cow Commitment is coming too; they'd like to be rid of him before then.

"I feel bad about it," says Matt MacSweeney. "He's not a bad guy if you get to know him. But people aren't helping him anymore — they're kinda leading him toward mistakes, kinda hoping he'll mess up. The attitude right now is, 'Hey George — here's a screwdriver, go see if that electrical socket is working.'"

After the eight-mile march, Calabanos removed his boots to show the cadre his black-and-blue, torn-up feet. It was George's responsibility to check his squad's feet, to make sure they didn't get as bad as Calabanos's were. "But that's first detail's fault also," explains Jonathan

Tullos, a cow in Bravo Company. "He's had those boots since R-Day, someone should have caught it before this." Now Calabanos is sitting pretty — he's on soft-shoe profile, no boots, no marches for a week. "But George could've known what to look for. I don't know, it just seems like any mistake he makes is getting put into the spotlight now."

Unfortunately, George's one bright moment occurs outside the spotlight. He does a fine job leading his squad of new cadets through Warrior Forge — a day of ambushes, reconnaissance, casualty drills in which all the summer's skills are tested together. But no one's there to see it except his new cadets, and their opinion can't help his standing with cadre or Vermeesch. He shows his squad how to move under fire, how to administer first aid to a fallen comrade, how to deal with EPWs, enemy prisoners of war. "First kick their weapon away," George says, "in case they're playing possum. Then give them a swift kick to the gender — you have to make sure they're down or dead." (George's technique receives some refinement when Rosenfeld, one of his new cadets, goes to check an EPW being played by a regular Infantry soldier. "If you kick me in the nuts," the soldier growls, "I will rip your ears off.") George slows the squad as they march down the side of a mountain, with the kind of caution soldiers appreciate. "These rocks are just *asking* for a twisted ankle," he says; Rash's instinct for self-preservation would keep other soldiers healthy too.

Tonight, Bravo Company will make a tricky nighttime patrol, spend an evening under fire in deep woods. There'll be a march to the site, probes by the Army regulars through the small hours, another march to Tent City in the morning. "I expect to see a lot of foxfire," George says with pleasure. I ask if that's a weapon. "No, it's basically when you get fungus on rotting logs and stuff, that glows phosphorescent in the dark. It's very pretty."

Army trucks called deuce-and-a-halfs (they can carry two and a half tons) ferry George's squad to the staging area at 2000 hours. Calabanos has found a way out of tonight's patrol: this morning, he showed George a new and engorged blister. But he's been on profile for a week, how could he have gotten it? "He hasn't *done* anything," George says.

"That thing was huge," one new cadet marvels. "Maybe he took a lighter to his foot. There's ways to get out of any training — don't put anything past anybody, especially Calabanos."

First Sergeant Ryan Southerland gives the order ("Let's *go*, Bra-vo") and George passes the word down to his soldiers: "Fourth Squad, get it up, get it on, follow me." They move out into the woods. A night march is an eerie sensory experience. Camo patterns work especially well in the dark; it's difficult to see anyone, yet you feel the heat of the cadets around you, smell the fabric and locker room smell of a unit on the move, hear the mash of boots. In the distance, through the trees, the company hears small-arms fire. Everyone goes into the prone position, a long line of shadows and green along the trailside — boots, helmets, sets of eyes palely blinking.

The smallest woman in his squad begins to labor and huff under her pack; George offers to ruck it for her. Bravo doesn't get probed during the night. (It turns out, in the morning, that the cadre marched too far; the Army units couldn't *find* them.) The cadets doze in long rows, crawling under ponchos when the sky decides to rain. At 0445, they're on their feet, ready to march back; darkness bleaches out of the sky. The cadre leadership again loses the route, going forward, stopping, marching back, pulling out the map, making Ryan Southerland slightly angry. But he walks the line, bucking up the new cadets. "This is a beautiful morning," he tells Rosenfeld. "Think what you just accomplished, think what you're about to do. What are your friends doing back home? Getting over a hangover is about the best thing they could be up to. But we're out here on this beautiful morning." George mutters under his breath, "This *sucks*." Then he says to no one in particular, "I'm going to have a field day with my feet after this."

Southerland is one of Bravo Company's most effective cadets. "He can make good stuff happen just by showing up," Captain Engen explains. When he pulls up beside a limping cadet, he makes the clearest appeal: "Like all the best things, this is you versus you. Get through this, you'll probably forget it. If you don't, that's what you'll remember, and you'll regret. So you have to minimize regret." Colonel Adamczyk will often describe the pre-Changes style of cadet leadership — with its threats and hazing — as "puerile, sophomoric and degrading." (It's one of his catchphrases.) His ideal cadet leader would be able to apply pressure without raising his voice; Ryan does this instinctively. "He's kind of an icon to us younger guys," a new cadet named Collins tells me. "When he corrects you, he always gives you something positive. He's not just there taking advantage of the power." Southerland is marching beside Fourth Squad as the rest of the cadre begin to nudge each other and grin. They know the signs. George Rash is limping, sweating; he's getting ready to fall out of another road march.

With every few steps, he drops farther behind his new cadets. This is the last thing George needs right now: word will go back to Engen, and through Engen it will pass to Super-V. All the cadre has to do, to push him closer to the edge of his personal cliff, is let him stop marching. But Ryan's instincts won't allow him to let George stop. "What's the problem?" he asks.

"My right heel," George says, "is on fire."

"Is new cadet Rosenfeld a member of the cadre?"

"No, First Sergeant."

"Then why is he leading your squad?"

George quickens his pace, catches up. "Oh, this sucks," he says. Ryan marches to the head of the column to consult with the rest of the leadership. George begins to pull back again, and soon Ryan returns to his side.

"My last one's right in front of me," George says quickly — meaning he's leading, just leading from behind. "My foot —"

"Get out in front and *lead*. Get in front of your doggone team. Where's your squad?"

"Just in front . . . God! . . . of me."

"Look at me. Why don't you get up there and lead them?"

"My fucking heel is getting ready to fall off my foot."

"No. Your *heel* is going to stay on. Your *heel* is attached to your *foot*, and your foot is inside your *boot*. Get in front of your squad."

George goes forward, begins to slide back. The ground along the side of the road makes its soft, inviting pitch. Ryan is with him immediately. "I'm not sure I'm gonna make it," he says.

"You're a leader," Ryan reminds him. "You need to lead your people. You better not be behind them."

Rash jogs up to his squad. And this time Ryan stays with him, shoulder to shoulder. George is fed up. Southerland decides to get George fed up with him. "You're angry?" Ryan says. "Thinking about hitting me? Keep thinking about that. Hit me by just leading your squad, one foot in front of the other. You're going to stay ahead of your people, and you're going to finish this ahead of your people." George glares, grits teeth; twenty minutes later he marches by Captain Engen, at the finish, leading his squad.

*

Three days later, Bravo reports to the Bayonet Course. The cadets won't actually train with rifles and bayonets; instead, they'll spar with pugil sticks — long, *Star Wars*–looking staffs with padded ends. They're less lethal than bayonets, but they can still inflict serious damage. Red Cross volunteers are there on a just-in-case basis. Calabanos removes his boot, hears gasps, receives his trench foot diagnosis. Captain Engen asks George when he last inspected feet. Rash says Friday — two days ago. As he talks it over with a female cadre member named Kim Wilkins beside the Red Cross table, he realizes the date was Thursday, just after the night patrol. He spends some time hunting down Engen and reporting his own error. The new cadets meanwhile practice their pugil technique on dummies composed of rubber tires and metal, firing themselves up by chanting "Kill! Kill! Kill!" Some new cadets lace into the model like it owes them money. In a few minutes they'll run the course and finally get what they've been waiting all summer for — a taste of combat against the cadre.

In the Old Corps, when cadets arrived at West Point they were separated into companies on simple terms of height. This approach made for better aesthetics during parades: rather than a mixed skyline of tenements and skyscrapers, you fielded a smooth and ascending progression of uniform heads. In later years, it also made for cleaner company photographs. Tall-man companies were "flankers," small ones were "runts." (The practice lingered on in various forms for more than a century, before cracking up against the hard shore of the 1970s.) One of the last places to retain any vestige of runts and flankers is the Bayonet Assault Course. New cadets pound down the lanes nine at a time, organized by height. That way, they will encounter a cadre member of equal size, guaranteeing a clean, fair fight.

By manufactured coincidence George is placed in a flanker lane. ("I don't know why or how," one of the leaders tells me. "He just happened to be on that lane.") During his first fight, George thinks it's a mistake. By the third and fourth — when every cadet running down his lane is a big head on a thick neck — he understands what's happened. He lifts his stick and fights it out. After an hour, George stumbles off the course with a concussion. ("He got his bell rung pretty good," the cadre tell me.) It's one of George's last acts of the summer. The doctors advise him to skip the fifteen-mile march back to West Point; he and Calabanos sit it out together. Whatever resolution George has picked up from the end of Beast won't matter. By the time he returns to post, he has learned he's being investigated for honor — the specific charge is lying about checking his squad's feet. The witnesses against him are cadet Wilkins, a woman from the Red Cross table and Captain Engen.

Acceptance

The Academy has the veteran host's exquisite gift for pacing and the appropriate gesture. Each class marks the end of summer training with a celebration. For the firsties, there are dates and the arrival of new military jewelry at Ring Weekend; for the cows, there's the gulp and promise of Cow Commitment. Yuks kick away their BDUs to waltz in dress whites at a ball called Camp Illumination. And new cadets march the Plain for Acceptance Day. It's the parade equivalent of osmosis. The new cadets cross the lawn — above the low shadows of noon — where three thousand fellow soldiers are waiting. Then the probationary *new* in *new cadet* falls away forever as they step forward, merge ranks with their elders, to become a single corps.

This is the first chance parents have had to examine their children since R-Day. Families choke sidewalks and lawns; there's a firing line of dads with recording equipment. Mothers wave signs. Some look professionally manufactured, with a mysterious sponsorship element: *BABY GAP Salutes Company A;* an Energizer bunny wearing cadet gray next to *Cadets Keep Going and Going.* Then there are patently homemade posters: a labor-intensive sign drawn like a Monopoly board, West Point inside jokes occupying the squares for each property: *AN-DREW — Welcome Back, You Are Now a Man. You Are Our MAN-opoly Champ.* Younger brothers squeeze off air horns, moms hug children, exclaim over weight loss, dads rub shaved heads.

The restaurants and supermarkets of Highland Falls host orgies of consumption. In the parking lots, parents exchange observations about poise and new confidence, but they are mostly astonished by the *gorging.* "She kept music — *blaring* — in the car. All. Day. Long. She told me what CDs she wanted us to bring. And just sat in the car playing music." "I have *never* seen him eat so much as he did at that cookout. He ate three hamburgers. Then he ate a chili dog. Then three or four cookies. Chips. Baked beans. And then homemade ice cream. Then he came back to us and said, 'Mom, Dad, I'd like you to take me to a restaurant.'"

A week separates the last march and Cow Commitment — seven days of mulling. Captain John Vermeesch receives reports on Huck Finn and George Rash. When the summer began, the two cadets were crewmates on the same foundering boat. Vermeesch can't get over Huck's transformation. "I was about ready to throw in the towel on that guy," Vermeesch says. "I mean, the jury's still out, but he is the biggest turnaround success story so far." Even Huck can't quite believe it; he talks about his old self the way you'd describe a person you didn't approve of in school. "Last year, I hated everything: didn't wanna be here, didn't wanna go in the Army. If I ever got stuck in the Infantry, I'd cut my trigger finger off — you know, whatever it took. Now I think this is a great place." He thinks it over, adds with surprise, "I'm not even ruling out the Infantry."

But if there's been a change in George Rash, Vermeesch can't see it. "The summer," he says, "fully met my expectations of what was going to happen. The whole notion of *quitting,* on a road march." Vermeesch knows all about the honor case; he knows it's not another cadet, it's Captain Engen who's charged George. "I'm not absolutely confident, but I'm pretty confident of what is going to occur. George will sit in front of a jury of his peers. And there's only one penalty for being found during an Honor Investigative Hearing — separation from the corps of cadets." Vermeesch would rather not see it come to that. "My hope is that he will assess his performance over the summer and say, 'This is not my bag. And I need to self-select out of this profession.'" Vermeesch squares his shoulders, glares as if Rash is in his office. "Because I have a very strong opinion about whether or not George Rash deserves to be an officer in the Army. But I don't know that I have a tremendous amount of *effectiveness* at influencing George Rash."

So Vermeesch sends Sergeant Tierney to George with the hard facts, in the days before Cow Commitment: You are being investigated for honor; if you take the oath and lose the hearing, you'll owe money (at this point, George would owe $125,000), or you're going to owe time as a Joe. The officers you'll meet in the Army, even if you make it through West Point, are like Captain Vermeesch and me: if you can't hang, that's like red blood in a school of sharks. George listens and nods.

At 1815, the cow class marches to Thayer Hall, laughing and singing cadence in the evening light: "Hail to thee, Infantry," "Wanna be *Airborne*, you gotta do it *my way*." They doff their caps as they enter Thayer Hall, rub what hair they have into place. As they walk the halls the joking begins: "I don't feel so good anymore — I'm *pushing* my feet down the hall." "Aw, don't even think about it." They take their seats by company, and G-4 is there: Jasmine Rose, Huck, Josh Rizzo, Maria Auer, Mark Thompson, Kevin Hadley, all the cadets who've made it this far. Before the Affirmation Ceremony, commemorative coins are handed to each TAC for presentation to the cows. There's a speech — "Your country calls on you, now, to take the handoff" — and then Colonel Adamczyk stands on the stage and leads the cadets in their oath. "Now, at ease. Raise your right hand and repeat after me: I — state your full name —"

George states his name along with a thousand other cadets. He stands near the end of G-4's row, with a look that's pinched and determined. "I acknowledge my commitment, if I am separated between now and the graduation of my class . . . ," he says with his classmates. When the oath is completed, cheers ring off the ceiling, and the TACs distribute the coins. Vermeesch shakes hands, says a few words to each of his cadets. To Finn he says, "Hey Reid — congratulations. Welcome to the profession of arms." When it's George's turn, Vermeesch's face turns cold, and he says, "You're staying, and you need to step it up. Now there are consequences."

The Corporation

Two cliques have emerged in G-4. The first consists of reckless cadets, always on the verge of trouble or just climbing out of it: Huck Finn, Josh Rizzo, Steve Cho, Will Reynolds, Huck's football teammate Cal Smith. Punishments at West Point come in the form of time — you get *hours,* in blocks of five, spent spiffing up the grounds or staring down the clock at the military version of detention. Huck's group is more or less the Hours Boys.

The second clique is the core of G-4 professionalism. One night Josh

Rizzo — an evening of beers still filtering through his system — rode the barracks elevator with a bunch of them. They stood firmly and dutifully, respectfully watching the numbers ascend from one to six. When Riz threw open the door to the room he once again shares with Huck Finn, he said, "I just rode up with the Corporation." "The who?" Huck asked. "That whole crew — Rob Anders, Eliel Pimentel, Matty Kilgore, Mark Thompson. You know — they're a fuckin' *corporation,* man."

The name stuck. The Corporation is composed of the patient cadets who understand that every chapter of life is also groundwork for the next chapter, that cow year is really an audition for firstie year — that all the good striper leadership positions will be handed out on the basis of their performance now. "They're way too 'Yes sir,' 'Yes ma'am,' whatever," says Cal Smith. "They just don't get any hours."

Eliel Pimentel is G-4's first sergeant, a likable cadet with the striking good looks of the young Marlon Brando. (When Eliel jackpots on girl-meeting trips, fellow Corporation members call him "Pimpentel.") Eliel's family emigrated from Puerto Rico to Orlando before he started sixth grade. "Eliel" was a tongue buster for the Floridians, so his teacher suggested the name "Eddie," which some Guppies use now. His father is a pastor with the Disciples of Christ, and his mother is also active in the church. This gives him some extra, celestial confidence. "My parents both felt, as I did, that God wanted me here," Eliel explains. "For some reason, it was part of God's mission for me."

God had some help: Eliel served with naval JROTC, came up through the West Point Parents Club of Central Florida (via the club, he already knew Chrissi Cicerelle and Jeremy Green, currently the number one–ranked cadet in the class of 2002). "When I got here, the central Florida upperclassmen came around and said, 'Anybody gives you trouble, we'll take care of you.'"

Pimentel is an odd mix. He listens to so much Dave Matthews he'll often drop the name "Dave," as if referring to a pal who just left the room — but he has never smoked pot, never sipped an underage drink. For cadets like Eliel, West Point involves not so much abandoning an old personality as raising the original self to the highest power.

During his first year, Eliel knocked himself out trying to perfect the role of plebe. "I tried to really do everything. Wake up early in the morning to memorize the meals and the newspaper for the upperclassmen. Sometimes I hated getting up — I was thinking, 'Damn, what are my friends back home doing right now?' But I worked really hard, and I thank God for how things have gone." When cadets like Eliel say "thank God," they really mean it: they are genuinely thanking God. If anything, Eliel would have asked that plebe year be even harder. "Not that I wanted somebody to *beat* me — but I read all the old West Point stories, and I did come here for that. I mean, if something's not challenging, then it's not that great when you're done. But if you're challenged and you still make it through, then it's that much better at the end. It takes pressure to make diamonds." As first sergeant, he wears a diamond-shaped insignia on his collar; he's responsible for checking rooms, checking uniforms, enforcing standards. In four other companies, first sergeants have already been relieved — "for doing stupid things, underage drinking, opposite-sex person in barracks" — but there's no chance of this with Eliel. "He's one of those guys I wish I could clone," Captain Vermeesch says. "Eliel's so mature, he understands everything that we're preaching here *already*. He's a stud all around, morally, ethically, without peer, really."

G-4's new company commander is another take-no-chances selection. Jeremy Kasper is a slim, pale firstie from the outskirts of the Corporation. He's an antidote to Jim Edgar, last year's commander. "The cadets say the company's running great," Vermeesch says, "because we have someone who upholds the standard, and there's never a question of what that standard's gonna be. If I could take one cadet from here to be a lieutenant with me out in the Army, it would be Jeremy. I trust him implicitly — with my kids, with my wife, on my right or left flank, wherever."

When the company commander is out for a good time, he knows where to turn. "When I really need to release some frustration and steam — I go to Barnes and Noble, buy a cup of coffee, sit there and read a book." On weekends, Kasper will kick back with a program called OPD, Officer Professional Development, screening movies for G-4's plebes. During films like *Glory*, *The 13th Warrior*, *Starship Troopers* and *U-571*, he hits Pause — stopping the fantasy in its tracks — and isolates the lesson. Before a frozen image of Antonio Banderas slugging a barbarian in the jaw, he'll say, "This is about what it means to sacrifice the comforts of your society in order to protect it."

Look closely and you can see something Rashian in Kasper — not in his appearance but in his deliberate, absorbed demeanor. But unlike George, he has consciously developed a soldierly manner. At OPD, he's showing plebes the road map he used to reach a leader's persona — how he shopped the culture for words, gestures, attitudes he admired and fashioned them into a self. He grew up watching John Wayne movies, and he moves with John Wayne's dismissive sway, gives the distracted half-grin Wayne would flash after two hours spent proving he was handy with a sidearm.

Jeremy grew up smart and solitary on a dairy farm outside Almond, Wisconsin. As a hobby, his mother painted portraits of horses; soon the portraits were earning as much as the dairy, then a little more, then the family was relocating to Lexington, Kentucky, home of the derby, "the horse capital of the world," Kasper says.

Lexington was culture shock. Jeremy walked into his prep school — "If your daddy was somebody, you went there" — wearing his dairy clothes. "Jeans rolled up farmer style and a flannel shirt," he remembers. The students weren't great about it. "If you didn't wear Gap you didn't fit in — the Gap was the minimum acceptable standard — and I'd never even heard of the store before I went there." The way his mother turned to painting horses, Jeremy began filling out the forms for West Point. "It was more of a hobby than anything else," he says, "so much paperwork to get through." He made his candidate visit in the winter. Snow everywhere, bleak and gray, "I was just having flashbacks to Wisconsin." He watched a rugby game, four cadets were carried off on stretchers, next morning he watched the medevac helicopters fly in. "I was like, 'I am not coming here, I don't know what these people are smoking, they are *nuts*.'" Six months later, Jeremy was marching the same fields on R-Day.

His father, Ray Kasper, was "shocked that he chose to go. He never was physical. He never played sports — just debate team, chess club, stuff like that. I think he wanted to see if he could do it. But immediately he stood straighter, he walked taller, had more confidence. The first Christmas he came home, he was bored, he said there were no physical challenges — he wanted to get back."

How West Point molds cadet personalities like Kasper's and Pimentel's is a topic for detailed analysis. "The outcome we're trying to shape here is their sense of self," Colonel Barney Forsythe explains. "The fundamental question is, How do you develop their professional self-concept?" Forsythe is West Point's vice dean of education — sandy hair, square glasses. The world of ideas is solid for him; when he refines a point he raps my notebook. Forsythe's father was Major General George I. Forsythe, who instituted the Army's last great shift, from a draft basis to a professional, all-volunteer force.

Colonel Forsythe has been working alongside Colonel Scott Snook on the new Cadet Leader Development System, a quieter sort of revolution. Instead of focusing on the *know* or *do* elements of "Be, Know, Do" (the Army's standard training pattern actually was devised by a friend of Forsythe's), they're focusing on the *be*. West Point, he says, is about "planned change — fundamentally changing people." As of 2000, that job is more complicated than ever, because there's no clear answer as to what types of conflicts they are preparing cadets for. "The argument is, we can't train them for every possible encounter," Forsythe says, "'cause we can't anticipate what those encounters will be like. Instead, we have to develop them to be the kind of people who can sort it out for themselves once they get there."

To that end, Forsythe and Snook rely on a framework created by the Harvard psychologist Robert Kegan, in an influential study called *The Evolving Self*. Kegan broke down the evolution of any self into five stages. Stage one is more or less how everybody acts as toddlers and children: impulse driven. ("I *am* my impulses," Forsythe explains.) Stage two is early adolescence: the formation of a personality, but one still devoted to serving your own needs. ("So if you ask a high school student why they do community service projects, the stage two answer might be, 'Well, I know it's an important way to get into college. And I sort of feel good when I'm doing it.'") Stage three is late adolescence: your values are defined by your group affiliation, whom you're standing next to. You're a team member with a team persona; before you answer, you look down the row to hear what the other guys have to say. ("So the stage three perspective on service projects might be, 'West Point is about selfless service, that's something we do here. If I didn't do it, I'd be letting my buddies down: it's what's expected of me, therefore I do it.'") Stage four is adulthood, the haven for the well-adjusted: you've internalized the values and made them your own. ("So you could articulate the value of service by what it means to you. You don't say, 'This is what my buddies and the profession expect of me.' You say,

'This is what I really stand for.'") Stage five is some kind of super-adulthood. Maybe your values are right, maybe they're wrong; they're just values. ("I'm not even sure I understand the stage five person — I've never met anybody like that.")

"When you look at West Point," Forsythe says, "we have a heavy stage three emphasis — be a team player, be part of the profession, be part of the group. What we really want to do is develop autonomous stage four people. So we push three and hope we'll mature them into four." Forsythe chuckles. "Well, we've been studying it for six years, and it turns out that the West Point experience is really about the transition from stage two to stage three."

This stall at stage three is receiving special emphasis now because of something that happened in Kosovo to a 1998 graduate named John Serafini. He was interrogating an Albanian prisoner; his NCOs suggested he get a little rough, and he held an empty pistol against the back of the Albanian's head until he learned what he needed to know. The story eventually made its way over the wires, to stateside papers and *Time* magazine (under just the worst kind of headline, "How U.S. 'Peace-Keeping' Became a Reign of Terror"), where it was described as "cross[ing] the line." There's talk of a court-martial for Lieutenant Serafini; his defense is that he was following the NCOs' advice, not values of his own. At West Point, this explanation set off alarm bells in every office. "This was clearly an officer stuck at stage two or stage three," Colonel Forsythe explains. "You can take advice from your NCOs, but then if you have your own values, you can say no. Because the *officer* is expected to be the one who sorts that out. That's why we've got to pay attention to this. It may well be that those who stay and color within the lines may be the least well equipped to deal with the challenges."

In G-4, at this year's Dining-in: the Corporation makes most of the challenges, the jokes are mainly inside-Corporation stuff. Eliel is forced to wear Mickey Mouse ears. "Because I'm from Orlando and I'm not a big fan of Disney — so instead of me drinking the grog, they had me wear the hat." Captain Vermeesch glows at the front table. "This crew could run the company," he says, "even if we were *never* here."

Happycadets.com

I f the Corporation represents stage three thinking, Ryan Southerland is an exemplar of stage four, with some of that inner Keirsey
too-muchness. It makes him a standout, a cadet other cadets look
to when he enters a room.

"He's just an outstanding dude," class vice president Carter Smyth
declares. "He cares about the right things, and he's one hundred percent genuine. He's inspired me to be a better person, because when you
see someone like him, you're just abashed. You're like, 'Why can't I be
like that?'"

Right now, Ryan's leadership abilities are lying fallow. Companies
follow a few Soviet-style nostrums ("Oh, it's an irony, we're very so-
cialistic around here," one officer tells me); command opportunities
are rationed like a commodity. If you've recently had a chance, as Ryan
did this summer, you can expect to warm the benches while someone
else takes a turn. In Ryan's case, he was picked Soldier of the Quarter
last spring, he got to be first sergeant at Beast. He asked for a platoon
sergeant's job, so he could have some effect on cadets. Instead, he
spends the term compiling intramural statistics as athletics sergeant.

When work shrivels, personal life balloons. During Beast, Ryan noticed Betty Simbert — the compact black junior who calls cadence like
a cheerleader. (Betty can't be over five feet tall, but her toned limbs give
her the look of a concentrated statue.) During the last weeks of Beast,
Ryan would make his way from talking to Betty's new cadets to talking
to Betty. By October, they're talking all the time by instant message.

MsBit [Betty]: what are you doing?
Grumpy [Ryan]: shining boots, we're having company inspections
    tomorrow . . .
MsBit: sounds like fun. us too. any chance to come over and shine
    them over here?

IMing has stormed the post. Cadet rooms thrum with the bells and
bleeps that announce incoming IMs. A few years ago, you'd see cadets
prowling the barracks before taps, hoping to scare up some human
contact. Now they're craned over their keyboards, hailing one another

over the Net. (TACs frown about it. "What bothers me when you look in the rooms is they have their backs turned to each other. A class can't get tight that way.") When they're away from their desks, cadets leave an "away message" on their IM, a gripe or a mission statement. One cadet collects them, posts the funniest and most telling at Happy-cadets.com. ("This site," a disclaimer runs, "is based and maintained in a neutral location so as to be in accordance with United States Military Academy Memorandum 93–01 . . . So far I am led to believe that this site has been a great morale booster.") Visiting the site is like strolling the Plain, reading people's minds.

giving up is a surprisingly good feeling

The phrase "high school hero, West Point zero" was developed in anticipation of my arrival at the academy.

"Get it together guys, I have a dog to kick and a wife to beat and I don't plan on being here all night."— TAC NCO

My parents keep asking how school was. It's like saying, "How was that drive-by shooting?" You don't care how it was. You're lucky to get out alive.

This week's MOPG [Moment Of Pure Genius] *again comes to us from the sweet dudes in the Brigade Tactical Department. The TAC came into my room and busted on me for having my gray blanket over the heater. He called it attempted arson. As if a radiator . . . heated by steam . . . could ignite a 100% wool blanket. It is now 120°F in my room because I have no control over the millions of BTU's that the heater is pumping out. He said he would authorize me to buy a wrench with my own funds to manipulate the knob that controls the heat.*

It's official, hell has frozen over— it's snowing

Top 5 Reasons Hell is Better Than W.P.
5. You can't get thrown out of hell
4. No one expects you to be perfect in hell
3. You wouldn't tell your friend to 'go to West Point'
2. There are more women in hell
1. Hell is forever, West Point just seems like it

So today in Beverly Hills, my Mom sees Brad Pitt, Jennifer Aniston, and Benicio Del Toro on the street . . . So today at West Point, I got to see George Rash . . . I definitely got the better of my Mom today.

Betty grew up in inner-city Miami, among palm trees and thunderstorms. Her parents came over from Haiti, her father went back soon after she was born. The year she was ready for high school, Miami Central established a JROTC program; as in many inner-city schools, the program was intended to keep students on the straight and narrow. "To build up people's self-esteem," Betty says. She's on West Point's cheerleading squad, the Rabble Rousers, and her words come in short cheerstyle bursts. "They wanted to start with freshmen. And they looked at me. 'You have the best grades and you look like you know what you're doing — you're the battalion commander.' I was like, 'What?'"

When Betty led her squad in competitions, they became famous as the team with the freshman leader. "I go back to my high school now and people I don't know say, 'There's Betty, oh my God, that's Betty Simbert, I want to be just like you.' I didn't do anything special. I just went to school." Her mentor, a retired major, directed her to West Point.

There are four regiments at West Point (G-4 is really shorthand for "Company G, Fourth Regiment"). African-American cadets jokingly refer to themselves as the "Fifth Regiment." Ogochukwu Obele, a big boxing-team champion from Boston with arms like truck tires, explains, "The Fifth Regiment is a way of saying the African-American population has to stick together." Of all the places I've been in America, including the thirty-five or so colleges I've visited as a reporter, West Point strikes me as the most successfully integrated, the least afflicted by racial tension. And it seems that way to most cadets as well. Yet the Fifth Regiment is distinguished by more than skin color. Many African Americans shun the post barbers — they're not great with blacks' hair — getting their hair trimmed in Harlem instead. They go clubbing off post more often than white classmates. And though they comprise 8 percent of the cadet corps, the gripe is they snag a much higher proportion of the leadership jobs. (TACs fret in their offices over meeting the "proper demographic distribution.") White kids bellyache about this affirmative-action disparity, but black cadets perceive it differently. They point out that while the percentage of women at West

Point exactly matches their numbers in the service, blacks make up far less than the 30 percent they do in the regular Army.

Another reason for the tight connection among African Americans: they're often directed to West Point's prep school — in Fort Monmouth, New Jersey — one final hurdle, a year to bring them up to academic speed. (It isn't just African Americans. Andy Blickhahn — the odds-on favorite right now for next year's first captaincy — did a prep school year himself. If you don't make C's there, home you go.) Even when a black candidate has exceptional grades, she'll sometimes cool her heels at the school anyway. "I had straight A's and twelve hundred on my SATs," explains Mary Tobin, a yuk from Atlanta. "I know people who entered West Point straight in with some significantly lower scores than myself. My year they were doing a huge push for minority females. So almost thirty of us entered the prep school together." With more minorities in the enlisted ranks, this becomes an important consideration; soldiers like to look up and see they're being led by a face that resembles their own.

The same holds true at West Point. Black cadets know how important it is to spot another black face in class, in the mess hall. Betty says, "We try to keep a close-knit family. When I see someone, I'm always like, 'How are your grades, make sure if you need anything, you come see me.' We've *got* to stick together, because if you don't see someone that looks like you here, then you start to think, 'I'm the only one,' and it gets harder."

For two years, Betty felt strongly that the Fifth Regiment's cohesion should extend to romance. She made fun of black friends who dated white cadet girls. "*All* of them did. And I just said, 'Why?' And they'd say, 'Because the black girls aren't coming across.' And I'm like, 'That's disgusting.' I'd tell them, 'You know, your mother would kill you if you brought a white beauty home.' So when I started dating Ryan, they started laughing, saying, 'Oh, you're a hypocrite.' And I know I am. Even now, I still give them a hard time about white girls."

And Ryan had never dated a black girl. He was just "a small-town boy," in Betty's words. (Her friends sometimes describe him as a "dorky-ass white boy.") The delicate issue of race crops up in their IMs.

MsBit (11:25:53 P.M.): hey can i tell you a secret . . . that i have been thinking about lately

MsBit (11:26:28 P.M.): well . . . you are the first white guy that i have ever thought about kissing, kissed . . . etc

Grumpy (11:27:00 P.M.): what have you been thinking about that? because i have thought about that a lot too.

MsBit (11:30:46 P.M.): i always thought that it would be weird, but its not. i have thought about my past opinions about stuff like this

Grumpy (11:33:34 P.M.): because as much as it is not an issue for me personally it is still something . . . aaarrrgghhh . . . you know?

MsBit (11:33:49 P.M.): yeah i know . . . it makes me nervous

Grumpy (11:35:05 P.M.): do you know why?

MsBit (11:36:34 P.M.): i dont know . . . that's just how it was growing up . . . i guess . . . i see it as an insult . . . when it's the other way round . . . it kind of hurts me . . .

Grumpy (11:38:43 P.M.): it makes me nervous too . . . I've never really been with a black woman before

MsBit (11:38:50 P.M.): why is it different? just weird jitters I guess

Grumpy (11:39:18 P.M.): maybe that's weird of me . . .

Grumpy (11:40:18 P.M.): in high school it seemed the w guys that had black girlfriends usually were just the kind of guys who really wished they were black

Grumpy (11:40:25 P.M.): and spent their waking moments trying to fit in with the black guys

MsBit (11:40:59 P.M.): most of my friends back at home would never date a w guy . . . my school had about 6,000 people, there were only 2 white people . . . but all of my new friends have all dated white guys

MsBit (11:41:09 P.M.): and i think they kind of change my perspective on things . . . then i wonder why we always come back to that one reason for being nervous

Grumpy (11:41:20 P.M.): what has that made you think about me?

MsBit (11:41:30 P.M.): nothing about you really . . . now i am thinking about . . . how my opinion makes you feel

MsBit (11:41:38 P.M.): does it change your perception of me at all

Grumpy (11:41:43 P.M.): no it does not

Grumpy (11:42:11 P.M.): i like you, and it doesn't matter to me. my real friends would not say anything in seriousness or think anything.

MsBit (11:42:24 P.M.): same here . . . my friends . . . would just
wonder if the kissing was good and if you were a totally good
guy

MsBit (11:42:34 P.M.): i can confirm the good guy part though . . .
lol

Grumpy (11:43:14 P.M.): ok. good night. you have to read this away
message

Auto response from Grumpy (11:44:02 P.M.): "Because there is
something in the touch of flesh with flesh which cuts sharp and
straight across . . . Let flesh touch with flesh, and watch the fall
of all the eggshell shibboleth of caste and color too." ~William
Faulkner, *Absalom, Absalom*

Grumpy (11:44:28 P.M.): I like the last part best

Toward the end of first term, Ryan is invited to meet with Sergeant
Greer, the adult NCO who's command sergeant major of the corps of
cadets. Greer is interviewing candidates for brigade command sergeant
major next term. This is the biggest job a cow can have (it's the job
Andy Blickhahn has now); you become the highest-ranking cadet in
your class. When Ryan arrives in Washington Hall, two cadets are already waiting for their interview slots on the bench outside Greer's office. Inside, there are coins and guidons and a life-size cutout of John
Wayne, squinting at some surmountable problem on the horizon.
Whenever Ryan turns his head, he finds himself meeting John Wayne's
eye.

It's a strange conversation. Greer asks if Ryan wants the job; Ryan
answers no — he'd really prefer to be a platoon sergeant. Greer asks
what he thinks about his fellow cadets. Ryan declares that there's a
problem with cynicism, and Greer asks what should be done to erase
it. Ryan points out that all cadets ever hear is that various actions are
unprofessional — no one ever tells them how they *should* act, beyond
just saying it should be professional, so instead everyone is sticking in
their rooms and playing on their computers.

The window goes dark outside, the conversation runs past the allot-
ted fifteen minutes. Thirty minutes pass, an hour. Ryan finds himself
talking about the Army values card that hangs around every cadet's
neck — how stirring ideals can become just a sliver of plastic that rubs
under your collar. "You just don't want cadets to say, 'This is the way it

should be' without proving it to yourself first," Ryan says. "You want to put that critical eye to things — not just trust something 'because the SOP says it.' When the Academy lets you get there under your own steam, and you've been down that road yourself, then you know it and believe it so much better."

When Ryan steps outside, the same two cadets are still waiting on the same bench, glares and worry on their faces. A few weeks later, assignments get posted, and Ryan is the new brigade command sergeant major.

Honor

It would be hard to estimate just where George Rash falls on the Kegan scale. In company, he's part of an anti-clique. Generally, once they're past plebe year, cadets gain some control over their housing partners. George bunks with cadets who've been shunned by their peers, who forget to list their picks on the sign-up sheet; he's G-4's roommate of last resort. This term, he's paired with Scott Mellon, a small, snarly TEDs wearer from Oregon. Mellon's a math-science whiz who's been on the service end of a lot of cooperate-and-graduate stories. Sharing plebe-year quarters with Huck Finn, he guided the big footballer through the hoops of each class. "Frickin' tutored me every night," Huck grins. "He's one reason I'm still here — the kid's a genius, man." "He got me through math," Huck's teammate Cal Smith says. "That kid cooperated with me, otherwise I'd have no chance of graduating." As George's honor investigation gears up, Scott has an idea for how George could cooperate with him. "Why don't you just quit and leave now?" Scott asks at night. "That way, I could have the room to myself."

The honor system that has snared Rash is one of the Academy's proudest achievements. As is often the case at West Point, higher notions spring from the practical. Early superintendents had good sound military reasons for stressing honor: in the field, under fire with lives at stake, an officer's word had to be his bond. In the cities, dredging expensive harbors and canals, graduates with unmonitored budgets would face the temptations of the ledger book.

The second reason had to do with the peculiar role early-nineteenth-century colleges began to play in American life. After the Revolutionary War, college attendance grew fashionable, and the campus atmosphere turned into a heady mix of hedonism and disorder; students went on one extended bender. University presidents complained of "riotous action," "profane swearing" and card-playing — the way contemporary deans will grouse about underage drinking and PlayStations — while urban students slunk off campus to attend horse races and the low-cost, ad lib entertainment of the public hanging.

New colleges took to the woods. The 1789 charter for the University of North Carolina, the nation's first public university, specified the campus be constructed no closer than five miles to a city; cities were thought to emit corrupting doses of what was quaintly called "vice." (The University of New Jersey had followed the same rationale years earlier when it relocated to tiny Princeton. Students, a trustee explained, would be "more sequestered from the various temptations" of modern city life, "that theatre of folly and dissipation.") This didn't spare Chapel Hill. Students were expelled for "firing pistols in the buildings" and "throwing stones at the faculty," for breaking a "window-glass" over a tutor's head, for attempting to burn down the trustees' house. In 1799, for a full week, students rioted; they went after the faculty. A professor testified, "They accosted Mr. Flinn with the intention of beating him, but were diverted from it, and at length uttered violent threats against Mr. Murphey and Mr. Caldwell . . . [they] waylaid and stoned Mr. Webb . . . they beat Mr. Gillaspie personally." When the university's president suggested an honor pledge "to suppress every species of irregularity," it sparked the Great Rebellion of 1805.

Up and down the states, students revolted to protest liquor restrictions, expulsions, bad food (Harvard had two menu incidents, a Great Butter Rebellion and a Rotten Cabbage Rebellion) and rules in general. A professor wrote they had "wild notions of liberty." In 1807, to protest suspensions — over cursing, liquor and "tavern-frequentation" — Princeton students seized Nassau Hall, repelling faculty members and concerned townspeople with banisters yanked from the staircase. A few years later, they jailed tutors in their rooms, nailed shut the doors and windows, set fire to the outbuildings. At the University of Virginia, when a professor tried to break up a drinking party, he was shot in the belly.

At Harvard, student-organized "combinations" kept informants from ratting on miscreants, and groups vandalized the homes of professors who handed out too much schoolwork. (Night watchmen who tried to stop the vandals got walloped too.) More than half of one class got booted out before graduation, and in 1821 about a tenth of the student body reported suffering from venereal disease.

In its early days, West Point wrestled with the same sort of student behavior that bedeviled civilian colleges. Early cadets went AWOL, fired muskets from windows, found professional women to service them on campus. In 1804, the second superintendent walked away from the job. A professor urged him to return, in a letter that is one of the first examples of corps-has: "Everything is going to ruin. Morals and knowledge thrive little and courts-martial and flogging prevail."

The fifth supe, Colonel Sylvanus Thayer, started bringing the Academy to heel in 1817. Thayer's solutions laid the groundwork for modern West Point. (Thayer is the sort of romantic, exacting figure historians write about this way: "He never married. The Academy was his only love.") One idea was the invention of TACs. Another was strictly limiting vacation time. (Thayer found that cadets on furlough would travel to New York and other cities, "there to indulge in dissipation and to contract disease, vices and debts. Others were put in jail and several of the young gentlemen I have not heard of since.") He curtailed their on-post free time too, scheduling nearly every moment of the cadet day, and greatly reducing the opportunities for delinquency. Thayer also prohibited smoking, drinking, gambling, spare-time novel-reading, cooking, chess, cards, subscribing to more than one periodical, playing a musical instrument, and swimming in the river.

Thayer's greatest innovation, the honor system, was somewhat at odds with these others. While the new restrictions severely limited cadets' actions — the theory being, as Thayer wrote President James Monroe, that any liberty offered a chance to misbehave — the honor system relied on cadets' moral strength and free will. Thayer streamlined the matter to its essence. If a cadet found himself accused of a regs violation, he was asked to confirm, excuse or deny it. Thayer accepted the statements at face value. Since cadets were gentlemen of character, he reasoned, their word was beyond doubt. He defined honor as the cadets' most treasured possession, which forced cadets to recalculate the value of any potential infraction. Would they trade their honor for a drink, a smoke, a game of cards?

The regulations and principles transformed West Point into a spartan, ethical ideal, and by the 1830s made it a popular tourist destination. Even Americans who would never live so correctly were relieved to know somebody still was, in the way agnostics get cheered up by Christmas. A midcentury Board of Visitors reported that cadets followed "a course of conduct that challenges the admiration of every beholder." Journalists swooned too. "Oh," wrote one 1870 *Boston Globe* reporter, "for such honoring of *honor.*"

At first, cadets enforced the code on their own. Known liars — or suspect, bureaucratic survivors of the process — were silenced. The old-time phrase was "sending them to Coventry"; breaking a silence constituted an honor violation in itself. If one cadet disturbed another's honor, they settled it by stepping outside. This evolved into semi-official "scrapping committees." If cadets lied about their whereabouts, or stole, they could find themselves shaken awake after taps. Cadet gangs would march them to the gate by lamplight, sometimes tar and feather them, sometimes force them into civilian clothes, sometimes hang a sign saying *Thief* around their necks, and send them packing. This evolved into a semi-official group with the menacing name "vigilance committee." In the 1920s the thirty-first supe, Douglas MacArthur — while restoring vacations and other contact with the outside world — organized them into Honor Committees with a formal hearing system. In 1947 General Maxwell Taylor drafted the honor code's terse mandate: "A cadet will not lie, cheat, or steal." In 1970 the phrase "or tolerate those who do" was added, in a sense enlisting every cadet on post as a member of the vigilance committee.

God, These People
Absolutely *Hate* Me

I n late August, two firsties from the Honor Committee, Balog and Mahoney, show up in George's room, posing deadly questions with FBI courtesy. George is facing two separate charges of lying: to Cadet Wilkins when he said he checked his Beast squad's feet "all the time," to Captain Engen when he reported he last checked them "on Friday."

Balog and Mahoney return a few days later for a sharper round of questioning — so it's clear different truths are being held up to the light, they want to measure George's word against others'. George writes and signs a statement after each interview, they carry it away for use at his hearing. Then they're back again, to introduce a term George has never heard before. "So, you're *self-admitting* that you lied?" George says yeah, he guesses he is.

Then, for a month, nothing happens. George walks the post in that eerie suspension that comes to any accused man, when it seems the authorities might simply have misfiled the paperwork, moved on, dropped the case. It's this period that nibbles away at many cadets on honor like acid. But George has already been inured by his West Point experience. "There are barriers that I've unfortunately built up," he explains, sitting alone in his room, "— fortunately or unfortunately, depending on how you look at it. To try to take criticism in stride. I might not do the job as well as they'd like to see me do it, but I can put up with a lot more shit than most people could . . . handle. When I came to West Point, the barriers were like clay, they were malleable and I could occasionally get around them. And the first two years were like the kiln that basically hardened them into bricks."

The hearing process doesn't start well for George. For some reason, the Brigade Honor Committee forgets to give him a copy of the packet containing the evidence against him. So George has no idea exactly what he's up against until he's sitting in the shiny, paneled hearing room at his preliminary hearing. There isn't enough time to proofread everything and make his objections, so they send him on his way.

Next morning he meets his JAG lawyer, Dan something, it could be Schimik, in the rush of events George never catches his name. First they go over the self-admitting botch. In fact, his lawyer explains, what he's told was not a lie but a *falsehood*. George had no intent to deceive anyone; he just got his facts wrong.

Then JAG Dan marks what's inadmissible and hearsay in the packet — about half the testimony. The words will be whited out on the photocopies for next week's hearing. No lawyer is allowed to assist there. George will serve as his own attorney: delivering opening and closing statements, cross-examining each hostile witness, defending himself. (At West Point, every cadet on honor is the lawyer who has a fool for a client.)

As he prepares his case, he rereads statements from cadet Kim Wilkins, from Captain Engen, from Mrs. Como the Red Cross volunteer; from members of his Bravo Company cadre and the new cadets in his squad. George's stomach sinks to his toes. "My God," he says, "these people absolutely *hate* me." The witnesses haven't stopped with George's performance; they've gone after his motivation, his character and drive. "They've basically called my whole existence into question. Whether I should be here, what kind of person I am, why I do the stuff I did. Basically they've called me a scumbag a dozen ways from here to Tuesday." Mrs. Como goes farthest: for her, George is an aloof figure, cold and menacing, a taskmaster who drove his squad past exhaustion into injury. "I met the lady for five minutes, ten at the *outside,* it sounds like she wants to put me on the stake and burn me."

Climb to Glory

As a *self-eliminate* at flight school, Whitey Herzog has to complete true-false psychology tests; the questions, soldiers joke, are the do-you-paint-with-your-own-excrement variety. The other phase of changing branches is an all-you-can-eat challenge. Whitey reports up the chain of command, from his captain to his battalion commander, downing another serving of reproach at every stop. The officers don't just want to make Whitey feel small — the aim is to make him feel small enough to stay Aviation.

He gives his salute in front of their desks, standing eyes-front, hearing the five-year-old echo of his words before the Cadet in the Red Sash: "Sir, Lieutenant Herzog reports as ordered." From there it's a kind of haze: Whitey ranks in the class's top half, he is leaving with only a few weeks to go. The officers ask, "Do you know how much money the government has paid to get you this far?" They ask, "Do you realize you're being selfish? Do you understand what sacrifice is?" They ask, "Do you want a kid someday? What are you going to say when that kid comes up to you and wants to quit something? You're going to be a real good quitter by then, aren't you?" One says simply, "I can't let you walk out of my office feeling good."

One of the final officers receives Whitey's salute, sends him to parade rest, then makes an invitation: "Let's both sit down on the couch. I know you're a strong pilot, it's clear you're working hard, everyone in your chain of command has good things to say about you." The tone surprises Whitey; they talk for half an hour. "There's no other branch like this," the officer reminds him. "Aviation goes everywhere, there's some real huah stuff, the shit we do is amazing." "I'm like, 'I know that, sir,'" Whitey remembers. "'I've got nothing but respect for this branch.' Then he says, 'Plus flight pay — but you know money's not what it's about.' I go, 'Roger sir, I know that.' He says, 'It's a great branch and a great career. I just don't want to see you having any regret. You have till Thursday to think it over.' Then he looks me in the eye and dismisses me, doesn't say a single bad thing. I wanted to tell him so bad — but you really can't say it — 'Sir, I appreciate you not giving me a hard time about this.' Because when something like that gets done, it's just done. You don't talk about it or say, 'Thanks for not being tough.' I just said, 'Sir, I appreciate your time.'"

Then Whitey heads off to Fort Jackson, South Carolina, home of the Finance Corps, for a four-month training course. (Finance's motto is the unassuming "To Support and Serve." It's one of the oldest branches — when you field an Army, you need an apparatus to pay it — and there's even a Finance song: "Pay Day, Pay Day / That's our special day . . . / When the Army gets the call / We'll be ready one and all / We'll be there when you hit that distant shore.") He has his own quarters in Dozier Hall, a kind of snug hotel room: sofa, microwave, TV. ("Victory starts here," a recorded female voice declares on the phone system every time a friend calls.) Studying in the Finance classes, Whitey finds friends among the sorts of relaxed people he never had time for at West Point. It turns out they aren't bad guys. There's one Academy grad who took his $25,000 cow loan, invested and day-traded it up past $1 million. There's an ROTC guy who shares a list of promising IPOs. Every afternoon, as soon as classes break, there's a stampede for the computers, students rushing to check on their stock portfolios.

Classes are a mix of Finance material — they learn to break down a paycheck — and general Army doctrine Whitey's taken before. They bond over Developing Unit Cohesion, worry together about Reducing

Vulnerability to Terrorist Attack (not that anything's on the fall 2000 radar, but with people like bin Laden around, it's something every officer should get used to considering). They admire the beautiful simplicity of the Military Problem-Solving Process. "It's a class I've had a million times," Whitey says. "But it's great, everyone should take it at least once. Any problem you have in life, there's seven guidelines to keep things rational." Difficulties, which come in a tangle, submit to assigned slots like cleaned dishes going into the pantry:

1) Recognize and Define the Problem.
2) Gather Facts and Make Assumptions.
3) Define End States and Establish Criteria. ("'Criteria' is how you know you've reached those end states," says Whitey. "That's one of the most important steps.")
4) Develop Possible Solutions.
5) Analyze and Compare Possible Solutions.
6) Select and Implement Solution.
7) Analyze Solution for Effectiveness.

There's only one *Recognized Problem* for Whitey. It arrives at the Finance field training exercise and awakens all his old Infantry yearnings. Whitey and the other LTs spend five days performing pay missions in the rainy South Carolina woods. Driving a Humvee, they deliver salary to an Armor battalion. Along the way, OPFOR — the opposition force, Infantry soldiers practicing their guerrilla techniques — harries them. This is part of everyone's training: in a forward area, Finance officers must be capable, essentially, of making change under fire. Whitey keeps his cool, helps his squad pin the OPFOR down and fight them off.

The last night, a captain named Greer — an infantryman who rebranched from Bragg, The Division — asks Whitey, "You've got Infantry experience, don't you?" Whitey thinks of those long-ago weeks with the Rangers. "It's relative," Herzog answers mildly, "but I know what I'm doing." Greer wants to unhinge the OPFOR: "We've been on the receiving end for a week. Let's take the fight to them." He details Whitey to take charge of part of the ambush. After dark, Whitey and seven guys cover the right flank of the field the OPFOR are aggressing from. They crouch all night in the turf at the woodline's edge. Rain turns to freezing rain, bits of ice catching on the grass like rock salt.

They change watch every hour. At 0350, Whitey's turn, there's the boom and flash of artillery simulators. The OPFOR is assaulting again, a jumble of shadows creeping across the field. Whitey and his squad open up on them. For the first seconds, the OPFOR don't even know where the attack is coming from. "They didn't know *what* was going on, it was obvious panic." Textbook stuff, Whitey and his team trading off among three SAWs (heavy squad automatic weapons) to maintain a constant rate of fire. In the morning After Action Review, the OPFOR are reduced to sputtering complaints about how Finance shouldn't go on the offensive.

The counterattack thrilled Whitey. "I got on one of the SAWs, it was great, it was a rush, we tore them up. It reminded me what I love about the Infantry." Then he catches himself. "But it's not something I want to make a career of."

Whitey has a plan. For step three, *Define End States*, he's aiming for the life Mark Matty didn't get: start a family, have a lot of fun. "I've learned I want a predictable life," he says. "And my family is gonna have the most wonderful father and the most wonderful husband." But for step six, *Implement Solution*, he doesn't pick a sunshine post like Europe or Hawaii. He requests Fort Drum, partly because Iggy Ignacio is there. But there's another back-of-the-mind reason. Drum deploys all the time; right now they have the best real-world detail, Kosovo.

Drum, on the snow prairies of upstate New York, is home to the Tenth Mountain Division — their symbol is two crossed bayonets above the motto "Climb to Glory." During World War II, the Army put together a force that could ski, climb and shoot. The roster was filled out with Ivy Leaguers and championship skiers. (In 1944 the Tenth broke the back of the Nazis' Gothic Line in the Apennine Mountains of Italy, sustaining 30 percent casualties, the highest rate of any American unit.) When the war ended, like disciples who'd been to the mountaintop, veterans fanned out across an America full of underused slopes and founded the U.S. ski industry — building resorts in Utah and Vermont, Vail and Aspen, spreading the gospel through downhill magazines and ski schools.

Iggy has come to Drum from Ranger school. His fourth day there, before a run in BDUs, lugging packs and weapons, an instructor asked to see raised hands from prior heat casualties. Iggy had gone down at

Airborne school. "I'm being honest," Iggy remembers, so up went his hand. "OK," the instructor said, "you run in back."

In the heat and the backwash of a hundred other joggers, Iggy had started to sweat, sweat a lot, started to bob his head. Instantly he had a Ranger instructor on him. "Put your head down one more time," the RI said, "and that's it." It stopped being about legs or lungs; for Iggy, the run became all neck. "And it's hard to maintain. Finally I couldn't do it no more, my head slipped." The RI said, "That's it, that's the end," and pulled Iggy aside to trees and cool shade while the line jogged into the scenery. Everyone had been warned about arguing with instructors — "they can get you for insubordination. So I look at him, I say, ''Scuse me, Sergeant, did I fail the standard?' He said, 'No, I just didn't want to see a heat casualty.'" Iggy shakes his head. "I knew what was going to happen right then. I'm not used to that — I've never not finished anything in my life. And I didn't even get to pass out, y'know? This is Ranger school — you're supposed to go till you're fuckin' *dead*. But they've had a lot of serious heat injuries, I guess they were protecting themselves, which I understand."

For an Infantry officer like Iggy, not having the Ranger tab can consign you to second-class citizenship. "You can't do without it as a mud crawler," officers like Jim DeMoss explain. "Ranger school is as close to the continuous strained experience of combat operations as we can come. When I meet another Infantry officer, that tab is the first thing I look for. If it's not there I feel like I wanna ask why." Captain Vermeesch wears the tab, but on his first try he got eliminated by the PT test before Ranger even started. "I consider that to be my greatest failure in my life," he says flatly, frowning. "You hear all the stories about when guys report in and, first thing, the battalion commander turns them around and looks on their left shoulder to see if they have the tab. I got sent off to my unit as a brand-new lieutenant without one, and that's an ugly situation to be in."

That's Iggy's situation now. When he sees his buddies from Ranger school at Drum, "they've all got the tab. I'm so happy for them, because they're my friends. But you know what it feels like to watch your guys move ahead when you're not getting to go along with 'em." He sighs. "Whitey knows. Guys who went straight to Vietnam — they never had the tab, they did fine. But I won't feel complete until I get it."

So here Whitey and Iggy are, roommates. They live in Watertown,

New York, such an Army company town the local waitresses perform the birthday song in cadence. ("I don't know but I been told / Someone here is getting old. / Sound off: hap-py, / Sound off: birth-day.") It's been more than a year since they said goodbye in Hawaii, and they've both met surprises and setbacks. They find an apartment, a floor-through in a weatherbeaten Victorian.

Whitey drives to Buffalo one weekend. He pays a call on the Mattys, shares a restaurant meal with his Buffalo crew. A cocktail waitress skims by, takes his attention. She's very good-looking, dressed like a cowgirl: pointy boots, suede skirt, leopard-skin Stetson. "Holy shit," Whitey says. "That's *Loryn Winter.*"

She's supposed to be in Los Angeles, enjoying the goods: good car, good job, the good civilian guy she dropped Donald for. It's the kind of meeting you rehearse in your mind a hundred times, and then the moment reduces you to ad libs. He stands and takes her arm. "Hey, Loryn," he says, "nice hat." Loryn's face actually goes white — something Whitey has read about but never seen in real life. She disappears behind the kitchen's swinging doors and doesn't come out.

But she must be watching, because as they're settling the check she's back at his side; Whitey smells her perfume, feels the old irradiation on the parts of his body that are facing hers. "I want to talk to you," she says. "I've been so sorry. I want to apologize for walking away that time."

"Don't worry," Whitey says. "I wasn't too concerned about it."

She brightens. "So how *are* you?"

Whitey starts to answer, but the perfume, smile, hat — it all sidetracks him. "You're . . . ," he says. "You're a — cocktail waitress."

Brave Soldier

Reporting for his honor hearing, George Rash looks more presentable than he's ever been. Even his eyeglasses appear creased and pressed, as if they've returned from the dry cleaner's. He has the job applicant's blank-slate look, the willingness to exhibit only what others want to see. By the end of the day, nine cadets will decide whether he gets to stay at West Point.

George is wearing his white-over-gray honor uniform. When the process kicks off at 0730 — the JAG representative sitting on a raised podium like a tennis umpire, making sure the hearing keeps within the lines, the honor president rubbing sleep out of his eye — George is alone. An accused cadet is permitted to bring one cadet adviser with him into the hearing room: the adviser can sit at his table, pass notes, offer strategy and the moral support of the raised eyebrow, everything but speak. George asked Steve Ruggerio (his bar mitzvah guest) if he could do it, but Steve is away from post. Then he turned to Phil Sacks, an H-1 cow who's his best friend from Jewish choir. "But he told me he didn't feel he could give it all his efforts, or help me as thoroughly as I deserved," George says and frowns. "Yeah, he pretty much backed out." So George meets his fate alone, the chair empty by his side.

But the G-4 crew does turn out. A good half of the company stops in for some of George's trial. Beyond the dependable fishbowl entertainment of any honor hearing, there's the historical factor to this one, like attending the Beatles' last concert. Scott Mellon spends most of his day; during the months of rooming together, the two cadets have patiently negotiated from what George calls "an armed truce to almost friends." Neither one is exactly the square-jawed West Point standard, which lends their bond a solid underdog basis. Even Sergeant Mike Tierney is here, drawn by the NCOs' helpless affection for soldiers, even soldiers they don't entirely approve of.

George seems surprisingly well rested. "I only slept five hours last night, but that's probably also because I took a three-hour nap yesterday afternoon, but that's beside the point." He cracks his neck, and the hearing begins. First comes jury selection, composing the nine-member cadet Honor Board. Who you pick could determine how you fare — and George is supposed to be on the lookout for any pro-officer or anti-Rash bias. He only rejects one guy, "just because he's sat on so many juries, it wouldn't be fair to force him to do another." During the 0930 recess — coffee, latrines — Sergeant Tierney can't watch in silence any longer. He takes Rash aside, stands him by the wall, "strongly suggests" he face this with a cadet adviser, any cadet adviser. "Heck," George says, "why not?" Tierney sends a cadet runner — and Jerry Davis, a steady, personable firstie, is nabbed coming out of a helicopter lab. He changes uniform, trots over, shakes George's hand, smoothes his hair, and George isn't alone anymore.

They're sent to cool their heels while the Honor Board reads

George's packet. Like most available West Point real estate, the Nininger Hall walls are trimmed with inspiration. There's a framed saber that once belonged to the "Brave Soldier," the class of 1951's honorary graduate, Robert A. Renneman. Renneman actually graduated Navy. But he'd grown to six feet seven inches — leaving him the wrong size for duty at sea; he commissioned Army and Infantry. During Korea, he led troops so hard he ended up far ahead and isolated, amid entrenched Chinese troops, batting away grenades with his free hand. When Renneman eventually fell, there was no safe way to retrieve the body. The next day, his unit approached his remains cautiously, expecting theft, violation, booby traps. Instead, the Annapolis ring was on his finger, his boots — one of combat's prime salvage items — were untouched. His face and uniform had been cleaned and repaired. A note from the enemy lay nearby: "Brave soldier. Take him home."

A cadet opens the door. "Everybody's finished. We're ready for you to come in now." George takes a breath, steps inside and delivers his opening statement. Being George, he has to use the time clearing up an earlier misstatement. His voice effortlessly slips into the legalese adopted by defendants on shows like *The People's Court*. "If you'll refer to the third board exhibit, which was my third written statement, you'll notice I self-admitted. This was because I was unaware of the true semantics of the definition of lying, which is telling a falsehood with the intent to deceive." That's the key to his defense. George sits down, Jerry gives him a sharp nod, and the witnesses begin.

Captain Chris Engen rolls in like a thunderhead, darkening the room for George. He takes his seat at the witness stand and provides a live version of his written statement. Rash watches closely, listens carefully. At an honor hearing, the board — the jury — also conducts the witness examinations. Engen explains that George waited three hours before changing his story. The Honor Board inquires, "Where were you during the remainder of the day, sir?" "Would it have been difficult for cadet Rash to find you, sir?" The delay has raised questions in the jurors' minds about George's candor. His own explanation was that the company had become so spread out it was difficult to track Captain Engen down. The captain says he was always nearby. Then the board tries to home in on George's demeanor. Did he seem nervous, guilty? The captain explains his voice did seem cautious and slow. (This line of questioning makes Scott Mellon snort. "Of course *anybody* talking to his TAC is going to think he's in trouble. He'll sound nervous whether he's lying or not.")

Then the board sets a speaker phone on the witness stand to relay Mrs. Como's testimony. For all the cadets know, she could be steering a minivan or sitting in a tree. It takes only five minutes for the Red Cross volunteer to undo all of George's diligent work at the preliminary hearing; she verbally reinstates all the objectionable language he had whited out. George, she says, is aloof and cold, and nobody liked him. Then she goes too far. George is also remorseless, and he scares people. The board members glance politely away from the phone, as people do when a voice has stopped commanding belief. They know George Rash has never scared anybody.

Then Mrs. Como reports the basics: cadet Rash failed to notice a case of trench foot in one of his squad members, and she overheard him lie about it to cadet Kim Wilkins. At their table, George and Jerry exchange notes, and George rises to cross-examine the phone. "Mrs. Como, do I have any medical training or basis for judging feet?"

Any basis?

"Do you believe that I have any specialized professional knowledge, to determine if somebody's feet are OK? Especially if the cadet had already informed me his feet are fine?" Jerry nods, writes on his pad where George can see: *Don't need to get more from this witness.*

The board thanks Mrs. Como, removes the phone and breaks for lunch. In the mess hall, George helps himself calmly to everything. He'll need to keep his energy up for the rest of the day, and it's incidentally a good menu — corn chowder, hot wings, chicken patties, bread sticks. Jerry Davis congratulates him on his composure; at other honor boards, he's watched cadets race into the latrines to throw up.

George strolls back into the hearing room, head held high, as if his case hasn't taken the beating it's just endured. Cadet Kim Wilkins takes the witness stand; the look she throws George is like a flashed knife. After cadet Calabanos's foot problem was diagnosed, she confronted George with the how-often-have-you-been-checking question. A few hours later she visited his tent to ask again, and that's when George downgraded his estimate to "most of the time." Her next move was reporting him on honor. The board snags on this issue. According to the honor code, if a cadet is aware of an honor violation but fails to report it, it's toleration — an honor violation of its own. But you're supposed to make a formal Approach for Clarification to the cadet you suspect before you file any charges. "Did you tell cadet Rash 'I'm here for clarification'?" a board member asks. "Did you say, 'I'd like you to clarify something for me'?" Looking stumped, Wilkins admits no, she didn't.

A different cadet might pass up the opportunity to cross-examine her. The board has already extracted good stuff, there's probably no more to find. (Jerry writes on his pad, *Don't need more.*) But George is suddenly curious, on a human level that transcends the hearing. Why *did* she ask the second time? He figures, as long as they've got her here, this could be his last chance to find out. Wilkins explains she was angry, she was hoping George would incriminate himself. It's the wrong thing to say. Noses wrinkle on the board. The word for this is *headhunting*, and the Army is a team. George sits down having finished off a witness.

The next witness is George's immediate cadet superior at Beast. He simply says there was no schedule for foot checks; the guidance essentially said "most of the time." George realizes if he can prove that's how often he did it, he's not guilty on honor.

The board pulls in George's old Beast squad one by one. George is up and about, asking questions and nailing down the timeline in his deliberate honking voice. So much is happening at Beast — bidding hello and goodbye to two different lives — that new cadets often have no idea how much time is passing. Days rise like cliffsides, the way a calendar might look to an ant. At first, they're no help, describing two-day gaps as lasting "a week and a half." Jerry is scribbling notes (*Ask when Warrior Forge was*), but George understands what he has to do. He sharpens the plebes' memories and soon they recall: George checked — spreading toes, examining heels barehanded, gloppy work — every other day. Cadet Calabanos, whose feet started all this, testifies that George checked "almost every morning."

Then George invites his character witnesses. There's Ahmond Hill, a G-4 cadet. (George asked him by chance a few days ago. "I was just wandering around the company, trying to learn to be sociable.") Then Jerry Davis turns to George, says "I'll do it," and he stands up and says a few good things he knows about cadet Rash. And then Phil Sacks shows up. He describes George's straight-and-narrow behavior on choir trips, dubbing him "the party pooper of the Jewish choir." He says he isn't surprised to see George at an honor hearing — which gets George's heart racing. He means that George gets in trouble for everything. But George never has trouble with maintaining his integrity; he gets in trouble, but he admits it, takes the hit, and drives on. "George is the cadet everybody knows *about* but nobody knows," Phil says.

Before George makes his closing statement, he glances at the nine faces on the honor board, hair short like his, uniforms like his. There's no way to tell if he's changed any minds.

The board deliberates for ninety minutes while George waits in the hall. They know that if George manages to graduate, he'll represent the Academy to anyone he runs into. People will adjust their impressions of West Point as a result. But they also know West Point has to remain a fair place. After the ninety minutes, they ask George to stand. The board president announces in a flat voice, "You are not found." Then they give George advice. To keep this problem from recurring, he should speak more clearly and concisely.

The path ahead is clear; three more terms at West Point, lower the head, grind it out, finish. Word ripples through the corps. For weeks people treat him differently; he's escaped from another locked room, he's demonstrated the soldier's fundamental attribute: endurance. George walks the post resolved and enlivened, like someone who's just eaten after a long fast. "For good or ill," George says, "I've become a survivor."

The Twelve Days of Christmas

A masked man has been sneaking into the rooms of West Point females, rifling their clothes, staring at the cadets while they sleep. Because the man cloaks his features with a terry cloth, cadets call him Towel Man.

West Point is a surprisingly open place. Most afternoons you could convene a model UN from the tourists photographing the monuments on Trophy Point — a plateau overlooking the river, dotted with cannon and statues — or a kennel club from locals who use the post to exercise their dogs. So Towel Man could be a cadet or a civilian, and most companies organize security details. Jeremy Kasper is working up the G-4 patrol schedule with a lively-eyed plebe named Patricia Teakle; Teakle has won a contest that allows her to shadow the company commander for a day. This is the part of the job Jeremy seems to like best, passing along his cadetness. They agree on which late-night hours to post cadets at stairwells and latrines, when to send them walking down the halls.

Jeremy trains his John Wayne smile on the plebe. "So we're done organizing. Now all we've got to do is give a snazzy name to this operation."

"Does it have to be a professional name, sir?" Teakle asks.

"No, it dudn't. But . . ."

She thinks hard. This is a big opportunity for a plebe, and she doesn't want to waste it.

"Come on," Jeremy says. "This should be the *easiest* part. What's your favorite animal?"

"How about Brain Stalker or something like that?" she asks brightly.

Long pause. He looks at her; both are learning a principle of military etiquette, that one's opinion isn't always welcome, even when it's invited. Finally he suggests, "What about Operation Jaguar? Hunts at night, drags things off. I like it. So we're going with Operation Jaguar."

When they're done and Teakle stands by the door, Jeremy says, "Please remember what we learned today, and try to use it to make yourself a better leader in the future."

"Thank you so much for the opportunity."

If some West Point conversations sound scripted, it's because they are, after a fashion. Cadets are screen-testing military dialogue on each other, gauging how persuasive they can sound. Kasper shakes Teakle's hand, walks down the hall toward another role: checking on cadets who took an APFT today. George Rash is among them. Kasper knows about the honor hearing, and harbors the usual mixed feelings about George. But he has no mixed feelings about the Academy. If the Academy says that George is meeting the standard, it leaves Jeremy in a pickle. "He still has a long way to go," Jeremy states carefully. "As long as he keeps his motivation high and he's willing to put forth the effort, then he will — he has every chance of becoming a leader for America's youth."

He gives George's door the double rap that announces official business. (A single or triple knock tells cadets a visit is social.)

"Enter, sir or ma'am," George says.

Jeremy ambles inside. "George. How'd you do on your APFT?"

Rash grins. "Passed it. Seventy-two push-ups, sixty-eight sit-ups." He grins again. "And fifteen-forty run."

"Congratulations," Jeremy says.

The cadets gaze at each other, like two sides of a mirror. Both arrived at West Point resembling each other far more than either one did the ideal cadet. Jeremy has worked ceaselessly to achieve that ideal; George has, against numerous assaults, fortified the personality he came in with. Each seems to see in the other an alternate reality, a path not taken. Then Jeremy swings his gaze down toward George's feet. "Shoes aren't lookin' *too* bad, George."

George treats this as the conversation starter it isn't. "Gotta shine my class shoes again."

"Keep up the good work," Jeremy says, with the slightly worried look of someone who's running out of prepared remarks.

"They got a little scuffed."

"You and me both," says Jeremy, stepping toward the door. "You and me both. Well, I don't wanna interrupt . . . I just wanted to say 'Outstanding.'"

"Thank you. It was a relief. I was running pretty hard. I didn't even look at my watch for the last two minutes of it." George is deep in his own persona, giving more information than anyone wants.

Jeremy deploys the Wayne smile. "Well, I'll tell you, George — you crossed two big hurdles these last couple of weeks. So hang in there, stay focused, continue to do the right thing. And you could make it out of here."

This should be the key that gets Jeremy through the door. "All I have to do is bring up the push-ups and the sit-ups to where they should be," George offers. "I know I can do better."

Jeremy reprises his exit line. "Well, hang in there. Have a good one."

"You too."

Professionalism has a limit, even for Jeremy. Every year, for the official Christmas dinner, all four thousand cadets enter the mess hall in full dress, red-faced from the cold air and excitement. At the end of the meal, they sing "The Twelve Days of Christmas." The verses pass to each wing of the hall, to each company, and as "five golden rings" arrives, cadets leap on the heavy wood tabletops while their dinner companions hoist the tables over their heads. "It's the *greatest* cohesion-building event," Jeremy explains. Song, effort, the sense of doing something in a huge, jolly group that no one else is doing in any other place in the world. This year, though, higher has been pondering how unprofessional and unsafe this tradition might be — asking what's really gained by exposing cadets to tired arms and the laws of gravity.

Fifteen minutes before Christmas dinner, an e-mail goes out to company commanders like Jeremy: cadets can sing, but they may not lift tables. "And we don't have time to prepare the cadets," Jeremy says, "for this whole change in the biggest holiday event of the year."

This year's first captain, a broad-backed, heavy-browed South Carolinian named Dave Uthlaut, mounts the poop deck in the center of the mess hall, above the din of talk and cutlery. "The corps is cordially invited," he says, with the measured flair of a joke, "*not* to raise their tables during this evening's singing." The hall buzzes hopefully: maybe Uthlaut's phrasing means that it's a suggestion, not an order. The singing begins. During the first verse the companies exchange looks, finger their tables, don't lift. But by the second stanza cadets jump aboard, and the thick platforms start to levitate. The BTO, Colonel Adamczyk, is here, along with the commandant and the TACs. They're running from table to table, yelling, as the cadets bellow and sing and the tables rise up together like spirit.

Afterward, every company commander is summoned to a bottom-floor day room in Eisenhower for what Jeremy calls "a *mandated* ass-chewing." The BTO offers a few stern words; the commandant, thin faced General Olson, describes how disappointed he was to see the entire corps violate a direct order. The comm asks the thirty-two company commanders, "If you were responsible for a lifted table, please raise your hand." Thirty-one hands go up; only one company commander abstains. The comm turns to her.

"Stand up, position of attention. Tell everyone here why, while they were failing to obey a direct — while *you* were in a sea of people doing things wrong — why you did the right thing."

"Sir," she says, "everyone at my table is female, and we couldn't lift it."

Shortly before Christmas break, Huck Finn gets a surprise gift. After Navy takes Army, 30–28, he's preparing for a relaxed, football-free second semester when he learns from Super-V that he's about to become a striper. He's been selected as next year's battalion command sergeant major. The job is a lunch-box version of Ryan Southerland's — a position that elevates Huck to first sergeant over four first sergeants. "If you can find out how I got picked for this," Huck tells people with a shrug, "you let me know."

Vermeesch knows. "People can change," he says. "And I feel pretty strongly about this: I think it's perilous to only recognize the folks who play right and stick within the limits. There is something to be said for someone who's willing to take a little personal risk. Now we'll see how Reid Finn performs with the spotlight on him twenty-four hours a day."

Bareass Is a No-Go

Since the days of Sylvanus Thayer, West Point has treated pop culture like a controlled substance. When prohibition succeeded, cadets became models of the unmediated life, showing what people might become once they're shielded from every uninspiring influence.

But that prohibition has now become unenforceable. For three years, TV has glowed in the barracks and DVDs have spun inside computers. The post bookstore — which retails airplane bestsellers, souvenir mugs, *Art of Camouflage* videos and soft-jazz CDs with misleading titles like *Sensuous Sax — Up All Night* — also rents videos to cadets. Shutting off the outside world now seems a noble, futile gesture, like blockading a country that's all shoreline. Higher picks its battles. MP3 download sites are embargoed on a solid intellectual-property basis. Internet pornography is prohibited on the theory that the American taxpayer, if consulted, wouldn't be thrilled to subsidize cadet tours of the erotic. Type in the wrong address, and the West Point helmet-and-sword logo fills your screen. The memo explains:

> To continue to access such sites is inconsistent with the central element of the USMA mission, with our stated Army values, and with our standing as the world's premier leader development institution . . . USMA has recently installed software which allows the Director of Information Management to monitor access to porno-

graphic web-sites around the clock. This program provides a real-time, detailed report of such activity, including the specific computer user, the web-sites visited, and the time spent on each site. Users are violating government policy by proceeding beyond this point and are subject to disciplinary action.

(It's not an empty threat. "The kid across the hall got ten hours for looking at porn," Huck Finn says, shaking his head, "and there've been about five others in the company." On Happycadets.com, complaints turn sociological: "I'm not sure if everyone recognizes how detrimental this is to four thousand men who are not allowed to touch girls. They must seriously assume that we are the only four thousand guys without any hormones, and therefore sexual activity is not necessary." One away message simply wails, "Unblock our porn!")

A cease-fire is declared each year on Hundredth Night. The event is a milestone for firsties: the start of their last hundred days at West Point. The Hundredth Night show — ninety minutes of nose-thumbing sketches and officer roasts — uses the culture cadets have left behind to lampoon the one that owns them now. This year, references to *The Matrix* and *South Park* predominate. Where Keanu Reeves is offered a red or blue pill to discover the truth behind his world, the show's main characters choose between two different flavors of Gatorade. Colonel Adamczyk generally casts a long shadow across the show: other years, he's been portrayed as an authoritarian and a kingpin. This year, his character is built around the mentally handicapped *South Park* character named Timmy, who can only repeat his own name.

The head writer, Max Adams, one of the Academy's hardy lit majors, watches from the Eisenhower Hall wings, grinning at the pre-rehearsal muddle. Cadets sit in long cross-legged rows, massaging the necks in front of them, stretching their lips around warm-up nonsense syllables: "Me-may-maw-moe-*moo*. Me-may-maw-moe-*moo*." There's the backstage strangeness of watching big-shouldered male cadets reach for the makeup box and patiently explain, "No — I need the *dark red* lipstick."

Adams watches with the critical half-smile of someone whose dreams are about to be inflicted on the world. He's prior service, from Florida, attending West Point through a kind of pop culture scholarship. "I was gonna go to Florida State film school — ever since high school I've been the kid with the video camera — but my SAT scores were in the toilet, I wasn't paying attention, I had my head too far up my own wazoo." Max ended up enlisted; he got sent to the Ranger battalion at Benning, where he entertained soldiers with long stretches of movie dialogue — *Rambo, Patton, Platoon, Heartbreak Ridge,* "any Clint Eastwood, John Wayne, tough-guy flick, that's what the Rangers love to hear." A Ranger mentioned Adams's name to a relative in the admissions office at West Point; a kid who could memorize movie scenes, he reasoned, was a cadet who could memorize Knowledge. One thing led to another. "They sent me to the prep school," Max says, "and here I am."

Since November, he's been working moonlighter's hours, running his script through what he refers to as "table-reads" and "tweaks" like a suntanned Writers Guild veteran. The show will run only twice: on Friday, March 1, for an audience of underclassmen and the BTO, then on Saturday, for generals, VIPs, the firstie class and their dates.

On Friday afternoon — nine hours before premiere — the head writer traditionally delivers a box-office pitch from the mess hall poop deck. Max climbs the staircase and steps forward. He looks out over the usual sea of high-and-tights, notices an island of generals, polished stars on their shoulders. (They're visiting post for an annual leadership conference, slipping into the mess hall like an old suit of cadet clothes.) Max tries to compose a pitch relevant to the sight: to compress his show's message to a few words, connecting all the work required to travel from plebe year to that big generals' table. He smiles and says, "I guess the key thing to remember is that West Point is a lot like anal sex. It starts out feeling great, but by the end it's just a pain in the ass."

His joke is a slow-motion bomb. Laughter and a crack of applause rise from the outer rim of tables. Then silence falls. Cadets are pretty sure they've just witnessed a first: a classmate separating himself over lunch. Then there's the scrape of a single chair pushing back. Colonel Adamczyk steams furiously across the hall toward the deck. Four hours later, Max Adams is seated on the chair outside Skeletor's office.

The Hundredth Night curtain won't go up until 2100, but down the hall another performance is already starting. This evening John Vermeesch will be promoted to major. About half of G-4 crowds into the ceremony, along with Vermeesch's wife, his family, his closest colleagues among the NCOs and officers. The winter has been snowy; the coarse, textile smell of wet uniform circulates through the Red Reeder Room — leather chairs, oak paneling — as Vermeesch's guests stand in their own slowly expanding puddles. Adamczyk, now in a much brighter mood, oversees the promotion. On the podium, Vermeesch moves with the hunkered, excited manner familiar from road marches. Beside him are his pregnant wife, Lynsey, and their four boys. The BTO clears his throat. The Army life that tonight's show will parody is being celebrated by eighty people inside Washington Hall.

"You cadets hear me say all the time that the Army is a family," Adamczyk begins, as the audience hushes. "And right here on my left you see a family in spades. Tonight they're being promoted together." Lynsey Vermeesch smiles. At Army promotions, it's never the officer alone. Husband and wife, who've shouldered the sacrifices together, rise in rank as a unit. "John relates that he and Lynsey met each other on a blind date, summer before his firstie year. John, I'd have to say that she was more blind than *you*." Big laughter from the room. Adamczyk has some small-town politician in his background; he knows exactly how long to hold the joke. "John also relates that they did not like each other at first." The BTO points out four children and a pregnancy with a nod. "It's really obvious these two like each other a whole lot *now*." Another swell of laughter.

"Now cadets, listen to this," Adamczyk says, voice picking up. "John Vermeesch, commissioned Infantry, 1990. He took over his platoon in January of 1991. And listen, guys: twelve clicks from the Iraqi border. All right? So when we say West Point is a leader development experience, and when we talk about being *ready* when you raise your right hand, here is a young officer who had to be absolutely ready on the day he accepted his commission.

"And this officer wears the marks of success — externally on his uniform, but more so within his heart and, as you see here, in the eyes of his family. He will go on to bigger and better things, for our Army and for our nation." He nods. "So John and Lynsey, thank you. It has been a privilege to participate."

Then, like a graduating cadet, Vermeesch holds still while family pin on his rank, his father working at one shoulder, Lynsey at the other.

John's voice is an assembly of croaks: each word swells big. "I wanna say I don't have any great profound wisdom to give anybody today," he says. "I just want to thank everybody who's ever been part of this experience. But I will say this: I'm gonna embarrass my father publicly. Emotions weren't allowed in the Vermeesch household. It was one of those things — you didn't cry growing up. If there was no blood, there were no tears. Good rule to live by. But my dad has been my hero my entire life, and if I've ever had a mentor, it was probably him. I learned more about values and leadership by his personal example than I've learned anywhere else. So Dad, thank you for all the hard lessons."

Then he turns to Lynsey, asks the pertinent question. "What can I say after eleven years of marriage, after four-and-a-butt kids?" He pats the pockets of his uniform. "I didn't know *what* to say, so I'm going to read you something that I once wrote — if I can find it. I wrote this back in 1991, on the eve of combat. And I just want to share this publicly, because Lynsey's never heard me say it before."

Lynsey points at herself, waves a hand by her eyes, mouths, "I'm gonna cry, I know."

John places his paper on the lectern. "'It's the morning of the seventeenth, 1991. I just said goodbye to Lynsey. And it was the hardest thing I have ever done. I tried to be outwardly cool, but on the inside I was crying as much as she was. I pray to God that I may see her again.'"

Lynsey's eyes spill over. John's voice goes wobbly as he continues reading. "'She has been so supportive. An Infantry officer — or any man, for that matter — could not ask for a finer wife.'"

He looks at Lynsey again. "That feeling — I just can't tell you how much stronger it is today than I felt it back then. Thank you, Lynsey."

She mouths something — it looks like "You too" — and John's gaze moves to take in the rest of the room. "To all my peers," he jokes, "all the officers and NCOs I work with, I'm sorry I got so carried away emotionally. But, you know, we hope in our lives to make a difference somehow. When you come into the Army, they tell you, 'Missions first, men always' — or *people* always. Sometimes you wonder what that means. Well, it's taken me a long time to figure out: in the Army, what we do is about people, about relationships you build." Vermeesch looks out at his cadets. "I know we all get down, and complain sometimes. But when you really peel back the onion, and think about the opportunities we've been given as Americans, particularly as American officers — man, there's just nothin' better going out there."

The room dissolves in a storm of applause. Vermeesch blinks at one edge, surprised by the unfamiliar power of words, how a handful of sentences can smear a room like tear gas. As the crowd breaks up, Sergeant Tierney is dabbing at his eyes. "If any of this gets out," he tells Vermeesch, "that I lost my shit, I'm gonna have to punch you out." Vermeesch jokes right back, "Man, you'll never see me tear up again."

By West Point standards, Max's show is a breakout hit. His speech packs in the first-nighters, and the cadet production team grasps one of the most heartening lessons of real-life theater: a sympathetic audience will laugh at anything. The script is a froth of inside jokes, expressed through movie scenes and scraps of TV dialogue. There are nods to *Bull Durham* ("I believe in using Napster and Audiogalaxy. I believe in lifting the tables for Christmas dinner"), *Fight Club* ("First rule of Firstie Club is, we do not talk about Firstie Club; second rule is, we do *not* talk about Firstie Club; third rule is, someone says 'Huah,' the night's over"), Animal Planet's *Crocodile Hunter* ("We're at remote Camp Buckner, stalkin' the wild yearling"). During musical numbers, rock songs follow the *Mad* magazine as-sung-to rule: "It's the End of the Corps As We Know It."

The Adamczyk character is the showstopper. When he crows "BTO!" or one of Skeletor's slogans ("Puerile," "Sophomoric"), cadet laughter shakes the auditorium. When he yelps the BTO's off-limits Christian name — "Joey!" — there's a hush, and when he then dives head-first into a prop desk, the cadets are ready to tear apart their seats. Fresh from John Vermeesch's promotion, the real Adamczyk watches from the first rows, his expression frozen and unreadable, eyes darting.

After the curtain, Adamczyk grimly climbs the stage risers to the platform. Each step reveals another slice of Adamczyk: head, blazer, chinos, loafers. Captain Noel Smart, the Hundredth Night officer in charge, follows his approach with a plebe's lock-kneed fear. After five years, the BTO has been involved with enough shows to master the idiom. "Obviously," he begins, "I have notes."

The show's director is a firstie named Dawn Drango, who moves with the bamboo springiness of a judo champion, which is what she is. She watches, hands twiddling the curtain, as Adamczyk does fifteen minutes of one-way talk with Captain Smart. Then Smart walks stiffly to her, and they hold an anxious conference. "We need to make some adjustments," Smart says. "This is gonna be difficult." First, there's a quick run of silencings: the word *bareass* was included in this evening's performance. "'Bareass,'" the captain says, "is a no-go. Also, you can't say 'honor nazi.'" "Right, sir," Drango says. "I understand. The BTO is thinking about the public image of the Academy we need to keep." Tomorrow, generals will be in the audience, joined by the supe, the comm, the parents. This is about West Point brand management. Second, due to Max Adams's speech, the cast is under orders not to acknowledge him Saturday night. Most important is the BTO character. "This is number one, the biggest challenge. Just don't make it look like he has bad, um, random, lack of muscle control," Smart says, picking his words so carefully you can see the thesaurus running behind his forehead. "Basically, don't take him to the point where he's drooling over himself. Make him more excited, *crazed* . . . as opposed to, well, y'know, mentally challenged or . . . retarded."

"I guess he can't ram his head into the desk anymore," Dawn sighs.

The production team spends the night with conferences, complaints, rewrites. It's a values clash: solid cadet instincts ("We've got to square this away") versus *Entertainment Tonight* ("We're sitting on top of a hit show"). Next night, the crew holds its breath before the BTO character's entrance. The show's versions of the supe and the comm say they've found a scapegoat, someone on whom to blame the West Point changes. The performers turn stage right, and the BTO comes wheeling out. There's a beat when the night could go either way. Then the actor squeals "*Joey!*" to the show's biggest laugh.

"That's pretty much all he says," the pretend supe explains. "He's taken a lot of head injuries."

"BTO! BTO!" the stage-Adamczyk chants, to whooping.

The show-comm shakes his head. "Here's a dictionary. Go look up some new words."

"Ho ho ho. *Puerile!*" Pandemonium. At the curtain call, Dawn says, "Most of all, we'd like to thank our head writer back there. We love you — thank you." This earns Dawn a brigade board, where she will contend that because she didn't mention Max by name, she's stayed within the guidance. (Dawn ends up losing rank and privileges, living as an underclassman for the rest of the year.)

Max receives so many hours they amount to complete days: there's no way to work them off and still graduate, cadets bet he'll be commissioned late, if at all. (The post is pulling for him. For months afterward cadets will chuckle over the performance, call it the best Hundredth Night they've ever seen.) As part of his rehabilitation, the Academy decides to find Max a new company and a new roommate, one who can teach him about discipline, professionalism, the pleasures of the straight and narrow. The cadet they choose is modest about his selection. He insists the reassignment was luck of the draw, but it's the pinnacle of his cadet career, a measure of how far he's traveled since watching a game of rugby on the snowy Plain. The Academy sends Max Adams to live with Jeremy Kasper.

The Right Reasons

The Hundredth Night show is produced by cadets from the West Point Dialectic Society and the Theatre Arts Guild. West Point sometimes has the rites-and-rituals feel of a large club, but it really breaks down into more than one hundred small ones. There's the Margaret Corbin Forum (the female cadet experience) and the Military Film Forum (lost squads), the Mountaineering Club and the White Water Canoe Club (ropes and paddles), and Officers' Christian Fellowship. (OCF is probably the best-attended club; cadets by the hundreds crack open their Gospels at Tuesday night Bible study. "God," says a slim yuk named Justin Pullen, "is a really popular guy at West Point.") Eliel Pimentel, from G-4, is a born joiner. He's toured the FBI through the Law Enforcement Tactics Club and test-fired advanced weapons with members of Infantry Tactics. As a part of the Domestic Affairs Forum, he's visited Rudolph Giuliani ("Great guy"), sat in on ABC News meetings with Peter Jennings ("Awesome — he's just, he's a presence in the room"), discussed constitutional reform in a Supreme Court side chamber with Antonin Scalia ("Just a very strong personality"). "I always say," Eliel explains, "West Point brings the world to you on a silver platter."

The platter holds the world's good and bad. Another element is illicit drugs, which deeply unnerves the administration. "It's taboo even to talk about it," a high-ranking cadet explains to me, after saying he can't have his name used. "Parents, the administration, nobody wants to hear about it." The Academy treats drug use seriously, conducting random tests, and punishes it harshly, with courts-martial and jail time. The honor code's toleration clause is nearly handcrafted to remind cadets of their responsibility to keep their post drug-free. There's higher's understandable concern with brand integrity. West Point's influence, its standing in the national community, derives from its absence of temptation, its ability to stay dry above the civilian bog. According to First Captain Dave Uthlaut, drug use can endanger more than reputation. "In our line of work, there's absolutely no place for distracters — for something like drugs, that's gonna take your mind off the job. You become a liability to your unit, not one we can depend on as a nation: out on the front lines, you're not gonna have access to that stuff."

But the first captain has noted changes since his arrival. "There *is* somewhat of a drug problem here. Obviously, I'm not the one the, uh, majority of the corps comes to with these issues. But my classmates will tell me, 'I could name you off ten people right now that are struggling with it.' I guess people slip through the cracks, or maybe they change once they arrive, either get disillusioned or fall in with the wrong crowd. I don't wanna give the response that we're a microcosm of society — 'there are drugs out there, so we've gotta expect drugs in here.' Because I don't *agree* with that at all. I think we are a cut above, and we need to hold ourselves to a different standard."

Adamczyk understands that West Point must do more than simply say no. The new plebes are coming, "and we're planning substance abuse classes. I talked to the yearlings yesterday. They've experienced things we're only reading about. They'll talk about designer drugs, club drugs, all the combinations and permutations in between. They could educate *us*. The kids who were doing drugs when I was growing up, they were kind of the deadbeats of society. Now it's mainstream."

Drug violations at West Point are enviably low. The Academy is rightly proud of its record — most years pass without higher seeing a case. To cadets, the question isn't whether classmates are doing drugs but whether the Academy is catching them. The cohesion that West Point painstakingly develops has a side effect: cadets rarely rat on each other. "You see, for *honor* violations, your loyalty is to the organization," a yuk tells me. "But for regs violations — are you gonna turn your brother in? You're supposed to stick together and help each other out, not screw each other over."

What some cadets have developed amounts to an early-warning system. Stripers get word when a urine test is in the pipeline; they need advance notice to work it into the schedule. "Put it this way," one staffer tells me. "Let's say I have word about when everybody in Second Reg is going to get tested. OK? Now, I'm not saying I'll hand that information around. But I'll explain it like this. If Joe Schmo is a good friend of mine, and I know he just snorted coke the weekend before, I'm gonna tell him: 'Hey, buddy, you might wanna chill out for the next couple weeks. Especially on post, here in the box. Now drive on.' So all of a sudden everybody finds out. 'The drug test is coming, the drug test is coming.'"

Many cadets will tell drug stories about a classmate, squadmate, roommate, a friend. "My roommate, last night he sneaks out of bed after taps, swings over to his girlfriend in Highland Falls, takes some E-bombs, runs back in before morning formation, hits class high as a kite." The cadets who use drugs have a simple explanation — a kind of reverse reaction to the Old Corps system Colonel Thayer put in place 180 years ago. "There's not a whole lot else to *do* around here," a cow says. "So people are kinda bound to do drugs. They won't let you go out drinking or keep alcohol. The easiest way to get messed up is to pop a chill pill and just cool out in your room. This place caters to it, because they just won't let you have fun any other way. Ecstasy is in and out of your system in seventy-two hours — they can't test for that."

Cadets shape their drug selections to fit West Point realities: what can be discovered, what can be concealed. Ecstasy, cadets explain, "looks like vitamin pills." The club drug GHB can be ordered online from the shadier art supply houses. It arrives in a can of rubber cement, and from there you can transfer it to any container; it's a clear liquid. Sit in a cadet room with the door open, another cadet will wobble in. "I'm drunk, I've got half a calzone, and I've got a whole bottle of GHB. If you don't come upstairs, I'm gonna drink all this G myself."

"Yo, you shouldn't be drinking that shit if you're drunk."

"I don't care. You oughta come upstairs."

"I don't want any G. But save me the calzone, I'm hungry."

"I was surprised by the reliance on stuff like that," a firstie tells me disapprovingly. I think he means drug use in general; what he's referring to is the substance hierarchy. "G and ecstasy. I mean, those are primarily club drugs. You take them to get messed up and that's all. Most people aren't comfortable enough with themselves to really break down the barriers of reality and go off to some other plane. It's disappointing," he says, in the voice of a Beast squad leader sizing up new cadets, "because they're not doing drugs for the right reasons. But that's a personal thing with me."

For firsties like this one, experimentation is about seeking higher truths. Dog-eared counterculture Baedekers by Aldous Huxley and Hermann Hesse still circulate through the West Point underground. "*The Doors of Perception, Steppenwolf*— those are life-transforming books. I wanted to experience things like that, experience myself." For these cadets, the challenge is making connections at West Point, locating the people who know people. Some let civilian friends do the work. "Because that's where you get caught, the selling and bartering. Someone catches my friends, they'll just go to jail. But if *I* get involved with it, the penalties for buying or selling . . ." He widens his eyes, lets it drop. Drug conversations on post are a cautious weave of euphemism and allusion. "First of all, you find out if you have the same interests. Look at their personality, sometimes check their CDs. After a while, you start saying, 'Hey, I know about this,' and they'll say, 'Hey, I know about that.'" For ecstasy, they substitute *Molly*— the telltale hard *e*— for mushrooms, they'll talk about *fungus,* like a road march hazard.

Cadets estimate that 3 to 10 percent of the corps use drugs. Those who do find a variety of rationales. "Kind of how I look at drugs is as a First Amendment issue. The law doesn't look at it like that, but that's ideologically how I do. And I'm careful with the work side. If you're hung over or stoned or whatever, you can't do your job. But I don't know, actually. In the Army, if you've done that stuff, how can you punish somebody for getting caught doing the same thing? What the hell do you *do* with that? My gut reaction is, you're a hypocrite."

Once they're comfortable, these cadets share risks and experiences. "Me and the guy I roomed with and another cadet got about an eighth of mushrooms — which isn't even that much if I want to do something crazy or hair-raising. I had two classes that afternoon, so I took a very large cap, which was probably the size of a quarter, I ate another two stems with that. And then I went to class," an upper-level mathematics course; theories, coordinates. All at once, the whole room began to bend theoretical. "Midway through class, I started tripping my *balls* off.

The teacher was pulling down graphs and the like, and I was seeing trails. And he called on me in the middle of class — I had to answer a question while I was seriously freaking out, holy shit, what am I doing? I wanted to get up and leave. And then I'm telling myself, 'No, wait a second, that wouldn't be cool.' I finally get back to my barracks. In the meantime, the two other guys I'd done it with, they've been sitting around staring at the damn carpet, seeing how cool *that* was."

Generally, cadets approach illicit substances with care. "You have to be responsible about it," a cow from the Southwest explains. "There are ways to be a responsible drug user, like a responsible everything else." They rely on the analytical skills they've perfected: testing the equipment, performing the risk assessment. They track which chemicals urinalysis is good at sniffing out; they're up-to-date on where evidence will reside in their bodies. (GHB and LSD will slip out of the record in twenty-four to seventy-two hours; hair can reveal ecstasy use for upward of ninety days.) After making a purchase, they'll check Erowid.org, a comprehensive listing of psychoactive drugs and their effects. When the substance has distinctive packaging — for example, ecstasy tablets stamped with the Pokémon character Pikachu — they'll click to Erowid's sister site, Ecstasydata.org, to learn the components. "And it turned out, that Pokémon stuff, it had a lot of PCP laced in — a good thing to know in case we got piss-tested. We gave it away."

Not all these cadets are as careful; as the Academy makes its checks and sweeps, there's no telling who'll turn up in the net. Jeremy Green is a cow from central Florida; he rose through the same West Point Parents Club as Chrissi Cicerelle and Eliel Pimentel. He's clear-eyed, big-built and smart — the ideal military starter kit. By the middle of his yuk year, he'd climbed to the number one spot in his class. He had the highest cumulative performance record across all three West Point areas — military, academic, physical — a kind of triple crown. On post, Jeremy became a celebrity, someone cadets watched from the corners of their eyes, wondering what he had that they lacked. Higher groomed him for feather-in-the-cap scholarships like the Marshall and the Rhodes. As a cow, he broke the academic bank, a 4.1 average. When he left for nights on the town, classmates thumped him on the back. "Hey — we've got the number one cadet right here."

A few evenings before Thanksgiving, Jeremy and four friends were lounging in his barracks after a night of clubbing. A firstie named

Chris Ward dropped something on the floor — it made a plastic *click* — which nobody gave much thought to. Jeremy was asleep when his roommate found the object. It was a transparent, bullet-shaped, single-dose container called a snuff rocket.

By midday, the Criminal Investigation Division of the Military Police was tossing Jeremy's room. Each item the CID turned up was another round fired into Jeremy's cadet career: a gram of cocaine, two bottles of GHB, a lick (a ten-milliliter bottle) of ketamine, a powerful veterinary sedative. Jeremy and his friends were charged before Christmas. As the sole cadet in possession, most of the weight fell on Jeremy; the others were allowed to quietly resign. The authorities, Jeremy says, "wanted to prove that I was *the* drug seller for West Point." Rumors had made it down to Florida, so he decided to call. It was the kind of conversation where the phone turns to lead in the hand. "Of everything that happened," he says, "having to tell my mother and my father was the worst. My mom did pretty good. She's a businesswoman, tried to stay calm and very professional about everything. I was so proud of her." Jeremy went home on administrative leave, kicked around Florida as his fate took shape a thousand miles north. He would be charged only with possession; there would be a court-martial; there would probably be time at Leavenworth. After a month, he returned to West Point.

A few nights before his trial, cadets take him to a divey bar called Firesides for a sendoff. Cohesion still counts, even at the end of the line. Jeremy is simply the friend who tripped up. Star athletes from several sports are there, standing him to drinks, slapping the table, bucking him up. But for all the assurances that he's not alone, Jeremy will have to walk the final steps by himself. He sits at the end of a long table as his buddies laugh and shout over the thump of the jukebox, observing the scene with the stone eyes of someone who knows he's already looking at a memory.

"We've got eight more Goldschlägers comin' . . ."

"Goldie shot? I'm *made* outa that."

"Yo, what's our tab gonna be?"

"It's *free,* the guy behind the bar said, because . . ."

Jeremy's face alternately darkens and lightens, thoughts passing like clouds. "I know I have to take the hit, because I know I screwed up in a hard place," he says. If there's anything about Jeremy Green that can still make the Academy proud, it's the way he stands to the charges and the prospect of prison. He sees it as a challenge, an unanticipated avenue for development. "It's like — it's a hurdle," he says, resting his big arms on the table. "Some people say you can't live life until you've hit the bottom. And that's what's happening to me now. I was at the top — I was given the chance to go farther and see things — and now I have to start all over. It'll be hard work. But I can't change it, so I'm going to make the best of it and try to learn from it. Benefit from it and build for the future. There's got to be something I can learn from this."

Even in his last hundred hours as a cadet, rules still apply. Jeremy and his friends rise, shake it off, prepare to head back to West Point for taps.

Jeremy is convicted of paraphernalia, of drug possession, of violating a lawful order. He avoids prison, but drug charges carry traps of their own: because of the conviction, he's disqualified from receiving a civilian college's financial aid. A year later, G-4's Cal Smith is spending spring break in Florida, he opens the door of a Miami bar. There's Jeremy Green, arms folded, working security. Cal Smith shakes his hand, says, "So this means I can't get in any trouble here?" Jeremy smiles, shakes his head. "Not tonight."

Hiding in the Middle

Gloom Period has slipped from cadet usage. This year, the pinched days between January and spring vacation have been one unbroken snowfall. Cadets are calling it *White Period.*

The weather feels Old Corps, a haze from above. Snow flickers by cadet windows thick and fast, pathways become a relief pattern of sharply incised boot prints. When the daylight dies out and the night lamps come up, West Point feels socketed in at the base of white hillsides, the last place in the world.

Huck Finn is a command sergeant major, which means he's on constant correction patrol. Taking a nighttime walk, he'll spot unaligned windows, milk cartons refrigerating on a sill. All of a sudden he's pulling open a warm door, squelching up a stairway, giving the kinds of orders he wouldn't have followed a year ago. "Some of my classmates are like, 'What the hell are you doing with that rank?' Well, I could give a goddamn what my position is, but now, after finally growing up here, I'm going to do whatever job they give me the best I can. This job requires me to enforce the standard."

Then he's back in his room, hammering out memos on the Alcove Policy and the Latrine Policy ("stuff I didn't even know there *was* before"). "Alcoves: One barracks laundry bag will be placed on the hook nearest the wall." "Latrines: Cadets may hang wet clothes in the latrines opposite the showers. Clothes must be removed no more than 12 hours after they were placed there . . ." Rizzo teases him in North Area when he catches Huck kneeling to grab a plastic bag frozen into the snow. "Goddamn if this ain't the new Huck."

George Rash is shifting too, even at the physical level: the year has filled him out, turned him stocky. The mess hall lards on the carbs during Gloom Period — fully loaded pizzas, fried everything — to maintain cadets in an up mood. (The DPE nutritionist explains: "There's a psychological boost that comes from eating a big, fatty, sugary meal.") George's cadet boss, Mark Thompson, says crossly, "Your uniform pants are fitting like they're painted on." George lands in the Army Weight Control Program. Once a month, he reports to Sergeant Tierney's office, strips down to his boxers for weighing and taping. Cadets take deep breaths, to bull out their necks and Schwarzenegger their pectorals, in order to meet body-fat limits determined by an algorithm of pounds and inches. Progress is defined as a two- to six-pound drop every four weeks; if George can't hit these Weight Watcher goals, he's out of the corps. "Laying off the cheeseburgers?" Sergeant Tierney asks, looping the tape around his throat. "Last time here you were two-oh-five." "Two-oh-seven, sir," George corrects. "I'm down somewhere around one ninety-nine point five right now, but who's counting?"

Crossing the ice to the computer lab, George can measure his internal changes. "I think I used to laugh a lot more when I was younger," he says. "I probably wouldn't even recognize the person I am today. I was a teenager, I got good grades, I could afford to be screw-the-world. Now I care what others think. Because I've learned the impressions I leave upon others reflect on how others treat me. Anyway, how easy is it to laugh when everything's gray and white?" He points at his uniform, then at the snow: white, gray.

And for the first time he's raising his eyes, looking ahead to graduation. "I ordered my ring last week." Rings, while not mandatory, are *strongly recommended.* "Only one or two people in every class don't buy one, and you have to go through your whole chain of command, all the way up to the supe, and explain your reasons to *him.* Personally, I think it shows you have absolutely no school pride."

Chrissi Cicerelle has been mulling over a different type of ring. She and Mark Thompson have been together for almost two years. "When somebody says, 'What do you wanna do after graduation?' I'm like, 'I can't wait to get married and have kids.'" Even her computer's e-mail alert has a marital subtext; it's clipped from the film *The Wedding Singer,* the scene where a suit-wearing kid sneers at Drew Barrymore, "You're a *bitch.*" (E-mail alerts can tell a cadet's whole story. Eliel Pimentel's program alternates between the Infantry slogan "Follow me!" and "Rangers lead the way," his roommate Matt Kilgore's computer coughs out the sound of an M-16 discharge, George Rash's mail is announced by a line from *Monty Python and the Holy Grail:* "Message for you, sir.") "Mark and I talk marriage — this is my first adult relationship, it's almost like playing house. 'Cuz we're *here,* this is a safe haven, you have to wait till you graduate to get married. I want more than anything for it to work, but there's so much baggage, so much history." They've been a couple so long, they've become a piece of landscape cadets monitor closely, watching for slips and flubs. "Oh, my Lord," cadets in H-4 say. "Thompson's so military, he bought Chrissi a *saber* for her birthday."

This would be a relief to talk about with her sister Marie, but Chrissi hardly sees her. "I don't know *what* she's doing. I was real excited having her here, but she's very independent. It kind of irritates me. When we try to have dinner, I can't find her, I have to IM: 'you're a plebe, you can't possibly have a life, where could you be?'" So the sisterly role falls to her roommate, Leslie Adamczyk, who doesn't approve of Chrissi's relationship. "Leslie doesn't like the way we fight," Chrissi says. "She doesn't like to see me hurt. She'll tell me, 'I want to shake you, it's not worth it, it's too hard, you shouldn't have to try this hard.'" The fights circle the same topic, like a plane with no place else to land. Chrissi has never dropped her yuk grouchiness; since Mark loves West Point wholly, there's a transitive principle: criticizing the post equals criticizing him. "I've become real bitter about this place. So I dwell on the rules and the regs. And he's very motivated. So it comes down to a professional argument — professionally, we don't seem to mesh."

Mark is a prior-service cadet from Los Angeles. He spent two years at Bragg, mastering a Joe's tricks: when to perform, how to sham. "You line up for formation in four squads. Well, when they're looking for people to go clean the latrines? The natural tendency is, they'll pick people out of First Squad: Boom! Boom! You guys, go clean latrines. So everyone stands in back — but see, after a while the platoon sergeant knows he keeps taking from First Squad. So he'll say, 'You guys in Fourth Squad, you're always hiding, lining up in the way back. Why don't *you* guys go clean latrines?' So you learn the best spot to be in is always Third Squad. Because you're not in the front, but you're not in the far back — you're kind of hiding in the middle."

Mark is sick of hiding in the middle. As winter begins its slow retreat from post, the Emerging Leader Review process begins — another series of elimination rounds. Each of the thirty-two companies picks its best cadets to send to a battalion review board. Eighty survive, move ahead to the regimental level. Forty head all the way to brigade, where the twenty-four strongest are picked for Emerging Leader positions. The first captaincy waits at the end like a Grail. Get there, and you become the public cadet face of West Point.

Mark has thoroughly handicapped the process. "You wanna get one of the four primaries," he explains, counting them off on his fingers. "For summer training, it's Beast commander first detail or second detail, Buckner commander first or second detail. Those are the ones who get considered for first captain." Vermeesch has picked candidates from the Corporation, to begin the process, which doesn't surprise Corporation member Rob Anders. "Me, Mark, Eliel, Matt Kilgore — we're all really damn good cadets and very competitive guys."

Eliel Pimentel has already lined up a foreign-exchange slot in Venezuela this summer; going for Emerging Leader means letting that go. Eliel told Super-V he wanted to pass. "So he asked me to think about it till 1500. I called at 1500. I was like, 'Sir, I think I'm gonna stay with my original decision.' He said, 'Well, I would like you to do it anyway.' We went back and forth, I told him I was sticking. Then, that night, after Officers' Christian Fellowship, he came up to my *room*."

Eliel's roommate, Matt Kilgore — a broad-shouldered, friendly kid from St. Louis — swivels around at his desk. "V was wearing civilian clothes — a turtleneck," he says. "Made me laugh. It was huge. I thought, 'What the hell is he *wearing?*' They had a pretty heated discussion."

"Not heated completely," Eliel says. "We got into it a little, but we maintained *respect.* He asked, 'Have you made your decision?' I said, 'Sir, I'm still going to stick with my original choice.' He said, 'Fine. If you don't wanna grow as a leader, that's OK. You can just maybe be company activities officer next semester — I'm not gonna guarantee you'll be company commander. You wanna stay at this comfortable level of leadership, don't wanna take the challenge — hey, that's fine.'"

"The reason," Matt says helpfully, "is that obviously Major V thinks Eliel's going to do well — as we all do. It was a funny conversation to listen to. Major V kept denying he was trying to push Eliel, just kept packing his bags for the guilt trip. 'I don't wanna tell you what to do — you know you could do great things, but I don't wanna tell you what to do.'"

"I gave him a few *sirs*," Eliel says. "'Sir, let's be realistic here.' 'Sir, plainly you want me to do this.'"

(Major Vermeesch smiles over his own memory of the night. "Eliel said, 'But sir, you know, what you think of me means a lot.' I said, 'Well, maybe *that's* something you need to think about.'")

The combined weight of the Lord and Eliel's parents won him over to Super-V's position. "My folks see this as God's mission for me in my life, manifested in this opportunity. And they said, 'Go for this. You owe yourself to at least try.'"

The first boards are held in a day room, TACs sitting behind a desk, running a kind of Academy beauty contest. First there's a judgment on appearance, then on bearing, then a talent portion where the cadet answers questions along the lines of "Provide three brief examples of Emerging Leader conduct" and "What one thing would you change about West Point?" The men come in with high-and-tights; the women sport the female equivalent, a sort of ear-hugging belle-of-Amherst do. You can see fingers and hands delicately trembling. A TAC will ask, "What's more important: accomplishing the mission or taking care of soldiers?"

"Ma'am, taking care of soldiers. The mission will be accomplished at its own pace, no matter what."

When cadets depart, officers quietly chuckle. "Yeah, 'The mission

will get done *eventually*.' You know — when the mission feels like it."
(The correct answer would have been "Mission first in the Army, people here at the Academy.")

"She forgot to salute! Just, 'See ya.'"

"I was getting ready to smoke her grade on that."

"I thought you were gonna fall out of your chair, trying to get a look at her shoes."

"How *were* the shoes, anyway?"

"Shoes were good, hair a little long."

A TAC-NCO shakes his head. "'The mission will get done *eventually*.'"

Ryan Southerland gets called to the boards too. He's got mixed feelings: "It's nice, but the jobs — anyone could do them. I guess it doesn't motivate me that much." Ryan is learning a soldier lesson early. The high-profile jobs are eating into his Betty time; the relationship suffers as long as he's brigade command sergeant major. He doesn't like going to the gym with Betty anymore because there are too many corrections to make along the way: untucked shirts, double-strapped book bags, not to mention what he might encounter inside Arvin Gym itself. At other hours, he's under a stack of work, the coal-shoveling side of leadership, all the ink-fed workings of the corps. All they can do is meet for hellos at night, in the small cliffside rock garden that's the couple's favorite spot on post. Betty and Ryan stand and watch boats move over the dark river, take the cold wind on their faces.

"But you wanna give it a shot," he says, reading the Emerging Leader e-mail, "to see what it's all about." At Ryan's first interview, a TAC named Major Custer is president of the board. The three other TACs watch Ryan salute, run their eyes up and down the creases of his uniform. Major Custer leads the questioning with "What one thing would you get rid of in the West Point system?" Ryan talks around it — he doesn't really have an answer, can't see the good in offering anything half-assed and official like "Cynicism, sir." The TACs bring him back, slanting the question toward the *Survivor*-style hypothetical. "OK, thirty-two TACs, the BTO and yourself are on an island. One of you has to go. Who goes?" Ryan thinks it over. "Well, Major Custer," he says, "out of thirty-two TACs, I think you're the worst, and I'm going to boot you off." Custer looks up. "I mean," Ryan tells me later, "he wasn't even paying attention until he heard 'Major Custer.' And then he asks why, and I say, 'Well, sir, I've heard so much about stuff you've pulled as a TAC and stuff you did at summer basic training. I heard you actually drove some new cadets to the point where they got injured. I just wouldn't want to have that on my island.'"

A few weeks later, when the results of the final boards are announced, Mark Thompson and Eliel Pimentel are in the final twenty-four; they've both earned good jobs, but neither has what Mark calls "a primary." Beast commander I is Andy Blickhahn. Buckner commander I is Ryan Southerland. The corps understands next year's first captaincy will be a dogfight between them.

The Blue Falcon

George Rash performs a personal rite of spring and bombs another APFT. He cramps up halfway through the run, eases off, finishes forty seconds late at a walk. Mark Thompson has become George's platoon sergeant. "A cramp — that's bullshit. You can say, 'As his platoon sergeant I feel bad, he's my responsibility to train.' But I take the hard line — surprise, surprise. He's a cow at West Point. If he can't internalize that and pass his APFT run, I have the attitude like, 'You don't deserve to be here.'" George has internalized a subtler principle. It's not that he can't pass an APFT run — he knows he can — he's learned that he can fail one without triggering any great tragedy. He's like a driver stepping away from a car wreck, with the conclusion that there's really no need to worry about seat belts.

TAC appointments run two years. Just when you have the situation under wraps, the call comes to move on. (This lends TACing a bittersweet flavor of parenthood: "You know you've done your job well," TACs say, "when your unit functions without you.") Major Vermeesch is *short*, which means he's preparing his G-4 goodbyes. You get the impression he wouldn't mind seeing George depart the company at the same time. So Super-V performs his own rite of spring, and warns his cadet that if he fails the makeup, he'll recommend separation from West Point.

Before he leaves, there's another sight Vermeesch would love to see. West Point hosts an annual military competition called Sandhurst. Britain's own military academy — also called Sandhurst — abstains from the academic classes that keep West Point a fully accredited college. Instead, it offers an intensive one-year military program — all four West Point summers with the intermissions snipped out, what the Academy would be like if cadets went right from Beast to Buckner and then straight on to Ranger school. Graduates leave Sandhurst as tactical demons. In late spring, the British academy ships two teams west. They compete against squads from every West Point company, in a timed and graded Warrior Forge. Teams run nine kilometers, shoot targets, build rope bridges, rappel down cliffs, scale walls and paddle assault craft along the route. Joining a Sandhurst team is what's known as a *gut check*. (The un-huah view it differently. "They're all masochists and sadists," they say.) Sandhurst means months of cold-weather training, a voluntary haze. No West Point team has beaten the Brits since 1993.

The Corporation will carry the flag on behalf of G-4. "I gave them a mission," Major Vermeesch says. Whether or not they can defeat the British, Vermeesch wants to see them win the corps of cadets. He thinks they've got a shot. "They're really quality people. Sandhurst is about sacrifice, overcoming adversity and winning — all those things that are great about the Army. They can exhibit to the company standing behind them that in our profession there *is* no second place. Second is that *dead or bleeding* kind of thing."

The squad — essentially, the Corporation plus Jeremy Kasper — train professionally. They run over the 0530 ice, tramp through the 1630 slush. Squad Leader J. J. Simonsen, a square-headed Kansan, swipes complicated workout tips from *Men's Health* magazine. They dine at their own table, banquet off post, swab rifles together outside the weapons room and celebrate training's end with wholesome spirit pranks like dunking each other in a lake.

The other subject on John Vermeesch's desk is Huck Finn. A year ago the cadet was ready to pack his bags. "Finn's story is one of those things that keep me going, you know?" Vermeesch says. "That makes me wanna come to work every day. You go, 'Hey man, all the bullshit, all this stuff that we do every day — somewhere in there, my fingerprints got left on somebody.'"

On the job, Finn brings a large-hearted Huckness to bear. The plebes George and Huck welcomed into the corps last summer are now being promoted; the promotion ceremony is the last formation where upperclassmen can officially push them around. The post hums and clicks like an engine room, plebes reciting Knowledge, pumping out push-ups. One streetwise plebe slides into formation just before the ceremony, sparing himself any last-call abuse. Huck spots it and applies the most forceful correction I ever see him make. He towers above the plebe, fists at his side, neck going red. "Why didn't you show your face the same time everybody else did? Everyone else was out here — thirty minutes ago. You're waiting behind and everybody else is getting *hazed*. You sit in your room and get by scot-free while your friends take the heat instead of you? That's called a Blue Falcon, and this place ain't about Blue Falcons!" *Blue Falcon* is a polite way to invoke the initials BF — a buddy fuck. It's about the lowest form of behavior Huck can imagine.

The Sandhurst competition runs on the last Saturday in April, and there's no second place for G-4. The team commits some errors, some oversights, finishes in the pack, far out of the money. They stagger back to North Area for the cadet barbecue, uniforms grimed, features smoothed with a look of honest, earned exhaustion. Huck watches the Corporation with guarded interest; maybe his not joining the squad was a kind of Blue Falcon of its own. He approaches Mark Thompson — the two have walked different cadet paths since sharing a room at Beast — while Mark loads a hamburger with iceberg lettuce and a tomato slab. He wipes his forehead with the back of a palm that leaves it muddier. "Hey, you think I could do this shit next year?" Huck asks. "Be like a Sandhurst squad leader?"

Mark laughs. "*No.*"

"Why not? Bro, I'm gonna do this shit."

"Seriously?"

"I'm serious. I wanna fuckin' do it. I know y'all are afraid to have an ox. I'll get in shape, I promise I won't hold anybody back. What do you think? You think I got a chance?"

Mark thinks it over. "Sure. If you do it, I'll do it. You a squad leader — that's a team I'd like to see."

Seven days before George Rash retakes his APFT, Major Vermeesch and Sergeant Tierney sit him down for a surprising offer. All George has to do is call it a day.

This is his first remedial APFT that carries major penalties; if George is separated, it's not just the end of West Point, it's repayment or some Joe years in the Army. Even if he pulls it out and grinds through firstie year, there's still military life waiting. "You're gonna have a company commander exactly like Major Vermeesch," Tierney reminds George, "and a first sergeant exactly like me. Spartans, who prey on the physically weak. That's reality. This is not your niche. You can either change yourself — or do yourself a favor and get out of here."

The TACs know the pattern; George will find a way to pass when he needs to. The only way to stop him is by getting him to stop himself. They offer George unqualified resignation, with no repayment, no penalties. A no-fault divorce: everyone agrees it was a mistake, everyone gets on with their lives. As the TACs view it, the consequences of George staying could be severe for West Point. "George leaving would be for the long-term good of the institution," Sergeant Tierney tells me. "If he makes it through, the credibility of this place will be seriously impacted. If civilians realize that people like cadet Rash can go through this system, then it's not the spartan atmosphere it's supposed to be or used to be."

They advise George to think it over; he does them the courtesy. He outlasted DeMoss, if he passes this APFT, he'll have outlasted Vermeesch. He's studied the TAC as closely as the TAC has studied him, and he has no hard feelings. "He hasn't specifically rooted against me," George says, "but I think the only time he ever rooted for me was right at the beginning. Shortly thereafter he pretty much said, 'OK, you're gonna probably be the problem child in the company. So . . . you're gonna sink or swim on your own.'"

George heads home from the library under lights going streaky in the fog, trees filling out with leaves. The offer is on his mind, shading whatever he sees like the bill of a cap. "I've fully considered it," he says, breaking it down to a series of questions. "Do I really want to leave my friends? Besides, I'm gonna have to keep physically fit, whether at West Point or elsewhere. So one way or the other I'm still gonna be running — just for health reasons, unless I want to be really fat or a slob. And as much as I hate it at West Point, I understand it. You never want to leave the familiar. And do I really want to basically invalidate the last three years of my life? Then everything I've done, all that I've learned and experienced, and my commitment that I swore to in August, would mean nothing."

George informs the TACs of his decision. The two men seem disappointed; they don't recognize how much George has internalized their system. He's learned that you may fail, you might get separated, but dead or bleeding, you do not quit.

A couple of days before the test, Rob Anders — who completed George's first remedial APFT with him years ago — takes George for a run, shows him where he's been using his arms improperly. They should *pump* in sync, providing some of the momentum. "As long as they're moving, your legs are gonna wanna move along with them," Anders says, demonstrating with a quick run.

At exam time, George throws on his gym alpha — the Academy PT suit — walks down to Gillis Field House and the track. An overflow crowd is taking APFTs today. A female cadet waves from the floor mats: "Hey, George." The DPE instructors, in their own tight version of the gym uniform, scowl like slim, moody Teamsters. Cadets wash out on the sit-ups, lose their grip over push-ups, wander off under the volleyball nets to count the consequences, plot their next moves, phrase their explanations. George breezes through the events, leans back to stretch his legs. The DPE officers say, "Ten minutes."

George blinks his way outdoors. The track, the sky, the noise of cars and a train. Major Vermeesch and Sergeant Tierney are standing by the wall near the stairs. George nods to them; the three have come to this moment together. Vermeesch pushes from the wall a little. He could say nothing, he could wait quietly to see how Rash does, but that would be another kind of Blue Falcon. He motions his cadet to stop.

"George," he says, "listen up. One thing I think is helpful is to break up the run in your mind." The major's eyes clench above his words, as if he can't believe he's doing this. "Instead of thinking of it as two long miles, think about it in three-hundred-meter jumps, say to yourself, 'All right, I see that tree up there. I have to maintain this pace to that tree.' Hit that tree, you have to maintain it to the fence post. Then, when you hit the half mile on the way home, I want you to tuck your head down and give it everything you have left. You get me?" Vermeesch watches George coolly, waits for his nod, then says, "Huah."

"Knock it out, Rash," Tierney calls.

Cadets in trouble bring friends. Cadets who are pacing each other sprint inside the pack, offering casino encouragement and stadium pleading. "Come on! Do it! You can do this, give me a little more, give it everything you have."

As George rushes to the line, his shirt is soggy, his breathing is ragged, cadets he doesn't know shout "*Rash!*" There's no taunt in it; George has earned something. He beats the clock by ten seconds, a 15:44.

"Usually," George says, sucking air, "I fall behind the pack by quite a bit. This time, I did what Major Vermeesch said, I started setting goals. 'By the time I reach that point, I have to catch up to them. By the time I reach the next pole, I have to stay even.' It felt better, kept me in a much better position. The relief is indescribable." Cadets walking upstairs clap George on the shoulder.

Major Vermeesch ambles slowly to George's side. George turns to face him, confesses his goal: to bring his run under fifteen minutes, where it was when he first arrived.

Vermeesch listens. "You oughta try and get there before you go out in the Army on troop-leading this summer," he advises. "Because your huah soldiers are going to want to see you run."

"I'll try to, sir," Rash says.

Vermeesch assesses his cadet one more time, turns to leave. "Take care, George," he says.

Surprise and Courage

As the class of 2001 prepares for graduation, the last two lights dim out of the West Point sky. First the supe boxes his personal mementos and his Pumbaa doll and retires from the United States Army. In the Washington Hall mess, General Christman charges the corps to deliver him one more rocket cheer. The cadets stand and roar, and then he's gone. The BTO, Joe Adamczyk, Skeletor, won't be haunting any more Academy pathways, ricocheting cadets back to their rooms. In May he accepts an offer to serve as commandant of Valley Forge Military Academy — the model for Pencey Prep in *The Catcher in the Rye,* and the location shoot for the military-kids-go-plumb-crazy movie *Taps.* He's approaching mandatory retirement for colonels, year thirty. Adamczyk jokes that he didn't quite meet the standard: "Twenty-nine years, five months — I didn't make the full career, there's some guilt. Honest to God, that's the emotion you get."

The post becomes a jumble of arrivals and departures. In G-4,

Major Vermeesch is clearing out his office, and Sergeant Tierney hangs up his stripes. Vermeesch set himself a goal when he arrived in company two years ago. He wanted to leave confident that his cadets were combat-ready, in case the call ever came — as it did for him, half a year after graduation. "I've talked about it with them. But I don't know that . . ." He pauses and squints. He can't know that in September, three months from now, the first contract in a long war will be made, fifty miles from where he and the cadets are standing. "No, I haven't met the goal, they're not all there. I don't know that I'm *capable* of getting them all there." He sighs, looks at a framed guidon on the wall. "To me, the part we've neglected is the military piece. If you're an egghead in the Computer Science Department, are you *really* capable of, you know, going out and sticking a bayonet in someone? Hopefully, the cadets get it by immersion — twenty-four hours a day, seven days a week, eventually they'll figure out the right thing to do."

Graduation — June 2, 2001 — is washed by rain. Security men patrol in gray slickers, families trot into Michie Stadium sharing umbrellas. Old grads shake hands and trade an old Academy saw: the class that graduates in rain goes to war. "But who the heck are they going to fight?" they chuckle. The supe and the comm read the thousand graduating names. When the supe calls "Max E. Adams" — the author of the Hundredth Night show — there's a mammoth cheer; Max made it after all. The morning's speaker is Deputy Secretary of Defense Paul Wolfowitz: a gray-haired man in a blue shirt and a blue tie, peering out into the gray from under a canopy. He compliments the supe, appeals to the cadets to give their parents a round of applause ("a fitting Army tribute"). Then he welcomes the graduates to the business.

"I want to challenge you," he says, "to think this morning about two words: surprise and courage."

He looks over the crowd, measuring the response. "This year marks the sixtieth anniversary of a military disaster whose name has become synonymous with surprise — Pearl Harbor. Interestingly," Wolfowitz points out, "that 'surprise attack' was preceded by an astonishing number of unheeded warnings and missed signals. Intelligence reports warned of 'a surprise move in any direction.' Military history is full of surprises, even if few are as dramatic or as memorable as Pearl Harbor. Surprise happens so often, it's surprising we're still surprised by it. Almost always there have been warnings and signals that have been missed — sometimes because there were just too many warnings to pick the right one out."

He pushes back an unruly bit of hair. "Perhaps the simplest message about surprise is this one: surprise is good when the other guy can't deal with it. Let us try never to be that other guy. A century ago, on a peaceful day in 1903, with great foresight, the secretary of war told Douglas MacArthur's class, 'Before you leave the Army . . . you will be engaged in another war. It is bound to come, and will come. Prepare your country.'" Wolfowitz grips the podium with both hands, takes in the field of young officers. "Be prepared to be surprised," he says. "Have courage."

Jeremy Kasper marches back to his room, showers, changes into his lieutenant's uniform. He threads his way around packed luggage and cardboard boxes filled with cadet gear. For Jeremy, the speech left something to be desired — too heavy on the motivational, too light on military career specifics. "I was kinda hoping to hear a little more about the Defense Review that's going on." Jeremy says, shrugging. The Quadrennial Defense Review — staffing, budget and systems — is the sort of item he follows on the inside newspaper pages, to keep up with shifts in the profession, to have information to mull over with TACs. "Where the army's headed, what the future of our stance on national security is, other than 'Be vigilant. Be *prepared*.' Heard that for four years."

In a big raucous party on the front lawn of retired lieutenant colonel Henry Keirsey's house, Hank swears his eldest son, J.D., into the Army. Then he pins one butter bar onto J.D.'s shoulder, while his own father stiffly pins the other. Hank welcomes J.D. into the military with a handshake. "I'm a very lucky man," Hank says, looking at his father, at his son, three generations of soldiers. "And I'm awful proud of what he's doing." J.D.'s guests — Ryan Southerland is there, eyes fixed on Hank — talk long into the night about Wolfowitz's speech. They debate "courage," ask themselves where and when those surprises might come.

PART FOUR

The Fourth Year

An Army of One

ONE SPRING AFTERNOON, Iggy Ignacio climbed and swung his way to the top of the splintery ladder on the Fort Drum obstacle course. He hooked his leg over, and for one of the first times considered the link between elevation and gravity.

"Whoa," Iggy thought. "This is like three stories down — this is high." He looked down over a landscape of activity. Soldiers were running, shimmying, hoisting. "When you're young," Iggy says, "you always go, 'Let's do this.' But as you get older your thinking is more, 'Well, wait a second.'" The height seemed to measure a passage of years: semesters with the Long Beach JROTC, hoping for the Academy; four West Point years, waiting on the Army; then ten months at Benning and a year here at Drum. Somewhere below was everything military life rushed you past, a home, a woman, a family.

Iggy has talked this over with his NCOs — soldiers in a unit who've already got ten, fifteen years under their belts. "Hey, First Sergeant," Iggy asked, walking into the man's office. "Knowing what you do now, would you have gone this far?"

The sergeant's mouth opened as his thoughts screened a quick montage of deployments and uniforms. "No sir," the sergeant said. "I have a sixteen-year-old daughter who doesn't even speak to me now."

Iggy joined the Army for family. But sooner or later your uniformed family will come into conflict with the one that runs through your blood. Iggy's people are waiting in California: his mom, his dad, two older brothers, all those uncles, a baby niece he hardly knows and a Filipina girlfriend named Corrine who he loves. Corrine has become just a whisper on the phone, raising patient, troubling questions: "When are you coming home?" Iggy wipes them aside the way an eraser pushes insoluble problems off a blackboard, makes promises about weeks of leave. "But it's more like," Iggy says, "there's a secondary meaning — home. Not 'When will you physically get here?'; 'When are you coming back to *stay* and shit?'" Catching his breath on the ladder, Iggy did calculations. "I've been in the military six years," he explains. "My mom and dad, my friends and brothers, Corrine, if you add it all up, it doesn't even come out to — ah, fuck — I haven't even spent a year with them."

When Iggy flies west on leave, the days pass at the tightly scheduled clip of hours in the Army: family functions, dinners with Corrine, all boxes he's got to check off. His brainy friends from high school rap the grate over his door, looking to talk Japanese anime and computers. His old gang-banger pals — neck tattoos and spooky fingernails — pull him out to clubs for shots and pool games. The last night, Iggy stands by his brother's Prelude in the parking lot, breathes the cool, spicy California air, gazes at the moon high above the palm trees. "I won't be here for another six months," he says. "It'd almost be easier not to come back. So you don't have to leave again."

It's been a challenging year. Iggy strolled to meet his platoon on a chilly 0630 morning, heading the formation with no Ranger tab, with nothing to officially reassure his unit but himself. Because the Army is short-handed, the platoon didn't contain the thirty-two soldiers West Point prepares you for; only twenty young faces blinked back. "I have four rules," Iggy announced. The first was integrity. The nature of the business, you don't lie: they shouldn't question him, he wouldn't have time to question them. "If you tell me," Iggy said, "that there's a bunch of fuckin' aliens flanking us on our left side, then that's what it *is*." Second rule was, don't sell out. "What I mean is, you know what's right: if you do what's wrong anyway, that's fuckin' selling out. Somebody makes a correction on you, and you get all bitchy but it's a valid correction, that's selling out." Don't point fingers was the third. "I'm less concerned with whose fault it is than with what we do to improve ourselves. I can tolerate mistakes; mistakes are how we learn." The fourth derived from news stories Iggy followed in *Army Times,* and from advice an old upperclassman passed along at Benning, about a growing problem in the Army. "Fourth rule is, we don't hit our children and we don't beat our wives. You're men and you're soldiers — men and soldiers don't act that way. If I find out any of you are doing it, I will hammer you."

Brotherhood came down to a simple equation: if they took care of Iggy, he'd do the same for them. Platoons get nicknames, Iggy's is called Mafia. Two weeks in, Iggy led Mafia through a nighttime blank-fire. "We got disoriented, shit happened and we screwed up," Iggy says, making a sour face. Next morning, Iggy's commanding officer instructed Mafia to report back as spectators; they would observe a platoon tackling the exercise successfully. The men Iggy is responsible for were squinting at their boots, at the clouds. "My NCOs are proud people," Iggy says. "They consider themselves good at what they do. And to be forced to watch another platoon that doesn't have any extra training . . . it was demoralizing." Iggy huddled with his platoon sergeant. Iggy was a new LT, a cherry, with no business second-guessing the commander. "Don't touch this one, sir," the sergeant advised. Mafia shuffled forward. "I took another look at my squad leaders, and I was like, 'Fuck this.'" Iggy walked to his commander. "Good morning, sir," he said. "Is it all right if we don't walk through?" The commander weighed it, told Iggy yeah, that was fine, Mafia could go and train.

Before climbing into uniform, Iggy was filled with apprentice enthusiasm. He's been learning a hard travel lesson, that the colors on the street don't necessarily match the ones in the brochure. When he was at West Point, his adult NCOs from JROTC would call to say they were packing it in. Iggy would disagree: they could be walking away from the one soldier who might have looked up to them. "Wait till you get inside," they told Iggy, "you'll understand." They explained about the Army's downsizing — how before Saudi the Army stood at nearly a million personnel, how after what's called the draw-down the service had contracted to a lean 490,000.

The result worked like a science experiment: halve the space and you double the competition. "My old platoon daddy would say how there was no room for promotions. That scared the shit out of people." It was like opening the door to admit one of the worst elements from the civilian world: there was no time to watch each other's back when you were busy watching your own. "He said soldiers were thinking, 'How can I make myself look good? By making somebody else look bad.' Which I believe is just stupid. The things my top sergeant told me," Iggy explains, "they might have happened before, just not to this extent. Back in the day, people looked out for each other in a heartbeat. Top said there had to be something wrong if we're losing so many people." Iggy understands all the five-and-fly stuff, but it can't just be about perks and salaries. "Civilians can say all they want to about money: soldiers back in the day weren't exactly getting paid either. So what made them stay? It ain't money — that's not what makes an Army."

Even the new Army ad slogan rubs many of his soldiers the wrong way, a four-word sentence of rankle. "'An Army of One,'" Iggy says. "Some focus study says it reaches the target group of high-school-age people. You don't come into the Army to be a 'one' — because you hope to be just another individual. That's for civilian life. You come to be part of something."

Mafia doesn't have Fort Drum's plum assignment, the Kosovo rotation. Iggy talks with his brothers about volunteering for deployment to the Middle East or switching to a company that will reach the Balkans. The phone goes silent.

"You're getting older," his brothers say. "Why would you want to do that?"

"Why?" Iggy asks. "Because that's what a military person does — you go where the shit is." It's the reverse of a question Iggy wanted to put to a sergeant during his last summer at West Point. The sergeant told him, "One thing to remember, sir: when you get here, I want you to keep in mind, your family comes first." Iggy tested the thought out. "I said I understood. At the same time I was thinking, 'Why? You should dedicate yourself to the Army.'"

His brothers say, "The family doesn't want you to go."

There's a voting bloc inside Iggy that always leans the same way: stick it out, go harder, get back to Ranger, try out for Special Forces — "if you're in," Iggy says, "go all the way in." But Corrine and his family campaign on the opposing platform: there are duties closer to home, jobs that can meet his brotherhood needs, organizations with fresh acronyms: FBI, LAPD, SWAT. When Iggy talks about maybe leaving, his voice goes gingery, testing out the syllables to see if they hold his weight. "See, if I leave this life, leading soldiers, I'm gonna miss the shit out of it. Part of me is gonna be so hurt, I wouldn't be able to explain it to you. And the suckiest thing about it is, it's not like you can do reconnaissance on the results. That's what sucks about the whole deal. You can't recon the bitch."

Iggy and Whitey hold a conversation all year that, though they never use the words, amounts to one question: Is it worth it? They have it at dinner, they have it watching videos at home — Whitey will give curveball rentals like *The Messenger* a shot, Iggy runs war movies, so that even TV becomes a kind of homework. Then it'll come up again at Applebee's, at Denny's for Saturday morning breakfast, waiting extra minutes for a table in the smoking section. And Whitey has the conversation with himself all the time. To prepare himself for the life he's adopted since Mark Matty's death, he's put his tongue on a special training program. Every time Whitey says something good about the Army, right away he's got to add something positive about civilian life. "I don't know, Igs," he says, "you've just gotta drive on. That's why military people always do so good out in the corporate world. We're prepared for anything."

But Whitey is fighting something he knows deep down. The Army offers experiences and feelings you can't match in civilian life. At Drum, Whitey's unit pushes through another combat simulation; they're an SSB, a Soldier Support Battalion. Five days of twelve-hour shifts in the computer room, allocating manpower to field units, arranging casualty evac, dispatching fresh troops. "That's part of the Army civilians never get to see," Whitey says. He pauses at the door of the simulation room after his shift: three hundred uniformed backs are hunched over computers, hands groping for phones, for coffee mugs, to massage a stitch out of the neck. "It's amazing," Whitey says. "You're not seeing anything fantastical like a guy charging down a machine-gun bunker, it's nothing gung-ho. What you see is people working their hardest and stressing their asses off — normal American people, practicing for war, who choose to do this. And it's not a job, I don't care who it is, everybody's in the heat of it. I don't believe one person is thinking, 'This is my career, nine to five.' Everybody's thinking, 'I gotta do my part.' You won't get perks or money or fame to compensate you, you'll just get a kind of satisfaction. Knowing you're practicing, because when there's a real war there's no room for error."

During the summer, Whitey learns that he'll be the first Goodfella at Fort Drum to see the elephant. His unit will deploy in November for a six-month tour in Kosovo.

Best Summer of Their Lives III

Signs sprout on post (*Welcome Class of 2005*), officers load moving vans, you can see all the way to the river through the front and back windows of the empty houses along Lee Road. Next year's firsties receive their summer rank, third lieutenant, and fan out into the Army on CTLT — Cadet Troop Leader Training — for a taste of officership, leading soldiers with regular units.

Ryan Southerland sticks around Highland Falls, a figure in the landscape. He will command the first half of Camp Buckner, overseeing one thousand yuks and a staff of upperclassmen. The assignment is his audition for first captain, just as commanding Beast I will be Andy Blickhahn's tryout. (Captain Engen, Ryan's TAC last summer, is rooting. "I hope Ryan gets it, he'd do a great job. He's just one of those guys — he's the only person who ever got George Rash to finish a road march.") Before packing for Fort Benning, Hank Keirsey's son J.D. leaves Southerland an old PT shirt — a West Point pass-down tradition that keeps graduated names circulating through the corps — then e-mails a pageful of advice. "And any time one of the Keirseys tells you to do something," Ryan says, stepping over rocks and tree stumps at Buck-nam, "that's pretty much the right thing to do."

J.D. has poured the problems of life through a single funnel and distilled the formula. It's a weight-room-and-bookcases mix, arranged in memorandum form.

Ryan,

Here are my departing bullet points of wisdom.

• Take care of yourself. Physically. Depression, malaise, etc., are all the result of a faulty PT schedule. Do this above all else. Avoid dessert.

• Read — it provides the background necessary for all disciplines. Cover the essentials: From Anton Myrer [his military novel *Once an Eagle* is a West Point bible: one of Max Adams's post–Hundredth Night sentences was a corrective study of the book] to Vonnegut, Pynchon, and Hemingway.

• Take care of subordinates. This is my only "leadership lesson."

You know what taking care of subordinates entails: it isn't being nice. It is presenting an attainable goal, a charismatic persona that they can aspire to.

• You are one of my closest friends ever. So I expect you to take a personal role in the development of my brother. I ask you to do so and would ask no one else. My gratitude in advance for making him a leader the way you are.

The new supe pays Buckner a look-in call and chats with Southerland. Officers often end up resembling their branches: General Bill Lennox is Field Artillery, a firm, blocky man with a look of contained force. Lennox invites suggestions on the new job — and Ryan, twenty years old, finds himself passing advice to the highest of higher. "Everybody loved General Christman," the cadet says. "But don't try to fill in on what he did, let us see who you are." Ryan admires Lennox: "He's trying to cut through the eyewash to see what's really going on," he says. "He's a *sharp* man. You know, some people are sharp, and some just played a lot of Hacky Sack in high school. I think he's focused on getting more Army into things." The general spends the months paging through the Academy like a thick book, making some of the discoveries Keirsey did half a decade ago. At summer's end, his verdict will become a West Point slogan: "We need to put the M — the military — back into the Military Academy."

Commanding Buckner gives Ryan a chance to return some of the glow from those three stars now gone out of the West Point sky. In the morning, when he stalks past the companies in formation, he calls out, "Warrior tough!" and a hundred voices cheer back, *Warrior proud*, cadets grinning like they've just spotted General Christman. Afternoons, when he visits the yuks' quarters, their eyes dart from boots to bed, as if they're squaring up to Colonel Adamcyzk. He approaches a sweaty yuk on a road march. "Having fun yet?" Ryan asks. "I just want to *die*," the yuk says, tossing away his rifle in frustration. (Ryan scoops up the weapon: "Well, I'll take it if you don't want it.") Then the yuk recognizes his commander, straightens and knocks out the remainder of the march, Ryan rolling by his side like Keirsey. "You're not getting ready to die on me again, are you?"

One of Ryan's command duties is organizing Buckner's celebration of the Fourth of July. Independence Day touches Army people in the same way Oscar night hits residents of Los Angeles; everybody walks taller, for one day the community's values and the nation's are the same. The detail work falls to Ryan's regimental training sergeant, a cow named Mary Tobin — five feet seven inches of staring TEDs, hair conked and pinned back tight. Mary arranges schedules, speakers, music. Like many cadets, Mary arrived at the Academy with clear driving instructions, then wandered off the main road. Her mother is not the kind of West Point mom who sat out the 1960s. She marched through Tennessee with Martin Luther King, stood her ground at whites-only diners, waited out the hours in southern jails, tried to join the Black Panthers — scouted around for forms to fill out — the year the organization collapsed. Stories passed from parents to children can harden into convictions. At her Atlanta high school, Mary Tobin was named the Student Most Likely to Restart the Black Panther Party.

"I had all these wild views about the government," Mary explains, testing the speaker system at the Buckner parade ground. "Plots against the black man. I was so angry and militant for so long — there was just *no way* in the world I'd ever join the military. My mother told me about Vietnam, how they sent all the black people to the front line, where they got shot." But Mary had joined the high school JROTC, risen to command. When she was a senior, her mentor summoned Mary and Mrs. Tobin to his office. "If your daughter wants to go to West Point," he said, "I've got her a scholarship." Mary's mother snapped back, "Well, she's not going into the military, so you can just give that scholarship to somebody else."

Mary arrived at the Academy with a plan. "I was going to infiltrate the United States Army, make my way to the top, bring in my own people through the side door and overthrow everything." Instead, during three years, the Army has infiltrated Mary. What she hoped to find elsewhere turned out to have been waiting here. "It's a beautiful place, where color's not a factor; it's all about getting a job done." She laughs. "So now you start getting impatient with regular people, worrying they don't understand. Instead of wanting to bring them inside, you want to protect it, you're like, 'No, you stay outside.'"

The festivities kick off at 0645. Mary calls cadence as the staff marches down the hill, Ryan taking over at the end: "Staff, halt." The eight Buckner companies collect on the cement ground. A thousand yuks in running gear; shirts catch the breeze, air carrying the summer smells of lake, gravel and pine. A cadet delivers the national anthem *a cappella,* with the moody pauses of a blues number, a story about a hard night that happened long ago. Everyone listens for the final two lines, with their stir and contradictions: a land where people want to be free, brave and back at home all at the same time. Ryan reads the prepared statement from the secretary of the Army. "'That our experiment in democracy has weathered the storms of history, to see yet another birthday, is a sign and a testament to the bravery of all those who have served on point for the nation.'" Ryan is dressed in gym alpha, because West Point celebrates July Fourth with a three-mile Independence Run. "'Soldiers have made today's celebration of independence possible. We thank you, and we salute you.'"

Ryan stares out at the one thousand yuks watching him. "Warrior tough!" he calls. The roar comes back: *Warrior proud!*

Ryan misses Betty Simbert, who's flown to Korea on CTLT, working with a Military Intelligence unit. When she finishes up, she'll go to South Africa, to serve at a nonprofit. "It's a weird, cool experience," Betty says; a paradox. "I got discrimination on both sides. From some of the whites because of the color of my skin. And then from blacks because I don't speak, like, *Zulu.* And when I say 'I'm African American,' they're insulted. They ask, 'Well, what part of Africa are you from?' I say, 'Well — Africa.' They say, 'Look. Then you're not African. You're an American. End of story.'"

Huck Finn is nervous about his summer assignment at Air Assault school, where he'll be roping out of helicopters, risking his money makers. He asks Rizzo, "You think it'll hurt my hands for fuhball season? Because they're sensitive. I gotta use 'em to snap a frickin' ball, you know? They're gonna earn me a million dollars in the NFL." But the new Huck is such a regulations devotee that he even arrives at Fort Lewis, Washington, in his formal white-over-gray uniform — as the travel orders specify — only to find every single cadet in the airport wearing civvies. His summer commander, a West Point grad, says, "I can't believe you're wearing that suit." But Huck enjoys CTLT. For one thing, it's like visiting a linguistic homeland, the soldiers swear just as much as he does, "they say some foul motherfucking stuff." The one thing he dislikes are the salutes. "I don't deserve a salute from these guys," he says. "I'm not a commissioned officer yet."

George Rash moves out for Fort Hood, Texas, another Military Intelligence unit. "It's very hot," he reports. The moment Rash-watchers have worried about — what effect George will have on actual troops — passes without difficulty, leaving no traces. "If you do what you're supposed to do, how you're supposed to, when you're supposed to, soldiers will respect you. And they'll overlook some of your minor inadequacies, help bring out your strengths." George grasps the lessons a TAC like Major Vermeesch has hoped he'd learn. "These people — or some other people, or at least people *like* them — will depend on me to take care of them. And do what I can to safely get them into and out of combat," he says. "Or, at least, as safe as combat can be."

Ryan will have his shot at CTLT after finishing Buckner. Before he leaves, there's a final round of first captain interviews, officers asking whether he'd like the job, what direction he'd go in. But in a sense the desk is stacked against him. Most of higher favors Andy Blickhahn. He's twenty-four, prior service, dependable; he talks, acts and reacts like the administration. Andy even has the stylized looks of a first captain: the square jaw, bright eyes and pretty chin of an illustration in the old-time *Saturday Evening Post*.

Ryan's last night at Buckner, Andy arrives all at once and asks for a tour. They ride together on a kind of golf cart (at West Point it's called a fast action vehicle) — commander and commander, jostling over the speed bumps. Andy will motion for Ryan to stop, they'll hop out, pose a few commander-type questions, pile back in. When Ryan asks a yuk, "How you making out?," he listens for the answer. But for Andy, the asking seems to be enough — getting an oar in, inserting himself into the other guy's thoughts. Andy's hand is cocked to slap the yuk's back before he's finished speaking.

"I just want to see what the attitude is out here," Andy says, stepping into a bay.

"Well," a male yuk says, "we're getting a lot of different points of view, of what we should expect next year, how to treat plebes —"

"So more than just 'This is what team leaders do,' it's 'This is what works'?"

The yuk closes his mouth. "Yes sir."

Andy slaps his back, translates their exchange into higher-speak. "So now you have a little bit more of a knowledge base?"

The cadet shrugs. "Uh, mm-hm."

Blickhahn asks another yuk, "What's the number one thing that could make you guys feel comfortable as part of the corps?"

"Well," he responds, "a motivated chain of command, I think. It gives you a positive attitude yourself."

"OK," Ryan says, "so you're saying that what comes down —"

"Well," Andy interjects, hand landing on back. "You're all doing great things. Really. Thanks for your time, guys." He heads back to the fast action vehicle.

"Have fun, fellas," Ryan says as he turns to leave.

At the end of the summer, Andrew Blickhahn is named the 143rd first captain of the United States Military Academy. Ryan is given regimental command; he'll head a thousand cadets. The firsties flood back into West Point, many driving the POVs they're now allowed to keep on post. "The Army," Huck observes, "is the only organization in the world that will replace a three-letter word like *car* with a three-letter acronym that takes longer to say."

And they finally receive their rings, small dense objects — stone, insignia and class motto compacted together like a memory. The firsties cross Central Area to barracks wearing their new jewelry; plebes patrol the concrete in scrums of fifteen and twenty, grabbing the upperclassmen by the ring finger, falling at their feet. Then, another Academy ritual, the plebes chant in unison:

"Oh my *God* — what a *beautiful* ring!
What a crass mass of brass and glass.
What a bold mold of rolled gold.
What a cool jewel you got from your school.
See how it sparkles and *shines?*
It must have cost a *fortune.*
May I touch it? Can I touch it?"

Firsties hide, skulk and dart away, to give the plebes a run or just to avoid the time-suck. Huck makes it all the way to his stairwell door, yanks the knob; a dozen plebes surround him, yelling in the sun: "Oh my *God* — what a *beautiful* ring . . ."

Out on the Plain, firsties stand for photos, rings by their faces. Others collect to pose "ring-style" — smiling at the camera, hands extended in front of them, as if each cadet is dunking an invisible head. "This is the biggest thing that's ever happened to me," one says.

The Ring

Ryan Southerland is completing the Myers-Briggs personality indicator at a long table inside the Jewish chapel; the test is part of a leadership conference, and Andy Blickhahn is here, along with the three other regimental commanders and cadet leaders from the Navy and Air Force. The Myers-Briggs is one more device for boiling the instincts and gestures of command down to measurable specifics — "just so you can understand what sort of person you are," Ryan says, "how you'll work with others."

> When you go somewhere for the day, would you rather
> 1. Plan what you will do and when.
> 2. Just go.

(Ryan darkens 2.)

> In daily work, do you rather
> 1. Enjoy an emergency that makes you work against time.
> 2. Plan your work so you don't need to work under pressure.

(Ryan fills in 1.)

At 0915, adult officers whisper, turn on the television. Cadets take in gray towers and charcoal smoke set against a coloring-book sky. "This fundamentally changes everything," Ryan thinks. "I'm looking into the future." Twenty minutes later, another jet arrows across Virginia to smash into the Pentagon's outer ring — and Ryan and the other cadets understand the country is at war.

Down the hill, across the warm Plain, in the classrooms of Thayer Hall, word is passing around, instructors are switching on TVs like parting the curtains on the same inexcusable view. "We're not going to stick with the syllabus today," one professor declares, replacing the chalk and folding his arms. "This is going to affect your lives more directly than any lesson I have to teach."

Huck Finn is walking the corridors between second-hour and third-hour classes. A cadet he doesn't know — quivering lips, swimming eyes

— tells him, "An airplane just crashed into the Trade towers," and ticks down the hall. Huck thinks, "What a stupid frigging joke." Another cadet hustles by, unfolding a cell phone. Huck hears the guy say, "Planes rammed into both buildings." Huck flexes his hands and begins moving quickly. As he thumps down the hallway, he catches sliced glimpses of sky and fires in every room. In his third-hour class, cadets are staring with parted mouths at the square buildings growing their ruffles of cloud. His professor switches off the TV and tries to conduct the morning's exercise, but he might as well be speaking in Aramaic. The professor is called outside for a few minutes. At 1030 he skims back. "Both towers just collapsed," he announces, voice shaky. The TV comes back on and the cadets watch scurrying pedestrians, the rolling wall of dust, ash and smoke. Professors begin releasing classes early: "I understand that many of you are going to have phone calls you'll need to make."

As Huck pushes across the Plain, he passes cadets walking private circles, spiraling around sweet spots where their phones can find reception. In his room, friends ding him over instant message.

GuinessMAN83: just heard. car bomb in front of State dept.
GuinessMAN83: somebody saying martial law in lower NYC.
Hucklberrry: fuckin martial law bro . . . never thought I'd live to
see the day. man I'm so pissed.
Hucklberrry: hold up. flight out of Newark to San Fran . . . Flight
93 . . . went down 80 miles outside Pittsburg. can't believe it's
come to this shit man.
GuinessMAN83: "this appears to be a coordinated terrorist attack
that appears to be going on as we speak . . ." CNN says it's
Ossama.
Hucklberrry: gotdamned right it is. He had his day and got the best
of us. I'm tellin you . . . we're going to do some shit . . . we're
Americans, we don't just sit down and take this.
Hucklberrry: hold up. riz phone ringing.

Huck's roommate, Josh Rizzo, grew up in Flatbush, a kind of feeder system for the New York Police and Fire Departments. Huck takes the phone, recognizes the voice of Rizzo's mom, doesn't wait for a report. "Y'all are OK?" he asks. "What about Josh's sister? How about his dad?"

Huck hears they're accounted for, and it's the moment he cries, fat tears inching down his cheeks. He's got to head for lunch formation. (Cadets will stand in jittery rows, eyes on the sky; a plane locating the Military Academy would remove four thousand prospective lieutenants.) Huck grabs a black Sharpie pen, scrawls over a sheet from his notebook, leaves it pinned to the door: "Riz: Family ALL OK."

Josh Rizzo is blond-haired, with sloppy good looks below bright, questioning eyes; as he makes his way through the cadet tangle along the Plain, the light drops out of his face. He presses upstairs, finds Huck's note. There are still the friends and neighbors who wear city uniforms or have other business that might have put them in the rubble. He went to high school with a cadet named Joe Quinn, worked at adjoining desks; they've stayed close. Quinnie's brother sells stocks for Cantor Fitzgerald, on the top floors of the North Tower. Rizzo races across post, yanking on doors and banisters. When he climbs to the room, he finds Quinnie sobbing with the chaplain.

West Point is placed on the highest alert, Threatcon Delta; the post clenches like a fist. Cadets can't leave, soldiers patrol the gates with automatic weapons and grenade launchers, five-ton Army trucks block the lots, heavy barricades protect the deep-porched residences of the comm and supe.

Rumors sweep the corps — plebes resigning, war isn't what they signed up for. Then that gets sorted out: firsties were asking to resign so they could enlist and fight. Word passes of terrorists staking out military bases. In the mess hall, General Lennox informs the corps that he's volunteered their services to the rescue — four thousand sets of arms, legs and able backs — but there's no need for additional workers, so cadets must exercise *battlefield patience*. The rescue crews eventually call, ask for something the cadets can provide: socks. Ryan Southerland organizes the sock drive for Third Regiment. "It's impossible to just sit there in your chair," he says, "and watch this on your TV, and know it's just down the road, and not be able to *do* anything. So this is our first bit of relief — they're going to end up with twenty times more socks than they could ever deal with."

The Firstie Club reopens Thursday night. The talk inside is a live, in-person version of the expert analysis on TV: asymmetric warfare versus total warfare, missile strikes versus ground troops, urban combat versus mass deployment, rushing to retaliate versus identifying the parties responsible. Cadets know that I grew up in New York, and before I can speak, hands reach for my shoulders and the questions turn to me: Am I OK? Are all my people — as if city life secretly consists of squads — accounted for? Same as in New York, their words are about morale, patriotism and determination, about preparing themselves and watching out for one another. Just as on the subways and sidewalks, people meet each other's eyes, looking for sympathy and trying to supply it at the same time.

During my three years at West Point, friends who don't follow the military have asked, "Do these guys know we're not fighting those kinds of wars anymore? Do they ever wonder if they're living in the past?" Now, as flags flap on cars and people bellow "America, the Beautiful" like a ballad and a threat, the country feels like West Point. It turns out that instead of living in the past, West Point has been living in the future, and now they've been joined by everyone else.

Huck and Rizzo enter the club. The past two days have twisted and wrung Josh like a sponge. Every call from home brings word of another death: a neighbor, somebody's brother or mom, a friend. "My mother is telling me, 'Don't come home, you don't wanna be around here right now,'" Rizzo says. "I feel physically sick from all these emotions. But I need to be there. I see pictures, I can't believe it — Huck, that's my home." Rizzo's phone rings again, the two cadets exchange looks; Rizzo finds a corner. When he returns, he's stowing the phone in his pocket. "This friend," he says, "her dad died in the fire." He squints. "I don't know, I hear it, but I don't feel it. It's so distant, it's like another news flash." Huck lifts a big hand to massage his friend's neck.

Huck and Riz carry plastic cups of beer outside, stare over the Hudson hills. There's a silent electrical storm, discharges spotlighting treetops and grassy hills from behind. The cadets on the back porch — smoking, murmuring — glance up, to see if something new has happened.

Huck and Rizzo's friends follow them outdoors. Everyone's heard from the home front — where news is shouldering its way out of its usual slots, spreading over the dial — voices stretched thin by anger and fear. It confuses the cadets; with their post at Threatcon Delta, they're safer in Highland Falls than the people they left behind to protect. The other fresh sound is something they never anticipated: friends thanking them for what the Army will do. "Our buddies," Huck says quietly, "who five days ago wouldn't of given a crap about the Army. It makes you proud."

For Megan Youngblood, a pale, doe-eyed cadet from Nashville who's branching Military Intelligence, the thanks carry a strange emotional responsibility, like salary for a job she hasn't performed yet. "I'm getting all these IMs and phone messages, they say, 'I feel a little safer knowing you're going to be helping do something to take care of this.' And honestly, I don't know how to *take* that. Because I don't feel that I know enough and can do enough right now. But I know I'll have to be ready in a few months — we're going to have to go out there and turn this whole dreamworld into a reality."

The toughest conversations have been with parents. Bryan Hart is from Baton Rouge; at the edge of high school graduation, he had advised Huck to stay away from West Point; they're friends now. "My dad called," Hart says. "He was choked up like I haven't heard him choked up in years. He said, 'If this is war, what if they graduate you boys early?' He said people around the coffee machine were talking about 'Let's go get the bastards' — but armed retaliation takes on a whole new meaning when it's your kids."

"Do it," Huck sputters. "Graduate me in December, send me to Ranger school, get me into the Army, I'm ready to go." He fingers his West Point ring. "I wanna die with this ring on me." Hart laughs ("I don't plan on dying, the bullet hasn't been made yet that can kill me"), Josh stares at his own hand.

Next morning, in Thayer Hall, the attacks thread into the lessons. Cadets discuss future military action in the cool, unruffled tones of cops predicting the Saturday-night blotter traffic in the station house.

"Ma'am," one addresses his professor, "I think we're in kind of one of the worst positions we've ever been in. Uh, we're looking at fighting an enemy that we can't really identify, in a land that we can't really identify. And we know at this point that nonretaliation is not an option. But we also know any retaliation is only going to breed more hatred against us in the Arab world. And like we all saw, it only takes four guys with knives to rain all this destruction on us. It's pretty easy to find four extremist people, if you go into a whole country full of 'em."

The professor nods. "Smart point."

Another cadet speaks up. "Ma'am, I think the only realistic option is: if we want to retaliate — which we know we have to do — we have to declare an all-out war on terrorism. And not just on Arab terrorists or on Islamic fundamentalists. On terrorism everywhere, Hezbollah, the Palestinians, even those who operate within our allies, like the IRA."

"That's excellent," the professor says. (As it turns out, this cadet has anticipated President Bush's formal strategy by several days.)

In another class, a cadet asks, "Sir, is there any information we shouldn't be . . ."

"Yeah. Let me talk about that right now. Who saw Senator Hatch on the news? He *really* screwed up. Did you see him actually tell the re-porters that we had transmissions saying Osama bin Laden was re-sponsible for this? Basically, he was releasing extremely sensitive" — the class chuckles — "intelligence information. What potential impact do you think that had on our collection apparatus?"

"Probably got shut down."

"Probably lost contact."

"Somebody probably got killed."

"Yeah," the professor nods, "the guy who was placing all those phone calls. For you future Intelligence people, it's very important to under-stand that." As he dismisses the class, he says, "I hope I'll see you at the Taps Vigil." At the ceremony tonight, the corps will honor the missing and dead.

In the afternoon, there's a barbeque for the Social Sciences Depart-ment, under a tent at the far end of the Plain. It was arranged weeks ago and would take weeks to reschedule, so the event goes ahead as planned. Smoke curls, beef sizzles, two fraternity-sized speaker cabi-nets woof out songs by Van Halen and the Grateful Dead. The barbe-cue rides on a thin edge of forgetting, on a willful, short-term amnesia. A cadet will swig Mountain Dew, smile, bend his neck to let the sun fall on his cheeks — and then a look of guilt will wince across his features. Colonel Jay Parker, the International Relations coordinator, watches cadets cross the grass to face the challenges of outdoor eating: how to take a bite of hamburger while balancing a soda and a plate. "These at-tacks are going to alter their generation of officers," he says, "just as surely as Pearl Harbor altered the Army of the 1930s, and Vietnam al-tered the Army of its era."

At the far end of the tent, another officer tells a group of cadets how he drove to lower Manhattan and had a police friend escort him through the barricades, how he spent the night working the long quiet bucket lines at the towers. The Brooks Brothers store across the street had been painted over with one word, *Morgue*. When people grew exhausted, they collapsed onto café chairs that had blown out the backs of restaurants. In the buckets' chunky dirt, he found an intact book, an unopened briefcase, a Palm Pilot. How when the rain came, it settled the dust.

Cadets start forming up for the taps vigil a little after 2300; they glide into silent rows along the Plain. Civilians — families from town — watch from the side as the lines grow thicker and deeper. The cadets' white shirts and hats take the light.

By 2330, four thousand cadets stand at attention. They stare across the flat grass toward trees, hills, clouds. Among the civilians, a young man wears a flag over his shoulders, a young couple curl four hands around a red candle, an older woman lowers her head to her husband's shoulder. The Plain lights snap off, and there's just the glow from the uniforms and the night.

For ten minutes there's nothing. Because this is a way to commemorate loss: with an absence, with stillness, with nothing. A steady sprinkler noise of insects rises off the grass, treetops rustle like the sound of approaching water. A truck bumps down a distant road, dragging a hole through the quiet. The cadets stare out to where the sky ends behind the dark, bulky hills.

The drill team fires a twenty-one-gun salute. Seven rifles, three shots apiece, each volley followed by a fluffy spreading echo. Then there's the night with its chilly smells of granite and grass and powder. The first slow notes of a bugle, a mournful taps: up the scale, over the scale, down the scale.

Then the cadet bagpipe team begins. Matthew MacSweeney is with them, playing "Amazing Grace," with its frills and edges. Faraway music, crimped by sadness, to escort the week's losses over the Plain.

After a moment, the cadets sing the alma mater. The sound is close to breathing, the faintest way four thousand people can sing one song. Then the cadets file out — the snap and click of shoes, a rush of gray and white, faces going visible in the light from doorways — and the night is left alone with itself.

A quarter hour later, Josh Rizzo is back in his room, staring at his hand. "I didn't know if I was ready," he says, "until this shit happened. I mean, I came here originally to play baseball. But I know now, I'm here to defend this nation. I have no fears, no qualms about going." He runs his fingers over his ring. "It's weird. When I first got this ring, I thought, 'Look at this cool ring. I can get any job I want.' Now I look at it and I think, 'We are *called*.' I've got a job to do. I've got to defend my home."

Guppies Never Quit

The new G-4 TAC is named Rafael Paredes, a craggy-featured, dark-eyed man with a grin that pries open his face. Just before Major Vermeesch left to pitch his office two buildings over, for a year of desk service with the Academy, he gathered G-4 in the day room. "There's good news, bad news," Vermeesch said. "The good news is, you're finally getting rid of me, if that's how you wanna look at it. The bad news is, you're gettin' another Infantry TAC — that'll make three in a row — Captain Rafael Paredes. A bit about him: he's five foot six — he's a little short guy — but don't take that to mean he's not big in spirit. He's one of the most fired-up guys I've met in a long time. What I'm asking is, I want you to support him the same way you've supported me."

By September, cadets see their new TAC barreling across North Area every afternoon. He'll plant himself in front of anybody — hulks, high-pockets, beanpoles — tilt his neck back, apply corrections. "I may be five-six," Paredes says, "but my ego's six-two."

The captain began pushing the Fighting Guppies onto a wartime footing even before September 11. He never posts a leadership philosophy — "I'm not big on a whole laundry list of rules," he says. But it's unnecessary, since nearly everything the TAC says is leadership philosophy. "We pamper cadets so much here — too many privileges, not enough responsibilities, spoon-feed the answers we want — that we spoil 'em." Staring through his window at some foul weather, he'll explain, "Taking care of soldiers is not necessarily keeping 'em warm and giving 'em food. It's giving 'em good *training*. Let's say there's rain. If you're just sitting around with your thumb up your ass, the only training effect you get is learning that being wet sucks, and a dirty thumb. But you could be out practicing battle drill in the rain." He shakes his head. "I tell my guys we're gonna stretch the threshold of pain a little bit, and sometimes that's gonna suck." He goes on, "We're not gonna train for a kick in the 'nads. But we *are* gonna try to be a little harder for a while. Leadership is a hard business."

Like many evangelists, Captain Paredes came to faith the rough way. As a young officer, he flew to a hot landing zone in the Mogadishu of *Black Hawk Down,* where he received an education in contrasts: smashed buildings, fine white beaches, starving locals, soldiers strolling the base in Teva sandals and shorts. Then he spotted the bandaged heads, the Joes on crutches: taking it easy is a bad habit, relaxing can get you hurt.

But for the firsties, kicking back is part of what the final year is all about. (Firsties, for example, are the only cadets allowed homey civilian touches like fridges and carpeting. Paredes's Health and Welfare inspection also uncovers a bunch of contraband George Foreman grills, which get confiscated.) The Corporation's early line on Paredes goes, "The new TAC is . . . a little more involved that we're used to. But we'll break him in." Firsties make pilgrimages to his office to explain that his approach isn't what they're used to; the captain's aggressive demeanor could put other cadets — not them — off. Paredes patiently hears them out. "Tough shit," he says. "I don't give a crap. Hey, suck it up." He grins. "I tell 'em there's a speech from *The Princess Bride:* 'Get used to disappointment.' I'll tell you what. The standards have not changed. Maybe the *enforcement* of the standards has changed. There's a new sheriff in town."

The captain has marched through so many challenges in his own life that what's left is a self-made man's impatience. He grew up in civil war El Salvador — crackdowns, assassinations, roving death squads like the Mano Blanco (a folded black sheet in your mailbox containing the white outline of a hand was a message that meant change, leave or die). What he's learned is that any obstacle you encounter, push it aside; that just leaves the shoving muscles stronger. He'd like to pass on this spirit to his cadets, so he changes the external things a TAC can. There's nothing to be done about the company's amiable, domesticated name. (When Paredes graduated West Point in 1991, G-4 had a scrappier handle, the Gladiators.) So he moves on to the company motto. He avoids saying "Go Guppies" — "It's kind of queer-sounding," he says — and combines it with the slogan from an old battalion: "Never quit." "So what I say now is, 'Guppies never quit.' I've got about half the company using it. I'm trying to instill the warrior spirit."

Then he turns his sights on two potential G-4 quitters, Scott Mellon and George Rash, the old roommates of last resort. He pores over their statistics like a baseball manager composing his roster. "George," he says. "We should've pulled the trigger on him a long time ago." Scott Mellon is a dicier issue. "He's super smart," Paredes says, turning to his computer. "He's got like a one-forty IQ — maybe he's too smart for his own good." Scott's away message is a G-4 favorite, a sentence he copied from a classroom evaluation. "Motivating: *IMPROVE*. Cadet Mellon sets a poor example for his classmates in demonstrating how little he can do and still get by." Scott has sized up West Point like a physics problem, calculating the minimum energy expenditure necessary to achieve graduation, the maximum result. Paredes pulls up records that chart Scott Mellon's decline. "He dropped from a three-point-six GPA to a two-point-four last year. I can't let people squeak by and graduate."

The two cadets have climbed and panted their way to firstic year. Another TAC might leave commissioning them up to the Academy. Paredes makes them both platoon leaders — they'll be responsible for thirty cadets, one of the most challenging senior-year assignments, the same job Jake Bergman ducked two years ago. If either cadet cracks, well, he can object about Paredes on his way out the gates. "Show me what you can handle," Paredes tells the two cadets. "I'm going to put a lot of pressure on you guys. Prove to me that you can do this job."

There won't be any Guppies squeaking by. In the fall, two G-4 plebes fall in love, embark on a mini, Bonnie-and-Clyde crime spree — boosting car keys, credit cards, money, checks. A colonel commiserates with the new TAC. "This is too bad," the colonel says. "You didn't come to West Point to kick cadets out, to put people in jail."

Paredes considers it for a few seconds. "As a matter of fact, sir," he replies, "I did. I came here to keep bad people out of the Army."

Branch Night

Firstie-year September is about the showroom hush of picking your branch. The Army word for practicing is *rehearsing* — that way, even the most hectic situation shapes up as a performance question of hitting your mark. In a way, firsties have been rehearsing this moment since the day they accepted their slots at West Point: "What would I do if it really came down to it — if the country sent the class to war?" The kind of what-if scenarios civilian friends test on each other over beers, after gun-and-chase movies, the firsties are facing now.

For the person Huck Finn has spent a year and a half becoming, the answer is obvious: Infantry, idiot sticks. In the weeks before branch selection, he's more agitated than he's been since yuk year. Everything that should be a relief — an article, some officer's advice — is just more sand in the mouth. He stamps around post, eyes hard beneath his brows. At football practice — everyone hitting tougher — all he wants is to get back to barracks, watch more CNN. In class, he's thinking about Afghanistan and pictures in the morning newspaper. The Sunday after the attacks, he heads for chapel. A man in a flag necktie takes the pulpit, raises a Bible above his head. "This has been a week like no other," the man says. "And I just want to remind you that, uh, this story right here? At the end, we win. OK? I promise, if you read all the way to the end, we win. We serve a mighty God." Religion has that soothing power to fold even the most disruptive colors into the comfort of an overall design, but it's not working on Huck.

His roommate's return from New York is more agitation. Rizzo tells about funerals and the odor hanging between the buildings of his neighborhood. "Riz says the wind blows straight across the river from Ground Zero into Brooklyn. He says it smells like dead people."

Nine days after the attacks, Riz and Huck watch shoulder to shoulder as President Bush addresses a joint session of Congress. There are moments when the commander in chief seems to be staring past the elected heads, down through the cables of the broadcast equipment, right at the firstie class. Huck keeps half an eye on Riz. For days, every time the eleventh comes up, Riz has pulled the same long face he wore all that Tuesday. But when the president mentions bringing justice to enemies, Riz brightens, mutters, "Yeah, hell yeah." Then the president turns to the lens, says, "And tonight, a few miles from the damaged Pentagon, I have a message for our military: Be ready." Josh jumps out of his chair, you can hear whoops and shouts from the windows of West Point.

Huck e-mails his parents that he's fixed on Infantry. There's no response. He e-mails again a few days later, adds an op-ed he grabbed online, some analyst making stabs about the Infantry's role. His mother finally writes back: Quit sending your dad stuff, he's a wreck thinking about you in the Army, are you kidding with this? "She's like, 'Cut out mailing that shit, ah'ight?'"

Huck is settled on it. "My class joined a peacetime army — we were gonna protect the Somalis, defend the Kosovars, hand around food. Now we're defending the U.S.A., and that's a fucking *great* feeling." Huck's grandfather fought in World War II, bumping over clouds and flak as a ball turret gunner. He got shot down over Austria — smoke, parachute, ground, capture — spent thirteen months in a POW camp that was liberated by General Patton. (Patton himself inspected Will Finn's Red Cross meal package, seven days' rations for seven people. "Well, damn, son," the general said, "*that* ain't enough.") Huck's dad was Field Artillery in Vietnam, loading guns with shells as big around as dinner plates. "Every Finn man goes to war," Huck says, "and I never expected I'd get to carry on the tradition. Now I'll have a chance to tell my children I defended the Constitution like my old man did." A frown clots his face. "Only thing that scares me is, I got that typical post-teenage thought that nothing's gonna happen to me, but I couldn't imagine anything worse than me saying to some kid, 'Go stand over there,' and he gets shot. I'm a frickin' emotional kid — I don't know how I'd handle it." So Huck spends off-hours compiling advice about combat: "Officers who can talk about Iraq." It's not always helpful. "They tell a story about Desert Storm, it's about kicking somebody's ass, because that's basically what happened." When he wakes up, he runs through maneuvers and hand signals in his room. "I wanna get geared up as best as I can. I want to be trained."

When Army plays at the University of Alabama in Birmingham, the Finns fly over from Baton Rouge. Before the game, Huck visits their hotel room. His father is in a chair, curtain drawn, no TV. He asks Huck quietly, "Have you decided what you're going to do about your branch?" Huck wanted to say — and didn't — that he'd been telling and telling him. He understood his father needed to hear the news from his face. Huck says Infantry, and his dad thinks for a minute. "All right, that's your decision," he says. "Go with it. Do what you have to do."

For three years, George Rash has harbored a climate-controlled dream: Ordnance, the single largest Army branch. Predictable hours, behind the scenes and behind the lines, maintaining ammunition, filling out forms under strong lighting. "I like tinkering around with stuff," George says. "Heck, I'd rather push papers than fill somebody with holes. I don't find going out and killing someone to be that much fun. I *can* do it, and will do it if I have to. But I'm not going to go out and deliberately look for somebody to shoot — communists or terrorists or whatever. As a person, I'd prefer to run an Ordnance shop and repair stuff." It's also a favor to his feet. "If you're dropped in, you basically drive everywhere."

But by the end of cow year, Ordnance had become the kind of warm dream you have to shake out of your head the minute you awake. George's rotten class standing ("I'm down near one thousand," he says, "out of one thousand") guarantees he'll tote a weapon. The Academy likes to promise each cadet a top-three branch choice. But it also follows the 80-20 rule: only 20 percent of each class is allowed a non-combat choice. If a whole class decides on support branches, Signal or Finance or Transpo or Ordnance, the bottom half get the saddle-up call whether they want it or not; they're *force-branched* to preserve the Academy's 80-20 combat-support ratio. This system could lead to what everybody has feared: George Rash in the Infantry. "Unless eighty percent of my male classmates pick combat arms of their own free will," he says, "I am going combat arms." So George prepares the best he can, by cutting weight and hanging around with huah cadets. "I'm hopin' some of it might rub off."

Pulling on his BDUs for Branch Night, George is hoping for Field Artillery; he could live with Combat Engineers, mine-clearing and bridge-building, it would put his aeronautical engineering major to good use. So long as he doesn't open his envelope tonight and find the scary brass X, idiot sticks.

Branch Night is mid-November — post crisp and dark, the moon reporting for duty early. G-4 falls in with the rest of the firstie class on the concrete apron of the Plain. A G-4 cow named Sam Kim strolls outside to slap Huck's back and wish him luck; Huck is too nervous to do anything but nod. His problem is the reverse of George's: he's so low in the class (the first two years sink his class standing like rocks) that Infantry might close out before it ever reaches "Finn." "If he gets it," Rizzo promises Sam, "you'll hear it all the way up here." Riz's heart is set on Field Artillery; he wants a part of the military action, and the branch's essential, royal pounding and smashing role in combat is there in it's motto: "King of battle." "My grandpa did it in Korea," Riz says, smoothing down his uniform pocket. "He got in a fight where he was firing his howitzers straight up in the air, because the enemy was so close. He asked me, 'Why don't you go for something not really right in combat?' I told him no, that's where I want to be."

Jasmine Rose stands a few boots away. She's hoping for Signal — stringing up phone lines, handling computers and other communications. "I always liked it since Buckner," Jasmine says. "The first thing that drew me, they said every time Signal goes out in the field, they're in an air-conditioned van, it keeps the equipment cool. Which isn't always true, but I was like, 'Wow, that's great, field air-conditioning.'"

There's never been a lot of doubt what insignia Ryan Southerland will wear; he's been aiming for Infantry since the first time he heard Lieutenant Colonel Keirsey speak. "There are just some people you meet," he says, "you want to measure up to them." Ryan is among his class's top thirty cadets, so Branch Night for him is mostly a formality. The high rank has also had its drawbacks. He and Betty finally broke up a couple of months ago. His cow job left him too busy to be more than a telephone boyfriend; regimental command is another ruckful of work, it doesn't even leave him time to be a friend. And a relationship would muddy the career choices he must make. "I didn't want to go into branch and post having that affect my decisions," Ryan tells me, "and I didn't want to force Betty to make those decisions thinking about me. But it's been very hard. There are still all these very powerful feelings. I was in love with her — I mean, as much as I know about love."

Remarks like this — over IM, in person — still irritate Betty. "Of course you know about it," she'll declare. Betty is hoping tonight for Military Intelligence; the rumor is that the branch will have a big part in whatever comes next. "At first I was, 'Oh shit, we're going to war.' There's that big you-can-die factor. But MI is a way for females to be involved with the whole terrorism thing."

Mark Thompson and Chrissi Cicerelle have called it quits too. They argued so long about regulations that separating turned out to be the one rhetorical position they hadn't occupied. After the attacks, Chrissi wept, softened, telephoned. "The bombings magnified it," Chrissi says, "showed me how important he was, fighting wasn't worth it. I told him I loved him." She sighs. "And he said, 'No, we fought for a reason and we broke up for a reason. I didn't make you happy.'" Mark, like the rest of the Corporation, is aiming for idiot sticks. Chrissi — as if their argument is still going on by force of momentum — is headed as far as possible in the opposite direction. Adjutant General, the Army's bureaucratic corps, is the one branch where there's no guarantee you'll command a unit. "I'm not sure I want to lead a platoon," Chrissi says. "I'm more into office work and organization, and doing my own thing."

At 1930, the drum corps arrives, works up its rattle, the firsties march off for Eisenhower Hall. Cows carrying their dinners in white takeout bags watch and give the thumbs-up. The firsties laugh and joke, meeting their careers in good humor, but if you look down, their legs are snapping in perfect unison. They march over the Beat Navy tunnel, clatter down the cement steps, to where they can see the big downsloping hills and the reflections on the water.

Inside Ike Hall, General Eric Olson, the commandant of cadets, takes the stage. Yesterday, the Taliban handed over the city of Jalalabad, setting off a general, messy retreat; military urgency backs the comm's words. "I've seen quite a few Branch Nights," he begins, "and I detect a certain quality to this one I haven't seen before. There's an anticipation, an excitement in the air. You're all thinking about the choices you're making, the contribution you're going to make to the effort that will almost surely be going on when you're commissioned."

His gaze sweeps slowly to take in the firstie class. "This is an Army in transformation," the general says. "Personnel, systems, equipment, doctrine, how we train — all that is being changed again. And you will help the Army make those changes. The Army needs people of your quality. It needs people like you perhaps more than it has in many, many years. I feel a tremendous sense of dependency on the quality of your service. Our nation will depend on you."

At a moment like this, the wide space inside cadet heads — full of anticipated trials and hopes for achievement — exactly matches the space outside them. Then the comm sneaks in a professional admonishment. "I expect you to celebrate tonight — and I'll expect you to celebrate responsibly." The moment condenses into one big laugh. "But as you celebrate, I want to give you something to think about. There's a message that's been out there on the e-mail. It's from an article that appeared in a Romanian newspaper, about the tragedies in America. The editorialist asks, 'Why are Americans so united? They don't resemble one another. They speak all the languages of the world and form an astonishing mixture of civilizations. Some are nearly extinct, others are incompatible with one another. Still, the American tragedy turned three hundred million people into one hand put on the heart. Nobody rushed to empty their bank accounts. Nobody rushed to accuse the White House, the Army, the secret services. They placed flags on buildings and cars as if in every place a minister or the president was passing.'"

The comm raises his head. "The editorial finishes this way — and I want you to listen to this. 'What on earth can unite the Americans in such a way? Their land? Their galloping history? Their economic power? I tried for hours to find an answer. I thought things over but I reached only one conclusion. Only freedom can work such miracles.'" The comm's face goes stern and optimistic at once. "It is freedom," he says, "that works miracles in the United States of America. And it is freedom that is being threatened, that is under attack. It's freedom that you are sworn to defend. And tonight you take another decision on the path to serve this nation, to protect that freedom. I am filled with confidence, because I know you will accomplish both very well. May I ask the TAC officers to distribute the envelopes, please."

There's the rumble of the class of 2002 rising to its feet. Captain Paredes shakes each Guppy's hand, presents the packet containing their branch insignia. "Hey," the TAC jokes, "I taped them extra to make it hard for you guys to open." Cadets squeeze their envelopes, trying to braille the contents.

Huck doesn't squeeze his. If it isn't Infantry, he's not ready to face the binding fact. "All the shit I've been through," he says, "it'd just be way too ironic if I didn't get stupid sticks." Someone announces "At this time . . ." from the stage, and there's a slash of envelope-ripping, followed by yells and backslapping down the aisles of Ike Hall. Josh Rizzo pulls out his king-of-battle pin — two crossed cannons. Jasmine Rose tilts the semaphore flags of Signal between her fingertips. Chrissi Cicerelle doesn't get AG. Instead, she finds the key-and-sword of the Quartermaster Corps; she'll be leading a platoon after all. The Corporation — Mark Thompson, Matt Kilgore, Eliel Pimentel, Kenny Wainwright, Rob Anders — is one long cheering row of Infantry. Each mud crawler pin is a plus for George Rash, a minus for Huck Finn. Hands meet for shakes behind Huck's back and over his shoulders as he sits scowling, palms folded over his envelope. Slogans and nicknames are being shouted, cadets testing how the new branch feels in the mouth. "We clear the way!" (Engineers.) "Queen of battle, baby!" (That's Infantry; on a chess board, the queen is the only piece that can go in any direction, take any foe.) "Silent war!" (Military Intelligence.) "The combat arm of decision!" (This wide load is Armor.) George splits open his envelope and lets out a big, relieved sigh as he examines a shiny, castle-like fort. If he graduates, he'll be an Engineer.

The firsties fall out to Ike's Café — a wide room, bargain-price beers on trays, prom-rock thumping from the speakers. They huddle at tables with their new branches and propose sloshy toasts. Cadets are pinning bright insignia on one another's lapels, standing up to the blink and flash of disposable cameras. Huck has walked in the opposite direction, to the quiet upper reaches of Eisenhower Hall, to prepare himself. Cadets shout more slogans:

"Spearhead of the Army!"

"First to fire!"

"We're Infantry, all we need is food, toilet paper and bullets!"

Two big cadets touch glasses, Coors dribbling over their thumbs. "Infantry can't survive without Armor," the first begins, and the second guy jumps in, "And Armor can't survive without Infantry."

Huck pauses on the staircase. He's thinking how his parents are worried about him, how his dad fought in Asia and his grandfather flew above Germany, and here Huck is sweating over a branch assignment. He rips open his envelope, shakes the pin out into his hand: idiot sticks.

The Corrections and the Hours

Cadet leadership is like traveling to a higher altitude; there's no way to predict the effect. You could get invigorated — wave your hands and talk in a loud voice — it might wear you out, it could make you delusional.

As Third Regiment's commander, Ryan Southerland acts pretty much the same as Ryan doing anything else. "I don't know if he's the best commander I've seen around this place," says cow Mac Davis, "but it's hard to imagine a much better one. I've never seen anyone get to a position like his who didn't act like a forty-year-old in a twenty-year-old's body, didn't mistreat his classmates or become a robot who shoots himself in the foot — didn't act, for lack of a better word, like a tool. It's why people get excited about Southerland."

To his own surprise, Ryan finds his assignment disheartening — "bittersweet," he explains, "emphasis on the first part." He has climbed far enough up the rank structure to peer into rooms where navigation is debated and course changes are settled on. But it's still a tour, just the deluxe version. "In cadet land, I have this position; in reality, I'm in charge of very little. The TACs are there at the company level, and what can I say to a TAC? Absolutely nothing." He frowns. "It's fake command."

It demoralizes him to watch Andy Blickhahn, because as some members of the corps anticipated, he proves to be higher's first captain more than the cadets'. "He really tries hard to please the officers," Betty Simbert explains; she and Andy have been close since the prep school. "Then he tries to explain it to the cadets, and the cadets are like, 'Yeah, bull.' I don't think they love him the way they did the first captain last year, Dave Uthlaut." Uthlaut expressed the ways of cadets to the administration — he was the firm, presentable cousin who steps upstairs at Thanksgiving to ask if the teenagers can all go see a movie. As cadets see it, with Andy it's the reverse: he's the cousin who comes downstairs to patiently explain why hitting the multiplex would be disrespectful to aunts and grandparents who've traveled long distances. Other cadets offer a balanced assessment. "Sometimes he seems great," they say, "and sometimes he's a butt-boy for higher."

But the most groused-about striper isn't the first captain; it's Chrissi Cicerelle's old boyfriend, Mark Thompson. Though he's not a regimental commander, Mark lands a glory position that's one of the most potent in the corps. As the operations officer, the S-3, Mark coordinates major events, arranging transpo and, this year, evacuation plans. S-3s also get tasking authority — meaning duties and punishments. "He's become a hated man," Huck Finn says. "Which isn't fair. I've known him since R-Day and he's a good guy."

The first signal is when Mark stops keeping time with the Corporation — no more Saturday afternoon basketball games, no more group dinners, no contact. It's not just Chrissi: much of his pre-leadership life he seems to see as weights, ties that must be snipped. "It's all changed," Eliel Pimentel says, shaking his head. "Last year, he talked about getting the cool office and stripes. This year, he made a decision to cut us off." When he gets engaged to a fellow firstie, he doesn't pass his old friends the news; instead, they hear about it through the fishbowl, which leaves scraped feelings.

At Academy events, he presses a white Secret Service–style earpiece into one ear; cadets can't remember seeing anything like it. They figure he's plugged into a constant stream of West Point logistical data, but as Huck says, "It's a mystery, man — nobody knows." To mock Mark, when they bump into him around post, cadets will press two government-agent fingers against their own ears.

What winds cadets up most about Mark Thompson has to do with the hours. In early fall, word comes down that all punishments will be served Old Corps style — on the Area. Walking tours, five-hour stretches of silent, back-and-forth marching across the hundred cement yards of Central Area. If you get quill, the TAC promises G-4, you will walk. To Captain Paredes's eye, the payoff will be measured in what's called *situational awareness,* a soldier's trained sense of where you are and what you're doing. If a cadet checks into a G-4 bathroom stall with an untucked shirt, that's an automatic five hours. A yuk attends Sunday chapel in her civvies, waves hello to Captain Paredes, spends a minute catching up — Monday morning the paper's waiting on her desk, five hours. Mark Thompson's hard innovation is what's called the three-gig rule. A gig is a mistake: unpolished brass, patchy shave, even misaligned chin-strap buttons on your hat. If you have three gigs, you've got another punishment. Now, before cadets can begin walking, they gather for a gig inspection. It becomes like one of those tricky Greek mathematical paradoxes: you could walk away from hours with more hours.

Then, what puts Mark over the top — cadets call it "the biggest 'holy shit'" — is when he shows up at hours formation and begins handing out extra hours to cadets for holding their rifles improperly, for marching bunched up. "He's not very well liked in the corps right now," Eliel says. You hear the concern for his old friend. "I think it's going to be rough for him next year in the Army, because he's made some serious enemies. But hey — decisions." Officers who've followed Mark's West Point career can't decide what to make of it. "I'm not sure what was up with Thompson," one says, shrugging. "If that's what he was always like, or if the job went to his head."

Even at the company level, leadership is what military planners would call a change agent. George Rash and Scott Mellon have been platoon-leading for a couple months when one of them springs a leak. It's not George. "George has done a great job," Captain Paredes admits. Disciplined and conscientious, George Rash is a standard-bearer; he's proved that he can do the job. It's Scott who catches Paredes's eye. A year ago, TAC-NCO Sergeant Tierney spoke about the cadet as if he were describing an unmemorable walk across a parking lot. "There's nothing great, there's nothing terrible; he's there. I would say Scott Mellon is a middle-of-the-road cadet." Scott has faced physical challenges. His shoulder was operated on last summer, so he's been on profile at fitness tests; plebe-year concussions — in barracks and in the boxing ring — have left him with complicated sleep patterns. (On the other hand, he did a fine job last summer with an Army tank unit.) The physical isn't what's getting under Paredes's skin; it's what's upstairs, the motivation, heart and head. He doesn't see Scott leading by example. A platoon is broken up into four ten-person squads. "Give them a vision and guidance," Paredes urges Scott. "Right now you've got four squads going in four different directions. When you've got them moving in the same direction, then you've got a platoon." Scott is doing the minimum needed to graduate. When Paredes visits his room to give more advice, he learns that Scott's formula even extends to the level of tidiness. "I told him to get his room clean," Paredes says. "Then I started taking privileges away from him."

The TAC puts Scott's room on *SAMI* — Saturday A.M. inspection — the maximum dust-free, white-gloved standard. "Before, he was initially very mild-mannered," Paredes says. "Always been, 'OK sir, yes sir.' But then he mouthed off to me. And that was it." Scott has fought back with the bright kid's strategy — going for cover in the rule book, shielding himself with fine print. When the captain returns and asks, "By the way, why isn't your room up to standard?" Scott replies, "As a matter of fact, sir, I've been meaning to talk with you about that. You can't put me in SAMI unless I see some paperwork."

It's the last thing a TAC wants to hear. "That pissed me off," Captain Paredes says. He told Scott's roommate to leave the room. Then he began a correction. "I yelled at him," the TAC says. "It was funny, I totally changed. I said, 'Lemme tell you something, monorail. Let me tell you something. We fuckin' *own* you. Listen, I have the power, we have so much power — why are you doing this?'"

The TAC casts around for other strategies. Paredes has been counseling Scott about his C average. The captain wants to talk the matter over with the Academy psychologists at the Center for Personal Development. "And Scott said, 'Hey, let them talk to me, they can tell me what's going on,'" the captain remembers. So Scott goes round to the building the cadets call the Center for Personal Destruction. Paredes monitors his progress. By midsemester, Paredes has an idea: to ask the CPD to perform a Scott Mellon fitness-for-duty evaluation. "When I saw him totally not meeting the — not succeeding," the TAC says, "I mean, do I want this cadet to be a lieutenant? Hell no! Hell no." Paredes shakes his head. "And Mellon could have graduated. He could've met the standard, he would've had a two-point-oh GPA, and he would've had a C military — he wasn't failing. Mellon could've squeaked by, and they would have graduated him. But *I* could not graduate him in good conscience." So Paredes got on the phone with the CPD. "And I'm not gonna turn around and rat out people. I mean, I'm the standard-bearer. So the only way you're gonna get him out is, I said, 'Hey, from a *medical* perspective, there's no way this guy — he's out there, right?'"

Personal Destruction

Before the attacks, cadet TV cards usually piped in *The Simpsons* or *Friends* or *Seinfeld,* light comedy recalling the contours of the old life like a postcard. The Grant Hall restaurant — it's called the Weapons Room and offers jam-packed sandwiches like "The Stinger Missile" — is where cadets line up for snacks and pizzas. Two big-screen TVs broadcast ESPN, guys lifting their eyes between swallows. Some nights, at 1930, a cadet will stand, switch stations, bring in pop news from *Access Hollywood.* For months, the Weapons Room TVs have been pinned to CNN, showing caves, hills, helmets, aircraft, a weather report of their future.

In December, Army takes Navy, 29–22. Mark Thompson patrols the sidelines wearing his white earpiece. President Bush watches from inside a scrum of Secret Service agents, visits both locker rooms. Huck Finn snaps the ball for the Black Knights' final punt; as he jogs onto the field, it hits him that he's playing his last down of big-time football.

A few days later, the Taliban surrender their last stronghold, Kandahar. The Grant Hall TVs function as a kind of West Point crisis index. You can pinpoint the moment the Academy returns to normal when a cadet puts down his sandwich, flips the channel, and the regular sports programming resumes. "Now it's like, 'Go back to daily life,'" Ryan says. "We've become such a fast society — we take things in, forget 'em just as quick." Civilian friends, however, learn that there's still a contribution they can make to the war effort, by hard-charging the mall at Christmas. This strikes Captain Paredes as "so . . . *weird.* Go shopping, like nothing has happened. You don't want to forget there are guys out there fighting. So I try to get my cadets to remember their mission."

During a January class, the TAC reminds the firsties they've only got five months left; it's time to start thinking like lieutenants. The change won't come by magic, he says, and uses the old Academy joke: there won't be any officer fairy-dust sprinkled on their shoulders at graduation. People expect to see them do great things; the work is not going to be easy. The firsties are back in the cadet mindset, complaining to him about papers due. "Guess what? You're in the big leagues now, guys. People don't go to a circus to a watch a guy juggle three balls. They go to see a guy juggle freakin' chainsaws on *fire*." That's what Captain Paredes intends to say. At the moment of decision, his tongue stumbles: "You don't go to the circus to see a guy with three balls." The cadets chuckle, raise their hands to say Yes sir, they would.

The CPD board reports back to Captain Paredes: Scott Mellon has been found unfit for duty. Their recommendation is for immediate separation, but Scott is still on post, awaiting final orders. The TAC visits his room. "On a daily basis," Captain Paredes says, "telling him, 'Scott, what do you wanna do? Hey, this is what the board decided. You're not fit. You have to ask yourself, "Did I meet the qualifications for the mission?"'"

The TAC also consults with colonels and the doctors from CPD. "We had a meeting with all the doctors; the colonel said, 'Hey, just tell 'em what you wanna do. You want to see Mellon out of here, right?' 'Yes sir' — he knew how I felt." Captain Paredes continues, "And I said, 'I'm not gonna tell Scott he's a pack of shit and he should get ready to go — not until we get the stuff. Because he's going to fight me every step of the way.' And then the psychiatrist goes, 'I agree with him. Scott's going to say, "Ha, I knew you were out to get me."' And so the colonel says, 'Oh, yes, you're right, good point.'"

Then, in early February, a rumor sweeps G-4. Scott Mellon, packing weapons, had planned to revenge himself on Captain Paredes. What really happened is simpler. Scott has been at West Point three and half years; he's taking dismissal hard. He tells his CPD therapist — as he later jokes to Huck Finn — that he's so depressed about it, the one thing keeping him from killing himself is he'd like to kill Captain Paredes more. Conversations at the CPD are not protected by the standard client-doctor confidentiality. The doctor phones Captain Paredes. "Scott Mellon has got homicidal ideations about you." (For the TAC, it's just another in his life's string of challenges: "Initially, I thought to myself, 'Tell him to bring it on.'") The rest develops by word of mouth. Scott likes to spend some evenings target-shooting with friends at an indoor range; another cadet overhears Scott talk about saving time by not leaving the weapons off post but stowing them in the trunk of his car. "You can have a weapon on post for four days before you have to register and store it with them," Scott says. The cadet goes to Captain Paredes's office.

"And I knew that I couldn't approach him like, 'Hey, where are the weapons?'" the TAC says. "So I said, 'Hey, let's talk abut this. What do you usually hunt for?'" Scott tells him squirrels. "'OK, what kind of weapons do you use?' Y'know — I started asking all these questions. Then, 'Oh, where are your weapons at?' He says, 'Sir, they're off post.' I told him, 'Tomorrow by 1700, I want you to register those weapons.'" There's no further communication from Scott. The TAC e-mails him, and Scott burrows back into the rules again, sends "a soliloquy" about his Second Amendment rights. Next morning Captain Paredes gets a warrant, calls Scott down to his office, tells him they're going to search his car. Scott looks at him. "You're right, sir," he says. "You've got me." They walk to the lot, look together at the .22 and .30-30 deer rifle locked in his trunk. A week later, Scott Mellon is erased from the Academy landscape. The day he leaves, Captain Paredes gathers his cadets, assures the company that Scott has left West Point to find the medical help he needs. The day before, the TAC had to visit the cadet in his room and ask for the return of his West Point ring.

A year later, during the run-up to the second Iraq war, Scott Mellon is studying at a civilian college. He's surprised to find himself missing West Point. "I'm living at home with my parents, and I dress like a dork," Scott reports. "I almost wish I still had a uniform, because at least I knew how to wear that." He passes the ROTC cadets on his campus, sees the jacked-up gear, has to hold off from stopping and making corrections. "It's really strange," Scott says, "because I hated West Point the whole time I was there, but now I feel guilty that I didn't graduate. Before I got there, I wanted to be in the Army; while I was there, I hated the Army; and now I feel really guilty about not being in the Army. Especially with the whole Iraq thing. The unit I would have been with is in southern Turkey right now."

Morning Star

Two years after leaving the Army, Hank Keirsey is standing at the Garrison station waiting for the Manhattan train. A kid is there in civvies, but the signs of cadetness are obvious: pressed chinos, newly mowed hair, casually correct bearing. Keirsey rumbles to his side, just as he approached hundreds of cadets on hundreds of West Point afternoons. "What're you looking at?" he asks.

The Garrison station sits a river's width away from the Academy. The platform offers a fine view: the Academy docks, pleasure boats bobbing; the hilly, climbing road; sturdy gray buildings growing out of the cliffside.

"Sir, I'm staring at that hill. It doesn't look so steep from here, but that hill has smoked me innumerable times." He turns to Keirsey. He sees a coat and tie, a small beard: a civilian in his middle forties. "You see, sir, I'm a cadet at West Point. And some of us there, we run that hill every day."

Keirsey's eyes sparkle. "Really," he says in his oak voice, "I hear they push you guys pretty hard in that outfit."

"Yes sir, they work us pretty good," the cadet says. "It's rough right now, because we're in this phase folks call Gray Period. Gray buildings and weather, plus, on top of it, we wear gray uniforms."

"I see," Keirsey says. You can tell how much it would mean for him to be recognized. Then he goes ahead and uncorks the old Keirsey vintage. "You pick a branch yet?"

"I'll do that next year, sir."

"Next year? Well, you look like an infantryman to me. You look hard. You've got the *shoulders*."

Keirsey steps a few feet away. He's been gone four semesters, he's no longer a figure in anyone's sky. "I guess I'm in disguise." He shrugs his own bearish shoulders. "That's the way I like it."

After two decades under idiot sticks, Hank's first civilian action was to declare a shaving moratorium. In the Army, facial hair is as forbidden as drugs or racial bias. "And you shave so long, you end up wondering about what the hell would come out of your face. So with this facial hair, I am entering the cocoon of civilization and will slowly emerge as a proper civilian." That first spring, Hank purchased an airy, long-decked house set back in the woods. He fixed it up, settled into the hermit's life of exile. He called the place a *hooch*, congratulated his big Labradors military-style. "Good dog — defecating outside the perimeter." When Kathy and Hank showed up for weekend officer parties — meat cross-hatching on the grill, fists wrapped around beers — a strange reserve clamped his tongue. Sure, the other guests were all wearing civilian clothes too. But come Monday, they'd have uniforms to climb back into. He didn't; this was Keirsey's uniform.

The change fell hard on Kathy: it was a forced excursion through foreign parts of the world she never planned to visit. She grew up in an Army household. "The military is the only way I've ever known," she says. "I liked my family, I liked Hank. I never wanted to not be in the military. That was the one part that really bothered me. I looked at my husband and I said, 'Honey, we're going to become *damn civilians.*'" Hank rolled out of bed each morning at 0530 — the body clock never quite gets relieved — to the same unanswered question: What do you do after the stands clear, the groundkeepers pull out the tarpaulin, you close your jersey in the locker?

He maintained military fitness, assigning his muscles different tasks like squads. An hour of roadwork each day for the legs, an hour on dumbbells for the arms. He hunted his dogs through the woods, tracking deer and fowl. He explained to Kathy why meat taken in action always tastes better than food captured at the grocery. "Take beef," he said. "That cow grows up thinking, 'The farmer is my buddy. He's always feeding me, he's always watering me, making sure I'm warm in the winter, cool in the summer. Here he comes now, what's he got in his hand? Wait a second, *I had this whole deal entirely wrong.*' That last instant of betrayal is what you can taste in every darn cut of beef. Deer, on the other hand, is meat that's never been lied to."

Army celebrity has about the same transfer value as fame in Japan. But there were people who knew about Hank. He delivered motivational addresses to unions and clubs, felt the old fire kindling in his chest. After that, he founded a business, teaching Army-style teambuilding to Manhattan executives — city-faced people who'd never shimmied across a rope bridge or rappelled a cliff. They stared at trees as if curious to see where they plugged in, and turned shy around Hank, like he was a 3-D effect stalking off a movie screen. (They appeared just as foreign to Keirsey. "You kind of gaze into their eyes," he says, "not sure what you're supposed to be looking for. And these guys don't seem to want to make eyeball-to-eyeball contact.")

Business often called him to the city, to shake the hand, close the deal. Manhattan never felt quite right to him. It was all clutter and gridlock, people living too close to and too far from each other at the same time. Opening doors on Wall Street, Hank became just another guy with a product to pitch. You never had to market yourself in the Army: your résumé was the patches and badges on your uniform, where you've been, what you've done, how hard you pushed yourself, how much it mattered. Not having to sell yourself — to hear true things turn suddenly false in your mouth — is a great ease on the heart. When they did buy Hank's service ("We are all very jazzed about doing this"), business guys often wanted to exchange some kind of trinket. Hank grew a wardrobe of shorts and logo sweatshirts.

When Hank got home, Kathy would ask, "How'd you do?"

"Excellent," he'd say, tossing his car keys on the counter. "I got a new hat."

The September attacks blasted Keirsey out of the commuting life. "I imagine it's the same as it was for guys after Pearl Harbor," he says. "You want to enlist immediately, get back in, do what you can do." Hank found himself in isolated terrain, another consumer of Army news — just when his neighbors felt their TVs turn participatory, as news became a show that could extend a big deadly hand. Some retired Army friends had partnered up with an international security outfit called Morning Star. "Our profession," the British Morning Star brochure reassures, "is your company's peace of mind. We offer specialised advice, training and experienced personnel. Our goal is to enable your organisation to operate safely in inhospitable environments." The firm's operatives are mostly ex-SAS — Special Air Service, the English equivalent of the Rangers. Morning Star's Washington headquarters "is two guys working out of their closet, basically," Keirsey says. He asks the firm to find him an assignment in the Middle East, where he knows the action is going to shift.

In February, there's a kind of on-the-job, inhospitable-environment audition. Morning Star's D.C. men fly him down to Washington, fix him with a visa, a digital camera, an international cell phone, then spend the afternoon combing bookstores for the relevant *Lonely Planet* guide. "They couldn't find it," Hank chuckles, "so I got a little brief from these two guys in their closet." A day later, he squints off the tarmac in Africa. His mission is to evaluate politics, security and stability in the large coastal city where an American firm plans to locate a refinery. "I'm reconning for extreme circumstances — if everything went into a Uganda scenario where people started eating each other, machetes come down off the wall, how are this company's employees gonna respond, where are they gonna go?"

He's entered into a strange shadow world — like the ghosts you get on bad TV reception — with no staff, no uniform, no weapons; and he's happier than he's been in two years. "It's a kick," he says, "like going into any other operation." The old situational awareness comes back, the tightness in the belly and the sharpened eyes. He noses around consulates, police stations, docksides and landing strips, taking notes, snapping photos. When local troops and police give him trouble, he takes their picture, shows them their likeness captured in the back of his camera. They smile and wave him along.

From his hotel room balcony he phones his son. J.D. is apprehensive, on the verge of Ranger school. As Hank stares over the baked, rotting town, he advises his son. "You cannot help but be amused if you try and remove yourself from your own unpleasant experience. And look at the other people suffering around you. You'll never learn more about human character. So you develop poise and dignity in tough situations, just by being in tough situations."

Hank's job has its own eye-fucking qualities. Dusty streets unmarked by road signs — they're pinched for use as roof shingles — French CNN murmuring above hotel bars, strange lizards and bats, sweating Europeans, Mad Max van drivers, year-old wrecks abandoned by the roadside, cat-eyed prostitutes, Muslims making the Hajj, sidewalk merchants offering to sell you shoes, snacks, water, animal hides, balancing the goods on their heads. Cabaret singers perform silky and perfect renditions of American pop; when Keirsey tries striking up a conversation, they know no English, they've memorized vowel patterns off the jukebox. And everywhere he finds a shifting backdrop of bulky men — with haircuts and experimental beards just like Hank's — conducting spectral missions like his own. "You pick them out automatically from a mass of faces," Hanks explains. "It's quite obvious. Just as I'm quite obvious to them. Then we go up like dogs sniffing each other's butt." He'll ask, "SAS?" They say yes, then ask, "U.S. Army? The Division?" "Yeah," Keirsey answers, "once upon a time."

At night, nobody ventures out on the roads — "that's the bad time" — so Hank curls at a seat in the hotel bar. There are South Africans everywhere, expatriates working the oil rigs, servicing vending machines, checking livestock. As they grow comfortable, their talk turns to the kaffirs — blacks: they are slow, lazy, hopeless. Hank puts down his drink. "Wait a second," he says, "that's not true. I went into combat with a lot of African-American guys. These were fired-up men, excellent soldiers. They woulda given their lives for anybody in the unit, and I would've done anything for them." There's a buzz at the table, the South Africans deciding whether to let Keirsey in on the truth. Finally one of the men nods, drops his voice. "Over in America," he says, "you got all of the good ones."

In the spring, Keirsey earns the job he wanted. Morning Star will deploy him to the Persian Gulf. He'll train local soldiers in anti-terrorism techniques. As the region braces for the war's next phase, Keirsey will do his bit to make things a little safer when Americans like his son finally arrive. He packs in his early-morning bedroom, chill drawing in under the windows. "I'll tell you what, there's a tension in the belly," he says. He pushes shirts and equipment — binos, compasses — into his duffel, along with lotion that will keep his hands from cracking in the desert. "Every time I used to deploy, I couldn't sleep. Not worrying that your unit was gonna get waxed, but that you were not gonna be able to accomplish your mission."

Kathy drives him to the airport; he'll be away for a few months, and the separation feels normal. When something happens, the abnormal thing would be for Keirsey to stay home. As they cut through morning traffic, Hank grows quiet. At the curbside he hugs his wife tightly without saying anything. Then he pulls on his cap, shoulders his duffel and walks through the automatic doors, heading out on a solo deployment because two and a half years ago he did a brave thing. He has instructed Kathy not to wait around, but she edges the car forward, trying to keep her husband in sight as long as she can. "There's his doggone *hat*," she says. "Now he's getting on the line." A few minutes later she says, "He's the only guy with a duffel." Then she says, "Now I can't see him anymore."

A few weeks later he phones J.D., to congratulate him on finishing Ranger school. When J.D. asks how he's doing, Hank jokes, "Just another day making the world safe for democracy" — what he always used to say in the Army. Then he thinks of the sort of kingdom he's consulting in. "No, wait, correction — scratch that. Making the world safe for a dictatorship."

Black Sheep

Last April, Huck Finn swigged Gatorade on North Area, watched the muddy survivors limp in from Sandhurst and guaranteed Mark Thompson he'd make the same walk next year. At West Point, promises cling to you like smoke; the only way to clear the air is by making good. In mid-January, Huck pushed into the day room for G-4's first Sandhurst meeting. The team waiting there was an anxious-eyed herd of plebes and yuks. Huck was a football player — an ex–football player — and Sandhurst isn't something football players do. "So who's the squad leader?" Huck asked.

The plebes and yuks stared back. "Aren't you him, sir?"

It's traditional for veterans to fill out team ranks with some been-there confidence. But the Corporation made their point last year; now they stick to the bench. (Major Vermeesch's response is a one-word shrug of surprise: "Huh.") The final semester can tag firsties like a tranquilizer dart. Matt Kilgore has a wedding to plan: a young local teacher passed him a note at T.G.I. Friday's, she'd spotted him and decided she wanted to sit across the table forever. Eliel Pimentel and Rob Anders have basketball and girls in mind (Rob is also acting in the Hundredth Night show); Mark Thompson hears the call of his earpiece. The only Corporation member to turn up is the group's brainiac — Kenneth Wainwright, a tall, elegant polymath from California, nearly bald, as if he's run the numbers and determined that hair obstructs a potential solar energy source. (Kenny will spend next year at Oxford through the Marshall Scholars program, exchanging Army greens for tweeds.) Matt Kilgore got the company commander nod from Paredes; he'll be the Guppy leading G-4 at the graduation parade. The first week, he sits in on a Sandhurst meeting, sizes up the squad. He pauses at the door to nod with Huck: "It looks like you've got some black sheep on your hands." Huck makes it the team name.

For a while it looks as if the team won't even qualify. A Sandhurst squad must have a representational makeup like Congress's: you need members from each class, and the Black Sheep don't have any juniors. Huck and Kenny buttonhole Sam Kim in his room; with a canny, three-pronged assault of shaming, bullying and begging, they get Sam on board. ("Huck kept saying, 'I know you don't want to, but bro, I need you,'" Sam says. "I'm thinking, 'This guy's just a dirtbag football player.' Finally I was like, '*Whatever,* dude.'") Then Huck's got to come up with a way to get everyone else just as motivated. He stands in front of the team, does first things first. "I'm Huck," he says, "hello. Not gonna try to hide it from you — Sandhurst, no experience, never been with it, nothing." He watches the cadets stare at each other: Why is this guy our leader? "Well, all right, I got one goal for this team. Anybody wanna take a guess what that shit is?" Nobody answers. Huck slaps his midsection, where he's grown his customary postseason gut. "By competition day, I want this motherfucker right here to be gone." The group laughs. "From then on, everybody got comfortable," Huck says. "They were like, 'OK, so what if it's Sandhurst, at least this guy ain't such a frickin' douchebag.'"

The team eats dinner at a separate mess hall table. Other squad leaders ghost by, scouting the competition. They see: a football player, a brain, one cow and a gift-box assortment of nervous plebes and yuks. Last year, G-4 finished in the middle of the pack, and that was with the Corporation and all their professional skills. The Black Sheep quickly become favorites to finish last in the corps.

The firsties pick their posts on a chilly night at the end of February. Their next years in the Army are already acquiring gravity and an address. Ryan Southerland, the Corporation, Huck and Huck's Louisiana buddy Bryan Hart crowd into Washington Hall to face Infantry selection and the Iron Mikes.

The class of 2002 has responded to wartime by putting 205 cadets in idiot sticks; it's one of the biggest groups in years. (Huck would have slept a little easier before Branch Night if he'd known higher's decision to give Infantry to any cadet who picked it first.) But with Keirsey, Adamcyzk and the old supe gone, nobody knows how to put their enthusiasm to good use: there are no speeches to get the blood racing, no reminders of soldiers in the field waiting to be joined and led. "When we're done tonight," the branch rep says mildly, from the front of the auditorium, "you can take off from here and enjoy the evening." Then selection begins, posts in Italy and Hawaii disappearing like seasons.

Ryan's last semester is shaping up as a trudge. A few nights ago, he sat down with some fellow stripers. "After last semester," one confessed,

"I have no passion left, no emotions for anything. This whole term is mechanical." Ryan couldn't believe it. "No," he said. "Think about it — when you lose that, you lose it all."

Plus, he's been butting heads with Andy Blickhahn, fighting the command mentality that stripers and corps are separate and the corps is wrong. Ryan is producing this year's Hundredth Night show — "just for the experience" — and he's borrowed uniforms from Andy and Mark Thompson. When the two hear they're being lampooned in some scenes, they demand their gear back. (They don't offer a reason, except to say it's a personal matter.) Word gets around, and it's a shock to the corps. After all, Adamczyk submitted to his annual lumps, and generals did too — two-stars like John Abizaid, who've returned to the Army to command whole divisions; General Christman even sent over his class-B trousers the year he was the show's villain. "It just became a fiasco," Eliel Pimentel says in his room. Matt Kilgore shakes his head: "Not many people took Andy and Mark's side at all. Historically, the show makes fun of recognizable personalities. Not joining in made them look a little like hypocrites, like they aren't supporting the corps." (Six weeks after Hundredth Night, when the firsties tilt together for their class photo and Mark tries to organize them, cadets will shout, "Where's your earpiece, man? Don't forget the piece." Matt Kilgore will wince at the image. "Everybody was just hating him, saying stuff to his face, ripping him *hard*. It got so bad I almost felt like crying for Mark.")

Ryan is the ninth cadet to choose at Post Night, when dream spots like Hawaii, Germany and Colorado are still available. He takes Fort Lewis, near Seattle — a new brigade is being developed there, one that will fight city to city, house to house, which is the direction Ryan understands the terrorism war is likely to go. Once again, cadet real-estate choices are based on a mix of huah and location, with everyone steering clear of buggy Fort Polk. Andy and Mark will take their striper competence to Fort Bragg, The Division. Matt Kilgore signs up for Fort Campbell's 101st Airborne, the Screaming Eagles; the assignment is likely to take him to Afghanistan or back to Iraq, a country professors are quietly telling cadets to keep an eye on. Eliel and Rob Anders opt for the pineapples and beaches of Hawaii. Huck and Bryan Hart are talking together as the board clears. "My palms are straight wet," Huck admits, and Hart whispers, "Stay South, stay in the South."

When Huck rises, late in the game, almost all the Iron Mikes have been picked clean. For anybody who knows him, it's a strange moment: the big cadet has nothing to say. If you can't select under pressure, a choice is made for you; Huck is the only cadet the branch rep has to invoke the ten-second rule on.

"Ten . . . nine . . . eight," the rep counts.

Oooooh! Take Polk!

"Six . . . five . . ."

A cadet starts to whistle the *Jeopardy!* theme.

"Three . . . two . . . one . . ."

"Korea," Huck says.

Yeeeeah! Wooooo!

When the last Iron Mike comes down, the air is charged with competition, support, good humor; but there's nobody there to shift the excitement toward the missions that await the firsties. "Make sure you sign the sheet before you leave," the branch rep reminds them. "OK, thank you and good night. This concludes the Post Night." Ryan remembers the kind of speech Keirsey would have given after post selection — then realizes he's one of the few cadets who does. "It's funny," he says, looking around the room. "He's passing out of the memory of the corps. People are already starting to lose him, to forget him."

Over at Thayer Hall, Chrissi Cicerelle runs dry on options and walks out of Quartermaster with Fort Bragg. She knows Mark Thompson is headed there, which is no inducement. "Also, I've always been terrified of Bragg," Chrissi says. The Eighty-second Airborne has "the reputation of being very male-dominated, very cocky, very Infantry — it's like, please, get over yourself. And look at me" — she holds both hands to her face: manicure, rings, earrings, great hair — "I don't exactly fit into the whole super-trooper mold." When she shows up at the Firstie Club, her friends have already heard. They're laughing before she sits down. "Airborne — *hooop!*" they call, and "Eighty-*deuce!*" Chrissi's face crinkles in exasperation. "You guys think it's funny, but it's not." She starts a letter-writing campaign and gets reassigned to Fort Campbell.

George Rash arrives at Engineer post selection with a loaded book bag. He takes a seat, cracks a book, starts doing homework. "What else am I gonna do for forty-five minutes?" he says. "I'm last." When 109 other Engineers have picked, George glances up to see what's left.

There's only one post remaining: George Rash will serve the next three years at Fort Polk, Louisiana.

Huck Finn gets some unanticipated help on hitting his Sandhurst target weight. He becomes fit walking the Area — Captain Paredes is handing out hours for everything.

There's frustration on both sides of G-4. Firsties believe they've earned the shy privilege of being left alone, and the TAC is spoiling their last months at West Point. This isn't an attitude Captain Paredes can support; he's developing them for the rigors of the Army. "What's gonna change in the next sixty days," he asks, "except the color of their uniform? They have the idea of 'It's almost over.' No, it's not, bro — it's just beginning."

From the captain's standpoint, punishment tours make perfect sense. "It's about expectations. We tell them West Point is going to be tough; if we don't meet that, they just become cynics. So hey, West Point is hard, motherfuckers. And I make it hard. Reach down, grab your balls, prove to me you can do this." With Scott Mellon gone, the captain looms in cadet minds like a movie crime boss, right after the scene where he proves he's serious by bumping off one of his own guys. When the Hours Boys aren't apprehensive on their own behalf, they're worrying about George Rash. Paredes now has a clear field of fire; George stands alone in the TAC's sights. "The TAC is just waiting," Cal Smith says, "and he wants to get Rash out of here *so* bad." But the others have plenty to worry about. The TAC comes to Huck's room to hash out some piddly violation, Huck raises his eyebrows, it sends the TAC over the top. "He told me, 'One more time, you and Cal Smith are both done — you're out of this school, you will not graduate.'" Huck is wrapped in a post-shower towel, but he marches straight for Cal's room. "I said, 'Look, dude, Paredes may be around the bend, but I'm definitely taking the man serious — he's seriously capable of screwing up my world. It's February, I'm gonna be good.'" It spooks Cal, too. "What he did to Scott," Cal believes, "he'd like to do the same to us. That's his deal, to ride you for everything until you snap."

Huck walks for poor shaving, lateness to class, sloppily executed parking jobs. Some tours run ten hours at a shot. "Doin' what I do best," Huck says, "walking the Area." Marching pitches him deep into himself. "I notice I'm singing songs in my head or looking if people I know are walking by. That's true West Point punishment, right there. I mean, if they wanted to devise a plan that would fuckin' teach cadets not to screw up anymore, they did a good job by bringin' back the walking tours. 'Cause that shit's *brutal,* man. It hurts physically and mentally, 'cause you get so frickin' bored — I mean, it's *boring,* dude. You can't talk. You've got that rifle on your shoulder, you got to switch it every five minutes. And I mean, hell, those damn *shoes,* bro." March a hundred hours at West Point, you've walked your way into what's known as the Century Club. Huck is already a Bicentennial Man — two hundred hours plus. And every Saturday he's on the Area, it makes the Black Sheep look sillier; they're the team being led by the ate-up firstie.

Huck is dead serious about Sandhurst — it's his best chance to get ready for next year. There's leadership practice: if he can motivate the squad to even a semi-respectable showing, that's way more than anybody expects. And there's mud crawler preparation: rappelling, rope-climbing, shooting and grenade-lobbing are the skills you'd list in an Infantry want ad. Huck pulls two weeks' worth of all-nighters to study up on each event. He works till streaks in the clouds tell him it's quitting time, Rizzo peeling back an eyelid every so often to murmur, "Huck's doing Sand-*huah.*" Huck translates Sandhurst into his second language, the X's, O's and dotted lines of football. When he's done, he's cooked up ten separate playbooks, one for each Black Sheep and a master for the squad. "When he handed us the playbooks," Sam Kim says, "that's when I thought, 'Hey, this might amount to something.'"

Training in North Area on a damp April Thursday — wind stretching and flattening the oily puddles — Huck understands he's also competing against his former image, the old Huck. He assumed command would mean acting more professional, but the too-bigness in his personality is finally paying off. He prefaces instruction with things like, "Another damn thing I forgot is" or "All right, I know you all hate the boat." Leadership, he thinks, is also a matter of spillover vitality — maintaining your enthusiasm at communicable levels — though that's just what the Academy has tried to drill and hour out of him. The Black Sheep are all spitting and all cursing, a squad of Hucks. When they ace a gas mask drill, they call, "Damn! We're frickin' *money!*" (Huck counsels them on the importance of gas masks: "OK — if you don't get your gas mask on in nine seconds, whoop-dee-fucking-doo, guys. Don't feel like we just lost the competition just because shit happens.") Every time the team says, "sir," spectators glance over their shoulders to see if an officer is passing, but the Black Sheep mean Huck. He tells them, "No one is taking us seriously, not even our own company. We're the squad that's been picked to finish dead last. But we're ready, and at 1420 on Saturday, we're winning this shit."

Sandhurst is a two-and-a-half-hour, greatest-hits version of four years of military training. It starts by testing the most basic housekeeping skill from Beast: at 1420, the Black Sheep muster for inspection. Huck employed an old Hours Boy trick, instructed the team to suit up last night in BDUs with all their kit, then spend ten minutes under the showerhead. At Sandhurst, you don't compete head-to-head against other teams. You fight mistakes — flubs cost points — and time, clock hands nipping at your heels. About forty cadets from G-4 turn out to run the nine-kilometer course alongside Huck's squad. And even though Bryan Hart has already run it with his own company, he comes back to support his hometown boy. "I wouldn't want to miss this crazy-ass football player trying to be a Sandhurst officer," Bryan says.

And then they're galloping off down the rocky orange path. Canteens flap, packs rattle, boots clack. At the boat site, Huck's plebe-year roommate, Kevin Hadley, cheers their paddling: "Way to go, Gups." He's headed for Korea, same as Huck, and frowns at the prospect; it's not the ideal post for a Christian. "I've heard there's a lot of drinking and prostitution," Kevin says. The Black Sheep change uniforms on the sand; as they're hustling down the trail, Major Vermeesch steps into view, one of his kids in his arms. "Go get some, G-4," he says, and the team thumps past.

When the squad fires too fast at the rifle site — a dusty spot where G-4 got cut points last year; the Black Sheep are already kicking up dirt with misses — Huck shouts them calm. "Yo, yo, stop." Then they squeeze off five quick shots in a row, sounding the carnival doink of hits. A cadet from another squad nods at Huck. "Hey, how many hours has that guy walked, anyway?" Then they clatter downhill to the grenade area, drop into the prone, blow the hell out of some plaster Ivan figurines. Then they're winding uphill again, the Guppies spreading out behind them like a big human wake. This stretch, to the one-rope bridge, is the longest run of the course. Boots catch on vines, puddles soak boots, fatigue starts clamping muscles. "Let's hear it," Huck calls to G-4, "we need some help back there." Shouts go mouth to mouth among the Guppies.

Keep moving.

Doin' great.

Let's move it, keep pushing.

Never stop pushing.

Good job, don't stop.

Don't stop moving now.

Keep pushing.

Guppies never quit! (This is from Captain Paredes.)

The words sweep under the team's boots like a breeze, giving legs some lift and play. The team shimmies across the rope bridge, backs sagging down close to the stream. Then the Black Sheep squeeze onto hands and knees for a crawl through a long culvert, water muddy and buttery under their palms. They pull each other over the twelve-foot-high Ranger wall, earn the highest possible score.

Every Sandhurst team includes at least one female member. Christina Cattley — a short-haired yuk with the nickname Cat — is crumpling under her ruck, eyebrows going fixed in the upright, pained position. Huck shoulders the pack, shouts, "Push Cat! One guy in front of her, two guys behind!" The team completes its rappel down the jumbled cliff face in big looping bounds, then the Black Sheep scramble over crunching leaves and molar-shaped rocks until they're back on post.

They catch their breath before the Gothic arches and casement windows of Arvin Gym, waiting on the team ahead to finish. The final event, the Commandant's Challenge, is always Sandhurst's worst haze. Last year, squads had to hoist a huge log on their shoulders, shuffling and grunting it back and forth. This year, the one big weight has been diced into thirty-seven smaller ones. The Black Sheep will have to lug five-gallon water jugs — the sloshing equivalent of forty pounds — two streets, from Thayer's statue to MacArthur's statue and back again, covering the distance between the old and modern Academies. The Black Sheep limp into the holding area, uniforms muddy, muscles stiffening. (Cat turns her camoed face to Huck. "Hey," she says. "Someone should snap a picture of me, we can post it on Hotornot.com." Huck rests his hand proudly on her helmet.)

If they blow this last event, they've blown Sandhurst. Their faces look as if they've been used to mop a floor, heads are nodding, the Black Sheep are staring more at their boots than at the sky. Huck steps in front of them.

"Hey," he says, voice serious, "I've had a great time with you guys, man. Not gonna lie. I can't believe this shit's over. In seven or eight minutes, man. The Black Sheep, all over."

The squad turns to Huck. "After all the shit we've been through, every fuckin' practice since January tenth, it all comes down to this right here. You don't think the whole corps isn't gonna be out there watching us, 'cuz we're the last team in? They wanna know how the Guppies are gonna do, how the Black Sheep are gonna turn it out. The team that's supposed to finish last at West Point, that's *us*. So we're all gonna be sucking it up out there — no walking whatsoever."

The team calls back, *Black sheep!* and *Suck it up!*

Huck swallows. "I've had a great fucking time with you guys, all the shit we've gone through. I never thought — most of you guys didn't know me two years ago. Back then, I *hated* people who did Sandhurst, I wanted to hit 'em in the face. Anybody military, I hated 'em. All right? Now I love this shit. You guys were amazing.

"All right, I hear them clapping down there, they're getting ready for us. We're going to suck it up."

It's late afternoon, shadows long, sun catching on the leaves. As the team moves forward, Bryan Hart steps close to his friend. "Hey, Huck. Seriously, way to go, man." The next chance they get to spend any real time together will be almost a year from now, after Ranger school, before Bryan drives down to the 101st Airborne to ship for Iraq.

Two hours later, at the award ceremony, Huck makes the long walk up the Washington Hall stairs to shake hands with the British commandant; his team has won the regiment. The Guppies get a streamer to put on their company flag. Late that night, legs going stiff, Huck e-mails Major Vermeesch. "Sir, I'd love to tell you this in person but I've got to get it off my chest. Today was nearly the best day in my life. I owe you a big thanks. If you hadn't pushed me and inspired me over the past three years, I would have missed out on knowing this team. Just between you and me, I have a satisfaction 10X greater than beating Navy."

The major responds at a decent hour. "I didn't have the words on Saturday, but please understand that I have never been prouder of — or happier for — any soldier than I was of you that day. That single event, and your team's success in it, are testimony to all that is right about West Point. Whether you want to believe it or not, you are one hell of a good guy, and you have the potential to be a great soldier. Your success as the Squad Leader will do more to eliminate the ghosts from your past than you will ever know. Be proud — and please know that it only gets better from here. God Bless, Maj V."

This would be the end of Huck's before-and-after story, except there's another after. Huck has gotten word through a sports agent. Huck's hands are basically fumble-proof, he snaps a couple hundredths of a second faster than the NFL standard, and the New York Giants are only fifty miles down the river. The team plans to offer him a contract if he can get out of the Army.

Whitey's Helicopter

The November weeks before Whitey Herzog deployed to Kosovo passed in a flurry of last things, each action sharpened by a kind of farewell awareness. Writing a check was sending his last rental payment; making a package of dog tags and insurance forms for his parents was his last trip to the post office; withdrawing travel money, he got his last smile at the teller's window. The day before he flew out, Whitey drove the hilly, pinched streets of Watertown, eyes camera-wide, logging enough footage — Tower Records, Applebee's, Wal-Mart, Midas, Denny's, Blockbuster, Target — to spell him six months away from the franchises of home.

That night, he piled uniforms, boots, compass, knife, CDs, neck guard, glove liners, knife sharpener, nail brush, ammo clip, a Bible trimmed with BDU colors ("in case you've got to pray in the jungle"), checking items off his packing list with a yellow highlighter. He put Hendrix and the Allmans on the stereo. Every so often, he reached around to scratch the small of his back, where his first tattoo was still healing: a hillside, a cross, a pennant with the initials *MJM* — Mark Joseph Matty.

In the morning, he pulled on BDUs, made coffee and stamped into the living room. Iggy subjected his ruck to an Infantry once-over, posing questions and offering anxious, wifely advice: "Make sure that cord's tied tight. Don't put your ammo on the side of the chem mask, 'cuz the way you got it rigged, you can't get at that shit. It would make things slower if you have to reload. Hey, have you got — did you pack your flak jacket?" They loaded Iggy's Honda, Iggy steered them onto Fort Drum, parked at the Rapid Deployment Facility, a low-roofed building with a wide-open entrance, soldiers inside stacking duffels and rifles, a flag on the wall. They both knew this morning would come; the surprise was that Whitey was leaving first. The Goodfellas shook hands, Iggy told Whitey, "You know how it is, brother — I'll see you when I see you." Whitey nodded and stepped through the doorway.

Then Whitey is in Kosovo, Camp Bondsteel. He jogs with other officers at sunup, clouds going pink, under guard towers where rifle barrels peek over the sides, climbing Radar Hill with its satellite dishes angled to the sky. For a few moments the landscape spreads itself below him: post, village, whitewashed Balkan houses with orange roofs. The region is like a smashed anagram of America. When he hits the Macedonian barbershop, the haircutters are always watching *Jerry Springer* — below the razor noise, there's that chant: "Jer-ry! Jer-ry!" Whitey slides off the chair to explain every time, "Guys, so long as you know — not all America is like that." His unit brings supplies to kids; Albanians and Kosovars are taught in separate schools, one building modern and heated, the other filled with dirty children and concrete floors; adults from the good school wait until the soldiers leave, then remove all the new gear from the underfunded place. He drives roads where Kosovars in Levi's — kids and parents — are rubbing their arms, sawing branches off trees. "You don't see too many intact trees around," Whitey says. "Because they're freezing, they need 'em to heat their homes. The thing you don't realize is, these people are not that different from us. This isn't some backward place — their ideal world would just be a night out in Buffalo."

There's a lot to get done. Whitey works till two in the morning, reports back to his desk at 0700. USAREUR — the United States Army in Europe — is preparing for the new currency, the euro; it means retooling spreadsheets, testing new systems, sending around the forms. People at home are watching combat footage on the news, the military is once again making them proud. A priest from his Buffalo high school e-mails, asks if Whitey would write about his experiences, he'd like to send word out to parents through the school bulletin. Whitey is happy to do it; of course, he can't reveal anything operational. The priest writes back, "Can I at least tell people you're in Afghanistan? Or is that a secret?"

It embarrasses Whitey. He explains he's in Kosovo, he's not doing anything dangerous, just necessary work. But writing helps him put something into words. For two years, he has lived his life with a whisper running at the same time, like bad reception on the radio: Wouldn't everything be easier as a civilian? Every month he's in Kosovo, that whisper becomes harder to make out. He'd like to share this with Iggy. "We're so tight," Whitey says. "He's my best friend, but he's hypocritical in this one way. He gives me advice, I listen, and it's always good advice — he totally squares me away. But he won't take any advice from me." What Whitey would say is that you have to treat the life you get as if it's the one you set out wanting. Whitey has deployed, but to Kosovo; he wanted Infantry, then Aviation, he's here as combat service support. But a lot of life is *almost* in the same way. You have to take the emotions and motivation you'd have if things were ideal and apply them in situations where they are not.

But Iggy doesn't need that advice. When he finished the rotation with his old platoon, Mafia, he got reassigned to staff. Two months later, Mafia deployed to Afghanistan. "My boys went without me," he says quietly. Iggy feels just what Adamczyk and Keirsey always spoke about: not necessarily wanting to be in combat, but a churned sense of standing in the wrong place while other soldiers are fighting. He understands the way back is by digging in, working long hours, telling his major, "Sir, I'd rather stay and knock this shit out rather than have it still be waiting in the morning." The war focuses him; he understands there's no other place than the Army. When Mafia returns to Fort Drum, his guys visit their former platoon leader at his office — the major tells Iggy it's a rare thing. In the spring, Iggy has earned his way back to a combat position. He begins talking about heading back to Ranger school, trying out for Special Forces.

One afternoon Whitey goes up in a helicopter, escorting cash reserves to a secured banking facility. It's funny, everybody always reminds you that the Army isn't about money, but there's more money on this Blackhawk than Whitey has ever imagined — bags of coins ("they're heavy as shit"), bills in duffels and boxes ("the bills are nice and light"). He's wearing body armor, has a pistol holstered under his arm, but the feeling is very different from four years ago with the Rangers. Back then, he was looking forward to something, the place where he is now. He stares out the window. A woman in a babushka is pinning laundry outside her house, two boys glance up at the noise of the helicopter, a dark road winds through the mountains. "It's very serene," Whitey says. "There's no drama to it, nothing glorious. I'm doing a simple job, but it requires extreme attention to detail. That makes you calm, because you're very focused." Listening to the rotors, Whitey realizes that if the Blackhawk malfunctions, if somebody shoots them down, it wouldn't bother him. "You know, the aircraft crashes," he says, "the money burns, no big deal. The Army would drive on. It'd suck to lose the equipment and money and lives — big loss — but it wouldn't be detrimental. I'd be glad to have given my little part to the effort. You know, the whole year at Aviation and afterwards, I lost that vision, because I had to concentrate on other things. Now I'm seeing myself more in the big picture, and it's a wonderful feeling."

A few days before he goes home, Whitey receives his Officer Evaluation Report from his commander.

Don Herzog executed his duties as my Disbursing Officer flawlessly. He was my right arm during a very difficult and challenging deployment to Kosovo as a part of Operation Joint Guardian. Don encountered some historical firsts, faced by no other leader on a tactical deployment. 1st Lt. Herzog's technical and leadership abilities exceed his years and experience. His performance as the Kosovo disbursement officer was simply spectacular, absolutely phenomenal for an officer of his junior grade . . . He possesses superior intelligence, communicates effectively and has demonstrated often his superior leadership qualities. His potential is limitless; select for below-the-zone promotion to Major and send to advanced civil schooling so that the Army can take full advantage of Lt. Herzog's multiple talents. He should command a finance company or detachment; he is a clear pack leader and in the top 1 percent of his peer group in ability.

When Whitey steps off the plane at Drum, Iggy is waiting in the crowd. "I'm fucked," Whitey says with a laugh. "They've got me for twenty." He knows he's staying in. "I've been there," he says, "I've seen it, and I want more." A few months later, he's offered a company command in Hawaii — a Finance plum — and he turns it down. He wants to try for Special Operations, get into Psy Ops — Psychological Operations; he knows how important it will be in the terrorism fight.

Iggy tells him something he heard from one of the TACs at West Point. "He said he never began it wanting to stay the whole time," Iggy says. "What he said was like, 'I tried my best not to do this, but I can't not do it.' There was just something about it he couldn't shake — loving soldiers, and knowing inside he was a soldier too."

The $250,000 APFT

Because the firsties are ready to graduate, they're out experience-hunting, dropping by each other's rooms, stockpiling West Point memories: sights, lessons, people. There's lots of reflecting on the achievements of George Rash. As the cadet who's survived everything, George is developing the broad-shouldered proportions of myth.

Huck Finn is sitting at his computer, checking reports on the latest round of hours, spitting dip into a Gatorade bottle. Dan MacElroy — the Black Knights' punter, with a kicker's sparrow build — crosses his legs on Huck's bunk. "That kid made it past so much," he says. "Every cadet at this Academy knows who George Rash is, and very few of them had good things to say. Just the fact that he could take the brunt of that — I think it's amazing." MacElroy grins. "And ironically, it seems to me that, throughout history, it's those type of people . . ."

Huck shakes his head. "George Rash is *not* that type of person."

"You watch," Dan says. "Give him a couple years. My point is, he's the triumph of everything, of cadets who make it through. Look at someone like MacArthur. When he came in here —"

"*No*," Huck says. "Don't put General MacArthur's name next to George Rash."

The conversation is being duplicated throughout the corps, cadet opinion flipping over like dominoes. "Actually, to be honest, I was a naysayer from the beginning," Steve Ruggerio tells his roommate, Marcus Genova. Steve ate whitefish at Rash's bar mitzvah two years ago, and Marcus survived a remedial APFT alongside George at Gillis Field. "I was one of the ones who said, 'This kid shouldn't graduate, can't graduate, won't graduate.'" Steve laughs. "But what can I say? The guy's tenacious. And he's not a bad guy either, once you get to know him."

One company over, in H-4, George's Beast roommate, Calvin Huddo — a small, tough-looking cadet with slitted eyes and action-figure arms — is discussing how much his own feelings have evolved. "At first I just wanted him dead," Huddo tells his pal Jared Fusnecker. "And then I was like, 'OK, George. You try it here. Just suffer.' You know what's funny? He tried his ass off. George is probably the biggest miracle that we've witnessed during our time at West Point. I love the kid. I have the right to make fun of him, because I put in the hours at Beast. But that doesn't mean I want to hear it from anybody else." George has become a milestone, something to measure their transition from civilians to officers. "I walked in on R-Day," Huddo says, "I was expecting my roommate to be six foot three, two hundred pounds, an athlete. I found George. It really set me back. I told him, 'Hey, we need to get ready for inspection tomorrow, start making your bed.' He's like, 'OK — how do I make the bed?' And then, because George didn't want to keep making it, he slept on top of the sheets every night in his BDUs. End of the summer, those sheets were more or less soiled *black*. The cadre were saying, 'New Cadet Rash, why are your sheets a different color?' And then by that point in Beast, his feet were *gone*, they were just hamburger meat. I wanted to say, 'Stop, stop, you can just quit.' He wouldn't."

Cal Smith is considering the matter with Sam Kim. "First semester, I said, 'This kid will not make it past plebe year.' Somehow, he manages. He gets through APFTs, goes before an honor board —"

"Falls out of road marches at two different Beasts," Sam adds.

"That's . . . tenacity right there. You know what? I *admire* George. For four years, he's taken the worst ass-ripping this place has to offer. People getting on him, telling him he's a shitbag, and he's stuck it out and hung around. Somebody was talking smack about him two days ago, I finally stopped him with my hand. I said, 'The kid's got a great heart.'"

And down in Eliel Pimentel and Matt Kilgore's room, they're laying odds on what's potentially George's final achievement. The cadet ranked at the absolute bottom of each graduating class earns the title Goat; it's considered a great negative feat, operating just at the edge of failure, like staying on a high wire by one toe. The class takes up a collection, each cadet kicking in a buck, and rewards the Goat with a

$1,000 bonus. "And George," Eliel says, "right now is the last person in the class."

"Dead last," Matt nods.

"So it looks like he's got Goat honors sewn up," Eliel says.

The prospect isn't appealing to George; it offends his sense of pride. "I don't *want* to be the Goat," he says simply. "The extra thousand dollars sounds nice, but it's not worth being the class's last guy. But most people think I'm trying to get it."

For four years, head lowered, George has observed his fellow cadets; his feelings toward them haven't varied. "There were people rooting for me who didn't think I would graduate," he explains. "And then there were those who figured I probably didn't need to be here, and hoped to see me get kicked out. And some of those, if you actually meet them, are amazingly decent people." George isn't certain how he's ended up a symbol. "I'm not sure I would consider myself . . . a charismatic individual. But I definitely leave an indelible mark on anyone I meet." He shrugs. "We've all managed to come through this together. I could not have done it without them. And I like to think, to a lesser extent, that some cadets could not have made it without me. Because my presence — my continued presence — has shown that anybody can move through adversity, if they're willing to put in the time and effort. And I like to think they view me as a success story. Because I've outlasted everybody who thought I wouldn't make it. Am I wrong?"

And then George bombs what should be his final APFT, undershooting the target by nine seconds. "He severely disappointed me," Captain Paredes says. "This semester he hasn't even done a bad job. But that was all he needed." The TAC knows George's file; whenever officers have said "pass or else," George has found a way to pass. "Every time he's on the hot seat," he says, "under pressure, he does well." But there must be other ways to de-motivate George. He calls the cadet into his office, sits him down at the opposite end of the desk. "You need to hear this from me face to face, man to man, so you'll know the way I look at things and where I'm coming from. I'm recommending you for separation now, whether you pass the APFT or not." George blinks. "And, as a matter of fact," he adds, "I'm also gonna recommend recoupment — that you pay the Army back."

George slumps out of the captain's office, no longer debating the pluses and minuses of Goathood; he's wondering how he could possibly come up with $250,000. "I don't know that many people my age who can afford that kind of debt," he says, walking to his room. "Unless they're rich. Or they got really, really lucky on day trading."

Throughout the year, TACs are counselors, role models, disciplinarians. In the weeks before graduation, they assume a final role: tailors. The firsties have received their Army uniforms, and TACs are subject-matter experts on how the uniforms ought to be worn. Cadets flicker through the day room one by one; Captain Paredes checks inseams, approves collars and buttons. "Looks good, looks sharp," he'll say. "The dimple in the tie," he explains solemnly to Huck, "is the sign of the well-dressed man." Then he teaches the cadet how to create one. "It's supposed to be the four-in-hand, what I'm showing you is the full half Windsor. Try that on your own now, huah."

George's last APFT is scheduled for the same afternoon as his uniform check. With two hours left, George buttons the shirt, knots the tie, pins on his branch insignia. It's the uniform he's worked four years to wear; if he fails his run, he won't get to put it on again. He clicks down the hallway to the day room. Cadets greet him cheerfully. "You look pretty spiffy, George — for a no-account butter bar." He stands at attention before the TAC, fists balled at his sides. Both men avoid what ought to be the only topic. What they discuss instead is shirt size.

"OK," Captain Paredes says. "This is very loose. This shirt is, what, eighteen–thirty-five? You want to try seventeen and a half." He hangs a few fingers inside George's collar. "Look at this: I should barely be able to get one finger in here."

He moves down to George's arm. "Just checking the sleeve length. Looks good." He slaps George on the stomach. "How's it feel here?"

"Pretty good, sir," George says. "I did just eat a large meal."

Back in barracks, George hangs up the uniform and changes into gym alpha. He sits and waits for the clock to tick around to his APFT. As he walks the halls, cadets give him the eye and a nod. "George, good luck."

After forty-seven months, the Army has finally caught up to George Rash. Cadets who turn twenty-two at West Point receive an APFT gift. George now has sixteen and a half minutes to complete the two-mile course. It's a gorgeous spring afternoon. Winds cool, sun high. George admires the conditions on a practical level. "I could've waited and taken this two weeks from now," he says. "But the weather's so beautiful, I'm probably not gonna get a better chance. Either way," he says, "it's my last APFT. Fly or die."

George steps downhill toward Gillis. There's the advice Jake Bergman yelled at him plebe year: "You *never* quit. You don't ever give them the chance to end your career. You never let them make that decision for you. Never." There's also the musclehead's old game plan: coast through the push-ups and sit-ups, conserve everything for the track. George enters the mats and echoes of the field house. It's crowded, a hundred cross-legged cadets fanning themselves with their APFT cards. "This is a record retest," the Department of Physical Education's Major Cuppett announces. "If you fail today, I will send up a packet, signed by the Master of the Sword, recommending separation from the Academy. This is your one shot. You will be tested on push-ups. You will be tested on the sit-ups. Then the two-mile run: this is a test of fitness and endurance. Troops, don't fail this test."

Push-ups come first. George removes his glasses, a passing DPE officer recognizes him by his neck and back, wishes him luck. George cuts off at fifty. Then he curls and grunts through sixty sit-ups, stopping with nearly a minute left. Another DPE officer wishes him the best on the rest of the exam.

George shifts to the final station. Cadets waiting for the run tug their bodies through an alphabet of stretches. "Last event," the DPE captain says. "OK, raise your hands if this is your final APFT." Arms go up, George's hand joins the thicket. "For most of you," the captain says, "this event should be the easiest. Now, I'll need to collect your scoring cards. George, please hand me that guy over there's card." Every officer at Gillis — a homey, frightening touch — knows him now.

"Guys," the captain continues, "when you are running the course, a lot of you might feel the need the get rid of some stuff that's in your stomachs. Huah, that's OK, I don't mind that. You're giving it all you've got, lactic acid is a byproduct. But please, *please,* don't do it near the finish line. Come across the line. Wait till fifty yards past the line. Because people behind you would greatly appreciate it if you do not throw up *on* the line. Huah? OK, you have exactly three minutes to complete your final stretches." George clicks his neck, pulls back his ankles; four hard years come down to this.

Outside, the officers announce, "OK, move over to the starting line. By our clock, you have one minute." George murmurs to himself, "I need to do it now." The officers call the numbers: "Five, four, three, two, one. *Go.*"

Fifteen minutes and twenty-six seconds later, when George Rash has beaten both his new senior's run standard and his plebe-year time, I ask how he feels. He smiles, wipes his forehead, answers with two words. "Damn good."

A few moments later he adds proudly, "That's my second-best time ever. No, wait, no. It's not my second best, but it's a high score. It's right up there."

Wherever he walks — across the Plain, through G-4 — cadets stop him, ask how it went, slap him on the back. Higher declines Captain Paredes's advice to separate George. As regimental XO, it falls on Major Vermeesch to make the call to his replacement, to explain the administration's position. "George met the standard. And that's all you can say. It's the standard, and you can't dispute it."

A day later, George rides up to the big PX to purchase the smaller shirt size Captain Paredes suggested. He knows he's going to graduate. "It's been a long four years. I took a bumpier path, but I got there. It's the path I had to take." I ask George how it feels to be leaving. I say it's been a strange year. I mean: the September attacks, graduating into a war, the new TAC, Scott Mellon getting separated, George nearly being separated himself.

George considers it, nods. "Yes it has," he says. "Very mild winter, very cool spring." He thinks some more, adds, "On average."

Once an Eagle

A few weeks before graduation, Huck Finn gets offered a free-agent contract to snap punts and field goals with the New York Giants. The nod comes while he's spending a weekend on Long Island. The NFL draft just concluded an hour before. "We've got you the deal," the sports agent says. "We just need to hear that you're not going into the Army."

It's the kind of large news that requires heavy telephone work for ballast. The agent calls Huck's coach, Huck's coach calls Huck, the agent calls again, Huck calls the coach. ("I'm going ninety miles a minute," Huck says. Fuhball is what brought him into the Army; it astonishes him to think that it will be taking him out of the Army too.) The agent calls back with specific instructions, "All we need now is confirmation from a West Point general, and you're suiting up for the Giants."

Huck goes at things straight ahead, freestyle; he gets hold of the commandant's number from information — "Eric T. Olson," he says, "General, West Point, New York" — phones him Sunday evening at 1900. The general invites him to come by the house. When Huck arrives it's after 2200, the commandant is dressed in pajamas and offers Huck a dish of ice cream. ("I said 'No, thank you,'" Huck says. "So he fixes himself a dish, sits down to it cool as can be.") They discuss the matter, the general grows quiet for a few moments. Huck says, "So what the Giants need *now* is a general's phone number, somebody who knows how the whole deal works with this thing." The comm says, "Well, I can tell you right now there's nobody here to talk to like that, because the current policy is two years active duty if you're going into the professional leagues." So Huck drives over and wakes up the football coach.

It isn't just the salary that's attractive, though it is a whopping figure: the league minimum, Huck learns, is $800,000 a year. Repeating the number to friends doesn't make it any more believable; he finally has to break the sum down to a per-play basis — "it's something like, uh, $25,000 a snap," Huck says — which helps turn things easier to picture. Sandhurst aside, football has provided every high point of his life. He still plans on serving as an officer; what he bargains for is a year. "Just one season, then I'll go do my Army shit. That'd be damn cool, if you ask me — to say I played for a season in the NFL." The coach tells Huck to arrange a graduate assistant's slot for the next academic year. Usually, the spots go to lieutenants with pressing reasons for sticking close to West Point — an injury, an ailing local relative, a fiancée finishing college at an area school.

Huck lines up a job with a sympathetic colonel in the Department of Behavioral Sciences and Leadership. (Huck is direct with the officer. "Sir, I want you to understand before you answer — I'm not asking to be a GA to help you out, I'm asking so I can play football.") Then he arranges to report to Benning on February 3, after his pro season ends. Since it's slightly larger than college size, he's got to find an NFL football for practice; he's got to memorize all new plays; he's got to pile back on the twenty-five pounds he dropped for Sandhurst. He buys creampuffs to keep on his shelf, scans restaurant menus for carbohydrates and desserts. "Banana chimichanga?" he asks, pointing. "Lots of calories in there, right? Fill it up, throw some topping on that, load it with whipped cream big-time, straight fat to the face. And have y'all got any cheesecake?" All he needs now is for the supe to sign his GA form.

And then, a week later, Huck gets scheduled for a 1330 meeting in the comm's office. The Giants' coach telephones at 1300 to read him his football itinerary. Practice starts the day following graduation. "June 2," the coach says, "here's where you're gonna be staying; here's what you're gonna be doing at Monday practice, Tuesday practice, Wednesday practice. We're sending up the drills and the blocking moves. And stop worrying about the footballs — we'll deliver a box of league-size balls in the morning." A few minutes later, Huck is sitting in a stiff chair, listening to the comm tell him there won't be any football.

"I wasn't going to go, 'Sir — but sir, please,'" Huck says. "Because this is the frickin' Army. When they make up their mind, there's no negotiation, it's done." Huck lists back to his room, places his last NFL business call. "To the agent," he says. "Man was in shock."

The cadet isn't a grudge holder. The way the rule works, he can try the NFL again two years from now. "But I'm not planning on it at all," Huck says, voice tired from phone calls to parents and friends back home. "Right now I've got Ranger school to think about, then Korea, then I intend on trying out for the Ranger regiment — high-speed stuff. That's the shit I wanted Infantry for in the first place." (Half a year later, Huck training at Fort Benning, the Giants will be knocked out of the playoffs because their long-snapper botches the snap on a field goal attempt, and Huck will receive e-mail from just about every person he knows.)

The NFL word speeds around the post. A few days later, when Huck is spending eight hours on the Area by order of Captain Paredes, a sergeant flags him down. "Hey, man," the NCO asks, "aren't you supposed to be a Giant?" A cadet — a bitter-looking yuk Huck doesn't recognize — stops him on the Plain and just looks him over. "Wow," the yuk finally says. "I realize I have no room anymore to ever complain about this place."

As graduation stops being weeks away, and cadets start measuring the time in days and then hours, a fear sweeps the class. The firsties have grown so close, the notion of breaking apart and living separately is painful. It hits Huck hard; he started out hating West Point — spent years kicking back every way a cadet can — and now he doesn't want to leave.

"No, I want to stay," he says. "This shit's fun. They feed us three hot meals a day, we get a nice bed every night, they even do our laundry." Walking home from another hours formation, he throws his hands open wide. "I mean, what do I got to worry about in this place? And how the hell do I make it on the outside in the Army? I know I've learned how to fuckin' keep my room real clean," he says. "I know I can fold my shirts and my underwear and roll up my socks right. But can I think for myself? I guess I've learned to rely too much on other people — Captain Paredes is right about that shit. Officers keep asking everybody, 'Are you all ready to get outta here?' Well, no, I'm not. I wanna stay in, bro. I love it here."

He lowers his big hands. "But then, every one of 'em are like, 'You're a whole lot more prepared than you think you are.'"

Cadets are changing. Eliel finds himself leafing through the old antiwar classic *Johnny Got His Gun* ("I don't agree with it, and a lot of it is a shock, but it's something you've got to expose yourself to") and shifting his position on marijuana use. "Not for me — I'll never do it — but for my friends, I think pot's great, better for the system than beer." Matt Kilgore finds himself worrying about his chosen field from an unforeseen angle. "My fiancée hasn't wanted to really find out exactly what I do yet," Matt says. "And she has yet to watch any movies like *We Were Soldiers* or *Black Hawk Down,* because she's not ready for that either. But I was at her house Sunday, flipping around, we started watching *Band of Brothers,* the HBO series. And she saw the patch the guys have on their arms, which is the same patch I'm going to wear. She asked, 'Isn't that the 101st Airborne?' Yep. And the scene was like some big artillery barrage, they were just getting the *crap* pounded out of them. She's like, 'Honey, what's all that stuff?' That's artillery. She goes, 'And what job is it you're going to be doing again?' I pointed and said, 'I'm like the little guy jumping into the foxhole to get away from all that shit.' And her mouth gets small and she goes, 'Oh.'"

And the post is changing. Rumors about regulations and privileges work their way through next year's firsties and cows. Tighter enforcement, tougher inspections, less time off post. The administration is even mounting a comeback for *pinging* — the fast-walking, tight-cornering stride that made plebes unmistakable in the Old Corps. "We all joke that we're escaping from the Death Star," Eliel says. "Just barely getting out in time. The pendulum has swung, this place is going back to spartan conditions." Eliel looks out the window. "I think West Point has just been going through an identity crisis for the last five years, people turning from one idea to another. And now they know where they want to go."

This new set of changes thrills officers on post. "I think we've been trying to anticipate what society wants from the Military Academy here," one explains. "And I don't think that's even necessarily what society wanted." For many of these soldiers, September 11 clarified exactly what society does want: technically competent and tactically superior leaders. "I think the supe and some others have started to look around and ask, 'What happened? What have we done to this place?' To Mom and Dad America — if their son or daughter is fortunate enough to come here, if they get that honor and privilege and all that — when those parents send 'em here, they don't expect them to be immersed in the same kind of culture they just left." The officer swallows. "It ought to be better than that. It ought to be special. And if it isn't, then we might as well lock the gates, run the place as a museum, ship the cadets to Central Arizona State and train them in ROTC. Not that there's anything wrong with that — I know a hundred great ROTC officers. But there's supposed to be something special about West Point."

Grad Week sets out with long days and crisp mornings, roaring industrial fans blowing the heat down the corridors. By Wednesday, parents are everywhere, walking on either side of their children like cadet assembly kits. Families watch the parades, forming colorful rows on the bleachers; with their civilian backgrounds, the bright uniforms and careful syncopation must make the same amount of ritual sense as *Riverdance*. For two years, Chrissi Cicerelle has never been far from her family; her sister Marie is now a yuk, and has been torturing Chrissi all week. "She keeps reminding me, 'This is your last Monday. This is your last Tuesday. This could be your last sandwich in Grant Hall. This is your last walk back from Grant Hall on a Wednesday.' But of course she's right. Come Saturday, this will all be gone. And I'm scared to say goodbye to everybody, considering what's going on right now. My friends in Infantry might well be in some kind of combat a year from now, and that terrifies me."

Chrissi is thinking about herself in Quartermaster, too. "I'm gonna be responsible for forty men and women. And that just blows me away. I really do think this place prepares us — but the thought just blows my mind." Chrissi is already staring down the line, to life after the Army. "I've decided what I'm kind of interested in is hair and makeup. I told my dad, he just threw his hands up. He's like, 'So you went to West Point and want to do *hair*.' I said, 'Yeah.' So I think there's a school — there's obviously beauty school, but that sounds so trivial. If I could, I'd like to go somewhere like Vidal Sassoon, or someplace else upscale, with a name that will carry me. I think it would be awesome." And when she thinks about West Point, she'll think about Mark Thompson. "Oh," she says, "he was my West Point. He really was."

Ryan Southerland and Betty Simbert say goodbye to each other a few days before the ceremony, exchange fresh e-mail addresses, part as friends. Betty is surprised by how few of her friends are graduating with her. They'll be present at the event, but as spectators, in the stands. Back at the prep school, she started out with seven close friends; one quit, another got kicked out before West Point, two got kicked out at West Point, the others are turnbacks — they're repeating firstie year. "I get mad at them," she says, wrinkling her forehead. "Just because of the fact that they aren't here. I'm angry. I say, 'We were supposed to be doing this together. Now I'm doing it myself. This sucks. It's just *my* graduation; it was supposed to be *ours*.' They say, 'As long as you're doing it. We knew you'd make it.' I'm like, 'Well, I thought you would make it too. Why am I up here alone?'"

The night before graduation, Ryan Southerland walks the post. He's spent the last semester sifting through classroom lectures, deciding what kind of officer he wants to be. "This one history professor," he says, the heels of his dress shoes ticking over the path, "he said you've got two courses. You can pick battles and fight them. And the other way is to accept things you think are really wrong, in the hopes of climbing to a position where you can make them better. But in exchange for that, you make a sacrifice. You can make that choice for your whole life, and then at the end, when you look back, you're a moral idiot. Because there's no guarantee you'll be able to make those changes, and in the meantime every decision you've made along the way has been wrong." He doesn't believe this is what West Point has prepared him for.

He pauses in front of the statue of Eisenhower, the gray figure seeming blue in the night. Earlier in the evening, Rudy Guiliani addressed the graduation banquet. "This is the first class in a while," he began, "that's graduated in a time of war. It's a war that started in my city. And you will have to finish this war." Ryan stares at the general, standing with one stone leg cocked as if getting ready to step onto the Plain. "He went through the same stuff we did," Ryan says, "just did it a few years earlier, on this long gray line. I mean, this place moves so fast, there's so much turnover. The firsties I remember when I was a plebe, nobody knows about anymore. When I mention Keirsey at my table, people say, 'Who?' And then when I leave, nobody will even mention him. Nobody will remember that he passed some time here, did some great things.

"But if you step back, you've got to appreciate that." Ryan looks back toward the barracks — rows of windows, a tiny door opening and shutting. "The train is still rolling. When you hop off, West Point keeps on going. That's what makes it what it is. My experience here is about six and a half hours from being over. But West Point keeps on going. The pace, energy, speed, the intensity, the consistency, that's what America wants from us. It's what it's prepared everybody to be used to the whole time." Back in barracks, Ryan goes room to room, hands around his own gym alpha T-shirts — just what J. D. Keirsey did last year, to leave something of himself behind, to keep his name circulating in the corps.

In the morning, firsties gather under powderpuff clouds for their last formation; class officers collect the Goat bonus in big Ziploc bags. (George has missed the honor by a few thousandths of a grade point.) Then they march together to Michie Stadium, where they reported for R-Day four summers ago. That morning, they had their names taken away; today they get them back, printed in diplomas.

President Bush delivers a speech congratulating the cadets. He says that the "war on terror is only begun," that "building a just peace is America's opportunity, as well as America's duty. From this day forward, it is your challenge as well, and we will meet this challenge together." Then the president squares up to the convivial challenge of shaking a thousand hands, as the reading of the names begins. Bush deploys a variety of handshakes: the Sidearm, the Hand-to-the-Elbow, the For-Ladies-Only. He is very game, playing it like racquetball, never letting a shot go by. One after the other, the cadets get their moment, meeting the boss. When there's a pause, the president lightly flexes his fingers, shoots his cuffs.

The names go on and on. First name, middle, last.

"Joel, R., Fulski."

"Jonathan, E., Algor."

Some names get huge applause. When "Ekkerhard, D., Stiller" is called, the cadets go wild; he's the Goat. The cadets approach the stage by company. When they stand in their long lines, tug on their hats, it's like a long white wave cleanly breaking. G-4 is the second-to-last company in corps; it's seated in the back rows. Huck sits with his cheek pressed into his hat, to shield his face from the sun. When cadets climb down from the stage, holding their diplomas, they tackle each other, laugh, hug. Then G-4 rises, hats on, begins its walk to the stage.

"Maria, J., Auer."

"Steve, J. M., Cho."

Eliel Pimentel salutes the president before they can shake hands. As George waits at the bottom, the supe — who has either never seen his name or can't quite believe it — calls, "George, R., *Rosh*." That's his goodbye from West Point. At the base of the steps, the G-4 hugs begin. George somehow stands just outside this commotion. Huck and Rizzo hug. Eliel and Rob Anders hug Matt. Jasmine Rose hugs Maria. George watches hopefully. Cal Smith hugs Will Reynolds. Riz hugs Kevin Hadley. Rob and Eliel and Kenny Wainwright hug Mark Thompson. Then the cadets turn and pull George in too.

The graduates return to barracks for the final uniform change, then spread out across the post for their swearing-in ceremonies. George is sworn in by the rabbi. Captain Paredes swears in a bunch of Guppies on the Plain. At a tent by the water, before his parents, Huck is sworn in by Major Vermeesch. His mother and father thank the officer for what he's practiced on their son. It's taken a long march to bring Vermeesch and Huck to this spot together. Before he leaves, the major hands Huck a gift, a copy of the military novel *Once an Eagle.* "Next to the Bible," Vermeesch says, "this is probably the best book ever written. Just read it, OK?"

A couple months later, when Huck actually starts the novel, a memo on official West Point stationery falls from between the pages. He's not going to read it — he assumes the major stuck it there as a bookmark and then forgot about it. Then he glances at the subject line: it's the official record of their counseling session, from February 2000. There were all the TAC's warnings about "discipline" and "separation" and "questioning your desire to be an Army officer." In the upper right corner, beside the date 6/1/02, Vermeesch has scribbled in, "What a transformation. Continue to make us proud."

SEEING
THE ELEPHANT II

A   S SECOND LIEUTENANTS (it gets written "2LT," but people just say, "Hey, LT,"), the cadets join the field Army, and run smack into what they were most looking forward to: more school. Every graduate must complete an OBC — an Officer Basic Course. Chrissi heads for Fort Lee, Virginia, with the Quartermasters ("Supporting Victory"); George Rash travels to Fort Leonard Wood to master Engineering ("Missouri is very hot — and I'm already hearing bad stuff about the mosquitoes"); Ryan, Huck, and most of the G-4 Corporation follow each other to Benning and the Infantry. In new uniforms and idiot sticks, there's arm-squeezing and reconciliations. Before a field exercise, Mark Thompson stands up and offers a general apology for last year, which gets accepted by everybody. The graduates are squinting together towards two approaching hills: Ranger School — a short, stark, foodless peak — and beyond that the massive, blurry hill of deployment during wartime.

Complete a book and it's like you've received an eviction notice from your desk; when it's over, you're obliged to hit the road. First there are weeks of spell-check and typo-patrol — which feels, in West Point terms, like taking accountability of the sentences. In the middle of this, Ryan Southerland and his buddy Carter Smyth knock on my apartment door. (When you get to know people in uniform, you enroll in the Informal Military Housing Society; your couch becomes everybody's.) Ryan laughs and snaps digital pictures of my junked-up desk, thick hair, deadline stubble. When this book appears — with its jacket and slab of photos sandwiched in the middle — I escort it around the country to meet readers. I drive upstate for West Point's R-Day, the landscape running flat and smooth. About ten minutes before post, the hills go clumpy and muscular, as if they've undergone some substantial PT. The R-Day mothers and fathers approach the book as a kind of road atlas for their expedition as West Point parents. (And I discover I am full of well-meant, distant-relative style advice: "Beast will sound worse than it is," "They will want to complain.") Parents who've read it hang near the signing table with questions: Whatever happened to that guy George Rash? What about Iggy and Herzog? Was anybody part of the war?

The same questions wait everywhere, like suitcases on the baggage carousel. In North Carolina, people ask about Chrissi. In Denver (where football is an export, and people compare John Elway sightings like a local comet) they want to hear if Huck ever suited up with the Giants. In D.C., I hear update requests for Whitey and Ryan. (One female executive wants their relationship status; I tell her Ryan's girlfriend is just then visiting him at Fort Lewis, Washington.) Readings coax veterans — shy and proud — out of every city. They cross the floor with square-shouldered confidence, and mostly ask about Keirsey. In Boston, grads do impressions of Colonel Adamczyk as a captain and TAC. ("He had this perfect thing of being able to shout without ever raising his voice.") I shake hands with lots of West Point parents — warm, upright people — which makes me want to spontaneously apologize for all the cursing. On a windy afternoon in Carmel, California, a World War II officer waits mildly until I walk to the car, then asks if any of the cadets have seen combat. "It will," the colonel finds the words carefully, "surprise them." Back home, letters and e-mail offer reminiscences and critiques (one woman protests the foul language by directing me to an article on Jehovah's Witnesses in uniform), and the same question: What came next?

They spend much of the year in school. Ryan completes Ranger with no trouble; the last thing he said at West Point was that once you stopped finding new things to test yourself, you were cooked. Ranger was what he had in mind, a sort of fuel experiment run on the body. Could you go all sixty days — patrols, mountains, swamps — minus food and sleep? "It was an interesting experience," he says when he finishes; then he flies to Rio for vacation, falls in love with an American college professor, heads for Fort Lewis to train with the Stryker Brigade. The Stryker is a sort of medium-weight armored vehicle, well-designed for peacekeeping in citics, which makes it just the thing to roll through streets in Iraq. As the war takes shape — and graduates can make out trees and people on that hill — friends want to talk politics. It was what they warned you about at West Point; you'd become a domestic Army ambassador. "It's about learning the vehicle, taking care of the soldiers, seeing how well you measure up to the job," Ryan says. "My friends don't get that my part isn't about politics."

Huck opens a February e-mail from Major Vermeesch the day before his Ranger class starts:

> Reid —
> Take your upcoming training seriously. Neither you nor I know what faces us in the coming months. But I'll bet you a month's pay (and keep in mind that MAJs make a whole lot more than 2LTs) that we will all need to be ready to face the elephant here in the near future. Studying history, I see exceptional similarities between our current situation and events that led to large-scale wars in the past.

As per his old TAC, Huck approaches the training seriously; as per Mark Thompson, he approaches it intelligently. He marches out to the first morning's PT test and hides in the middle. Ranger Instructors size up the crowd. "All right, we've got too many guys bunched up in the center. Everybody who's now up front, move around to the back." This leaves Huck in the first row, squeezing out push-ups right under the RI's nose, and he fails a couple minutes later. The training moves on without him, a car he watches from the distance. "I am getting into bed until tomorrow morning," Huck says. "This is the most embarrassing day of my life."

He's on snowbird duties — desks and papers — when the war begins. "God damn if Major V wasn't right," he says. There are phone calls from home: Huck assuring his mother that, posting to Korea, he won't even be able to *hear* the war. Hanging up, Huck isn't sure how he feels about that. A couple of weeks later, he gets a command over e-mail. Alaska is short of lieutenants. Huck is supposed to find thirty-six LTs willing to switch posts and go up north. Huck walks the post, making the pitch. He knows Alaska has units that will deploy. He sits back at his computer, thinks it over. "Sir, I was only able to find sixteen people," he writes back. "But please add my name to make it seventeen."

Huck isn't the only grad filling out change of address. (That whole year, e-mails come around, with innocent subject headings meaning Afghanistan or Iraq: "Address Change," "Updated Data," "New Mailing Info.") For months, rumors circulated about George Rash. Hard luck at Fort Leonard Wood — poor attitude, flubbed runs, George has gotten kicked out of the Engineers, he's resigned. The LTs whistle and shake their heads: "So Rash finally went down." G-4 grads have a counterargument: George is one of those people, he will never let trouble get that far, and wouldn't ever quit. Word floats back: Rash has done fine with the Engineers. "Well, either way, he's going to be stuck at Fort Polk." But Rash knows his approach: if you narrow the eyes, lower the head, and let fortune do its work around you, who knows what good things might happen? In Missouri, he finds a guy with reasons to want Polk. They swap posts and George heads for Korea. When he finishes, he heads to Fort Lewis; he'll be there when Ryan Southerland returns from Iraq, for a kind of Beast II summer cadre reunion.

Hank's son J.D. leads a platoon with the 101st Screaming Eagles, the second Keirsey to cross the desert into Iraq. Keirsey opens his letters at the kitchen table, staring at dogs and trees. J.D. waiting with his platoon at the Line of Departure, the LD. ("Gas alerts," he writes, "cause much sweating in the pro-mask. I got Mom's package and read it on guard last night, and watched anti-aircraft and listened to cruise missiles.") The letters chart a progress from expectation to experience. J.D. prepping. J.D. drawing fire in Karbala. J.D. and his platoon overrunning an Iraqi headquarters, kicking in doors, ducking RPGs. Hank reads the letters aloud to guests, rolling out the maps and markers to fix his son's precise location. Kathy Keirsey rests a hand on his chair. "As a parent," she explains, "you don't want to hear your son is anywhere near this stuff. But as a wife and mother of Infantry officers, you want to know your son is doing his job." The Army doing what it can to balance a wobbly peace, J.D. and his platoon inspect farm equipment in towns, making sure no single group — Sunnis or Kurds — is threshing an unequal proportion of wheat. Then J.D. heads back to the States and tries out for the Ranger unit. He makes it through the physical stuff;

there's one final test, a character evaluation. Rangers sitting around a table, lobbing out the questions: Was J.D. just doing this to please his old man? Did he enjoy following in somebody else's footsteps? And what was he doing away from his platoon in Iraq? J.D. answers coolly, "I'm doing this for myself, not for anybody else. And if you believe I'm deficient for being absent from my unit, then you are duty-bound to put me on a plane to Iraq, I would love to be with my soldiers again." The Rangers break out in grins, say they'd just been giving him shit. J.D. ships back to the Persian Gulf as a Ranger.

For many officers, home becomes a restless, difficult place, a bed you can't get comfortable in. It's not, they explain, that you want combat, but when you know something is happening, you want to bring it your skills. John Vermeesch moves through Command and General Staff College at Fort Riley, Kansas. "Sitting here in the land of academia," he sighs. "While my friends deploy around the world, I am keeping my powder dry."

Colonel Joe Adamczyk manages two years as commandant of Valley Forge Military Academy. They're the wrong two years to be away from the Army, watching soldiers and maneuvers on the news. Then he retires from civilian life — a sort of de-retirement — signs with an outfit called MPRI (Military Professionals Resources Incorporated), and flies to work with the transition team in Iraq. Not a uniformed colonel anymore, he says, "I am now just another 'shirt.' Still, it's an opportunity to serve." Somewhere in Iraq, a soldier is passing by with a bad uniform, with sloppy hair, and Joe Adamczyk is deciding whether or not to bite his tongue.

Hank Keirsey leaves for Iraq a few months after his son; Morning Star dispatches him out among the flat-bellied and the steely-eyed. "Back into the mix," Keirsey says. He found stuff to enjoy in civilian life, but there he is, packing another duffel, stepping into another airport. "You know," he says, "when you live in great comfort, you sit around, you ask yourself, 'Well . . . why would I want to leave and go do this? But other times, you wonder, is it possible to fully enjoy the taste of victory, without heading back out to get the stink of the shithole in the nose again?"

Iggy Ignacio makes captain, returns to Benning, and for the third time in his career narrowly misses a chance to deploy. It's too much. There's the tangle of wanting to prove yourself, and never knowing if the chance will come — and then the knots come undone, as he realizes he can't wait on outside proof any longer. Iggy's five are almost up. He signs forms and prepares to remove his Army uniform.

Six years ago, during their last West Point fall, Iggy listened as Whitey Herzog chose his Army branch. He helped him step away from his ideas about Infantry — Iggy asked, "Are you sure? I'm not sure you're sure" — then promised to support his decision. It's on Whitey's mind as he picks up the phone from Germany. Whitey helps his friend break the broad choice down to a clipped equation: costs and gains, what will hurt, what won't. Iggy says he worries it might not be the right decision; Whitey tells him the emotional math holds up. After a minute Iggy says, "I wish I could be there with you."

Whitey has posted to Ansbach. (Part of Bavaria, "which is like the Texas of Germany," Whitey explains. "People never say they're Germans. They say, 'I'm from Bavaria.'") He's a captain now, training NCOs and Joes he'll lead for a year in Iraq. He throws his approval behind Iggy's plan — it calls for Long Beach, his girlfriend Corrine, and a badge with the police. "Police is good," Iggy says. "But they don't deploy." Whitey disagrees: policemen deploy every day. "Anyway, Igs, the first deployment is great, it's everything people talk about. But the ones after that, it's just time away from family."

Whitey thinks of what he wants to say, what he's learned in six years; being a cadet instead of a student, leaving for Alabama instead of staying with Loryn Winter in Buffalo, serving in Kosovo with the Army instead of living as a civilian anyplace. It's been about letting go of all the other places you might be. "You're not just the sum of your decisions," Whitey tells him. "There's a you that doesn't change, just because you happen to be standing in one place instead of another."

Iggy sounds more at ease than he has for a long time; Whitey is careful not to jostle anything by saying how happy he feels. Around Ansbach, he's a veteran, someone LTs and soldiers can come to with questions and anxieties. For most, Iraq will be their first time out of the gate. Whitey, training hard, has the confidence of a man who's memorized the timetable. "My desk sergeant and I were talking. We're like, 'Yup, I know just what they're goin' through.' I told my guys, 'You're thinking about charging in there and getting everything established quick, setting up your personal shit, getting into a rhythm.' I said,

'Calm down, get that outta your head, it's not going to happen. The first four weeks are gonna be the hardest. So don't worry about when we'll get comfortable, that'll come.'"

Finance missions have been ambushed, so Whitey spends his time brushing up on the company's military basics: nighttime exercises, maneuver, commo, live fires. As their skills sharpen, Whitey grows happier. He's so motivated it's sometimes hard to sleep; at night, his brain keeps whirring through training he wants to get nailed down. "War isn't something any human being ever really wants to go to," he explains, "but the bottom line is, this is a duty, it's something the country has asked us to do. That's a good feeling." Six weeks before deployment, he gets a last chance to visit Buffalo. His dad studies him on the ride back to the airport. "I remember listening to you talk about this when you were ten years old," he says. "Now you're really going to do what you've always wanted to do." Mike Ferlazzo — his old friend from H-4, who burned cigarettes with him in the last hours before graduation — is stationed a car trip away. Ferlazzo trained in Rucker with Aviation; they're headed together for Iraq. Mike will be flying Apaches over the same terrain where Whitey will be working. Mike's girlfriend is visiting him in Germany, and some nights Whitey heads over to his couch; they polish off beers, talk about where they've been, what's coming next.

Whitey has been alive long enough to see the ways any life resembles a movie; the same kinds of scenes keep rolling around, and once you recognize the pattern, you have a chance to shift how the reels unspool. When he was back for the captain's course at Fort Jackson ("Victory Starts Here"), he met a woman named Tiffany. They've been together twelve months, and Whitey is in love. Once again, he'll be out of the picture for a year. He thinks of everything he didn't say to Loryn, and on his last night he calls Tiffany. He tells her he appreciates that she'll be shouldering most of the burden. "It's my life that's going on pause, yours isn't," he says. "So I'm asking more of you than you are of me. I don't want a decision from you — I know I can't ask that. One thing I can ask: Whatever you decide to do, don't let the fact you're alone dictate your choice. Whatever you do, do it because of the way you feel about us, not because I'm not there." Tiffany listens, says a deployment isn't something she's used to, that she feels sick to her stomach. "It's going to be the number-one challenge," Whitey says, "being alone. I kind of feel like everything is working against us on this one, because being alone is not something our society is geared toward."

And the next morning, Whitey and his company deploy. Within two weeks, Whitey's seen three sandstorms, and has grown used to wearing goggles and a bandana to keep particles away from his face. Within three weeks, his unit is ambushed for the first time. The attack comes at night, and the training carries. Whitey empties three magazines returning fire. "No one was hurt," Whitey says proudly. "We did well."

Wartime Iraq and Afghanistan are like the twin hub cities for the military airline. Nearly every Army career is either heading toward them or just flying back. The graduates hear stories from Bryan Hart, Dave Uthlaut, Matt Kilgore, Mark Thompson, Carter Smyth: Somebody is surprised by how different the mission is from the training; somebody else is surprised by how exactly it's like the training; everybody is surprised by the heat. The landscape becomes a mental map, cities identified by faces. They hear Jake Bergman — who virtually lifted George Rash through his first APFT — is serving in the tiny village of Taji, still finding time to work out. Then they hear that Jake's group is with the Fourth Infantry Division, which has lost several soldiers, and that he's learning to deal with life and death. Even Max Adams, who got himself in Dutch over the 100th Night Show, rolls in and out of stories, leading a Transpo unit in Kuwait.

Kuwait is where Chrissi Cicerellle also spends a year. Heat, sand, filling out reports, cracking open the cargo boxes, supporting victory. Hard work: "We go twelve hours on, twelve hours off," she says. "This was supposed to be a fourteen-day detail. Here we are 105 days later, but who's counting?"

At West Point, when Chrissi imagined herself leading a platoon, the pictures had the weightless quality of a future painted by science fiction. She couldn't be sure whether she had become the officer the Academy wanted her to be. In the desert, Chrissi finds her legs. "If anything," she says, "they over-prepared us." And Chrissi discovers something else, when Joes seek her out with the spats, gripes, and back-home money worries that get classed as *soldier problems*: her inner civilian, the old sore spot with Mark Thompson, has left her an edge, a gift for understanding them.

Kicking off work, she laughs about the landscape — "nothing but powdered dirt, sand, highways and telephone poles for miles. Overall,

I'm not impressed" — and watches *Sex in the City*, mentally recasting the exteriors as a montage of all the things she's missing. She realizes that instead of working in a salon ("I've decided to save it for personal relaxation instead of business") she mostly wants to visit one. "I haven't cut this mane since last Valentine's Day."

To her surprise, her thoughts slide back to West Point. "I miss the feeling I had when it was all brand-new," she says. "That overwhelming mixture of pride, awe, and patriotism. I'd give anything to do it all over again. I'd do a lot of things differently. And I'd appreciate the little things more — like the walk back from Thayer Hall, when the leaves are starting to change. I never thought I'd miss it as much as I do."

In December, Ryan Southerland ships to Iraq from Fort Lewis. IEDs — Improvised Explosive Devices, bombs that detonate as vehicles pass — have been claiming lives, and moods have darkened. A couple nights before he leaves, Ryan keeps spilling an imaginary pair of dice from his fist onto the table; if it happens, it happens — no training can prevent it. Then he's on the ground in Iraq; facing a whole new series of tests; Ryan moves with the same deliberate, interested excitement he had at Beast. "The platoon," he says, "is pulling together." At West Point, even before the September attacks, officers assured cadets they'd some-day lead a deployment; now they're here, as if they've stepped into someone else's prediction. For many of them, Iraq follows a familiar track. First it's a milestone, then a routine. They've spent four years be-coming champion complainers. Now, they've got all-new material. "Every day, we do the same exact stuff at the same exact time — it's *Groundhog Day*." "This is the beach without the water." But beyond the missions, there's the strangeness. Ryan spends Christmas Eve in the town of Balad, staring up to find the Iraqis have done a nice thing of positioning green lights at the top of a minaret. In somebody's front yard — Ryan and his unit are following a lead — he watches as an Iraqi woman shoves an Iraqi man so hard he flies out of his shoes, the shoes just standing up right behind him. Turning down a street in Mosul, where bombing has leveled a police station, he finds the air hanging with unfamiliar smells.

Back home, the politics of the war are shifting, which makes some LTs question themselves. There are Iraqis who look on them as occu-piers; it gets hard to ignore. Cadets are trained to see their work as be-yond politics. One of the other LTs says that, on some level, the job has become jumbled with decisions made elsewhere; maybe in the past you could ignore the question of where you got sent, but now you had to factor in politics before putting on the uniform. Anything else is blind nostalgia. But then the LTs remind themselves that soldiering is a universal role — in every culture, somebody has to be willing to take it on. And the work itself isn't political; it's about motivating soldiers and pushing yourself to do a difficult task safely and well. Iraq is just where Ryan's class and the classes behind will have to spend some time, the next stop on the West Point train. Ryan says, "As Keirsey would say, you have to keep up the fire."

Twelve weeks after failing the first time, Huck Finn sucks in a breath and heads back to Ranger School. He knocks out his push-ups right in the front row, passes — then realizes he's left himself in a pickle. "My only worry was that PT test. I hadn't given any thought to the military stuff. Being hungry? I starved myself for Sandhurst. Not sleeping? I never sleep much anyway. I kept thinking, 'All I gotta worry about is sticking those push-ups. Then I'll have the Ranger tab.' So right when I stand up it hits me: Holy shit, now I've got fifty-nine more days of this. I hadn't prepared myself at all."

They're a long fifty-nine days. By week four, half the class has washed out. The second phase, in the mountains, is when the sleep deprivation starts to tell. At night, everyone knows to expect hallucinations — walking dreams, the subconscious gobbling what mental airtime it can. A grad hears trees talking to him, flags down the Ranger Instructors. "I'm out of here," he says, "I'm done." But after some nights, the hallucinations turn manageable, become a portable entertainment. In the final weeks — patrolling through swamps in Florida — Huck's Ranger buddy carefully eyes the sun as it drops behind vines and leaves. "Let the fun begin," he says. Huck's worst one comes while he's squad-leading. He becomes certain that some type of aircraft — a spaceship — has landed beside him. He turns to his Ranger buddy. "Damn, dude," he says. "I'm gonna fail this patrol. I'm gonna get kicked out." The other LT tells him he'll be fine. "No I won't," Huck says. "They're following us." "Who?" "Little green aliens. I'm gonna get kicked out of here." "And that's how Ranger School screws with you," Huck laughs. "I wasn't upset because little green men are following us. I'm worried because I was gonna fail my patrol. What's that about?"

On day sixty-two, Huck stands at graduation with his tab. Then he piles gear in the back of his truck, covers the 4,500 miles between Baton Rouge and Fort Richardson, Alaska, south to all-the-way north, riding across the seam of the country. Halfway there, he pulls in for a visit with Major Vermeesch at Fort Riley, excited and proud to shake hands with his former TAC again, one officer to another.

In Alaska, Huck learns details of his deployment. His battalion — the 501st — will head to Afghanistan in November. Two years ago, Huck watched the World Trade Center on television, flexing his hands, itching to leave for Afghanistan. Now he's getting that wish. Huck asks his commander, "Is the mission peacekeeping?" No, the captain tells him. This is direct; they'll be hunting after terrorists. It will be classic Infantry work: crossing terrain, sleeping under the stars. To keep their worries low, Huck tells his folks the mission isn't combat. "Nothing dangerous," he says. "Our battalion will be there on a humanitarian basis." A few weeks later, his commander mails a promise to all the families. The 501st will have state-of-the-art air and ground support; there'll be helicopters, mortars, A-10 warthogs. It's meant to be reassuring, but within a few minutes, Huck's mom is back on the phone, asking why his commander is mentioning bombs. "So I had to tell her, 'Yeah, it's just, we'll have to be dropping stuff on them if they won't accept our food packages.'"

In Anchorage, before the deployment, restaurants whip up free dinners for the soldiers, bars stand them drinks. His last morning, Huck spots a store offering a free Bowie-knife-sharpening to soldiers headed for Afghanistan. He drives home to grab his Bowie knife. It's only when he's stowing the thing in his duffel, a few hours before flight time, that everything hits him. He'll be away seven months. He's flying to one of the world's places where anything can happen. "I'm actually going," he says. "At Army-Navy, I didn't realize I was playing my last football game until the kickoff. This is the same deal." It's been a long time since plebe year, when he said he'd slice off his trigger finger if he ever got forced to ship out with the Infantry. "I can't believe this shit's really here," he says. Then he laughs. "It just not normal, is it? Most of the population goes and sits behind a desk all day. It just ain't normal to go to a place where people you don't know will want to kill you."

Then Huck hoists his ruck, shoulders his duffel, loads onto the plane for Afghanistan.

"So we left in October," Huck tells me, "and flew from Anchorage over the North Pole and then into Forward Operating Base (FOB) Salerno. That entire process took about thirty hours total, so it wasn't too bad." In the company newsletter, another officer writes of stepping from the aircraft at the second-to-last stop, Kyrgyzstan: "For those of us who have been in the Army since before the collapse of the Soviet Union, it was very strange to be staying at what was once a Soviet military airfield. There were even old Russian planes and helicopters all over the place. Who would have thought that one day our enemies would be our allies?"

Then Huck and his platoon reclaim their gear, head to quarters:

I live in a tent twenty-by-ten with six other guys (my RTO, Platoon Sergeant, Weapons Squad-Leader, Platoon Medic, and both Forward Observers). My platoon is broken up into four of these tents. We've got thirty-five total so their tents are a little more crowded. They've got wooden floors, one fluorescent light and an electrical outlet. That was much to our surprise, since we were expecting to land and sleep under the stars with no hope of electricity. We've got four "bathrooms" that have toilets but 90% of the time the water isn't running to flush the "surface laid mines." There are showers, but hopes of hot water are slim-to-none. I don't take showers . . . at all. I've been about sixty-five days without one now, and the FOB pretty much knows me as "the dirty LT" but I could give a damn. I don't see the point. Anyway, we usually get two hot meals a day and it's typical army food, but I won't complain since I wasn't expecting much hot food at all while being here. The FOB has hired about a hundred local Afghani men to do the general day-to-day labor around the base. They wash laundry, scrub toilets, help cook food, fill sandbags, etc.

There's new lingo: local Afghanis get called *Hadjis*, from the Hadj, the annual Mecca pilgrimage. When platoons roll off base (*outside the wire*) they're accompanied by *terps*, hired Afghanis serving as interpreters. Huck gets to liking them. The terps are volleyball demons; when they challenge the Americans, the match runs so lopsided, a terp drifts under the net to Huck's team. "I come over to help out," he says. "In a gesture and spirit of friendliness."

Afghani merchants establish a bazaar just outside the gate; sheds on sticks, selling a 7-Eleven's mishmash of gear, mats, DVDs, pillows. Troops throw on body armor, cross the ground to the Hadji-mart. "You've got to bargain with them," Huck says. "The guys speak good English, too. Some of these motherfuckers speak better English than I do." Huck heads into the mart looking for a pillow.

"How are you, my friend?" the man asks.

"I'm good, thanks. How much for that blue one?"

"For you, special price: ten dollars."

"Ten? I can get it for five, at a Wal-mart."

"Oh, my friend, but this is silk."

"Burlap. It's damn burlap."

"Oh yes. But this was made by hand."

"Hand? What's that tag say? 'Made in the Taiwanese Republic.'"

"OK, two dollars. Sold?"

The Afghanis are indispensable in many ways, as well-intentioned as people back in Anchorage.

Our food/fuel is driven in from up north by contracted Hadji truck drivers. Our front gate guys check all the trucks and scan the drivers . . . then let them in to deliver the goods. Outside of our wire are Afghani Militia Force (AMF) towers. The AMF are local Afghanis that volunteered to fight against the Taliban with Americans. During my first time on FOB security, I met frequently with the head AMF soldier to discuss security issues. These guys are amazing . . . they would rather die to save an American life than one of their own. After getting to know the head AMF commander, I realized how these guys think: they see Americans as men who have traveled the entire way around the earth because of what Taliban did to our people on September 11th. And he's exactly right — that's part of why we're here. The AMF go out on missions with us . . . but I'll get to that in a second.

The typical patrol starts in the early A.M. local time and ends when the sun goes down at night. We drive in a convoy of vehicles all day, stopping along the way to check various different things out — caves along the road, suspect homes with antennas on them, locals carrying equipment ("Why you got those weapons on you, hand-grenades on you, satellite phone on you?" et cetera). Caveclearing has become second nature to us by now. One out of every ten caves will have some type of unexploded ordnance (UXO) in it — 99% of the time it's an old Russian mine or mortar round. The Taliban jerry-rig these types of UXO into remote control bombs that they place along the side of the road in bushes to detonate when we drive or walk by. For the most part, locals within twenty miles of our base are extremely pro-American and want to help us out. But there are always bad guys here and there . . . it's just next to impossible to find them because they go from shooting at us one minute to being a farmer blending in the next. It's very frustrating. We always have engineers with our patrols, so whenever we find UXOs, they just slap a stick of C-4 down on it and blow it up. That's always cool to watch.

About two weeks into our patrolling, my platoon was tasked to move to the northwest for ten days. The local government was holding their first democratic elections, and the commanders asked for a platoon to provide security and patrolling in the area. It was nice being up there away from the wire. I was my own commander and I decided what we did every day. Within thirty minutes of our arrival, some Taliban shot a 107mm rocket at our base. By that point I'd been in country for almost a month and a half so it wasn't a big deal — they shoot these 107mm rockets at our base all the time. They never get close at all . . . but this one landed about fifty meters from where I was standing. The cargo truck I was next to had a piece of shrapnel go through the windshield and back cab of the truck — too close for comfort.

Come to find out later on, there were five more rockets pointed in the same direction, all set on timing devices. Some local AMF soldiers saw where the first rocket was launched from and drove out to the site to investigate. When the head AMF guy gets out of his truck, the second of six rockets starts firing up for take off. The guy jumps on top of the rocket as it's burning and taking off to keep it from hitting near our base again. He got severely burned on the face and hands, but the rocket never came anywhere close to us. That's the type of men the AMF are . . . the guy literally jumped on top of a rocket taking off to redirect it from our position.

After ten days up there we started making the nine-hour drive back here. (You can't ever go very fast because the roads aren't paved and they go through some big mountain passes. The road is synonymous with ambush. We had heard about an eighty-vehicle Russian convoy; they ambushed and killed every damn one of them.) Along the way someone set off one of those remote control mines on the vehicle behind me. I heard a huge explosion and looked in the rearview mirror to see nothing but a huge cloud of dust rising behind me with shrapnel shooting into the air. I couldn't even see the vehicle that was behind me and I thought they were all goners. My first thought was that this was the initiation of an ambush so I started getting ready for direct attack. It never came but we never halted the convoy. Over radio we all got accountability of the platoon and drove on toward home. It was the second closest I've come to getting blasted over here.

I'll say this for the Army as a whole — it has done a great job training me for the missions we've done. I can spit out an OPORDER in my sleep from Infantry OBC and Ranger school, and I can come up with good and clear tactical plans. I had enough stress on me, pulling shit together for that first time we left the wire. And it was second nature — Ranger School, I never would've been able to do without it. Here's what we're doing, here's where we're going, all right motherfuckers, let's move out.

But surprising to me at this point, we have not had to fire a single shot directly at the enemy. I know they're here and I'm sure I come face to face with them every day. But they do a good job of hiding in the local population. Our third platoon got four of them last week when they drove up on them firing on a local government official. I must admit that I was jealous they'd made direct contact before we had. For the most part, we detain possible bad guys, bring them back to the FOB for the intelligence guys to figure out.

And now for the next three weeks we've rotated back onto FOB security. So we won't be going outside the wire for that time. It's been an experience as a leader and a human in general. To be honest, I'm kind of glad we're staying in the wire for a while. Continuous missions for five weeks really started getting to me physically. I had a thousand decisions to make every time we left the wire and that really takes its toll on a man after a while.

He opens letters from friends — including Bryan Hart, who graduated high school with him, and who yelled Huck on at Sandhurst.

Bryan and Huck shared West Point advice; a fellow lieutenant, Bryan now passes on advice for patrols. There are many uses, he explains, for the plugger. The plugger is a big handheld GPS unit — it indicates your position by bouncing a signal off a satellite — which most locals have never seen before.

Next time outside the wire, Huck gives it a shot. His platoon walks into a house — adobe walls, ladder going upstairs — to conduct a weapons check. The rule is that residents are allowed one automatic rifle per household. They can have an AK-47 or a shotgun, but no pistols. They can keep two magazines and that's it. Huck explains, "So I'm here to pick up the other stuff. I know it's in here, so bring that stuff out."

"I only have one gun," the Afghani answers through the terp.

The search begins, Joes nosing and checking; the Afghani hangs close by one wall, keeping his body between the Americans and a big storage chest. Huck switches on his plugger, points in that direction. "Now," Huck says, "this unit I'm holding is a weapons detector. And it's telling me you've got the other stuff right there in that chest."

"Oh no," the Afghani says. "Yes, you got me. I have four other weapons, but that's it."

One of the Joes nods to the ceiling. "Hey," he whispers, "he's got grenades up there." Huck swings the plugger around to the ceiling, squints for the reading. "I'm getting another signal right here," he says. The Afghani climbs up, returns holding a box. "And he's got fifty-three new, still-packed-in-Styrofoam grenades in there." When Huck's platoon heads back to Salerno, the entire village believes Americans have a weapons detector.

The TV series *Friends* was one chunk of the world outside that fell into West Point after The Changes; Huck never much watched it then. But at Salerno, his entire platoon is big on the show. They purchase DVDs at the Hadji-mart ("I see you've got season three of *Friends*; when will you get season four?") and screen them on Huck's laptop computer. "It's good because it makes everybody laugh," Huck says. "And bad because it makes us think of home and shit. We throw it in there, I'm at Salerno and I start thinking about home."

Another base is located nearby; Huck and his platoon pull security there. Huck runs into some Special Forces teams. The SF guys are like SF anywhere — long hair, civilian clothes, beards, casual off-duty.

"Great guys," Huck says. There's a satellite phone, which gives Huck the chance to call his girlfriend in Chicago. He tells her about unpaved roads and the mountains, how the night sky is amazing because you can see every star. He doesn't talk about patrols or shrapnel because he doesn't want her leaving the phone worried. Just when it's working, Huck hears the boom of a Taliban rocket. These attacks come in spurts. Huck tells Heidi, "Hold on real quick a sec." Huck listens; there's another bang. "Oh, I gotta go," Huck says. Heidi asks, "What was that?" "Don't worry, it's nothing, somebody else needs the phone, I gotta go."

He calls his mom the next evening, tells her he's safe, that the time will fly, and he'll be back before she knows it. "So don't worry," he says, "I miss you all immensely. I'm just the next Finn in line, doing the right thing."

A few days before his next run of missions, Huck gets me on the satellite phone. We talk together over G-4: DeMoss, Vermeesch, Paredes. We talk about Keirsey, and about Josh Rizzo and Eliel Pimentel. We laugh over the cold nights of Navy Week, how the winter river winds could stand you straight up, how it'd get so hot in summers you'd see dots of wet on people's foreheads, but all the uniforms stayed clean. It's strange to think that when I put down the phone I'll walk outside, gulp a soda, and Huck will step out to the night sky of Afghanistan. I think about Huck walking all those hours at West Point; it makes me remember one of the last things George Rash told me, explaining what carried him through four years. "It's just, you have to adapt to life. You've got to do that here — or anywhere, really. Learn to grow up, and get past your difference or difficulties. Otherwise, at best, you'll end up leading a lonely life."

Huck tells me when he gets back to his tent, he'll fire up the stove, throw on his West Point blanket. He brought it with him. "You know I wasn't going to leave home without my green girl, didn't you? I've hung on to that shit. It's the same one I had in barracks the whole time, the same one they handed out to us on the first day of the first year."

Huck in Afghanistan

BIBLIOGRAPHY

Agnew, James B. *Eggnog Riot: The Christmas Mutiny at West Point.* San Rafael, Calif.: Presidio Press, 1979.

Ambrose, Stephen E. *Duty, Honor, Country: A History of West Point* (revised edition). Baltimore: Johns Hopkins University Press, 1966, 1999.

Atkinson, Rick. *The Long Gray Line.* Boston: Houghton Mifflin, 1989.

Barkalow, Carol, with Andrea Raab. *In the Men's House.* New York: Poseidon Press, 1990.

Battle, Kemp. *History of the University of North Carolina, 1789–1868.* Raleigh, N.C.: Edwards & Broughton, 1907.

Bugle Notes, various years. Annual publication of the U.S. Military Academy, issued to cadets upon first entering West Point.

Cowley, Robert, and Thomas Guinzburg, editors. *West Point: Two Centuries of Honor and Tradition.* New York: Warner Books, 2002.

Crackel, Theodore J. *The Illustrated History of West Point.* New York: Harry N. Abrams, Inc., 1991.

Cullum, George Washington. *Biographical Register of the Officers and Graduates of the United Sates Military Academy.* New York: J. F. Trow, 1850.

Custer, Elizabeth. *Boots and Saddles.* New York: Harper & Brothers, 1885.

Donnithorne, Larry R. *The West Point Way of Leadership,* New York: Doubleday, 1994.

Dupuy, R. Ernest, *Men of West Point: The First 150 Years of the United States Military Academy.* New York: William Sloane Associates, 1951.

Ellis, Joseph J., and Robert Moore. *School for Soldiers: West Point and the Profession of Arms.* New York: Oxford University Press, 1974.

Fleming, Thomas J. *West Point: The Men and Times of the United States Military Academy.* New York: William Morrow, 1969.

Flipper, Henry O. *The Colored Cadet at West Point.* New York: H. Lee & Co., 1878.

Forman, Sidney. *West Point: A History of the United States Military Academy.* New York: Columbia University Press, 1950.

Grant, Ulysses S. *Personal Memoirs of Ulysses S. Grant.* Introduction by Geoffrey Perret. New York: Modern Library, 1885, 1999.

Huntington, Samuel P. *The Soldier and the State.* Cambridge: Harvard University Press, 1957.

King, Charles. *Cadet Days: A Story of West Point.* New York: Harper & Brothers, 1903.

Kirshner, Ralph. *Class of 1861: Custer, Ames, and Their Classmates after West Point.* Carbondale: Southern Illinois University Press, 1999.

Lovell, John P. *Neither Athens nor Sparta: The American Service Academies in Transition.* Bloomington: Indiana University Press, 1979.

Malone, Paul Bernard. *West Point Cadet.* Philadelphia: Penn Publishing Co., 1908.

McCaughey, Robert A. *Josiah Quincy: The Last Federalist, 1772–1864.* Cambridge: Harvard University Press, 1974.

McCrea, Tully. *Dear Belle: Letters from a Cadet & Officer to His Sweetheart, 1858–1865.* Foreword by Bruce Catton. Middletown, Conn.: Wesleyan University Press, 1965.

Myrer, Anton. *Once an Eagle.* New York: Holt, Rinehart & Winston, 1968.

Norton, Aloysius Arthur. *Study of the Customs and Traditions of West Point in the American Novel.* New York: Columbia University Press, 1950.

Pappas, George S. *To the Point: The United States Military Academy, 1802–1902.* Westport, Conn.: Praeger, 1993.

Rapp, Kenneth W. *Whistler in Cadet Gray and other Stories about the United States Military Academy.* Croton-on-Hudson, N.Y.: North River Press, 1978.

Ricks, Thomas E. *Making the Corps.* New York: Scribner, 1997.

Ruggero, Ed. *Duty First: West Point and the Making of American Leaders.* New York: HarperCollins, 2001.

Schaff, Morris. *The Spirit of Old West Point, 1858–1862.* Boston: Houghton Mifflin, 1907.

Simpson, Jeffrey. *Officers and Gentlemen: Historic West Point in Photographs.* Tarrytown, N.Y.: Sleepy Hollow Press, 1985.

Stewart, Robert. *The Corps of Cadets: A Year at West Point.* Annapolis, Md.: Naval Institute Press, 1996.

Todd, Frederick Porter. *Cadet Gray: A Pictorial History of Life at West Point as Seen Through Its Uniforms.* New York: Sterling Publishing, 1955.

Truscott, Lucian K., IV. *Dress Gray.* New York: Doubleday, 1977.

Webb, Ernie, John D. Hart, and James E. Foley. *West Point Sketch Book.* New York: Vantage Press, 1976.

ACKNOWLEDGMENTS

IN A BOOK like this, where so many people were generous with their attention, hospitality and time, a proper Acknowledgments page could run as long as the closing credits of a special-effects movie. This is a proper Acknowledgments page.

To begin with, I'd like to express my gratitude to the many cadets who shared with me their impressions and experiences, and who answered all my plebeish questions. ("Why do people use the number eight for 'eight-up'?") As much as anything else, I appreciated their good company, whether driving me in a Humvee or assaulting me on the Bayonet Assault Course or taking me to meet their parents or sitting with me over beers at the Firstie Club. Thanking them individually would be impractical; instead, I'll say that this book would not have been possible without the generous cooperation of the United States Corps of Cadets. I'm grateful to any cadet who wore an as-for-class uniform between 1998 and 2002, and I'm especially indebted to those whose names appear in this book. Their time, their honesty and their stories have given this book whatever you like best about it.

Similarly, I would like to express my appreciation to the officers in the West Point administration who so graciously tolerated the sight of a rumpled journalist crossing the Plain or stepping in and out of barracks. In particular, my thanks to General Daniel W. Christman (retired) and General John P. Abizaid (First Infantry Division), who first invited me to West Point. (Colonel Kerry Pierce, who answered many of the first questions I had about the West Point system, passed away after a long illness in November of 2000; he was generous with his time as well.) Alan Aimone, chief of Special Collections at the U.S. Military Academy Library, was a good sport about the many West Point history books I kept from his shelves for far too long. More importantly, he was an excellent source of information about both the modern Academy and good spots to dig for material on the historical one. Dr. Stephen Grove, the West Point historian, was also a valuable guide as I picked my way through West Point's past.

Civilians visiting West Point usually check in at the blocky Welcome Center down the road; for journalists, the welcome center is the Public Affairs Office. The staff there is a healthy mix of officers and civilians, uniforms and chinos working side by side. I owe special thanks to its director, Lieutenant Colonel Jim E. Whaley III, for years of question-answering and door-opening. Mike D'Aquino escorted me with good humor and endless patience during my first week at West Point. Andrea Hamburger was almost spendthrift with information and suggestions and forbearance, and likeably hardheaded when I wanted to do something stupid like go skydiving with the parachute team. Theresa Brinkerhoff arranged my tickets to football games and banquets and, when she ran into me, always pretended to think I was a real card, which was even nicer. Major John Cornelio was an excellent host during my first months at West Point, and Lieutenant Colonel William H. Harkey (retired) was also generous with his time. Pat Brown and Lieutenant Colonel Kirk Frady were also helpful and gracious. As with the officers and cadets noted above, this book would not have been possible without the help of the Public Affairs Office.

Turning to the civilian world, my editor at Houghton Mifflin, Eamon Dolan, shares the dedication of this book with Company G-4, in gratitude for the great dedication he has shown for me and my work. He was more intelligent, patient, thoughtful and more of a friend than any writer has a right to expect. Janet Silver was generous to this project in many ways, and gave me great advice for a speech I was anxious about delivering in South Carolina; she runs a tight ship. Bridget Marmion is full of smart ideas about marketing, and Lori Glazer and Whitney Peeling, in publicity, were both very intelligent and helpful and charming people, in a field where part of the job is perfecting a kind of cultured yelling.

At the Wylie Agency, Andrew Wylie and Jeff Posternak have been exactly as advertised, which if you're familiar with the ads is about as large a thank you as a writer can offer.

At Vintage Books, Anjali Singh has been exceptionally intelligent, what David Mamet would call a *closer* — comes in for the sit, puts in the hours, doesn't walk away without the papers in hand. Marty Asher is the sort of gentleman who makes you wish you could find ways to act, day-in, day-out, more gentlemanly yourself. Russell Perreault and Sarah Hutson have been like a publicity reveille; they know how to get you up and out there fast. Leah Heifferon offered her time and ideas, Marla Jea reminded me how much more we all have to learn about grammar, and Jon Fine proved as good as his last name.

This book began as stories I wrote at *Rolling Stone* magazine, where I've spent eight years. Jann Wenner, Bob Love and Will Dana have been great friends to the project and to me. Jann Wenner is publisher and editor of the magazine; I want to express my gratitude for his patience, faith and training. (When I mentioned this to him, he asked if I could add "glacial patience.") Former managing editor Bob Love brought me to the magazine, smoked with me through a lot of long nights and taught me the supreme importance of good reporting; if there's nothing to tell, it doesn't matter how you tell it. Will Dana was an immense help to the stories as they came together; his enthusiasm about the Academy was a boon at the point in any story where a writer is apt to confuse irritation with the process with irritation about the subject. Danielle Mattoon was also helpful during my first months at the Academy.

I owe Lisa Bankoff at ICM a great debt of gratitude. She's been extremely wise about business, people and prose, which is just what you want from an agent. Beyond that, Lisa has proven to be an excellent, steadfast friend. Patrick Price at ICM was also helpful, a keen reader and a steady voice at the end of the phone.

At Goldberg-McDuffie Communications, Lynn Goldberg and Camille McDuffie have both proven invaluable assets (*force multipliers,* as they'd say in the Army); Sarah Trabucchi has shown great dedication and warmth to this project, and has also been a good, patient friend.

Because this book took so many years to research and write, I keep thanking people for *patience.* The woman who has displayed that virtue most is my girlfriend, Evie Shapiro. She was patient with my absence and even more patient when I was back home, with pages of transcript on the sofa, tapes everywhere, books with torn pieces of paper marking the relevant passages like little prayers. Jean Brown was an incredibly valuable ally; only Jean has witnessed the director's cut of this book, as she transcribed hundreds of hours of tape. My mother, Pat Lipsky, helped in many ways; Heather Mabis Chase was a great help too, both as a reader and as a friend. Lots of other people offered their assistance and advice at various stages: Jeff Giles, Captain John Hillen (retired), Stephen Sherrill, Emily Little, Michael Rubiner, Mark Seliger, Shaune McDowell, Shelter Serra, Elizabeth Wurtzel, Rachel Clarke, Stacey Greenwald, Carol Dittbrenner, David Samuels, Chris Heath, A. C. Adornetto, Jane Kennedy, Bruce Keith and, for an invaluable contribution, Eric Easterly. It's an old saying that a book has friends before it has readers; this book was fortunate to find such good ones.